DEVELOPMENT OF EDUCATION IN INDIA

CONCEPTS IN COMMUNICATION INFORMATICS & LIBRARIANSHIP (CICIL)

For a list of titles in this series, see pp. 443-447 at the end of this Book

Vol. I : Development of Education in India : A Survey of Educational Documents Before and After Independence
A. Biswas and *S.P. Agrawal*

Vol. II : The Second Historical Survey of Educational Development in India : Select Documents 1985-1990
S.P. Agrawal and *J.C. Aggarwal*

Vol. III : Third Historical Survey of Educational Development in India : Select Documents 1990-1992
S.P. Agrawal and *J.C. Aggarwal*

Vol. IV : Development of Education in India : Select Documents 1993-94
S.P. Agrawal and *J.C. Aggarwal*

About the Authors

S.P. Agrawal (*b.* 1929) was Director, National Social Science Documentation Centre, ICSSR, Government of India and Member Secretary, Indian Association of Social Science Institutions. He was also the Vice-Chairman of the Asia and Pacific Information Network in Social Sciences (APINESS). In 1988 he was awarded the degree of Doctor of Philosophy in Education (*Honoris Causa*) by International University Foundation. Presently, he is Member, IFLA Round Table on Research in Reading, International Committee for Social Science Information and Documentation, Board of Studies of National Archives of India and Hindi Advisory Committee, Ministry of Coal, Government of India. He is also Fellow of the Society of Ethnobotanists. Born and brought up in the cradle of freedom movement, which he joined at the tender age of twelve, he gained an insight into political problems and developed a sense of responsibility which bore fruit as an information scientist. He has written extensively on various aspects of Education, Indian Polity and Library and Information Science.

J.C. Aggarwal (*b.* 1928), former Deputy Director of Education/Executive Director of Delhi Bureau of Textbooks, Delhi Administration has a varied experience in the field of education. He has singly/jointly authored about 130 books on Education, Social Sciences and current problems. In collaboration with S.P. Agrawal, he has written *Documentation Encyclopaedia of UNESCO and Education* (in two parts); *Women's Education in India; National Policy on Education, Agenda for India 2001;* and *Vocational of Education in India; Uttar Pradesh : Past, Present and Future; Modern History of Punjab; Modern History of Jammu & Kashmir*, etc.

His other recent publications include : *Year-book of Indian Education, 1991: World Overview; Ramamurti Report 1990 on National Policy on Education in India;* and *Survey of Educational Documents in the World since 1983*, etc.

CONCEPTS IN COMMUNICATION
INFORMATICS & LIBRARIANSHIP-77

GENERAL EDITOR : **S. P. AGRAWAL**

DEVELOPMENT OF EDUCATION IN INDIA

SELECT DOCUMENTS 1993-94

VOLUME-FOUR

S.P. Agrawal
former Member Secretary
Indian Association of Social Science Institutions,
and
former Director, National Social Science Documentation Centre (ICSSR)
New Delhi

J.C. Aggarwal
former Excutive Director
Delhi Bureau of Textbooks, Delhi Administration, Delhi

CONCEPT PUBLISHING COMPANY, NEW DELHI-110059

ISBN 81-7022-661-9

First Published 1997

Published and Printed by
Ashok Kumar Mittal
Concept Publishing Company
A/15-16, Commercial Block, Mohan Garden
New Delhi-110059 (India)

Phones: 5554042, 5504042
Fax: 091-(11)-5598898

General Editor's Introduction

Development of Education in India (First volume of the Historical Survey) was published in 1986. Volume 2 entitled *The Second Historical Survey of Educational Developments in India* covering the period 1985-1990, and Volume 3 under the title *Third Historical Survey* covering the period 1990-1992 were brought out in 1991 and 1994 respectively. It is of great consolation that all these volumes placed in the hands of the discerning educationists as also reviewers have been well received. In all humility, we assume that the surveys are fulfilling long-felt need.

This fourth volume covering the period 1993-1994, is a sequal to *Third Historical Survey of Educational Developments in India : Select Document 1990-1992*. A few significant documents relating to the years 1991 and 1992, not already covered, have also been included. The material has been grouped in four parts. Part one presents an overview of educational developments. Part two includes select documents covering diverse facets of education. Part three is devoted to educational statistics. Part four consists of appendices relating to topics not covered earlier.

Acknowledgement

Main documentation sources are : Ministry of Human Resource Development, Department of Education, Government of India, New Delhi; University Grants Commission, New Delhi; National Council of Educational Research and Training, New Delhi; National Institute of Educational Planning and Administrative, New Delhi; and Association of Indian Universities, New Delhi. We are grateful to all research institutions/organisations for using their documents in this publication.

S.P. Agrawal

CONTENTS

PART-THREE

EDUCATIONAL STATISTICS

PART-FOUR

APPENDICES : SIGNIFICANT DOCUMENTS NOT INCLUDED IN THE PREVIOUS SURVEY

PART-ONE

DEVELOPMENT OF EDUCATION

1

Development of Education An Overview

1.1 ELEMENTARY EDUCATION

Universalisation of Elementary Education

Provision of free and compulsory education to all children until they complete the age of 14 years is a directive principle of state policy. Recognising the need for literate population and provision of elementary education as a crucial input for nation building, the policy of the Government has been to provide free and compulsory education to all children at least upto the elementary stage. The resolve was spelt out unequivocally and emphatically in the National Policy on Education (NPE), 1986 and the Programme of Action (POA), 1992.

The target for the VIII Five Year Plan has been divided into the following three broad parameters :

(1) *Universal Access* : (i) Universal enrolment of all children, including girls and persons belonging to SC/ST;

(ii) Provision of primary school within one km., of walking distance and facility of non-formal education for school drop-outs, working children and girls who cannot attend formal schools;

(iii) Improvement of ratio of upper primary to primary schools from the existing 1:4 to 1:2;

(2) *Universal Retention* : (iv) Reduction of dropout rate between classes I to V and I to VIII from the existing 46 per cent and 60 per cent to 20 per cent and 40 per cent respectively;

(3) *Universal Achievement* : (v) Achievement of minimum levels of learning by almost all children at the primary level, and introduction of this concept at the upper primary stage.

Progress Over the Years

Concerted efforts towards UEE have resulted in manifold increase in institutions, teachers and students as shown in the Table below :

TABLE 1.1: No. of Institutions (in lakhs)

	1950-51	1993-94
Primary Schools :		
(Classes I-V)	2.10	5.73
Upper Primary Schools :		
(Classes VI-VIII)	0.13	1.55
	2.23	7.28

TABLE 1.2: No. of Teachers (in lakhs)

Primary Schools :		
(Classes I-V)	5.38	17.03
Upper Primary Schools :		
(Classes VI-VIII)	0.36	10.80
	5.74	27.83

TABLE 1.3 : Gross Enrolment

	1950-51	1993-94
Primary Stage		
Total Enrolment (in millions) :	19.2	108.2
Gross Enrolment Ratio (%-age) :	43.1	104.5
Upper Primary Stage		
Total Enrolment (in millions) :	3.1	39.9
Gross Enrolment Ratio (%-age) :	12.0	67.7

As a result of this growth, Indian elementary education has become one of the largest education systems in the world, providing accessibility within 1 km., of walking distance to 8.25 lakh habitations covering 94 per cent of the country's population. Growth in enrolment during the last decade has brought rates close to 100 per cent at primary stage.

In the endeavour to increase enrolment and achieve the target of UEE, all state governments have abolished tuition fees in the government, local body and aided schools upto the upper primary level.

While the Gross Enrolment Ratios (GER) at the primary stage in the country as a whole and in most of its states exceed 100 per cent there are quite a few states where the ratio is considerably lower. These include Uttar Pradesh, Bihar, Rajasthan, Haryana, Jammu and Kashmir and Meghalaya. At the upper primary stage these states and in addition, Andhra Pradesh, Orissa and Sikkim have GERs lower than the national average. Most of these states have literacy rates lower than the national average. There is thus a strong regional dimension of UEE.

The problem gets more complicated as the drop-out rates, though declining, continue to be high. Nearly half the children who enter Class I drop out before reaching Class V, and two-thirds of the children drop-out before reaching Class VIII. Regional disparities also abound in rates of the dropouts.

Gender Disparities : As with any educational indicator, gender disparities are conspicuous in regard to enrolment and retention. Girls' enrolment has grown at the primary stage from 5.4 million in 1950-51 to 46.4 million in 1993-94 and at the upper primary stage from 0.5 million to 15.7 million. The rate of growth of enrolment of girls has been higher than that of boys but disparities still persist—girls still account for only 45.7 per cent of the enrolment at the primary stage and 37.73 per cent at the upper primary stage. The drop-out rates of girls at the primary as well as the upper primary stage are higher than those of boys.

Regional disparities are also conspicuous. High female literacy states (i.e., those above 50 per cent) have by and large universalised primary enrolments among girls. Even in regard to upper primary enrolment Kerala, Goa, Pondicherry and Lakshadweep fare very well. In states with medium female literacy status (40-50 per cent) enrolment of girls appears to be satisfactory at the primary level. The situation in low female literacy states (20-40 per cent) causes concern. These states have more than half of the country's population, with just four of them (Uttar Pradesh, Bihar, Madhya Pradesh and Rajasthan) accounting for 40 per cent of the country's population.

Scheduled Castes and Scheduled Tribes : According to the 1991 Census, the population of Scheduled Castes (SCs) was 138.12 million (16.33 per cent) and that of Scheduled Tribes (STs) 67.8 million (8.01 per cent) of the country's population.

Both SC and ST populations are not homogeneous target groups in all respects. There are wide variations between different SC and ST groups regionally. Thus SC girls in Kerala are likely to be better placed than non-SC boys in some of the more backward states and districts.

Because of the affirmative policies of the government, the enrolment of SCs and STs has increased considerably at the primary stage. The participation of SCs and STs is now more or less in proportion to their share in population at the primary level. Drop-outs, though declining over the years, are significantly large. Gender disparities are very conspicuous among SCs and STs also.

Content, Process and Achievement Levels : The issues of content vs concept, understanding vs rote memorisation, unachievable content load vs achievable set of competencies have been integrated into the new Minimum Levels of Learning approach.

Minimum Levels of Learning have been specified in terms of competencies expected to be mastered by every child by the end of a particular class. The emphasis is on :

(a) relevance and functionality in primary education.
(b) lightening the curriculum load by emphasising competencies rather than content.
(c) ensuring acquisition of basic competencies and skills;
(d) promoting mastery learning not only by the brighter students but by all children in the class; and
(e) introduction of continuous and comprehensive evaluation in the class room in order to give teachers a diagnostic tool and facilitate remedial teaching. 19.

Following are the major activities under the programme :

(a) Adaptation of MLLs by the State Govts and translation into the regional languages.
(b) Conducting pre-test to ascertain existing levels of achievement.
(c) Orientation of teachers enabling them to adopt activity-oriented child-centred and competency based teaching learning process.
(d) Review of existing textbooks and preparation of competency based text-books and work-books.
(e) Preparation of handbooks for teachers;
(f) Development of competency based teaching learning aids;
(g) Preparation of competency based test items.
(h) Implementing a system of continuous and comprehensive evaluation.
(i) Emphasis to be placed on identifying learning levels, learning difficulties leading to remedial teaching.

The programme is being initiated in the current year throughout the country with the help of Voluntary Agencies, Research Institutions, SCERTs and District Institutes of Education and Training. As on date 12 states are implementing the programme through 100 DIETs and would be gradually expanded to cover the entire elementary school system by 2000 A.D. Since this would be a key component in the DPEP, more intensive work would be taken up in these districts.

Simultaneously the MLLs are being laid down for the upper primary stage by a national committee chaired by Prof. R.H. Dave.

Non-Formal Education Programme

Coverage : Although the focus of the programme is on the educationally backward States viz., Andhra Pradesh, Arunachal Pradesh, Assam, Bihar, Jammu & Kashmir, Madhya Pradesh, Orissa, Rajasthan, U.P. and West Bengal, it also covers urban slums, hilly, tribal and desert areas and projects for education of working children in other States as well. The programme is, at present, in operation in 20 States/UTs.

Strategy

(a) Condensed course of about two years duration;
(b) Part-time instructions at a time/place convenient to learners in small groups;
(c) Part-time honorary instructor/supervisor locally recruited and trained;
(d) Emphasis on flexibility and decentralisation of management;
(e) Use of curriculum and teaching-learning material comparable to the formal system and relevant to local environment and learners' needs; and
(f) Testing and certification of NFE students to enable their entry into formal system.

The programme is implemented through State Governments as well as Voluntary Organisations. The Central Assistance to State Government is provided on sharing basis i.e., 60% for co-educational centres and 90% for exclusively girls centres. The Central assistance to NGOs for running NFE Centres and Experimental and Innovative Projects is provided on 100% basis.

Monitoring and Evaluation : The programme of NFE is being monitored through quarterly progress reports, periodic evaluations conducted by Joint Evaluation Teams and field visits of Central Government and State Governments Officials. Moreover, 7 external agencies evaluated the programme in 8 States viz. Andhra Pradesh, Bihar, Gujarat, Madhya Pradesh, Orissa, Rajasthan, Uttar Pradesh and West Bengal. On the basis of the feed-back received, remedial action is being taken for effective implementation of the programme. It is proposed to decentralise monitoring, appraisal and supervision of NFE programme. A system of concurrent evaluation of the programme is proposed to be evolved.

Implementation in 1994-95 : In the state sector, grant amounting to Rs. 94.25 crores has, so far, been sanctioned to 14 States/UTs for running 2.26 lakhs NFE centers in the year 1994-95. Under Voluntary sector, grants amounting to Rs. 16.69 crores have been sanctioned to over 425 voluntary agencies for running about 29,000 NFE centres and to 37 voluntary agencies for implementing experimental and innovative projects for achieving the UEE. Against the budget allocation of Rs. 131.27 crore, an expenditure of Rs. 110.94 crore has, so far, been incurred and the remaining funds will be utilised by the end of the financial year. In view of the special emphasis on girls education, the number of exclusively girls centres have been increased to 99,252 which accounts for 44% of the total centres. The estimated enrolment capacity of the programme is about 63 lakh children.

An outlay of Rs. 704 crore (Rs. 625 crore for State Sector and Rs. 79 crore for voluntary sector) has been approved for the 8th plan period. The emphasis is on consolidation of the existing programme rather than its expansion. Efforts are, therefore, being made to improve the quality, allow greater flexibility to implementing agencies, re-locate NFE centres on the basis of micro planning/area survey, and promote more experimentations and innovations in the field of Elementary Education. Development and scaling-up of effective. NFE models that can help the learners to learn at their own pace is a major thrust area in the 8th plan period.

Operation Blackboard

The National Policy of Education, 1986 recognising the unattractive school environment, unsatisfactory condition of buildings and insufficiency of instructional material in primary schools, which function as demotivating factors for enrolment and retention, called for a drive symbolically called "Operation Blackboard" for substantial improvement in the quality of primary schools. The scheme was started in 1987-88 to bring all existing primary schools in the country to a minimum standard of physical facilities by providing them with :

(a) At least two reasonably large all weather rooms alongwith separate toilet facilities for boys and girls.

(b) At least two teachers—one of them a woman as far as possible; and

(c) Essential teaching and learning material including blackboards, maps, charts, a small library, toys and games and some equipment for work experience.

100 per cent Central assistance is provided for procurement of Teaching Learning Equipment and appointment of additional teacher in single teacher schools. Construction of school buildings is the responsibility of the State Governments.

In order to operationalise the Revised Policy of the Government regarding school facilities, the scheme of Operation Blackboard has been expanded to provide third room/third teacher to primary schools where enrolment exceeds 100 and to extend to Upper Primary schools and has been launched from March, 1994. Following criteria have been suggested to State Governments for implementation of the expanded Operation Blackboard :

(i) It will be limited to rural areas only during 8th Plan.
(ii) Girl schools will be given first priority.
(iii) SC/ST areas will be given preference over other areas.

It has been made mandatory to the State Governments, that at least 50 per cent of the teachers appointed in future should be women.

Construction of school buildings is the major problem that State Government, have been facing. This problem, has, however, been sorted out with Ministry of Rural Development, who have agreed not only to continue central funding for construction of school buildings under Jawahar Rozgar Yojana (JRY), but also make it a high priority item under newly introduced Employment Assurance Scheme and the 120 backward districts identified under the intensive JRY. According to this formula, 48 per cent of the funds for construction are provided by Ministry of Rural Development, if States allocated 40 per cent Non-JRY share and 12 per cent State JRY share.

TABLE 1.4: Achievement under Operation Blackboard

(Rs. in crores)

	Physical			Financial	
	Coverage of Schools	Sanction of teachers	Construction of class rooms	From 1987- to 6th March '95	During 1994-95
TARGET	522909	152848	263616	1156.79	215.00
ACHIEVEMENTS	522547	146557	140373	979.18	124.13

Out of 1.46 lakh teachers sanctioned 1.18 lakh posts have been filled up.

Expanded OB:	8th Plan Targets		Achievements
Third teacher	42,000 (30%)	**	14535
Upper Primary schools	14,000 (10%)		7335

** The coverage could however, be enhanced subject to availability of funds.

It is proposed to sanction teaching learning equipment to remaining 0.1 per cent primary shools, about 15,000 upper primary schools and sanction third teacher to about 14,000 primary schools during 1994-95.

The expenditure during 1993-94 was Rs. 179 crores while BE for 1994-95 are Rs. 215 crores.

Teacher Education

The Centrally Sponsored Scheme of Restructuring and Reorganisation of Teacher Education is being implemented since 1987-88.

TABLE 1.5 : Achievements under the Scheme during the period since 1987-88

Sl. No.	Nomenclature	Comulative Achievements (upto 28.2.1995)
1.	Amount spent (Rs. in crores)	401.30
2.	Number of Teachers oriented during 1986-90 under the programme for Mass Orientation of School Teachers (MOST) (in lakhs).	17.62
3.	Number of District Institutes of Education and Training (DIET) sanctioned.	384
4.	Number of Colleges of Teacher Education (CTEs) sanctioned.	56
5.	Number of Institutions of Advanced Study in Education (IASEs) sanctioned.	24
6.	Number of States/UTs covered.	28

During the Year 1993-94, 33 DIETs, 2 CTEs and one IASE were sanctioned. During 1994-95, it is proposed to sanction 46 DIETs and 10 CTEs/IASEs.

Setting up DIETs/CTEs/IASEs is a long-gestation activity, in view of the time it takes to put up necessary buildings and create and fill up posts. Yet about 300 DIETs have become operational and have started conducting training programmes.

Under the component relating to strengthening of University Departments of Education, UGC has selected Departments of Education in five universities under Special Assistance Programme at the level of Departmental Research Support. These universities are Kashi Vidyapeeth, M.S. University of Baroda, Osmania University, Rohelkhand University and Punjab University. The UGC has also decided to assist some distinguished university departments on regional basis for taking up M.A. course in Education.

Special Orientation Programme for Primary Teachers (SOPT) is going on almost in all States and 1.14 lakhs teachers have already been covered.

National Council for Teacher Education (NCTE)

In accordance with the provisions laid down in the National Policy of Education, 1986 and the Programme of Action for its implementation, the National Council for Teacher Education (NCTE) has been conferred a statutory status and brought on the Statute Book as NCTE Act No. 73 of 1993. The Act provides for the establishment of NCTE with a view to :

(a) Achieving planned and coordinated development of teacher education system throughout the country; and

(b) The regulation and proper maintenance of norms and standards in the teacher education system and for matters connected therewith.

Shiksha Karmi Project

Rajasthan Shiksha Karmi Project (SKP) is being implemented since 1987 in Rajasthan with assistance from Swedish International Development Agency (SIDA) to the tune of 52 million SEK. The Project was to be implemented initially for a four-year period from 1-7-87 to 30-6-1991. Ninety per cent of the project outlay is being funded out of Plan budget of the Central Government which is subsequently reimbursed by SIDA.

Keeping in view the anticipated saving of 35 M SEK, it was decided to extend the project for a further period of three years i.e., from 1991-92 to 1993-94. The mid-term review has been held on 4.3.1994 in which SIDA has recommended to Swedish Government a further assistance to India of 60 million SEK to be allocated for the first three years of phase-II of the SKP from 1.7.94 to 30.6.97.

The project aims at universalisation and qualitiative improvement of primary education in remote and socio-economically backward villages in Rajasthan with primary attention given to girls. The project identifies teachers' absenteeism as a major obstacle in achieving the objective of UEE. The project is being implemented by Government of Rajasthan through Rajasthan Shiksha Karmi Board (RSKB) with the assistance of voluntary agencies.

SKP is an innovative intervention which aims to overcome major problem of poor enrolment and high drop-out of children, particularly girls. The SKP runs Prehar Pathshalas, Angan Pathshala, Mahila Shiksha Karmi Training Centres. An innovative aspect of the project is the development of locally relevant curriculum related to the environment of the child and its effective transaction in the classrooms for increased enrolment, selection and participation, especially of girls.

As on 30th September 1994, the SKP is functioning in 25 districts and 67 blocks/units in 1066 villages in Rajasthan. There are 1066 Day Centres and 2105 Prehar Pathshalas in which 2514 Shiksha Karmis (male 2244 and female 270) are involved for imparting education to 1,02,454 children between the age-group of 6-11 years out of which 21092 are attending non-formal classes (Prehar Pathshalas). Another 20 blocks/units in 300 villages are proposed to be covered upto 31.3.1995. 3274 Shiksha Karmis are expected to look after 1366 day schools by the end of March, 1995. A budget provision of Rs. 500 lakhs has been made for the year 1994-95.

District Primary Education Programme

In keeping with the NPE, 1986 (as updated in 1992) and its Programme of Action, a new initiative to achieve UEE has been evolved titled, "District Primary Education Programme" (DPEP). The DPEP seeks to operationalise the strategy for UEE through decentralised planning and disaggregated target setting.

The Concept DPEP is a beachhead for effecting improvements and full scale development of the entire elementary education sector. The overall goal of the programme is the reconstruction of primary education as a whole in the districts instead of the piecemeal implementation of schemes. The fundamental principle of DPEP is capacity building at all levels, be it national, state or local level and to evolve strategies which are replicable and sustainable.

National experience with the pursuit of UEE had established the following :

(a) UEE is contextual. The contexuality varies widely across the country. Even in states like Kerala where participation is near universal much requires to be done in respect of quality and achievement. In such states the pursuit of UEE would be mainly in the areas of quality, facilities and achievement. In other states participation and demand aspects need more attention.

(b) Contexuality entails local area-planning with disaggregated targets and decentralised planning and management. Planning for UEE had hitherto been mainly at the national and state-level. Barring some states and union territories, these entities are too large and heterogenous for effective planning; they cannot provide contextuality. Ideally the planning should be from below, right from the village upwards but given the objective conditions, a beginning has to be made with district as the unit of planning. The district plans are to be prepared through an intensive process of interaction with the local bodies, teachers and NGOs so that it is "owned" by all who are to be associated in implementation and it reflects the ground-level realities.

(c) Resources are an important but not sufficient condition for achieving UEE. A host of measures, both financial and non-financial, both on the supply side and on the demand side, need to complement higher allocation of resources.

(d) The strategies for UEE have hitherto emphasised, mainly access in terms of construction of class rooms and appointment of teachers. This has been inadequate and needs to be augmented by :

(i) a holistic planning and management approach which goes beyond implementation of a disjointed set of individual schemes, perceives the task of UEE in its totality, integrates all the measures needed for achieving UEE in the specific context of the district;

(ii) this holistic planning incorporates a gender perspective in all aspects of the planning and implementation process and is an integral part of all measures needed to achieve UEE;

(iii) addressing the more difficult aspects of access, particularly access to girls, disadvantaged groups and out-of-school children;

(iv) improving school effectiveness;

(v) strengthening the alternatives to schooling, particularly the non-formal education system;

(vi) stressing to participative processes whereby the local community facilitates participation, achievement and school effectiveness;

(vii) toning up teacher competence, training and motivation;

(viii) stressing learning competence and achievement;

(ix) stressing the need for improved teaching/learning materials;

(x) overhauling planning and management in respect of both routine and innovative areas; and

(xi) convergence between elementary education and related services such as ECCE and school health.

Consequently, the strategies for the Eighth Plan adopt a dis-aggregated approach, with focus on preparation of district-specific, population-specific plans for UEE within the broad strategy frame of micro-planning through people's participation and introduction of MLLs in schools to improve learner achievements. Micro-planning will provide the frame work of universal access and universal participation while MLLs would be the strategy frame for universal achievements. DPEP seeks to operationalise this strategy.

The Programme also builds upon the experience gained in —

(i) the implementation of the Bihar Education Project (with UNICEF assistance) and the Lok Jumbish Project (with SIDA assistance);

(ii) the planning of Basic Education Project in U.P. (with IDA assistance); and

(iii) the implementation of the Andhra Pradesh Primary Education Project (with ODA assistance), Shiksha Karmi Project (with SIDA assistance) and Mahila Samakhya (with Dutch assistance).

Objectives : The objectives of the programme are :

(i) to reduce differences in enrolment, dropout and learning achievement among gender and social groups to less than five per cent;

(ii) to reduce overall primary dropout rates for all students to less than 10 per cent;

(iii) to raise average achievement levels by at least 25 per cent over measured baseline levels and ensuring achievement of basic literacy and numeracy competencies and a minimum of 40 per cent achievement levels in other competencies, by all primary school children; and

(iv) to provide, according to national norms, access for all children, to primary education classes (I-V), i.e., primary schooling wherever possible, or its equivalent non-formal education.

Management

State Level

The programme would be implemented in a mission mode. Implementation at the State level would be through registered autonomous societies with the Chief Minister as ex-officio President of the General Council and Chief Secretary/Education Secretary as Chairman of the Executive Committee.

National Level

A national level structure is being set up on the lines of NLM which would oversee the implementation of the programme throughout the country and provide the necessary technical support to states and districts. As DPEP will cover several states and more than a hundred districts, and being a logical sequence to the externally-aided basic education projects in Bihar, Rajasthan, Andhra Pradesh and Uttar Pradesh, there is reason to provide for a regular system of monitoring, information sharing and dissemination of experiences at the national level.

Village Education Committees (VECs)

Village Education Committees are a key feature for localised participative management in DPEP. Comprising representatives of local village panchayats, women activists, educators and guardians, the Committees will play a key role in local school management and ensure people's participation for enhancing enrolment of primary school children, their retention and regular attendance.

Capacity Building and Technical Support : The national level technical assistance will include the following :

(i) Development of state capacities for plan formulation;

(ii) MIS including school statistics, project indicators and building of a data base, would be developed, tested and installed in DPEP;

(iii) Development of In-Service Teacher Training including prototype training designs and materials and competencies in multi-grade teaching and MLL;

(iv) Development of prototype materials for teaching Reading and Mathematics for classes I-III and evaluations of impact;

(v) Development of prototype training materials in educational planning and management and the training and the training of teams in DPEP assisted States/Districts;

(vi) A unit for programme research, studies and evaluation to organize research activities for better DPEP implementation and evaluation, as well as establish a net-work of research institutions for primary education;

(vii) Intervention strategies for tribal education;

(viii) Development of cost-effective designs for primary schools; and

(ix) Provision for international exchanges and training for capacity building.

Coverage : As of now the process of planning has been completed for 42 districts in the States of Madhya Pradesh, Assam, Haryana, Maharashtra, Karnataka, Tamil Nadu and Kerala. The planning process has been initiated in five districts each in Andhra Pradesh and West Bengal.

Funding : While funds made available by European Community Programme assistance to DPEP are being applied to 19 districts of Madhya Pradesh, the other 23 districts are funded by IDA. ODA has expressed interest in funding five districts each in Andhra Pradesh and West Bengal. A unique feature of DPEP is that though multiple agencies fund the GOI share, the approach is common. GOI would be an equal partner in the process of appraisal and supervision. DPEP is likely to develop as a technical and resource organisation for primary education development in the country on the lines of the IDBI or HDFC.

A sum of Rs. 94.00 crores has been provided for implementation of DPEP during 1994-95 in the Department of Education's budget. A sum of Rs. 32 crores has been released to the seven State Implementation Societies as the first instalment of GOI share for the implementation of DPEP in 1994-95.

Baseline Studies : A significant achievement of the project formulation process under the District Primary Education Programme so far, has been the condcut of a large baseline study on achievement levels amongst primary students. These studies were conducted by the National Research Institutes, e.g., NCERT, NIEPA and an NGO in 46 Districts spread over 8 States of Assam, Haryana, Tamil Nadu, Karnataka, Kerala, Madhya Pradesh, Orissa and Maharashtra. The objective of these studies was to assess the present status of primary education development in the selected districts so as to provide an empirical basis to the district plans and define better the relevant strategies for project implementation. Over 50,000 children from 1718 schools spread over 106 Blocks were tested on a sample basis. These tests were so designed as to have access to the information on achievements of different segments of the students such as boys, girls, SC and ST among them. The specific details now available would be used for tailor - made designs for training and class transactions. These tests should be repeated every three years so that the assessment of the impact of DPEP on the learning achievement levels of students could be made. The findings of the studies revealed that learning achievement levels are quite low across several districts. These studies will be used for developing district-specific interventions in keeping with area-specific nature of DPEP. These studies are being shared further in the districts with teachers, parents and public representatives and suggestions are being invited on how to improve standards of school effectiveness and learning levels.

Lok Jumbish

An innovative project called "Lok Jumbish" : People's Movement for Education for All : with assistance from Swedish International Development Authority (SIDA) has been undertaken in Rajasthan. The basic objective of the project is to achieve Education for All by the year 2000 through people's mobilisation and their participation. The Government of India approved the first phase of the project for a period of two years, 1992-94, to cover 25 blocks spread over several districts with an estimated cost of Rs. 18.00 crores to be shared by SIDA, GOI and Government of Rajasthan in the ratio of 3:2:1. The first phase of the project has concluded on 30th June, 1994.

During the first phase the target for project coverage was achieved (25 blocks) and project interventions were made in several components of primary education like teacher's training, minimum levels of learning, opening of new schools, non-formal education centres etc. The salient achievements of Lok Jumbish Project are :

- Lok Jumbish has been able to set up innovative management structures incorporating the principles of decentralisation and delegation of authority as well as built partnerships with local communities and the voluntary sector.
- Community mobilisation and school mapping

- Innovative and community centred buildings development
- Focus on girls and socially disadvantaged groups

During the Phase I 204 primary schools were opened; 144 primary schools were upgraded; 339 posts of additional teachers provided; 2120 schools were provided with equipment and teaching-learning material; 650 NFE centres were opened; 30 training camps for Master Trainers and 198 camps for teachers were organised; mobilisation activities were undertaken in 1,096 villages; 50 field centres were opened and 294 women groups were organised.

Bihar Education Project

The Bihar Education Project is a basic education project aimed at bringing about qualitative improvement in the educational system and through it, in over-all socio-cultural situation in the state of Bihar. It comprises all components of basic education and is envisaged to cover, in a phased manner, 150 blocks spread over 20 districts over a five-year period, 1991-92 to 1995-96. The estimated outlay of the project over 5-year period (1991-92 to 1995-96) is Rs. 360 crores with an agreed funding pattern of 3:2:1 between UNICEF, GOI and GOB respectively. Special emphasis has been laid on the education of hitherto deprived sections of the society such as SCs/STs and the women. Bihar Education Project (BEP) is an evolving project with Block as the unit for most of the programme activities. Participatory planning and implementation are the important characteristics of the project. Generation of demand for educational services, capacity building and development of participatory management structures are the other crucial elements of the project implementation.

A State level body Bihar Shiksha Pariyojana Parishad (BSPP) has been registered to plan and implement the BEP. The Parishad has two organs—the General Council with Chief Minister as Chairman and the Executive Committee with Education Secretary, Government of Bihar as the Chairman. The Government of India, Government of Bihar, UNICEF, Teachers, NGOs, etc., are represented on these bodies. It has its branches at the district level wherein a District Executive Committee, with partnership of the GOI/GOB/UNICEF/Teachers and NGOs look after the project planning. For implementation of various components of the project activities, task forces have been set up. At the village level, the Village Education Committee (VEC) is envisaged as the crucial unit which would assist the basic education system in securing the cooperation and participation of the community and oversee educational inputs. The project is being implemented in a Mission Mode.

The project coverage upto 1994-95 was 98 blocks in the seven districts of Ranchi, W. Champaran, Rohtas, Muzaffarpur, Sitamarhi, E. Singhaboom and Chapra.

The major activities undertaken/proposed during 1994-95 included setting up and operationalisation of Village Education Committees (VECs) and training of the VECs functionaries; distribution of free of cost textbook kits to children; organisation of workshops at District and cluster level on Universalisation of Primary Education; taking up of baseline studies in project districts; workshop on microplanning and school mapping; conferences with Teacher Organisation construction/repair of school buildings; provision of toilets and drinking water facilities in schools; special orientation of teachers; in-service training of teachers; training of Head Masters, inspecting officers, etc.; organising Gurugosthis and bringing out quarterly magazine; study tours of teachers; establishing block/cluster level resource centres; establishing more NFE centres; expansion of Mahila Samakhya Programme to more areas; setting up of Jagjagi Kendras and MSKs; convergence of ICDS, PHED, health and welfare schemes with the educational inputs; bringing out a news magazine *Pratyush*; organising ensembles, puppet show and broadcasting of regular programmes; participation of the community in the enrolment drive resulting in enhancement of enrolment, particularly that of girl children; arranging orientation workshops for selected voluntary agencies; support to NGOs for innovative micro-projects; paintings, posters and panels; exhibitions; *Nukud Nataks*; etc.

A work plan of Rs. 42.4 crores has been approved for 1994-95. A Budget provision of Rs. 20 crores (GOI share) exists for the year 1994-95 for this project.

1.2 SECONDARY EDUCATION

Vocationalisation of Secondary Education

In accordance with the priority accorded to vocationalisation of education in the National Policy on Education, a Centrally Sponsored Scheme of Vocationalisation of Higher Secondary Education was introduced in February, 1988. The main objectives of the scheme are to enhance individual employability, reduce the mismatch between the demand and supply of skilled manpower and provide an alternative for those pursuing higher education without particular interest or purpose. A Centrally Sponsored Scheme of Pre-Vocational Education at Lower Secondary Stage has also been introduced from the year 1993-94 primarily to impart training in simple marketable skills to the students of classes IX to X, to develop vocational interests and to facilitate students in making a choice of vocational courses at the higher secondary level. The target laid down in the revised policy is to divert 10 per cent of higher secondary students to the vocational stream by 1995 and 25 per cent by 2000 A.D.

In order to provide expert inputs in policy formulation and implementation on a continuing basis, a Joint Council of Vocational Education (JCVE) has been set up at the national level under the chairmanship of Minister of Human Resource Development, with counterpart organisations at the State levels.

A Central Institute of Vocational Education, named as "Pt. Sunderlal Sharma Central Institute of Vocational Education (PSSCIVE) was set up at Bhopal on July 1st, 1993 under the overall umbrella of NCERT. The Institute acts as an apex level research and development/organisation in the field of vocational education and provides technical and academic support to the programme."

The scheme at +2 stage is implemented through the State Governments/UT Administrations. So far all the States/UTs, except Lakshadweep, have joined the programme. Up to the end of 1993-94, 16450 vocational sections have been approved in 5701 schools, creating capacity for diversion of 8.22 lakh to the vocational stream at the +2 stage. The actual enrolment is, however, likely to be less as optimum utilisation of facilities created may not be achieved. During the current year, i.e., 1994-95, main emphasis is, therefore, on consolidation and qualitative improvement of the programme.

The courses are selected by the State Governments on the basis of assessment of manpower requirement through district vocational surveys. About 150 vocational courses have been introduced in six major areas, viz., agriculture, business and commerce, engineering and technology, health and para-medical services, home science services and others. It has been recommended that 70 per cent of the total instructional time be devoted to vocational theory and practice, and the remaining to the study of general foundation courses and language course. On-the-job training forms an integral part of the curricula.

The scheme at the +2 stage envisages setting up an administrative structure at the Centre, State, district and school levels. The Bureau of Vocational Education is operating at the Central level to oversee the implementation of the programme. In the major States/UTs separate structures at the State level have been created.

The policy emphasises the need for making available non-formal, flexible and need-based vocational programme to school drop-outs, neo-literates, etc. The scheme, therefore, provides for funding of innovative programmes in the field of vocational education undertaken by voluntary organisations. So far 25 voluntary organisations have been assisted under the scheme.

The scheme lays considerable emphasis on practical training of students both during the course of study as well as after completion of the course. 60 vocational subject fields have so far been covered under the Apprentice Act to enable the vocational graduates at the +2 level to avail of the benefit of the Apprenticeship Scheme.

Efforts have been made to introduce need-based courses to ensure ready employment for the vocational students. Collaborative arrangements have been worked out with the Ministry of Railways, Ministry of Health, Handicraft Board, etc. A large number of industrial enterprises, in both public and private sectors, were also addressed by the Ministry with a view to involve them in the vocational education programme. From the responses received it was felt that some linkages could be forged for providing on the job training facilities to vocational students and in devising curricula and learning material. To pursue the matter further, a workshop was organised by the PSSCIVE in October, 1994.

A computerised Management Information System has been developed for vocational education to obtain necessary information on different aspects of programme implementation. The National Informatics Centre (NIC) in collaboration with this Department and NCERT has prepared two guidelines—one for filling up the format and the other for feeding the data through Computer software prepared for the purpose.

Educational Technology

This is a Centrally Sponsored Scheme combining certain elements of a Central Plan Scheme. The Scheme seeks to provide the entire cost of Radio-cum-Cassette Player in primary schools and 75% cost of colour TV in upper primary schools to provide access to quality education. To enable production of suitable programmes for these schools, six autonomous State Institutes of Educational Technology in U.P., Bihar, Orissa, Maharashtra, Gujarat and Andhra Pradesh have also been funded under the scheme.

The scheme extends financial support to the Central Institute of Educational Technology (CIET) for producing programmes for the school sector for broadcasting through Doordarshan and Akashvani.

At present all the programmes for the school sector for broadcasting through Doordarshan are produced by CIET and SIET system, and are funded under the scheme. For the Akashvani also the programmes are produced by the schools sector.

Radio-cum-Cassette Players and 51507 colour TVs have been

distributed. CIETs and SIETs have together produced 3921 TV and 1100 Audio Programmes for the school sector. CIET has also produced cassettes for teaching Indian language to the school children.

Under the aegis of the Indo-US Sub-Commission on Education and Culture, an innovative and experimental project in Distance Education coupled with inter-active learning, "Classroom 2000 AD" was launched in May 1993. This involved live teaching through a central facility to schools located in different places in the country. The students in the schools covered were able to interact live with the teacher and were also able to solve multiple choice objective type questions through computer key pads. On evaluation this project was found to be successful.

National Open School

National Open School (NOS) was es-tablished in November, 1989 as an autonomous organisation with the objective to provide quality education, through distance education mode, upto secondary stage for the school drop-outs and children who cannot attend formal schools. This school is vested with the authority to examine and certify students registered with it upto pre-degree level courses. The certificates issued by this school are recognised for admissions for pursuing higher education and also for employment.

The students have the freedom to choose the set of subjects according to their needs, interests and abilities. The students are also encouraged to choose vocational subjects in combination with academic subjects.

Central Board of Secondary Education

The Central Board of Secondary Education deals with multiple activities relating to affiliation, academics and examination that fall in its ambit. At the end of December, 1993, the Board had 3857 schools affiliated to it and about 500 cases under consideration. The major concern of the Board is for improving the quality of education in the schools affiliated to it. An All-India exercise of reviewing the courses in all subjects of teaching at the secondary and senior secondary levels was taken up. Action to review 41 vocational trades at +2 level and develop syllabi and courses in each trade was initiated.

Boarding and Hostel Facilities for Girl Students

The Scheme for Strengthening Boarding and Hostel Facilities for Girl Students in secondary and senior secondary schools was launched in 1993-94 to boost retention of girls in secondary and senior secondary schools, particularly in rural areas where schools are scarcely located and the girls are not able to cover considerable distance between their homes and schools. Under this scheme, assistance is provided to the existing hostels run by Non-Governmental Organisations (NGOs).

Improvement of Science Education in Schools

This Centrally Sponsored Scheme initiated during 1987-88 aims at improving the quality of science education and promoting scientific temper as envisaged in the National Policy on Education, 1986. Accordingly, 100 per cent assistance is provided to the State/UTs for upgradation of science laboratories in Government and Government aided secondary/higher secondary schools, provision of science kits to upper primary schools, provision of library assistance to secondary/higher secondary schools and training of science and mathematics teachers. Another component of the scheme is to provide assistance to voluntary organisations for developing innovative teaching and learning methods.

TABLE 1.6 : Science Education : Achievements (1987-88 to 1994-95)

	7th Plan	1990-91	1991-92	1992-93	1993-94	1994-95*	Total
Amount spent (Rs. in crore)	80.03	20.59	18.98	24.94	22.08	22.70	189.32
No. of States/UTs covered	30	24	12	14	15	15	32
No. of Schools covered							
(i) Upper Primary (Science kits)	42,398	5,791	7,880	11,678	5,756	5,000	78,503
(ii) Sec./Higher sec.(library assistance)	16,382	3,843	3,671	5,179	3,874	3,250	36,199
(iii) Sec./Higher sec.(Laboratory assistance)	15,073	3,981	3,783	5,849	3,914	3,250	35,850
No. of institutions assisted for setting up of District Resources Centres**	115	57	26	—	—	—	198
No. of Vol. Orgns. covered (for innovative programmes) cumulative	13	7	14	7	12	12	30

* Anticipated.

** This component does not qualify for assistance during the 8th Plan.

Environmental Orientation to School Education

The scheme started in 1988-89 aims at providing infusion of environmental information and concepts in the general syllabus and curriculum. The scheme initially catered to the requirement of the elementary sector. During the VIII Plan, however, it has been extended to the secondary and senior secondary levels. Assistance is given to State Governments for reviewing syllabus and textbooks for providing environmental orientation. A major thrust under the scheme is to fund NGOs for developing innovative teaching methods and reading material for school children in the field of environment.

Another salient feature of the scheme is the "Nodal Agency Approach" wherein larger voluntary organisations designated as nodal agencies guide and assist smaller voluntary organisations in formulating suitable proposals for Environmental Education. Funds are released in the first instance by the Government to the nodal agencies and are, in turn, passed on to the smaller voluntary agencies.

The States/UTs are provided assistance under this scheme on project basis which includes review and development of curricula on various disciplines at primary, upper primary, secondary and senior secondary levels with a view to infusing environmental concepts therein; review and development of textbooks at primary and upper primary levels; review of strategy for imparting environmental education at upper primary level, development of teaching and learning material; organisation of suitable innovative work experience activities, etc.

TABLE 1.7 : Environmental Orientation to School Education Achievements (7th Plan to 1994-95)

	7th Plan	1990-91	1991-92	1992-93	1993-94	1994-95*	Total
Amount spent (Rs. in crore)	3.57	2.00	1.81	1.80	1.12	1.95	12.25
No. of States/UTs covered	20	8	9	17	5	10	25
No. of projects sanctioned	32	6	9	1	11	10	70
No. of voluntary bodies assisted	10	7	5	4	9	10	25

* Estimated

International Mathematical Olympiad

The International Mathematical Olympiad (IMO) is held every year with a view to identify and nurturing talent in mathematics at school level. Indian delegation participated in IMO-1994 held in Hongkong during July, 1994. India was ranked 16th out of 69 participating countries. The Indian team won 3 silver and 3 bronze medals. IMO-1996 will be held in India.

Cultural Exchange Programme : Under this scheme financial assistance is provided to meet the cost of travel and stay of Indian delegation going abroad and foreign delegation coming to India.

Computer Literacy and Studies in Schools (CLASS) : A pilot project on Computer Literacy and Studies in Schools (CLASS) was initiated in 1984-85 in consultation with Department of Electronics. The broad objectives of the pilot project included, demystification of Computers and to provide 'Hands on' experience. The project has been continued upto 1992-93 on adhoc basis and fund to the tune of Rs. 4.5 crores were provided each year. 2598 schools were covered upto 1992-93. The CLASS Project has been evaluated by a number of agencies, Ministry of Human Resource Development and Comptroller and Auditor General of India. The C and AG report identified multiplicity of agencies, diffused responsibility, inadequate monitoring etc. Keeping these drawbacks in view, a modified scheme has been prepared and is being implemented as a Centrally Sponsored Scheme from 1993-94.

An amount of Rs. 146.00 crores has been provided for implementing the scheme during the Eighth Plan. This amount is for maintaining 2598 schools already covered under the old scheme as well as for including 1820 additional schools during the Eighth Plan. 218 additional schools were covered during 1993-94.

The National Population Education Project (NPEP)

The National Population Education Project was launched in April 1980. It completed its first cycle in 1985 and the second cycle in 1992. Its current third cycle which has started from January 1993, will be coterminus with the Eighth Five Year Plan.

The project is directed to attain the objective of institutionalising population education in schools and non-formal education system. As an educational response to population issues, population education aims at making learners aware of the interrelationship between population development, resources, environment and quality of life, developing in them rational attitude and responsible behaviour and initiating in them positive value orientation so that they may take informed decisions on various population issues according to small family norms.

The NPEP is funded by the United Nations Population Fund (UNFPA). The UNESCO provides technical support through its country Support Team (CST), based in Kathmandu (Nepal). The NPEP is being implemented by the NCERT. The Ministry of Health and Family Welfare is the nodal agency.

The Project is being implemented in 29 States and Union Territories, the States of Goa and Meghalaya and the Union Territory of Lakshadweep remaining out of its fold. The Akashvani and Doordarshan, Family Planning Association of India and other non-government agencies are involved in relevant project activities at national and state level.

The main activities of the project include (i) development of curricular and instructional materials to ensure effective integration of population education in the curricula of school education, non-formal education and teacher education; (ii) development of training materials and audio-visual materials; (iii) development of materials on emerging concerns; (iv) orientation of teachers, teacher educators and other functionaries; (v) organisation of co-curriculum activities in schools and NFE centres; (vi) promotion of research and evaluation studies in population education; and (vii) monitoring of project activities at national, state and local level.

Integrated Education for the Disabled Children

The Centrally Sponsored Scheme of Integrated Education for the Disabled Children which was launched by the erstwhile Department of Social Welfare in 1974, was transferred to the Department of Education in 1982. The Scheme is framed on the premise that children with mild handicaps make better progress academically and psychologically if they study in common schools along side 'normal' children. The Scheme provides 100 per cent financial assistance to State Governments/UT Administrations/Voluntary Organisations for creating necessary facilities in schools. Assistance is also given, through UGC, to selected Universities/ Institutions for running training courses in special education for teachers of the handicapped children. Training facilities are also provided by NCERT in the four regional Colleges of Education.

A UNICEF Project Integrated Education for the Disabled (PIED) is also being implemented which envisages development of specific strategies for education of children with disabilities in general schools. One block each in the States of Haryana, Madhya Pradesh, Mizoram,

Orissa, Rajasthan and Tamil Nadu and the Municipal Corporations of the Delhi and Baroda are covered under this project.

So far 24 States/UTs have been assisted under the Scheme. About 40,000 children spread over 9,000 schools have been covered. A much larger number are receiving indirect benefit through special teachers and other learning material. A large number of voluntary organisations have also been provided financial assistance under the Scheme.

Yoga in Schools

Keeping in view the provisions of NPE, 1986, a Centrally Sponsored Scheme for Introduction of Yoga in Schools was launched in 1989-90. Under the scheme, financial assistance is provided for training of teachers in Yoga and for building the infrastructure necessary for the purpose. In addition, institutions of all India character are given assistance for maintenance as well as developmental expenditure for promotion of basic research and/or for teachers training programme in various aspects of Yoga other than the therapeutical aspect. Financial assistance to Yoga institutions for promotion of therapeutical aspect is being extended by the Ministry of Health and Family Welfare.

National Award to Teachers

The Scheme of National Awards for Teachers was started in the year 1958-59 with the object of raising the prestige of teachers and giving public recognition to the meritorious services of outstanding teachers working in Primary, Middle and Higher Secondary Schools. In 1967-68 the scope of the scheme was enlarged to cover the teachers of Sanskrit Pathashalas, Tolls etc., run on traditional lines. In 1976 the scheme was further enlarged to cover Arabic/Persian teachers of Madrasas run on traditional lines. From the Award Year 1993 the Scheme has further been enlarged to cover teachers from Sainik Schools, Navodaya Vidyalayas and schools run by the Atomic Energy Education Society. Each award carries a certificate of merit, a cash payment of Rs. 10,000 and silver medal. The number of awards given have been increased from 296 to 302 from the award year 1993.

Two hundred and seventy teachers were selected for the National Award for 1993.

National Council of Educational Research and Training (NCERT)

The National Council of Educational Research and Training (NCERT), an autonomous organisation, was established in 1961 to bring about qualitative improvement in school education and teacher education. It functions as a resource centre to the government in the field of school education and teacher education. The NCERT undertakes programmes related to research, development and training extension and dissemination of educational innovations etc., through various constituent Departments at the headquarters in New Delhi and 17 Field Offices all over the country.

Kendriya Vidyalaya Sangathan (KVS)

The Kendriya Vidyalaya Sangathan was set up in 1965, primarily for catering to the educational needs of the children of transferable Central Government employees, including defence personnel, whose education was handicapped owing to frequent transfers of their parents from one linguistic region to another and the resultant change in the course of study. The organisation is fully financed by the Government of India.

During 1994-95, 23 schools were opened making the total number of 818 Kendriya Vidyalayas having an enrolment of more than 7 lakhs while the teaching and non-teaching staff is around 43,000.

Navodaya Vidyalaya Samiti (NVS)

It is universally accepted that children with special talent should be provided opportunity to proceed at faster pace, by making good quality education available to them irrespective of their capacity to pay for it. The National Policy of Education—1986 envisaged establishment of pace setting schools intended to serve this purpose in the country on a given pattern, with full scope for innovation and experimentation. In pursuance of this objective to provide good quality modern education to the talented children pre-dominantly from the rural areas, the Government of India have launched in 1985-86 a scheme to establish Jawahar Navodaya Vidyalayas (JNVs) in each District throughout the country which are being managed by an autonomous organisation called Navodaya Vidyalaya Samiti. The broad aims of the Samiti are to serve the objectives of excellence coupled with equity and social justice, to promote national integration by providing opportunity to children from different parts of the country to live and learn together, to develop their full potential and to become catalysts to the national development.

The Vidyalayas are fully residential and co-educational in which admission to the children from urban areas is generally restricted to 25 per cent of the seats. Efforts are made to ensure that atleast 1/3rd of the students in each Vidyalaya are girls. Reservation of seats in favour of children belonging to SCs and STs is provided in proportion of their population in the concerned Distt., provided that in no Distt., such reservation is less than the national level.

The Vidyalayas provide education in the streams of Humanities, Commerce, Science and Vocational upto +2 level and are affiliated to CBSE. There are at present 359 sanctioned Vidyalayas in the country operating in 30 States/UTs. The State of Tamil Nadu and West Bengal have not yet opted for implementation of the Navodaya Vidyalaya Scheme.

The Samiti has 8 Regional Offices at Pune, Bhopal, Chandigarh, Hyderabad, Jaipur, Shilong, Lucknow and Patna. Each of these Regional Offices monitor the Academic, Financial and Administrative functioning of the Vidyalayas under its jurisdiction.

Central Tibetian Schools Administration (CTSA)

The Central Tibetian Schools Administration was set up as an autonomous organisation in 1961. The main object of the society is to establish, manage and assist schools in India for education of the children of Tibetian refugees.

To Keep the Tibetian community abreast of all aspects of modern education and development while retaining the essentials of their traditional system and culture, the organisation set up these schools. In the year under report 11,129 students are receiving education in 94 schools including 13 Grants-in-Aid Schools and 51 Pre-Primary schools spread all over India.

1.3 HIGHER EDUCATION AND RESEARCH

Growth of the Higher Education System

At the beginning of the year 1994-95, the total student enrolment in universities and colleges was 50.07 lakhs accounting for more than 2.02 lakhs as in the previous year. The enrolment in the university departments was 8.29 lakhs and that in the affiliated colleges was 41.78 lakhs.

Enrolment in the Faculty of Arts constituted 40.4% of the total enrolment. In the faculties of Science and Commerce the percentage was 19.6 and 21.9 respectively. Enrolment at the first degree levels was 44.11 lakhs (88.1%); at the post-graduate level 4.76 lakhs (9.5%); at the research level 0.55 lakhs (1.1%); and at the diploma and certificate level 0.65 lakhs (1.3%). The total number of teachers increased to 2.86 lakhs during the year. Of these, 0.65 lakhs were in the university departments/ university colleges and the rest in the affiliated colleges. Of the 64847 teachers in the universities, 8300 were Professors, 16990 were Readers, 36963 were Lecturers and 2594 were Tutors/Demon-strators. In the affiliated colleges, the number of senior teachers was 30695, the number of Lecturers was 180418 and that of Tutors/Demonstrators was 9717.

Upto November, 1994 the total number of universities eligible to receive assistance from UGC in the country was 162 and the total number of institutions deemed to be universities was 36.

Higher Education among Women : The enrolment of women students at the beginning of the year 1993-94 was 16.64 lakhs as against 15.90 lakhs in the previous year. At the post-graduate level, the enrolment of women was 35.1% of the total enrolment. The enrolment of women students was the highest in Kerala (53.4%) followed by Punjab (48.6%), Delhi (46.7%), Haryana (42.6%), Meghalaya/Nagaland/Mizoram (39.5%), Tamil Nadu, West Bengal/Tripura/Sikkim (38.9%). The enorlment of women was the lowest in Bihar (16.9%).

University Grants Commission (UGC)

Some of the major thrust areas pursued during the years were : Autonomous Colleges, Academic Staff Colleges for Orientation of Teachers, eligibility test for recruitment of lecturers, Inter-University Centres and Consortiums, Distance Education. Fellowships/Scholarships, COSIST, Adult Education and National Literacy Mission, Spread of Mass Communication and Educational Technology Network, Vocationalisation of Education at the first degree level, Environment Education, Curriculum Development/Redesigning of Courses, Computer Education, Education for Scheduled Castes/Scheduled Tribes and for the Minorities and Weaker Sections among the minority communities, Education for the Women and Handicapped, Population Education. A brief account of the efforts made by the Commission in respect of various schemes is given in the following paragraphs.

The setting up of a National Accreditation Board for Higher Education as an autonomous body was approved.

Environment Education : The Supreme Court *inter alia* directed the UGC to take appropriate steps to prescribe a course on environment and consider the feasibility of making environment a compulsory subject at every level of college education. In pursuance of this, the UGC invited proposals from the universities for introduction of courses in Environment Education and the following programmes were approved.

(i) Proposals for organising workshop/seminar/refresher courses on environment awareness.

(ii) Projects on "Fly-Ash Accumulation and Comparatives of finding avenues for its Mass Scale Utilisation."

(iii) Introduction of special paper on Environment Education at PG level in different areas like History, Physiology, Chemistry, Rural Economics, Economics Studies and Planning, Mathematics, Botany, Zoology, Sociology and Geography, B.Ed., M.Ed.

(iv) Introduction of M.Sc course in Environment Education. Programme to telecast nearly 100 episodes on environmental awareness through its 'country-wide classroom' programme and preparation of a booklet for colleges as foundation course at under-graduate level, and popular literature like handouts, pamphlets on environmental awareness.

Autonomous Colleges : The Commission has been promoting and encouraging the concept of autonomy through its scheme of autonomous colleges which it has decided to continue in the VIII Plan period. At present the total number of colleges which have been granted autonomous status is 108.

Plan Grants to Universities : At the beginning of the year 1994-95 the Commission provided plan grants to 100 eligible universities (excluding Agricultural universities) amounting to Rs. 6684 lakhs, as part of the total commitment for the VIII Plan period. While the quantum of outlay for general development for each university is decided at the beginning of the plan period and is determined on the basis of the state of development of that particular university, grants for schemes are provided on the basis of recommendations of experts after scrutiny of such schemes. Also at the beginning of the year 1994-95 plan grants amounting to Rs. 3006 lakhs were released to Central Universities.

Development of Colleges : VIII Plan grants to colleges are being given on the recommendations of expert committee and in consultation with college principals and state representatives. An outlay of Rs. 26528 lakhs has been approved for about 3900 colleges so far for the VIII Plan.

Special Assistance Programmes : The Commission continued to provide assistance to 41 centres of Advanced Study and Special Assistance to 115 Departments of Science, Engineering and Technology and 16 Centres of Advanced Study and 118 Departments of Humanities and Social Sciences upto November, 1994. In addition 84 Departmental Research Support Projects in Science and 47 in Humanities and Social Sciences were under implementation upto November, 1994. The

Commission also dropped two departments for their failure to implement the schemes sanctioned and derecognised one department as its performance was not found to be of the requisite standard.

Strengthening of Infrastructure in Science and Technology (COSIST), Programme : Departments supported under COSIST have been given functional autonomy. The infrastructural facilities extended through COSIST support have improved teaching instructions at post-graduate and research level and have enhanced the quality of teaching, particularly experimental part of the courses. As a result of the review of the Special Assistance Programme (SAP) and COSIST, it has been decided *inter alia* that SAP and COSIST will be an integrated programme and COSIST level support may be provided only to those departments which have completed atleast one phase (five years) of SAP and have been reviewed.

Super Conductivity Programme : The UGC programme on super conductivity has been in operation since 1987 for assisting universities in developing education and research capabilities in both basic and applied areas of superconductivity. The Commission was supporting 38 universities upto November, 1994 in both basic and applied areas.

Common Facilities and Services : Modern computer-based information/documentation centres have already been set up at Bangalore, Bombay and Baroda. These Centres have improved the information accessibility to teachers and students. During the year, Eastern Centre for Research in Astro-physics was set up with a view to establish a world-class Astrophysics groups in the eastern part of India. The Centre would build up experimental facilities, particularly in the field of solar radio astronomy in the initial stage with future projections to cover galactic and extra galactic radio astronomy as well. Also during the year, the MST radar at Srivenkateshwara University was made fully operational in MST mode for a detailed study of the middle atmosphere dynamics. The Indian Institute of Advanced Studies, Shimla has also been functioning as an Inter-University Centre for humanities and social sciences on behalf of the UGC. These Centres are in addition to the Nuclear Science Centres, New Delhi, Inter-University Centre in Astronomy and Astrophysics, Pune, Inter University Consortium, Indore, Crystal Growth Centres, Anna University and Inter-University Consortium for Education Communication.

Media and Educational Technology : The UGC has taken the initiative to utilise the time slot given for higher education by televising the TV programme in higher education and entitled "Countrywide

Classroom" which has taken higher education to remote areas of the country. The Commission is at present supporting Educational Media Research Centres (EMRCs) at various Universities and Central Institute of English and Foreign Languages (Hyderabad). Audio-Visual Research Centres (AVRCs) at various universities, are being supported for training of personnel and production of software. The Consortium for Educational Communications (CEC), an autonomous organisation under UGC, provides programmes for transmission through the enrichment channel of Doordarshan. The Commission has also established Consortium for Export of Educational Material as a project mode of CEC.

Adult, Continuing and Extension Education Programmes : The Commission is providing assistance to universities for the implementation of Total Literacy (TLC) through their departments of Adult, Continuing and Extension Education. Such assistance is also provided for population education and planning forums.

AIDS : An action plan was also drawn up for prevention and control of AIDS with the help of the university and college community through the introduction of self-study courses, dissemination of information with the help of PERCs and medical experts, provision of community services through NSS and NCC, publicity through countrywide classroom programmes, preparation of course material, and by providing additional grants to universities and colleges for purchase of books on AIDS, population education, environmental and drug abuse.

Indian Council of Social Science Research (ICSSR)

The Indian Council of Social Science Research was established in 1969 as an Autonomous organization to promote and coordinate social science research in the country.

The Council provides maintenance and Development grants to 27 research institutes to enlarge the knowledge of social science by improving the quality of research and promoting inter-disciplinary perspective. The ICSSR at present has six Regional Centres.

Under the Tribal studies programme 36 review papers were selected for publication in four separate volumes.

Scheme of Financial Assistance to Institutions of Higher Learning of All India Importance

The Scheme of Financial assistance to Institutions of Higher Learning has been continuing. Under the Scheme, financial assistance is provided to voluntary organisations/educational institutions which are outside the university system and are engaged in progsrammes of innovative character.

Assistance is also extended to institutions offering programmes of particular interest to rural community and are of innovative character. During the year : (i) Shri Aurobindo International Centre for Education, Pondicherry; (ii) Shri Aurobindo International Institute of Educational Research, Auroville; (iii) Lok Bharati Sanosra, and (iv) Mitra Niketan, Vellanad, Kerala are being extended financial assistance.

Association of Indian Universities (AIU)

Association of Indian Universities (AIU) is an apex voluntary educational organisation of universities with the major objective of promoting and coordinating the activities of higher educational institutions, which are its members. Some of the major activities of AIU in the field of higher education include disseminating information, carrying out research studies, publication and promotion of literature, cooperation among institutions in the area of cultural sports and allied areas, conduct of conferences of Vice-Chancellors and organisation of training programme for University Administrators.

AIU is substantially financed from the annual subscription paid by the member universities and proceeds from the sales and publication of literature pertaining to higher education. The Association receives Plan and Non-Plan grants from the Government for the research programmes conducted by the Research Cell.

A project entitled "Accreditation of the Institutions of Higher Education in India : An Empirical Study of JNU" has been completed. The study has attempted to develop indicators of accreditation and assessment for institutions of higher education in India, especially the central universities. Based on data gathered from the Jawaharlal Nehru University, the following indicators appear to be promising: mission and key inputs of the university, performance of students, performance of teachers and efficiency in the use of resources. Another project on "Status of Question Banking in Indian Universities" has been completed and the findings have been published in the Journal of Higher Education Vol. 17, Nov. 3, 1994. The study explored the use of question banks developed either by AIU or by the concerned university, and the further possibility of using question banks in various subjects at the undergraduated level in colleges and universities.

1.4 ADULT EDUCATION

National Literacy Mission (NLM)

The mandate of the National Literacy Mission has been enlarged at the national level now to cover 100 million persons by 1997. The Mission which was originally launched with the objective of imparting functional literacy to 80.00 million adult illiterates in the 15-35 age-group by 1995, has now been extended upto 1997 i.e., by the end of the 8th Plan and its coverage enhanced to 100 million. Apart from covering its target clientele in the 15-35 age-group, children in the 9-14 age-group would also be covered wherever there is a demand.

The Total Literacy Campaign which has now been established and accepted as the main strategy for eradication of illiteracy under the Mission has now been extended to 338 districts in the country and of these 130 districts have entered the post literacy phase. So far an estimated 71.1 million learners have been enrolled in the programme and 44.70 million persons are reported to have been made literate.

Review by Prime Minister in the Conference of Chief Ministers : A conference of Chief Ministers of all the States and Union Territories was held under the Chairmanship of the Prime Minister at New Delhi on 15th February, 1994 to consider the reports of the National Development Council Committee on Literacy and CABE (Central Advisory Board of Education) Committee on Decentralised Management of Education and proposals regarding Education for All. A summary of the discussions at the Chief Ministers Conference in so far as they relate to Adult Education, is furnished below:

There was complete unanimity at the Conference that EFA should be placed high in the country's development agenda. Welcoming the announcement of the Prime Minister to enhance the outlay on education to six per cent of the National income from Ninth Plan, the Chief Ministers agreed to supplement the efforts of the Central Government in the mobilization of resources and to accord higher priority to primary and adult education in State Plans. It was also agreed that along with higher allocation of resources it was necessary to ensure better utilization of resources through effective implementation and monitoring of programmes in their States. The Chief Ministers would periodically review the progress in this area so that the right signals are sent all over the State about the high priority attached to EFA and management of educational services and programmes more effectively. The need to enlist the cooperation of NGOs, teachers' unions and socially conscious individuals come out very clearly in the discussions. The shared perception was that without proper decentralisation of educational administration and greater community participation, universalisation of elementary education (UEE) cannot be achieved. The school should be an important social organisation once again as it used to be. The Chief Ministers also agreed that special efforts would be made to promote convergence of primary education and related services like Early Childhood Care and Education (ECCE), ICDS, school health and nutrition. It was felt that apart from improving efficiency such a convergence would promote enrolment and reduction of drop-outs. It was felt that specific efforts are needed in educationally backward States like Bihar, Uttar Pradesh, Rajasthan, Madhya Pradesh and Andhra Pradesh. The programmes in these States would be periodically reviewed by a group of Chief Ministers with a view to sustaining the tempo and achieving synergies in implementing the programmes in the related fields of education, health, women and child development and nutrition.

As a follow-up of the Conference of Chief Ministers taken by the Prime Minister, a meeting of Chief Ministers of Bihar, Madhya Pradesh, Rajasthan and Uttar Pradesh was held at Bhopal on 1st July, 1994 to discuss progress of Total Literacy Campaigns and Universalisation of Elementary Education under the Chairmanship of the Minister of Human Resource Development. The recommendations of the meeting of Chief Ministers, in so far as Adult Education is concerned, are as follows :

> The four States will accord priority to primary education and Literacy Programmes. Expenditure cuts due to economy measures will not apply to these programmes. During the currency of the Plan period efforts will be made to enhance allocations to 6 per cent of the gross national product for the promotion of education. For the implementation of Primary Education and the Literacy programmes by State Governments, services of talented and dedicated officers will be made available for a sufficient period. The District Collectors of TLC districts would not be disturbed during the implementation of the programme except extreme public exigency.

Total Literacy Campaigns : After successful conclusion of the Total Literacy Campaign (TLC) in district Ernakulam (Kerala) in January 1990, the TLC has become the principal strategy of the National Literacy Mission which has the objective of making 100 million citizens functionally literate in the preferred age-group of 9-35 by the end of the Eighth Five-Year Plan.

The TLC is marked by certain positive characteristics that it is area-specific, time-bound, delivered through voluntarism, cost-effective and outcome-oriented. The campaigns are implemented by Zilla Saksharata Samities (ZSS) specially constituted under the District Collectors. The ZSS, with its membership drawn from all sections of the society, ensures its participative nature. Besides the task-specific sub-committees of the ZSS, popular committees are also constituted at all levels from the district down to the village panchayats, which are animated by the culture of equality.

The TLC presupposes the generation of a positive demand of the people for literacy through appropriate environment-building programmes. The initial effort at environment-building is closely followed by a door-to-door literacy survey during which potential learners and volunteers are identified. Suitable primers are developed through the State Resource Centres in accordance with the pedagogic technique of Improved Pace and Content of Learning. Primer-specific training is provided to the Resource Persons, Master Trainers and Volunteer Instructors. Two activities, namely, environment-building as well as monitoring and internal evaluation, are continued through the teaching/ learning activity which account for a total of 200 hours spread over a period of 6 months. An external impact/summative evaluation is made at the conclusion of the teaching. Post Literacy Campaigns (PLC) are launched to mop up the left-over illiterates and to consolidate the gains of literacy acquired during TLC, and to enable the neo-literates to develop abilities for self-learning.

The literacy campaigns are implemented through direct funding to the ZSS by the Central and State Governments in the ratio of 2:1 (for normal districts) and 4:1 (for districts under Tribal-Sub Plan areas). Besides the funding arrangement, the active involvement of State Governments is ensured also through the identification of the District Collector with the ZSS. The enlarged role of the collectors has ensured their active leadership for the TLC. The TLCs, by and large, have enlisted the enthusiastic participation of all sections of the society, especially the women, the weaker sections, etc.

On the question of continuation of the Total Literacy Campaign Scheme during 8th Five-Year Plan, the Union Cabinet has, inter alia, approved the following :

- Funding pattern for districts under Tribal Sub-Plan areas revised from the usual ratio of 2:1 to 4:1.

- Inclusion of children in 9-14 age-group for coverage under TLC. The children who are being covered under NFE Scheme would be excluded for coverage under TLC. Strategy for covering this age-group would now be an essential part of the TLC proposal, with separate primers for 9-14 age-group.
- Provision of extra funding for restoration of projects which do not do well in the first phase of implementation due to circumstances beyond the control of ZSS, e.g., natural calamities, political upheavals, etc.
- Constitution of a Project Approval Committee of the Executive Committee of National Literacy Mission Authority to enable speedy approval of the projects. In order to increase the participation of State Governments in the process of project formulation and approval, it has been decided to include the Education Secretary of the concerned State as Member of the Project Approval Committee of the NLMA.

So far 338 district TLCs and 130 district PLCs projects have been approved.

The focus of the Total Literacy Campaigns has now shifted to the Hindi-speaking areas where bulk of the illiterate population resides. It is expected that in the remaining period of the Eighth Five-Year Plan, a continued input of TLC can cause a major dent in the problem of adult illiteracy. So far 93 districts under TLC and 13 districts under PLC have been sanctioned in the Hindi-speaking States.

Post-Literacy and Continuing Education : Since the launching of the Scheme, over 22,000 JSNs have been sanctioned in different States/ UTs and of these, around 18,000 JSNs were operational during 1994-95. These JSNs essentially cater to neo-literates of Centre-based Adult Education Programmes. Each JSN is expected to cover a cluster of 4 to 5 villages with a population of about 5,000. JSNs set-up under the Scheme are designed to provide opportunities and facilities for reinforcement and upgradation of literacy skills.

Voluntary Agencies : The Central Scheme of Assistance of Voluntary Agencies in Adult Education came into operation under the National Literacy Mission (NLM) in 1987-88.

146 TLC projects including 38 approved in 1994-95 have so far been sanctioned to 141 VAs for making a total of around 20 lakh persons literate. One project is being implemented in Andhra Pradesh, 8 in Assam, 23 in Bihar, 1 in Haryana, 7 in Madhya Pradesh, 1 in

Manipur, 17 in Orissa, 3 in Punjab, 9 in Rajasthan, 13 in Tamil Nadu, 59 in Uttar Pradesh, 1 in West Bengal and 3 in Delhi.

Directorate of Adult Education : The Directorate of Adult Education (DAE, a subordinate office of the Department of Education) continued to function as the National Resource Centre in the field of adult education and total literacy campaigns. The Directorate has 6 units with identified professional and administrative functions.

1.5 TECHNICAL EDUCATION

During the past four decades, there has been a phenomenal expansion of technical education facilities in the country. But, a lot still needs to be done in the field of technical education in respect of increasing its coverage and enhancing its accessibility to the needs of organised as well as unorganized and rural sectors and in improving its relevance to productivity. Moreover, the changing scenario by the turn of the century in socio-economic, industrial and technological areas needs to be considered to enable the system to play its role with greater relevance and objectivity. Based on these considerations, several initiatives were taken to further revamp the technical education system. These include: modernization and removal of obsolescence, promoting institution-industry interaction, providing continuing education for upgrading the skill and knowledge of technical personnel working in industry and service sector, transfer of technology to the rural sector/setting up of Technology Development Missions to meet the emerging challenges in Science and Technology.

The year under report witnessed some significant developments in the field of technical education. A considerable progress was made in implementing the various programmes and schemes. A major project has been undertaken with the assistance of World Bank to upgrade the technician education system in the country for enabling the polytechnics to improve their capacity, quality and efficiency. Vested with statutory authority, the All India Council for Technical Education (AICTE) continued to fulfill the tasks assigned to it.

Indian Institutes of Technology

The five Indian Institutes of Technology (IITs) at Kharagpur, Bombay, Madras, Kanpur and Delhi were set up in the country as Institutes of National Importance and premier centres of education and training in engineering and applied science at the undergraduate level and to provide adequate facilities for post-graduate studies and research.

The IITs conduct four-year undergraduate programme (Bachelors-Degree) in various fields of engineering and technology. They also offer integrated Master's Degree courses of five years duration in physics, chemistry, mathematics, biochemical engineering and biotech. One year and a half M. Tech. degree courses in various specialisations and one year post-graduate Diploma courses in selected areas. In addition, the Institutes offer Ph.D Programmes in different branches of Engineering Sciences, Humanities and Social Sciences. There are also advance area of training and research in each Institute in identified areas of specialization.

During the year under report, the Institutes continued to modernise their laboratories with funds provided by the Government of India for the purpose.

A special preparatory course of 10 months duration continued to improve the intake of SC/St students in the IITs. Those SC/ST students who fail to qualify the joint Entrance Examination (JEE) for admission in the IIT's but score a certain minimum percentage of marks are offered admission to the preparatory course. At the end of the preparatory course, the students are subjected to a qualifying test on the basis of which they are offered admission to the B.Tech. Programme without having to appear in the JEE again. This has improved the position of intake of SC/ST students in the IITs. The SC/ST students also continue to get financial support from the Institutes by way of pocket allowance, loans and discretion grant, apart from free messing.

As per the Assam Accord, another IIT has been set-up in Assam, the Sixth in the chain of IITs. For declaring the IIT, Guwahati-the Sixth in the fraternity of IITs as an Institute of National Importance, the Institutes of Technology Act, 1961 was amended and came into effect on 1st September, 1994.

Indian Institutes of Management

The four Indian Institutes of Management (IIMs) located at Ahemedabad, Bangalore, Calcutta and Lucknow were set-up by the Government of India with the objective of providing education, training, research and consultancy in the field of management. These Institutions are the premier centres in these areas.

The three Institutes in Ahemedabad, Bangalore and Calcutta continued their usual academic programmes, viz., Post-graduate Programme in management (equivalent to M.B.A.), fellowship programme (equivalent to Ph.D), Management development Programmes, Organisation

Based Programme and Research & Consultancy for Industries as in the past.

The fourth Indian Institute of Management at Lucknow started functioning from 1985-86 session.

As a Follow-up of NPE, these Institutes have established Research Centres to meet the needs of other non-corporate and under managed sectors like Agriculture, Rural Development, Public Systems Management, Energy, Health Education, Habitat, etc. These Institutes have also set up computer-aided Management Centres with the objective of promoting the development of application of software in the area of Industry-oriented Management Techniques.

Indian Institute of Science, Bangalore

The Indian Institute of Science (IISc), Bangalore is one amongst the premier Institutes in the country carrying out research work in Engineering Sciences and allied field. The Institute was established in the year 1909.

Revised Funding Pattern of Indian Institutes of Technology, Indian Institutes of Management and Indian Institutes of Science : A Revised Pattern of Funding has been implemented beginning with the financial year 1993-94. The Non-Plan grant of the Institutions is fixed at the level of grant in RE 1992-93 plus 10 per cent thereof, and maintained at that level for the next four years (Till the end of 1996-97). The Institutions will retain revenue receipts to augment the funds provided by the Govt. of India, as cushion against normal escalations over the four year period. The savings, out of the Non-Plan grants, and the revenue receipts will be retained and carried over by the Institutions. To encourage and accelerate the creation of an adequate level of Endowment Fund, the Government of India will provide 100 per cent matching grant for savings out of the Non-Plan grant, revenue receipts and net earnings from consultancy and continuing education programmes, to the extent these are transferred to the Endowment Fund.

Technology Development Missions

The Prime Minister, during the first meeting of the Planning Commission held in September, 1991 observed that institutions of excellence like IITs and IISc., Bangalore need to concentrate on technology assessment and forecast so that futuristic approaches could be re-oriented to take up the development of emerging science and technology trends in the country. Sequel to these observations of the Prime Minister, Directors of IITs and other experts deliberated in different meetings arranged by

Planning Commission and identified the following 8 generic areas of strategic significance :

1. Food Processing Engineering
2. Integrated Design and Competitive Manufacturing
3. Photonic Devices and Technologies
4. Energy Efficient Technologies
5. Natural Hazards Mitigation
6. Communication Networking and Intelligent Automation
7. New Materials
8. Genetic Engineering and Biotechnology.

An amount of Rs. 60 crore for eight missions has been provided towards Plan Outlay during the eighth Plan period, out of which Rs.2 Crore has been released to five IITs and IISc., Bangalore during 1993-94. The budget provision for the year 1994-1995 is Rs. 33 crores.

All India Council for Technical Education

The AICTE set up in 1945 as an advisory body was given a statutory status through an Act of Parliament in 1987. The Act came into effect on March 28, 1988. The main functions of the statutory AICTE include proper planning and coordinated development of technical education in the country, qualitative improvement at all levels in relation to planned quantitative growth and regulation of the system and maintenance of norms and standards.

In order to streamline the system of approval of new courses and programmes the Council has issued regulations for establishment of new institutions/starting of new courses, etc.,

The Council has come to an understanding with the Council of Architecture (functioning under the Architects Act) and the Pharmacy Council of India (under the Pharmacy Act) in the procedure for assessment of courses and institutions in their respective fields.

The Council has laid down norms and standards for diploma, degree and post-graduate courses in various fields. In pursuance of the Supreme Court judgments, the Council has issued regulatious fixing norms and guidelines for changing tuition and other fees and providing guidelines for admissions of students to professional colleges.

With effect from 1.4.1994, the following institutions/schemes have been transferred to the Council :

1. National Technical Manpower Information System (NTMIS)
2. Technical Teachers' Training Institute (TTTIs)
3. National Institute for Training in Industrial Engineering (NITIE)
4. National Institute of Foundry and Forge Technology (NIFFT),
5. School of Planning and Architecture (SPA),
6. Development of PG Courses,
7. Development of Management Courses at Non-university centres.
8. Research and Development (R&D) in selected higher education technical institutions,
9. Modernisation and Removal of Obsolescence.
10. Thrust Areas of Technical Education,
11. Institution Industry Interaction,
12. Continuing Education,
13. Sant Longowal Institute of Engineering and Technology,
14. Quality Improvement Programme,
15. Indian Society for Technical Education, and
16. Entrepreneurship and Management Development.

Regional Engineering Colleges (RECs)

Under the scheme of establishment of Regional Engineering Colleges, a Central Plan Scheme—seventeen Colleges have been established one each in the major states to meet the country's growing requirement for trained technical manpower for various development projects. Each college is a joint and cooperative enterprise of the Central Government concerned. While all the seventeen colleges offer Ist Degree Courses in various branches of Engineering and Technology, fourteen of these have facilities for Post-Graduate and Doctoral programmes. The present admission capacity in all the Regional Engineering Colleges is of the order of 5354 for Under-Graduate and 1440 for Post-Graduate Courses.

PART-TWO

DIVERSE FACETS OF EDUCATION : SELECT DOCUMENTS, 1993-1994

2

Report of the UGC Funding of Institutions of Higher Education (1992-93)

Introduction

On November 11, 1992, the UGC appointed a Committee under the chairmanship of Justice K. Punniayya to examine financial situation in regard to Central Universities, Deemed Universities, Delhi Colleges and Technical Institutions funded by the Government of India and to make recommendations about their financial needs and systems for the future. The Committee submitted its report on November 30, 1993.

The Committee met 13 times in Delhi. It also visited 8 Central Universities for getting feedback from various recognised associations, like Teachers' Associations, Students' Unions and Non-teaching Staff Associations. It interacted with 25 academics and eminent educationists, 12 Principals of Colleges of Delhi and Banaras Hindu University. It also interacted with the Union Minister of Human Resource Development. The Committee also obtained the perceptions of the several Vice-Chancellors, the officials of the Ministry of Human Resource Development, Government of India, U.G.C. and others associated with higher education.

Members

1. Justice (Dr.) K. Punnayya, Chairman
   B-2-351/1/12, Road No. 3,
   Banjara Hills, Hyderabad,
   Andhra Pradesh.
2. Prof. Tapas Majumdar,
   Zakir Husain Centre for Educational Studies,
   Jawaharlal Nehru University,
   New Delhi-110067.

Report of Justice Dr. K. Punnaya Committee, 1992-93: University Grants Commission, New Delhi, 1993.

3. Professor Emeritus (Dr.) M.V. Pylee,
Moolamattam House,
H.M.T Colony Post, Cochin
Kerala-683503.
4. Shri M.R. Kolhatkar,
Adviser (Education)
Planning Commission,
Yojana Bhawan, Sansad Marg,
New Delhi-110001.
4A. Shri R.C. Tripathi,*
Adviser (Education),
Planning Commission,
Yojana Bhawan, Sansad Marg,
New Delhi-110001.
5. Prof. N.S. Bose,
94, Ramakrishnapur Lane,
Howrah
West Bengal-711102.
6. Shri P.K. Umashankar,
Meenakshi, Plot No. 857,
13, Main Road, Anna Nagar West,
Madras,
Tamil Nadu-600040.
7. Prof. C.S. Jha,
Department of Electrical Engineering,
Indian Institute of Technology,
Hauz Khas, New Delhi-110091.
8. Prof. S.C. Dube,
D-504, Purvasha,
Mayur Vihar Phase-I, Delhi-110091.
9. Prof. S. Izhar Husain,
Professor of Mathematics,
Aligarh Muslim University, Aligarh,
Uttar Pradesh-202001.

Terms of Reference

1. To examine the present policy, norms and the pattern of providing development and maintenance grants to Central Universities,

---

* Shri R.C. Tripathi was inducted in place of Shri Kolhatkar's w.e.f July 1993.

Deemed Universities, Delhi Colleges and Technical institutions from the University Grants Commission/Ministry of Human Resource Development and to suggest policies and norms for determining grants in future.

2. To examine the inter-university variations in development and maintenance grants (per student, per department, and any other relevant criterion) with a view to develop objective parameters governing such grants.
3. To examine the pattern of utilisation of the grants.
4. To examine the pattern of allocation of grants between teaching, research and non-teaching functions and to suggest norms relating to expenditure on the above functions.
5. To examine the feasibility of developing norms for individual items of expenditure under the development and maintenance grants and to suggest such norms; and specifically, to examine whether students/research students strength should be related to faculty strength and the strength of non-teaching employees or any other criteria in this regard.
6. To consider the extent to which flexibility should be available to the institutions for increasing or decreasing expenditure on the individual items under the maintenance grants.
7. To explore and recommend ways of improving overall cost efficiency of the institutions.
8. To study the extent to which the institutions are raising their own resources, and to suggest specific measures for augmenting the proportion of resource raising by the institutions.
9. To recommend incentives to institutions that raise a higher proportion of internal resources and to develop norms for utilisation of internally generated resources.
10. To review existing schemes, of financial assistance for needy students such as free studentship, scholarships, students loans and to recommend measures for initiating such a scheme with a view to assisting students from disadvantaged sections of the community, and promoting equity in higher education.
11. To consider any other item ancillary to the above which the committee may consider relevant.

Dr. P.B. Tripathi, Joint Director in the UGC was the non-member Secretary of the Committee. He was assisted by Shri R.L. Sondhi, Under Secretary in the UGC.

Extracts from the Report

The funding of a University must have a direct relationship to its objectives and should be designed to promote quality, efficiency, autonomy, accountability and relevance. (2.17)

However, global trend is increasingly to make institutions of higher education be dependent on large share from fees and sales of services both to students and to other users, such as industry and government. (3.2)

All over the world the state makes substantial funding for higher education. But the states increasingly feel that equity and social justice can be ensured better through direct support of students through scholarships and grants. Similarly, accountability and pursuit of national priorities in higher education and research are seen to be secured more through contractual agreements with institutions and through selected programmes and specific projects rather than through open-ended subsidies to institutions. (3.3)

TABLE 2.1 : Teacher-Student Ratio

University	Teacher-Student Ratio
Aligarh Muslim University (AMU)	1:9
Banaras Hindu University (BHU)	1.98
Jawaharlal Nehru University (JNU)	1.10
Hyderabad University	1.8
Visva Bharati	1.9

(7.52)

(The Committee suggested that this ratio should be 1.12)

TABLE 2.2 : Ratio Between Teaching to Non-Teaching Staff

University	Teaching and non-teaching staff
AMU	1.4
BHU	1.5
JNU	1.3
Hyderabad University	1.5
Visva Bharati	1.5

(7.56)

(The Committee suggested the ratio to be 1.3)

TABLE 2.3 : Work Load of Teachers (Recommendations of the Committee)

Activity	Average No. of Hours Per Week		
	Professor	Reader	Lecturer
Teaching	6	8	10
Testing/Examination	1	1	1
Tutorials	1	2	4
Preparation for Teaching	6	8	10
Research/Research Supervision	14	14	10
Own Reading/Admn. Work	12	7	5
Total	40	40	40

Delhi Colleges

The teacher-student ratio ranges from 1:7 to 1:22. The cost per annum varies from Rs. 6000-9000. The expenditure on salaries exceeds 70 per cent of the expenditure and items like equipment, furniture and library services receive negligible share. (12.6)

TABLE 2.4 : Work Load of Teachers

Activity	Average No. of Hours Per Week		
	Professor	Reader	Lecturer
Teaching	6	8	10
Testing/Examination	1	1	1
Tutorials	1	2	4
Preparation for Teaching	6	8	10
Research/Research Supervision	14	14	10
Own Reading/Admn. Work	12	7	5
Total	40	40	40

For science subjects or where field work is involved the work distribution can be suitably adjusted. (7.57)

SUMMARY OF RECOMMENDATIONS

(Appendix 1 of the Report)

1. Any additional resources generated by a university/institution may be kept in a separate fund to be utilised for furtherance of the objectives of the university/institution. (1.12)

2. UGC may provide a matching grant as an incentive to universities generating additional resources. (1.12)

3. There should be 100 per cent income tax concession on all endowments and contributions made to the universities, and additional

concessions to donors sponsoring selected research projects in the universities. (1.12)

4. While universities should be encouraged to augment their resources for covering a larger proportion of costs of education than what prevails now, the increased burden must be borne mainly by those who can afford. (1.13)

5. State or Government funding must continue to be an essential and mandatory requirement for support to higher education. The Government/State must continue to accept the major responsibility for funding the essential maintenance and developmental requirements of the universities. (1.14)

6. The basis of funding of a Central University may be linked to its specific objectives and to its pursuit to excellence, innovativeness, all-India character, and ability to provide access to weaker sections. (5.6)

7. Research funds may be provided in the development grant as special inputs for strengthening the university's research infrastructure. (5.6)

8. Central Universities may switch to appropriate mix of input funding and student funding systems which may be standardised for comparable courses of study by UGC over a period of time. (5.7)

9. In regard to student funding consideration of merit as well as social and economic backwardness should be taken into account. (5.8)

10. Quality, efficiency and innovativeness must be consciously rewarded and institutions failing to improve financial and academic discipline should face disincentives. (5.9)

11. The unit cost system of calculation of eligibility for grants should replace the existing incremental system which may be retained till the end of the current Five-year Plan Period (5.10)

12. From the Ninth Plan onwards, grants should be related to unit cost of activities as a rule except for new programmes for which unit costs are not determined, or would be difficult to determine. (5.10.II)

13. The Government must ensure that the maintenance grant covers the wage bill of universities including periodical increases in increments, D.A. and other service charges. (5.10)

14. Heavy subsidies in many of the activities covered under maintenance grants, such as supply of electricity, transport, water supply etc., and in many other items have to be reviewed and reduced to a substantial extent so that the maintenance grant can be stabilized at a certain acceptable level. (5.11)

15. Maintenance grants to a university based on unit costs of its activities would require periodical revision. (6.1)

16. Expenditure due to increase in the number of staff has to be reviewed and curbed firmly wherever necessary. (6.2)

17. An optimum division between academic and non-academic costs should be arrived at to help in stabilising the maintenance expenditure. (6.2)

18. The universities should be competent to operate their maintenance grant flexibly except for the creation of any new post of any category. (6.3)

19. 20 per cent of the annual maintenance grant may be released to the universities in April-May, 60% in September-October and remaining 20 per cent in December. (6.4)

20. Part of the development grant may be provided for organisation of new academic programmes and development of existing programmes.

21. Development grants should be linked to an academic audit system and performance indicators to be developed by each university (6.5)

22. Central Universities must avoid offering conventional courses except when they are specially needed. (6.5)

23. In viewing academic infrastructural facilities, no distinction should be made in regard to the Plan and Non-Plan grants and the entire system must be viewed as a whole. (6.5)

24. Each university must have a perspective plan which must be linked to its objectives, environment and potential. (6.9)

25. UGC must have a well-developed system for defining objectives and profile of each Central University and also of monitoring their development. (6.9)

26. UGC should constitute a Standing Advisory Committee of experts who would continue on a reasonably long-term basis for evaluating the perspective plans drawn up by Central Universities and monitoring them. (6.9)

27. UGC should have special provision of funds in the plan for which all universities may compete to organise new courses of study and undertake research in identified areas. UGC may identify areas for such courses of study and research. Selection of institutions for funding must be on clearly identified parameters. (6.9)

28. The Vice-Chancellors may be provided with specified discretionary fund to be used for promoting excellence in teaching and research without incurring any recurring liability. (6.9)

29. Once the Five Year Plan of a university is finalised, the university should be competent to implement these schemes within the broad guidelines of UGC. (6.10)

30. Each university should have a Statutory Building Committee

and it should not be required for universities to seek the approval of UGC for construction of building, once plan and estimates are approved by the Building Committee. (6.11)

31. The university must have an efficient system for dissemination of information regarding deployment of resources and implementation of academic and non-academic plan programmes. (6.12)

32. The development plans of the universities should be linked to the perspective plans of the universities and there should be a statutory Planning and Monitoring Committee for each central/deemed university. (6.13, 6.14)

33. The universities and UGC must improve their organisation of an efficient reliable and prompt information system of storage, retrieval and analysis of the same. (7.1-7.3)

34. UGC must develop a system of presenting annually a set of selected information on academic, administrative and financial parameters of the institutions, particularly which are fully funded by it. This information should be utilised in decision-making processes. (7.12-7.13)

35. Two parallel quantitative norms for determining the Non-Plan grants viz. (a) the optimum proportion of total maintenance grant for particular activity and (b) the optimum per student recurring cost p.a. have been suggested. (7.19)

36. The academic cost i.e., expenditure directly related to teaching and research should be 60-65 per cent, academic administration should be 10-12 per cent, and on other departments, auxiliary services etc., be within 20-25 per cent of the total maintenance grant. Till further refinement in calculation the basis of maintenance grants is calculated as under: (7.47)

	Activity	Social Sc./Humanities	Science
		Cost per student per	
(i)	Academic/Teaching Cost	Rs. 11,680	Rs. 21,640
(ii)	Academic/Admn. Cost	Rs. 4,500	Rs. 4,500
(iii)	Other department/ auxiliary services and miscellaneous expenses	Rs. 6,070	Rs. 6,070
Total		Rs. 22,250 or 22,300	Rs. 32,210 or 32,200

37. ADA, Pension, Arrear pay etc., be provided on actual basis. (7.41)

38. The maintained institutions in A.M.U, B.H.U. and Visva-Bharati be paid maintenance expenditure on incremental basis till meeting the same from other agencies is finalised. (7.50)

39. The student teacher ratio should be 1:12. (7.52)

40. The teaching to non-teaching staff ratio should be brought to 1:3 and employees like gardeners, safaiwalas, watchward etc., be engaged on contract basis to the extent possible. (7.55)

41. The minimum work-load for Professors, Readers and Lecturers should be 40 hours per week and the work distribution for actual teaching and tutorial, examination, research, own reading, administrative work, assistance to students have been spelt out in detail. (7.57)

42. On the pattern of the U.K., the Indian Universities should adopt Academic Audit system and UGC may give highest priority to it as this will not only promote academic efficiency, but also cost effectiveness. (8.19)

43. Priority should be given to introduce a monitoring system for Performance Indicators. (8.20)

44. While the Government/UGC may continue to be the major funding agency, the universities must generate internal resources which should be sizeable in course of time. (9.2)

45. The tuition fees may be revised upwards with immediate effect and may be periodically adjusted, keeping in view the rate of inflation. The tuition fee may have to be different within a university, for different courses of study. The revised fee should be made applicable to the new entrants. (9.8)

46. Fees for library, laboratory, sports should be revised upwards to recover a significant part of the recurring cost. (9.9)

47. Hostel fees should be revised with immediate effect to meet all the actual recurring cost and in due course of time, a part of capital cost as well. The student community should be involved in the discussions to raise resources where their interests are affected. (9.10)

48. There is a need to review the municipal, civil and other services which are extended to individual members of the university, in their personal capacity and they should be charged appropriately to recover the cost. (9.11)

49. The income derived from enhancement of fees should be utilised to augment fellowship and scholarship programmes for ensuring access to weaker sections. (9.12)

50. For generating income, the universities should let out their infrastructural facilities like playgrounds, auditoria etc., and also organise

short-term courses for which there is demand. They should also solicit endowments, contributions and actively participate in consultancy without affecting the academic activity of the institutions. (9.13)

51. The resources generated by the universities should constitute at least 15% of the total recurring expenditure at the end of the first five years and at least 25% at the end of 10 years. (9.19)

52. With a view to mobilising resources from within the country and abroad the Alumni Association may be set up in each university with the assistance of an Advisory Body consisting of the well wishers of the University. (9.20)

53. A significant proportion of the internally generated resources and incentive grant from UGC for the purpose be put in a corpus fund. UGC may also provide corpus fund grant to institutions in addition to maintenance and development grant. (9.24)

54. The income from the corpus fund be utilised for infrastructural development of the university. (9.24)

55. Income generated by the university be used to build up the basic academic infrastructure without having any recurring liability (particularly staff appointment) besides providing support to needy students. (9.25)

56. UGC may comprehensively look into expanding and/or appropriately targeting the existing schemes for providing fellowships, scholarships, freeships and student concessions. (10.1)

57. The existing scheme of the Department of Welfare to provide tuition and living expenses to SC/ST students needs streamlining. (10.2)

58. There is a need to strengthen the "Book-Bank" scheme in institutions. (10.4)

59. UGC may introduce broad-based student scholarship schemes for postgraduate students studying in Central Universities; this may be extended to 20% of the total student enrolment at postgraduate level. (10.9)

60. Central Universities should award freeships or admit students at concessional rate of fee to meritorious students belonging to socially and economically weaker sections of the society. (10.12)

61. UGC may explore the possibilities of introducing soft loan scheme in collaboration with the nationalised banks. (10.14)

62. Government in course of time may shift the funding of universities to a system of students funding for ensuring access of higher education to socially and weaker section of the society. (10.17)

63. In respect of institutions deemed to be universities the present mode of determining the maintenance grant may be replaced by grants based on input cost, the modalities for which could be determined by a group to be set up by UGC. (11.16.i)

64. The pattern of provision of development grant suggested for Central Universities should apply by and large to the institutions deemed to be universities. (11.16.ii)

65. A statutory body for extending financial assistance to Delhi colleges be constituted and UGC may not directly fund Delhi colleges. (12.10)

66. The Governing Bodies of Delhi colleges should be reorganised and conferred adequate powers and authority. (12.11)

67. UGC in consultation with Govt. of India should set up a Committee regarding the future set-up for the Delhi colleges in light of the foreseeable demand for new colleges in the National Capital Territory of Delhi. This may inter-alia require multi campus structure or alternatively starting new universities. (12.12 & 12.13)

68. Recommendation made for resource generation in respect of Central Universities should be applicable to Delhi colleges. (12.12)

69. The Academic Audit System and Performance Indicators should be finalised in consultation with the colleges and made applicable to them. (12.15)

70. The 4 colleges affiliated to BHU may continue their affiliation to BHU until they voluntarily relinquish it. (13.2)

71. A Banaras Hindu University College Funding Council be constituted under the Chairmanship of Pro-Vice-Chancellor, BHU, which will receive funds both from UGC and U.P. State Govt. for disbursement to these colleges. (13.3)

3

Summary Record of Discussions in the Workshop on Performance and Accountability in Higher Education (1993)

Introduction

The Workshop was jointly organised by the University Grants Commission and Indian School of Political Economy at Pune on March 10-11, 1993 on Performance and Accountability in Higher Education. The Summary Record of discussion presented here was prepared by Prof. V.M. Dandekar on the basis of notes and written comments sent to him by various participants. List of participants is given at the end of this chapter.

SUMMARY OF RECORD OF DISCUSSION

10 March, 1993

Prof. G. Ram Reddy

The workshop was inaugurated by Prof. G. Ram Reddy, Chairman, UGC. Prof. Reddy admitted that, for various reasons, the performance of the system of Higher Education had fallen short, not only of the socio-economic needs of Indian society but also of the minimal expectations regarding routine functions such as organizing admissions according to predetermined schedule and timely holding of examinations. Taking an over-view of the state of higher education, Prof. Ram Reddy thought that, there was a crisis of objectives, quality, relevance, and equity. Considering the manifold challenges, he emphasized that the

---

UGC Performance and Accountability in Higher Education : Discussion Papers and Summary Record of Discussions on the Workshop, University Grants Commission, New Delhi, 1994, UGC Occasional Papers.

participants in the Workshop must go beyond re-stating the oft-repeated prescriptions and address themselves to how the system of higher education could be made to work and work better.

There were severe constraints of resources; it was going to be increasingly difficult for the Central and State governments to provide resources not only to meet the normal cost escalations in the existing institutions but also to expand them or set up additional institutions for new cohorts pressing claims for higher education. Hence, all possible ways to enhance incomes and cut down costs had to be considered. There were severe limitations on the extent to which fees could be raised, especially because the relevance and quality of programmes of studies in most institutions was far from satisfactory. He advised that, while considering various measures, besides taking cognizance of the recent pronouncements of the Supreme Court, it should be remembered that the present level of participation in higher education could not, in any way, be considered adequate.

Moreover, one must bear in mind the relevance of extracurricular role of the universities with regard to personality development. Prof. Ram Reddy wondered whether limiting the interaction between the students and teachers within the narrow confines of given subjects, as implied by Prof. Dandekar's proposals, would not abridge even further the already marginalized role of examination-oriented education.

Prof. V.M. Dandekar

Following the opening remarks of Prof. Ram Reddy, Prof. V.M. Dandekar presented the main points of this paper on 'Reforms of Higher Education'. He explained that the immediate context of the Workshop was the severe financial constraints under which the Government of India and the State governments were functioning and that his proposals should be seen, not with reference to the system as it should ideally function, but in the particular context of financial constraints and the actual state of affairs in higher education.

If may be said that education should be free, in other words, should be fully subsidized. In fact, in a recent judgement, the Supreme Court has declared that Right to Education is a fundamental right derived from Right to Life. He would not comment. The fact is that the country cannot afford to make education at all levels free for all. Therefore, it is necessary to ponder on the question whether any part of education should be partly or fully paid for by its beneficiaries.

To judge this question, he would formulate a general principle. Whatever cannot be given free to everybody at public cost and therefore, where the beneficiaries are only a few and selected, the full public cost should be recovered from the beneficiaries. For instance, primary education is in principle free to all but higher education is not. Hence, the student beneficiaries of higher education should pay the full cost. He would state the same principle somewhat differently. Where there are private benefits arising from public expenditure, and where the private beneficiaries are identifiable, the costs should be recovered from them, not necessarily immediately, but at least over a period. If this is not done, those who get the benefits, get them free and often at the cost of the non-beneficiaries. This is particularly true of higher education.

Apart from the question of cost, he thought that there was a real danger of the entire system of higher education coming to a grinding halt under the mounting burden of students entering or wanting to enter the system because it costs very little while its economic benefits are considerable. There is concern regarding the non-descript character of the graduates that the universities are turning out every year and the large unemployment that prevails among them. It is widely recognized that at least one reason for the unemployment among the graduates is that a great number of them are plainly non-employable; in other words, the university degree and diplomas they have taken are not worth much. Nevertheless, a university degree or a diploma continues to be a requirement for any job and consequently, the colleges and universities continue to be crowded with students hunting or fishing for a degree or a diploma.

Obviously, the remedy lies in making the higher education recognizably more useful. In his opinion, this can be done only by making the teachers accountable to the students and the students responsible for their studies. The students will become responsible for their studies if they are asked to pay the full cost of their education and they may agree to do so provided they can be assured that they get their money's worth.

The present system of higher education does not ensure this because the teachers are not accountable to the students. If the teachers cease to be employees, with salaries, etc., guaranteed by the government, and instead, become independent professionals who must earn their living by their services to their clients, they will become accountable to the students.

On their part, the students have become less and less responsible and serious for their studies. An atmosphere has grown in which its seems that virtually anything can happen, with publicity always close at hand. If the students are obliged to pay full cost fees from their own resources, with access to loans if necessary, they will begin to give higher priority to their studies.

Thus, there were two key elements in Prof. Dandekar's proposal. First, that the teachers in colleges and universities should not be supported by an assured monthly salary but, instead, should earn their living by service to their clients, namely, the students; in other words, they should subsist by the fees the students may pay for the courses they will teach. Thereby, the teachers will become accountable to the students and hence, he thought, more honorable in their own right. Second, the students should pay the full cost of their higher education so that they will become more responsible to their studies; if they neglect, it will be at their own cost.

Prof. Dandekar then turned to the role of universities and colleges in the proposed system. The universities may construct or formulate a set of courses which will be taught by teachers attached to the university, on terms and conditions mentioned above, and not as salaried employees. Some colleges may also arrange for the teaching of these courses by attracting or otherwise arranging with the teachers who are willing to teach the courses according to the syllabi prepared by the university. If they are useful, the students will attend the lectures and pay the prescribed fees. The university may then award degrees or diplomas to students successfully completing certain sets of these courses after duly evaluating their performance. If the university degrees have any market value, the students will take the examination and pay the examination fees. But to appear for these examinations, it should not be obligatory for a student to attend a certain number of lectures in a university or a college.

The primary function of universities and colleges will be to provide the needed physical facilities, classrooms, laboratories, libraries, study rooms, etc., for the use of the teachers, and to conduct examinations of students wanting to be examined in these courses. They shall charge the teachers a certain fee or a rent based on the full cost of the facilities and services they shall provide. A teacher may give lectures at one or more colleges and/or in his own premises.

The students may enrol for particular courses delivered by particular teachers and pay the fees prescribed by the respective teachers. The colleges or universities should collect these fees and pass them on to the respective teachers after deducting the fees or rent to be charged to them. The colleges and the universities shall not charge any fees to the students for attending any lectures delivered in their premises; the students have already paid for them. But they may charge some fees directly to the students for library and reading room facilities, for conduct of examinations in particular courses, and for any extramural, extracurricular facilities, and hostel accommodation they may provide. This should be quite independent of whether a student attends any lectures delivered in the particular college or the university. A student may attend some lectures in one college and some lectures in another college paying the respective fees; or he may not attend any lectures in any college. Nevertheless, he may avail of any of the facilities of library, reading room, examinations, etc., offered by a college or a university for a fee if he can afford it and if he considers the facility worth the price. As the students will bear the full cost of higher education, they will bear the cost only of what appears useful to them.

Research will have to be funded either by the users, such as the interested industry, or by the government. It will be the responsibility of the teacher to bring in research funds by placing his project proposals before appropriate funding agencies. If any equipment comes along as part of the project funding, it will come on loan from the funding agency and shall remain in the exclusive custody of the concerned teacher. The function of the college or the university shall be to provide the needed library and other facilities together with any equipment which it may have of its own and which may be useful to the project for which it will charge a certain rent. If the teacher does not find the facilities or other environment in the particular college or university agreeable or if, for any personal reasons, desires to move to any other college or the university will have the option to buy the equipment at book value; otherwise, it will return to the funding agency. Thus, while the funding agency shall provide the necessary funds and equipment, the college or the university must provide an honorable research funds first and then appoint a researcher. When they do, they think that they have obliged the researcher and do not deem it necessary to treat him any more honourably. This is the reason why there are research funds, some competent researcher, but little research environment and therefore, little research on our campuses.

Prof. Dandekar then turned to possible objections which will be raised to the proposed system. One objection will be that the proposed system will convert the universities and colleges into coaching classes preparing for certain examinations. In his opinion, there would be nothing wrong if this happens; in fact, he thought that it will upgrade the universities and the colleges if they perform as well as some of the coaching classes at present do. Moreover, it is not necessary that all colleges confine themselves to coaching students for the university courses but conduct their own examinations and offer their own degrees or diplomas to successful students. Or better still, those with greater vision and more dynamism, may formulate their own courses, attract necessary teachers, conduct their own examinations, and offer their own degrees or diplomas. In either case, they shall be judged by the quality and utility of their product.

Another objection will be that the higher education in the proposed system will have no standards. This is true, if by 'standards' one means uniformity. In his opinion, the bane of the present system of higher education is that it tries to standardize the teacher and the taught by means of regulation. Even the Open Universities have not been able to escape this mania for standardization. As a result, the outcome of the universities, both open and closed, is a standardized but nondescript product stamped with degree and diplomas by the universities because the government has given them the exclusive license to do so.

He said that to make higher education more useful and relevant to the student, it was necessary to discard the notion of a standardized education and allow variation in the subject coverage, in the subject combination, and in the level at which each subject is taught and learnt. Even if a university constructs a hundred courses in a subject, they will all be standardized and no standardized course can provide the same variation as an individual professional teacher can provide to suit the needs of the class of students which he attracts because, even in the same branch of learning, the competence of teachers as also the needs and the capacity of students vary greatly.

The third objection will be that, in the system being proposed, subjects and courses which have some economic value only will survive and thrive. This is of course true. But, with limited resources and the rising cost of higher education, a large part of higher education will have to be justified only on grounds of its economic returns. True, everything that the market will not support is not socially or culturally worthless. These things shall not survive unless supported by the state, that is, by the government. With very limited resources, such a support will necessarily have to be highly selective and with a maximum eye on economy. In the field of higher education a number of subjects will need such a support. It will then be difficult to avoid the question of priority, selectivity, and economy. Subjects which are socially and culturally valuable, but which the market will not support, certainly deserve and need support from the government; but they also need to be taught by teachers who pursue scholarship and who conduct their profession with an innate pride, dignity and honour.

A legitimate objection to the principle that the students should bear the full cost of higher education is that it will be harder on the poorer students. This is indeed true. There is no denying that something should be done to compensate for the disadvantages of the poor. But the remedy is not to make the higher education free or highly subsidized for all as at present. Instead, the government should make available long term loans for higher education to any student who is willing to borrow and repay on given terms and conditions but without any restrictions on this choice of subjects, teachers and institutions, provided, of course, he studies at an institution recognized for the purpose and the teacher is one attached to such an institution; if a student chooses to study with an unattached teacher, he must pay the teacher's fees out of his own funds.

In certain deserving and needy cases, there should be a provision, to convert some of the loans, either partly or wholly, into grants, It is out of these loans or grants, that the students shall pay the chosen teachers for the chosen courses and to a smaller extent to the colleges and universities for the services they provide. The colleges and universities will subsist mainly on the fees or rents they will charge to the teachers and to a smaller extent to the students for the facilities they will provide, there will thus be a total accounting of public costs of higher education, by subjects, by courses, and by sections of the society; an accounting of who provides which services and at what costs and who bears and shares these costs. Obviously, an appropriate financial institution such as a National Bank for Educational Development will have to be created.

Prof. Dandekar recognized that so radical a reform cannot be done in one sweep; that it will have to be brought about gradually. For this purpose, he suggested the following: First, public assistance to higher education in the form of grants to the universities and colleges, staff strengths and salary scales, etc., should be frozen at their present levels. An existing teacher in a university or a college will continue undisturbed in the present pay-scales and according to the present terms and conditions of service; but these will not be revised anymore whatever be the prices and whatever be the revisions in pay-scales and conditions of services in government and other places.

In return, a teacher will be allowed to charge and collect, through his university or college, a fee from the students attending his course of lectures subject to the condition that a part of the fees so collected, say one half or one third, will be surrendered to the government. The university or college may also ask for a share of the fees so collected as rent for the facilities it provides. Whatever of the fees is left to the teacher should not be meagre and should provide sufficient incentive for him to gradually shift from the old to the new basis of living : that is, from the salaried to the professional manner of existence.

Second, the government shall not sanction any new universities or colleges with any sanctioned staff nor shall sanction new positions of teachers in existing universities or colleges. Vacancies occurring when a teacher retires or otherwise leaves the service will be filled not by new recruits but by existing teachers moving from one position to another or from one institution to another. This will make the universities and colleges competitive in their bid to invite and retain good teachers; they will try to improve their facilities and work environment. It will also gradually reduce the number of salaried teachers in universities and colleges.

Third, all new entrants to the teaching profession will enter on terms and conditions mentioned above; briefly, they may attach themselves to a university or a college, if allowed by the institution, but shall earn their living from the fees which the students shall pay. New universities and colleges may be opened but without any sanctioned posts of teachers. The government may initially sanction small capital grants or preferably loans, like seed money; but, ultimately, they must build their assets from the fees and rents they may charge to the teachers and students making use of their facilities.

Fourth, funds saved because of progressive reduction in the number of salaried teachers as also new and additional funds provided for higher education will be used mainly to give loan scholarships described above.

It will be thus that the existing system will be gradually replaced by the reformed system. Undoubtedly, many details will have to be worked out. But, it is necessary to initiate a process which will seep into the present monopoly structure of higher education and eventually bring it down.

Prof. Nilakantha Rath

After Prof. Dandekar, Prof. Rath presented his paper, 'Higher Education : Plea for Reorganization'. He began by pointing out that twenty-five years ago, the Education Commission of India began its report by saying "The Destiny of India" is now being shaped in her class-rooms. Since then there has been very considerable quantitative expansion in the 'class-room' facility and enrolment. The share of expenditure on education in the net national product has nearly doubled. However, partly because of this quantitative expansion, there has occurred serious deterioration in the quality of the product. This has been particularly so in higher education.

Writing in 1966, the Education Commission observed, "There is a general feeling in India that the situation in higher education is unsatisfactory, and even alarming in some ways, that the average standards have been falling and that rapid expansion has resulted in lowering quality. The examination results, the views of employers and the assessment of teachers themselves, the results of research done—all seem to support this conclusion. Many of our educationists and publicmen, however, have not fully realized, how serious are the act not conditions, academic and physical, that obtain in the colleges and universities. Even those who are broadly aware of the situation, fail to notice its poignancy because they have become used to such conditions." The Commission made a number of recommendations but, in spite of trying twenty-five years after, the situation has not improved; in fact, it has deteriorated further.

It has now become obvious that the entire structure of higher education calls for a change. It must begin with putting the responsibility squarely where it belongs, namely, the college and its teachers. What is required is not selective autonomy, but universal and compulsory autonomy. Every affiliated college should be autonomous in its academic work: the college should prepare the courses of study to be offered to the student in the undergraduate classes, do the teaching and design and arrange for the assessment of the students. No common courses or syllabi and no common examination should be prescribed or imposed by the university. Each college should have its own method of selecting pupils for admission, as long as it is on merit, decided by any special examination and interview, besides the total background of the student. Indeed, the entrance test should be at least as stiff as the exit test, in order that only students, with the necessary background and competence, benefit from the types of courses offered by the college are admitted and frustration due to failures is minimized.

The university, instead of assessing the students, should assess the teachers and the several departments in the affiliated colleges periodically, say, once in four or five years. Failure of a college, or a particular department, or a teacher, to improve should result in the withdrawal of affiliation of the college/department/teacher by the university. Except for these three aspects, every affiliated institution should be completely autonomous.

Autonomy to the colleges would immediately raise the spectre of unequal standards. But, even today, we know that degree of an university, even in the same class or grade, does not mean the same with all successful candidates. With autonomy, this hidden difference will tend to become open. The market for graduates will almost immediately recognize the great differences and begin to check and choose. The postgraduate teaching institutions shall begin to conduct their own admission tests, instead of depending on the university (i.e. autonomous college) grades.

Moreover, there is no reason why different colleges should not design their recruitment, courses and assessment, to suit different requirements in the society. Given complete freedom to experiment with such teaching programems, the autonomous colleges will learn to take up the challenge.

A group of autonomous colleges may prepare common courses of study and hold common examination. Indeed, in the beginning, many colleges may do this. But gradually the more enterprising and innovative ones will formulate their own schemes. An important merit of the autonomy scheme is to enable those colleges, subject departments and teachers, who feel smothered and even suppressed in the present scheme of things, to come out and stake their reputation in the academic field. Gradually others will follow.

Complete autonomy to colleges raises the question of financing of higher education. Today, in large part, it is being done by the state and central government by giving grants to universities and colleges. A better way would be to make widespread provision for scholarships and loans to students admitted to different educational institutions. The institutions should charge full fees and the student can choose the institution of his preference. Of course, such a sharp change can be done only in stages. Therefore, to start with, the government may freeze its total monetary grant to the colleges with further stipulation that not more than half the grant can be used for the salary of teachers, about 25 per cent for library and laboratory purchases and the remaining for other expenses. The colleges, in turn, should be allowed to charge differential fees for different subjects, a part of which (say about half) can be used to pay salary (supplementary) to the teacher and the rest for library, laboratory and other purposes in fixed proportions. Most important of all, the teachers' salaries should be variable and negotiable and no teacher should be given a permanent tenure unless he has put in at least seven years as a teacher.

Such an altered approach to the organization of higher education would result in greater variation in the quality of colleges, as well as in salaries of teachers and fees of students. It does not necessarily follow that the number of students seeking admission would come down or entirely deny them higher education. The Open University system provides opportunity for students seeking higher educational qualification at an easier pace and lower cost. Indeed, some colleges and college teachers might find it financially more rewarding to convert themselves into private tutorial colleges and teachers preparing students for the Open University degree. Many sections of our society have been traditionally kept out of any education. In the new social environment, they are demanding and will continue to demand access to all fields of education. It will be well-nigh impossible to restrict or control this. While the abler amongst these will get scholarships and loans to seek admissions to full-time higher educational institutions, with at least a minimum quota fixed for them, the rest shall be free to use the facility of the Open University.

Such a reorganized system of higher education would fix responsibility and provide accountability; these are conspicuous by their absence in the present situation. It would provide incentives to different institutions to try to become institutions of excellence in their chosen fields, while the present system smothers all initiative in the direction. The institutions can cater to a wide variety of needs, when at present an undifferentiated mass product not tailored to any particular need is causing frustration all round. It is high time our material and human resources in higher education are used more productively. But that can happen only when the direct beneficiaries are made to realise the cost of it.

Prof. S.P. Sathe

Prof. Sathe, Hon. Director, Institute of Advanced Legal Studies, Pune, thought that the present state of higher education in India, reflects, on a smaller scale, the chaotic state of the Indian society itself. In behalf of the State, it is being increasingly argued that it should concern itself only with primary education and the higher education should become more and more privatized and should be funded by its beneficiaries as well as from their sources such as industry or philanthropic institutions. Privatization of professional education had already started in the eighties when high fee/capitation fee medical and engineering college were allowed to be opened in states like Andhra Pradesh, Karnataka and Maharashtra. They met the desire of the higher income classes to provide greater opportunities to their sons or daughters to join these socially and economically privileged professions and of the educational entrepreneurs to make large profits at a minimum investment. When some persons, offended by the inequity of the capitation fee system, moved the Supreme Court, the Court declared it to be unconstitutional and void.

The Court held that (i) right to education was a fundamental right comprehended by article 21 of the Constitution which guarantees right to life and personal liberty; (ii) the taking of capitation fee for admission to a professional college was violative of the above right to education and also of the right to equality guaranteed by the article 14 of the Constitution and (iii) it was the duty of the State to provide education at all levels.

Soon after, the Supreme Court, dealing with review petitions, held that (a) while the right to primary education was a fundamental right, right to higher education was subject to the economic capacity of the State; (b) the taking of capitation fee was unconstitutional; and (c) while a college could take higher fee from 50 per cent of the admitted students, the other 50 per cent must be admitted at the fee charged in government colleges. What should be the higher fee chargeable for the 50 per cent of the students would be decided by a committee to be appointed for that purpose in accordance with the scheme suggested by the Supreme Court.

This has created more problems while trying to resolve some created by the earlier decision. If 50 percent of the students have to be given education at the fee prescribed in a government college, (called free seats) the remaining 50 per cent will have to bear the burden of meeting the deficit caused by such low fee of the free seats students (called payment seats). This will create two classes in the same institution. Up till now, private engineering/medical colleges charged higher fees than the government engineering/medical colleges. There were thus differential fee rates between government colleges and private colleges. Now, even within a private college there would be two rates of fees, 50 percent would pay fee at the rate payable in a government college and the remaining 50 per cent would have to pay higher fee. How high should such fee be? If an institution is not to take any capitation fee, such fee would be quite high. There would thus be no equality of opportunities between the poor or middle class students and those belonging to affluent classes.

In fact, the objection against capitation fee would be equally valid against such high fee. Since all the students are to be selected according to merit, it will only mean that those who come in the list of first 50 per cent would be lucky to get their professional education at government rate of fee. Such students would not necessarily be from the poorer classes. At least some of them could be from the affluent sections. The two fees are applicable not on the basis of any classification of students on the ground of their financial capacity but any on the accident of their having secured more marks in the examination.

Having had such sad experience of the examination system, one doubts whether such discrimination for charging fees should be based on such a dubious factor as performance in the examination. When the difference in fees payable between two categories would be so vast, would there be not greater efforts to manipulate the examination results? In this also, the rich would have an advantage because of the higher resources they can mobilize such as extra tuitions, approaching the right people for having question papers leaked, getting more liberal evaluation, etc.

Funding higher education has become a complicated matter. If such funding is to be raised from student fees, the fees would have to be quite high and that would make professional education beyond the reach of a large number of students. The social and political costs of such exclusion of a large number of people from opportunities of higher professional education would be enormous. That would generate social discontent and would ultimately lead to worsening of the law and order situation. Monopolization of opportunities of higher professional education by the affluent sections of society would perpetuate the disparities of wealth and adversely affect vertical social mobility. It would also sharpen antagonism between those getting free seats and those getting payment seats.

In our new mood of liberalization, it seems that the State is thinking of privatizing the education as well. The slogan that every one must pay for his education must be applied selectively to those who really can pay. But any educational policy which restricts education to a small number of economically privileged is bound to have deleterious consequences. The rationalization of the fee structure, therefore, will have to be done very carefully and if this is to be done without sacrificing social justice, the State will have to intervene meaningfully and more discriminatingly. The State must increase its outlay on education. Primary education must be its highest priority but there should not be an excuse for its withdrawal from higher education. If primary education is necessary for making human life meaningful, higher education is necessary for supplying manpower for rendering various services for human welfare. There should not be overemphasis on any branch of knowledge. All branches of knowledge must be accessible. Society needs not only good engineers and doctors but it also needs scientists, linguists, social scientists, lawyers, creative writers, and artists.

The fee structure should be so organized that education should not be so cheap that people can have it for whiling away their time and it should not be so costly as to be prohibitive for a person of modest means. Various facilities for loans and scholarships will have to be provided. The cost of education also could be reduced by making optimum use of the buildings and infrastructural facilities. The State should make it clear that all those who deserve and who have interest shall get an opportunity to pursue education of their choice.

Prof. S.K. Kakkar

Reacting to the views of Prof. Dandekar and Dr. Rath, Prof. Kakkar of the Delhi University Teachers' Association (DUTA) stated that, the two speakers had failed to appreciate the true essence of higher education. He strongly objected to any sort of privatization of colleges/coaching classes. Autonomous colleges will cause only insecurity of service and will not help the teachers in any manner. Role of Universities as stated in the judgement of the Supreme Court is relevant; it is to develop human personality and character. Instead Prof. Dandekar and Dr. Rath have tried to present students and teachers in a client and respondent relationship.

Prof. Kakkar said that any teacher committed to education would refuse to enter into a commercial transaction with his students. A good teacher not only teaches the subject in which he has special expertise but also attempts to develop the personalities of his pupils and awaken in them the spirit of enquiry to seek knowledge on their own initiative. He mentioned that a committee of DUTA had prepared not only a Code of Conduct for the teachers but also made recommendation for revamping the system of education and examinations. For instance, it had recommended that marked answer scripts should be returned to the students because it should contract unethical practices in evaluation.

No educational system can be left to the vagaries of the market system. Market forces will drive out those who cannot pay. For instance, he mentioned that, a good college in Delhi University with 2000 students (Arts, Science, Commerce) has an annual budget of Rs. 1.7 crore which is Rs. 8,500 per student (Rs. 6,000 for Arts and Commerce and Rs. 12,000 for Science) and hence, even with heavy subsidization, only 2 per cent of students go in for higher education.

He advised that we should press for greater allocation of funds for higher education and suggested that these would be available if a concerted effort was made. For instance, he mentioned that the order of UGC freezing grants of all Central Universities for 1993-94 at the same level as in 1992-93 was reversed and the original grants restored because of the collective representation made by all the Central Universities fully supported by their Teachers' Associations. He asked, why did the other universities not do this?

He thought that the autonomy of the Central Universities was continually eroded into. For instance, the UGC prepares guidelines to govern salaries/appointments, etc., of all employees of the Central Universities and the Visitor functions on the advice of the Ministry. Nevertheless, he suggested that it was advisable to continue with present model and improve it selectively: for instance, rational fee structure allowing gradual raise in the fees, examination reforms by agreeing to return the marked scripts to students as suggested by DUTA, assessment by peer group, etc. He asked for greater democratization of university bodies with 50 per cent representation for teachers in the academic council.

Prof. (Ms) A.S. Desai

Prof.(Ms) A.S. Desai, Director, Tata Institute of Social Sciences, Bombay, thought that the proposal to shift the entire burden on teachers requires much more soul searching to see whether it will improve the quality of higher education because it was not clear to hear as to who, will formulate the syllabus. She warned that every system has its own corruptive influence and it may all end up in teaching shops. There was no guarantee that the best students will enrol themselves with the best teacher.

She thought that raising fees will never be enough to meet the full cost. As to the loans, borrowers will be from the disadvantaged sectors. In particular, it will affect women's education and in the social milieu, the women will be the losers.

Instead, she suggested that educated employed should be taxed to raise the needed resources. She also suggested that the participation of teachers in decision-making should be increased and that good teachers should be adequately rewarded but asked for evaluation of teachers by students after every semester.

Prof. A.S. Nadkarni

Prof. Nadkarni of the Indian School of Political Economy suggested that the autonomy of a university had two aspects. One is autonomy vis-a-vis the Government. To regain this, the universities must reduce their dependence on the Government. He agreed that the students should have a feeling that they are financing their expenditure on education by taking a loan. But, he thought that the grants to the colleges were not adequate and that therefore, the proportion of expenditure on education should not be reduced. His suggestion was that such assistance for supporting higher education should flow from the Government to the students and from the students to colleges and universities. The second aspect of autonomy is internal to the university which is made up of a number of interdependent interests, departments, etc. All these should have scope of participation in the internal activities of the university. The election principle, as it has worked in several universities, has resulted in small caucuses managing and controlling the working of the universities. Some other principle, such as rotation/ex-officio, may be found more desirable.

Prof. A.P. Bhupatkar

Prof. Bhupatkar, Director, Institute of Management Development Research, Pune, said that students still attach a great deal of importance to university degrees. Therefore, at least initially, autonomous colleges will face some drop in the number of students and hence in the number of teachers. Nevertheless, he thought that having small autonomous institutions was a step in the right direction. However, the problem then would be how to stop commercialization of higher education.

He thought that an assessment of teachers by students was not advisable because this can bring in an element of coercion and it may also sour the relations between teachers and students. He said that an educational system cannot be made to work without taking into account aspirations of teachers, students, etc., and the socio-cultural meaning we attach to education. He believed that, in general, there was little of intrinsic value offered to students by way of relevant knowledge. That is why only a minority of students were interested in it. In his opinion another matter of immediate relevance was to develop capability for managing of large systems.

Prof. M.I. Savadatti

Intervening in the discussion, Prof. Savadatti, Vice-Chancellor, Mangalore University, thought that the following points were obvious: there seemed to be a crisis in quality, confidence, credibility, relevance, leadership and productivity. This has led to failure in performance; some universities are not performing even at the minimum level. There is no doubt that higher education has been heavily subsidized; nevertheless, it is an investment which promotes upward social mobility for people and therefore, it should not be treated as a business proposition.

Prof. Savadatti reminded that the existing system did produce reasonably competent people for the past 50 years. Its non-performance now is essentially a phenomena of large numbers of affiliating colleges, teachers and students. The best people of the system are still as good, or possibly better than, those of the earlier period, but now their proportion is small and the reason is that enough inputs are not there for the large number of people in the system. This is evident when one sees IITs and Deemed Universities where the input is very high. These institutions attract quality students and teachers and show overall quality performance. We are asking for quality without providing adequate inputs. However, financial realities are such that larger inputs are not possible. In the circumstance, is there anything we could do?

It had been suggested that affiliation system should be scrapped. Prof. Savadatti thought that it was a sound suggestion but that in the socio-political context, it would not be accepted; neither the institutions would accept it nor the teachers would accept it. UGC had tried the experiment of autonomous colleges but it had not met with much success. By and large colleges would not like to be autonomous; they have not been built to be independent.

He suggested an alternate model which he called cluster autonomy. Essentially this would be a group of institutions, say 10 to 20 colleges in a region, which together would be autonomous. These colleges could belong to single faculty or be a multi-faculty set up, excluding professional colleges. Professional colleges could form a similar cluster. These clusters would provide enough resource persons, infrastructure, and confidence to be on their own. Once these clusters become successful they could transform themselves each into a university.

The University will hold independent examinations without assuming the responsibility for the development of courses and supervising the functioning of the colleges. The examinations could be taken by the students of the colleges at their free will as external candidates in the present set up. This would help the colleges to have confidence in their teaching programmes and students would feel happy that they are having a university degree. This should be so, particularly during the transition period.

Prof. Savadatti emphasized that the important component in the system were the teachers and suggested that something has to be done to enable them to have communication skills and confidence in their ability to teach. He mentioned some efforts made by UGC through Academic Staff Colleges but thought that they did not make much difference. Therefore, he suggested that a Resource Development Centre should be organized by each university with emphasis on developing communication skills and to enable teachers, to take greater interest in students and develop greater confidence in handling teaching and also students. This will require identification of resource persons and giving a new direction for the teachers to develop themselves into knowledgeable and competent teachers.

He agreed that there was some room for increasing the fees but not enough to recover the entire cost of higher education.

Prof. V.G. Bhide

Prof. V.G. Bhide, former Vice-Chancellor of Poona University thought that Prof. Dandekar's proposal was a distorted view of higher education, that, in fact, a university is a totality of all disciplines. But, he admitted that there was a crisis of relevance, performance, etc. More generally, he asked as to what were the aims and objectives of university education and said that no thought has been given as to its quality and relevance of its product.

A large number of affiliated colleges with wide disparity of relevant structure and infrastructure has distorted the system. Deterioration of standards at the first examination is the most serious. He asked that the system of affiliated colleges should be abolished because it tends to distort, pressurize, and dictate to the university resulting in lowering of standards. He complained that science education was in a mess and that there was a sharp drop in standards at B.Sc. level because of the teaching imparted in affiliated colleges without any facilities of laboratories, experimentation, etc. He agreed with Prof. Dandekar and Prof. Rath that no effort at standardization need be done. Colleges should be completely autonomous and may prepare any number of programmes; if they need any academic assistance, the university should give it. University should act as resource centre for all these colleges, nurturing and nursing talent wherever it exists.

Prof. R.M. Honawar

Prof. R.M. Honawar, Hon. Director of the Indian School of Political Economy, said that there was merit in Prof. Dandekar's suggestions but it is not possible to implement them if the social realities remain as they are. Persons involved in the process have no great interest in reforms. Students require education for a variety of reasons; in few cases, to achieve excellence; in a majority of cases to secure a job. They want a degree. Teachers are happy; popular and good teachers are not really the same. Interest of those in authority is in expansion of the system while quality would require a reduction in numbers.

11 March, 1993

Shri Anand Sarup

On the second day of the workshop, Shri Anand Sarup, Hon. Editor of the Journal of Higher Education, presented his paper: 'University Autonomy and Accountability' Through many examples, he argued that, the manner in which Vice-Chancellors were appointed and removed, the university bodies were constituted, the power to provide or withhold grants or sanction posts was exercised and the political, law and order and other support was given or withdrawn, showed that the university autonomy was no more than a myth, to which, the academic community and the Vice-Chancellors refer only when it suites them. In this connection he cited the cases of dozens of poorly equipped capitation colleges to whom affiliation had been guaranteed by the universities under political pressures. In reality, with the induction of so many nominated and elected persons representing particular sections or interest groups in the Academic and Executive Councils and the introduction of time-bound automatic promotions and rotational appointments of Deans and Directors, the Vice-Chancellors and the university managements enjoy less freedom of action than the chief Executives and the Boards of Management of the much maligned C grade public sector companies.

Shri Sarup drew particular attention to the unenviable condition of the Vice-Chancellors who had great difficulty in getting university bodies to take unpopular decisions: they had to resort to emergency powers ever so often to implement important policy measures or enforce executive decision. In many universities, year after year, the state governments fail to provide funds even for routine maintenance and payments of staff salaries. With professionalism and a sense of discipline at such a low ebb and casteism and parochialism prevailing everywhere—equally among teachers, staff and students, none could hold out for long for objectivity and academic discipline.

He said that, while things were bad everywhere, the condition of universities with large number of affiliated colleges were truly pitiable. The institutional culture, the academic priorities and the power equations in the degree colleges in far flung areas ware very different from the relatively refined environment of university campuses. This resulted, on the one hand, in the neglect of educational process in colleges and on the other, in the frequent dislocation of work as well as the abridgement of the parameters for innovation in respect of curriculum development, internal assessment, conduct of examinations etc., on the university campuses.

In the circumstance, he thought that university communities and the Vice-Chancellors should give up their prior claims to autonomy as an inalienable right and instead, carry forward a determined bid for freedom of action, in managerial as well as academic matters, for performing the tasks assigned to them. For this purpose, it would be desirable to make a clear distinction between the managerial autonomy of the Vice-Chancellor and that of the university as a whole. Rather than looking at the Vice-Chancellor as a colossus towering over the university system, it would be better to regard him as a manager with a mandate to carry on the administrative and academic functions of the university, with the support and concurrence of various university bodies. This would, besides rescuing the Vice-Chancellors from their perilous perches, provide for a framework for making members of various bodies, who at present exercise power without accountability, administratively and morally answerable for their decisions. This, inter alia, would pave the way for decentralization of authority and responsibility to the departments and faculties. Whatever decisions may be taken for enforcing accountability, it is essential to accept the undeniable fact that the old system of university management has failed and a new system of corporate management has to be evolved to respond to the changes in the internal and external environment of universities.

While discussing the issues of performance and accountability of various sections of the university community, the question of the leverages available with the Vice-Chancellors, various authorities of the university and even the UGC, was pointedly raised by many participants. In response, Shri Sarup made the plea that the various academic, managerial and extracurricular functions of each institution should be identified and grouped together on a functional basis. These should be assigned weights on the basis of their role and the expectation from them. Thereafter, data should be obtained from each institution, complied according to a predetermined framework, appraised on the bases of weights assigned and made public at the end of each academic year. In his opinion, this was the minimum which the system of higher education must do to justify its existence and strengthen its claim for the provision of necessary funds. The idea put forward basically aimed at creating an awareness of accountability by establishing certain quantitative and qualitative co-relates between inputs, processes and outcomes.

Prof. M.I. Savadatti

Reacting to Shri Anand Sarup's presentation, Prof. Savadatti offered a brief but candid and graphic description of the chasm between the conventional image and the objective reality of the role of the Vice-Chancellor. As he put it, the Vice-Chancellorship is an illusion. Important aspects of the role seem to result extensively from a process that decouples problems and choices and makes the Vice-Chancellor's role more commonly sporadic and symbolic than significant. Compared to the heroic expectations he and others might have, the Vice-Chancellor has modest control over the events of university life. The contributions he made can easily be swamped by outside events or the diffused process of decision-making in the universities.

Indian Vice-Chancellorship is a reactive rather than a pro-active job. Vice-Chancellors define their role as a responsive one. They worry about the concerns of Government, community leaders, students, faculty members and law enforcement officials. They see themselves as trying to reconcile the conflicting pressures on the University. They allocate their time by a process that is largely controlled by the desires of others. Though they are for the most part, individuals of considerable energy, they often become tired.

The Vice-Chancellorship is a parochial job. Vice-Chancellors are normally not strangers to the institutions that choose them. Although they have typically worked in one or two other universities, these universities are similar in type and close in geography. Insofar as a Vice-Chancellor compares his performance with other Vice-Chancellors, he tends to compare it with a group of Vice-Chancellors who are in his own experiential 'neighbourhood'. Insofar as invisible through the media, he is ordinarily visible only to his local community.

Vice-Chancellors are normally academics. Their careers are almost entirely in academic institutions; their values are those of the academe. The details of their values vary considerably. The academic creed of a small school, confined to a marginally surviving subject, is not the same as that of a major prestigious University and Vice-Chancellors reflect that difference. Since the academic creed is not completely different from the general organizational creed, Vice-Chancellors are similar in many ways to administrative heads of other kinds of institutions. Nevertheless, they are recognizable as products of the academe.

The Vice-Chancellorship is conventional. He comes to his job through a series of filters that are socially conservative vis-a-vis his major constituents. He sees his job in the standard terms reported in the academic and management literature. He allocates his time in response to a series of conventional expectations. He enters and leaves his job in a manner that has strong normative components. The Vice-Chancellor cannot effectively argue with conventional claims on him nor does he really wish to do so. His actions, his activities and his self-perceptions are constrained within social expectations which he accepts as essentially legitimate.

The Vice-Chancellorship is important to the Vice-Chancellor. It is the peak of his career. He obtains the job as a reward for his previous record. It is the best job he has ever had or is likely to have. It is a mark of his success. Although the route to the job is clearly not random, each Vice-Chancellor's 'career' tends to be a post factum construct. His self-esteem depends on being viewed as a good Vice-Chancellor, but his reputation depends on the reputation of University.

In a way, these major features of the Vice-Chancellorship and Vice-Chancellors need to be elaborated and interpreted within an understanding of the University as an organization. The University is a prototypic organized anarchy. It does not know what it is doing. Its goals are either vague or are in dispute. Its technology is familiar but not understood. Its major participants wander in and out of the organization. These factors do not make a University a bad organization or a disorganized one: but they do make it a problem to describe, understand and lead. As the head of such an organization, how can a Vice-Chancellor set specific organizational goals? What can he accomplish? How can he use his experience? And finally, how does he measure his success or failure? He is human. His capabilities are limited. Nevertheless, there are modest gains to be made by making some changes in the perception of his role so that he can be more effective and more relaxed.

Prof. A. Gnanam

Prof. A. Gnanam, Vice-Chancellor, Pondicherry University put forward the view that University autonomy was the creation of universities which could survive only if those outside and inside the system assiduously safeguard its fragile structure in order to enable it to achieve human resource development. He said that, in principle, a university is supposed to be autonomous; in practice, autonomy means performance as expected and required by the Government. Structure of management, financial powers of various bodies of the university, even the powers and functions of the Vice-Chancellor are all governed by an Act of Government. He was of the view that even Teachers' Associations, when they interfere as associations in matters which do not concern the welfare of teachers, contribute to the erosion of autonomy.

He suggested that part-time teachers such as highly qualified housewives may be involved in the functioning of universities and also suggested that leaders of professions may be invited to give lectures for which the students may pay and attend if they find them useful.

Prof. K.B. Powar

Drawing upon his experience, Prof. K.B. Powar of the Association of Indian Universities (AIU) gave several instances of the state government curtailing the powers, in other words, the autonomy of the university either by executive order or simply by freezing posts and placing embargo on the filling up of vacancies or by not sanctioning funds even for improving the ongoing academic programmes. A state government, for instance, had laid down that universities must seek prior permission to start even those courses for which the state would not have to assume any burden by way of financial assistance.

He thought that it would be difficult to create a culture of accountability without establishing a system by which the UGC, the AIU, the State Governments and Central Ministries would have access to organized information regarding the performance of individual in situation. For this purpose, appropriate parameters could be evolved and a scheme of rating could also be worked out. In this context, he emphasized that the institutions which failed to come up to the minimum level of performance must forfeit the right to receive funds from the government and the UG. As far as the evaluation of the performance of teachers is concerned, Prof. Powar proposed that reliable and objective criteria could be worked out to assess them for Teaching, Research, Extension and Contribution to the administration of the institution.

Prof. Powar did not agree to the cutting off affiliated colleges from universities—they could continue to work under the umbrella of the university. He thought that there was need for at least one section in the university with under-graduate teaching.

Prof. P.K. Ghosh

Prof. Gosh, Director, Jamnalal Bajaj Institute said that Management education is able to cover its total cost and some management institutes, such as the Jamnalal Bajaj Institute, produce even a surplus because they produce a product which is required by the society. If general universities and colleges must depend upon governmental assistance, they must ask themselves as to what ultimate good they are able to do to society. If not, interference from politicians and bureaucrats becomes un-avoidable because they are not academics.

He said that the picture of university today is one of organizational chaos involving procurement and use of resources requiring sanction and approval at several points. Departmental heads fail to give leadership within their own departments. Orientation of teachers in academic staff colleges have not proved successful. These are the failures of the present system of general higher education which need to be corrected.

Prof. B.M. Udgaonkar

Prof. Udgaonkar, former Professor in the Tata Institute of Fundamental Research, said that management/teachers/students of colleges cannot be improved if they do not want to improve. UGC also faces pressures from Ministry of Education. We are deep in a debt trap and funds may not be available. Image and credibility of the university system has gone down so much that to say that the students in higher education form only a small proportion of population, in itself, does not make much sense because, what the system produces, both in numbers and quality, is not needed by the society. Hence the question arises whether time has not come to give up the University system which has such a large compliment of affiliated colleges.

One solution is to separate graduate education from post-graduate education and research. Universities should confine themselves only to post-degree education and research while the collegiate education may be vested in boards (B.A/B.Sc/B.Com) like 10+2 boards. Holding examinations, correcting papers, announcing results in time, etc., requires pride and not so much money.

Shri T. Rajgopalan

Shri Rajgopalan of Hindu (Madras) mentioned that, in Kerala, a large number of parallel colleges have been set up and the teachers are shifting from regular colleges to these parallel colleges.

Prof. S.C. Gupte

Prof. Gupte, Vice-Chancellor, Poona University, said that University was the creation of law—no educationist was consulted before passing the University Act, 1974. Senate has representation of management, students, teachers, local bodies, etc. Appointment of the Vice-Chancellor is by a peers Committee. Under the University Act, the policy making structure is really more participatory. But, in practice, it is dominated by bureaucrats and politicians, including management of affiliated colleges; it lacks checks and balances required to make it accountable. The situation has deteriorated to such an extent that agents of administration are openly indulging in the leakage of question papers.

Prof. V.G. Bhide

Prof. Bhide said that there was need to look into the recruitment procedure for the teachers. He said that there was hardly any accountability on the part of the teachers whether in class-room teaching, examining, or evaluating. He mentioned that after an orientation programme we do not have any feed back and suggested that the teachers should be examined every 5 years.

As to the resources of the university, Prof. Bhide pointed out that the budget for garden in the National Chemical Laboratory equals the budget of 4-5 science labs/departments., of the university and suggested that functional linkages should be established between national laboratories and universities so that fuller use may be made of available physical and manpower resources for higher educations. At the same time, he emphasized that the Universities must become self sufficient by (a) some increase in fees, (b) consultancy, transfer of know-how, testing of technical parts, (c) tax free donations from alumni Association and industry and business, etc. He thought that rather than the industry establishing private colleges such as the Maharashtra Institute of Technology, there should be developed a symbiotic relationship between industry and the universities.

Prof. Bhide said that the autonomy of the university system was continuously being eroded and that the factors responsible were both external and internal to the university. For instance, the State Government recognizes affiliated colleges as part of the University without consulting the university; new courses are not permitted by government. Internally, the ideas of the Vice-Chancellor are not accepted by the Executive or the Academic Council whose members are either government servants or vested interests/people with little academic interest in university. He suggested that a member of the Executive or the Academic Council should be in charge of any one subject either examination or administration and agree to take decisions and shoulder the responsibilities together.

Prof. S.M. Bhave

Prof. S.M. Bhave of the Poona University Teachers' Association (PUTA) commented on papers of Prof. V.M. Dandekar and Prof. Rath. He said that the conclusion and the arguments in the two papers were the same, namely, that the field of higher education must be thrown open to market mechanism. The argument supporting this conclusion was to two-fold. The first, which may be called the economy argument, was as follows: The field of higher education has grown enormously in recent years. The number of students flocking to the system is so large that there is real danger of the system collapsing under sheer weight of numbers. This has come about because education is heavily subsidized.

Under the changed economic situation and economic thinking this may not be possible any more and hence the system of higher education must generate its own resources which will ultimately allow market forces to operate freely.

The second argument, which may be called the accountability argument, may be summed up as follows: Students get practically free education but, in the bargain, they have no freedom to choose the type of education they need and the type of institution from where to get it. They are passive recipients of whatever is dished out to them. There is no authority which decides whether what is being taught and how it is taught is good or bad. The teachers are not accountable to students and students are not responsible for studies. The situation will change if a wide variety of courses and competing class of institutes are allowed to flourish. Then students have the choice of courses to offer and the choice of institutes from where to receive instruction. The system will be an open market.

Prof. Bhave thought that to examine the economy argument, it was necessary to look into the historical development of higher education, more particularly, the general higher education as imparted in the degree colleges in arts, science and commerce, which forms a large and core component of the system. He illustrated his point with reference to Maharashtra hoping that it would more or less apply to other states as well.

He wished to point out that the inception and growth of higher education took place under the aegis of the Government. The Government established the universities by passing the necessary legislative and administrative measures. In several states, even today, a large number of colleges are fully conducted by the Government. Early leadership and administrative and academic guidance were also provided by the Government. Finally, the Government extended its patronage to the products of the system by offering them jobs in its service. In short, higher education has been dependent on the Government right from the beginning and its expansion, which Professors Dandekar and Rath and other educationists bemoan, took place with the approval of and encouragement from the Government.

After independence, as a part of its policy of inaugurating a socialistic society, the Government decided to reach higher education to masses. Consistent with this goal the Government of the then Bombay State announced, in 1958, that all students belonging to the Economically Backward (E.B.) classes would get education free i.e., their fees would be paid by the Government. Two aspects of this policy are notable. First, the concession did not depend on the performance of the student, nor was it confined just to say, to the first degree. Even if the student failed the facility was discontinued only for one year and would be revived if passed the examination later. Secondly, the system was not consulted to assess whether it was equipped to receive in its fold the influx of a large number of students whose academic background was vastly different from that of the students who were till then registering for degrees.

In Maharashtra, the first batch of E.B., students passed out from schools in 1965. A large section of them, which would otherwise have left education, demanded admissions to colleges. In response to this demand, as many as 159 colleges were opened in Maharashtra in that year alone. The expansion has continued unabated since then.

An important component of Government's patronage to higher education has been the financial assistance in the shape of grant-in-aid. The amount of grant before 1966 was not more than 50 per cent of the annual expenses of a college. But the salaries of teachers and non-teaching staff were revised in 1966 and 1973. At each revision the Government agreed to meet the increased expenditure through equivalent increase in the grant-in-aid. Non-salary expenditure also rose due to inflation and the Government was obliged to take care of that too.

At this stage, the Government could have insisted that the colleges raise their own resources. This would have meant either a rise in fees or assistance from business and industry. The first alternative did not imply any relief to the Governments once it paid fees of 80 to 90 per cent of the students in the mofussil areas. There was no flourishing business and industry in the countryside which was enlightened enough to make endowments to colleges. The co-operative sugar factories did open many colleges but it is doubtful if they would have done so if the grant from the Government was not forthcoming.

In order to stream-line the method of giving grants to colleges, the Government revised the grant-in-aid code in 1979 by which the Government undertook to meet, in effect, all the current expenses of colleges. Thus, in practice, the colleges are Government undertakings like the State Transport Corporation, etc.

There is already some experience of what happens to non-aided colleges. In 1983, the Government announced that all colleges started in that year or later would have to function without grants during the first three years. The colleges believed that, implicit in this announcement, was the assurance that they would get grants from the fourth year. With this bait, many colleges were started. Prof. Bhave had visited a number of them and he thought, that their condition was, to say the least, most deplorable. Regular salaries were not paid to teaching and non-teaching staff. There were no libraries, not to speak of laboratories. Even sanitary blocks were absent in some cases. The staff clung to jobs in the hope that once the grants from the Government started flowing in, they would get regular salaries. But even after three years, the Government has not given grants on the specious plea that it had never made such a promise. The colleges launched an intense struggle and finally, in 1990, the Government agreed to pay the grants in phases.

In the old grant-receiving colleges, many courses were started during these years on no-grant-basis. Though the Government modified its policy in the case of arts, science and commerce colleges from 1990, these courses have still remained on a no-grant basis. Thus, in many old, established and grant receiving colleges, there is a sizeable component which receives no grants. The situation in this component is not much different from the one that obtained in non-aided colleges. No separate teaching staff is appointed to engage the classes in this component unless it is extremely necessary. The staff from the aided component engages these classes either without extra payment or at best with a token honorarium. The facilities accumulated over the years in the aided component are now extended to students in the non-aided component stretching the facilities to the breaking point. This is especially true in the case of the office staff.

The colleges charge higher fees for courses in the non-aided component. These courses, such as the computer science, are designed to meet the demands of the employment-market. Yet so far, in the highly industrialized state of Maharashtra, no industrial house has offered financial assistance to any renowned college to run such courses. Therefore, the hope entertained in some quarters that industry and business will share the burden of financing higher education appears untenable.

In conclusion, Professor Bhave said that Professors Dandekar and Rath suggest opening of the system of higher education to forces of the market and believe that this will be consistent with the new market friendly climate of thought in the Government. Market-friendliness is assumed to be a sound economic policy. But a sound economic policy may turn out to be unwise in a given situation. As already said, the higher education has always been dependent on the largesse from the

Government and withholding of the Government's financial assistance invariably results in worsening the situation. Moreover, it was the Government, unmindful of the economic and academic costs involved, that has allowed the expansion of the education system. Now, if the Government disowns its financial responsibility to the system, it will be a cruel betrayal of millions of poor students who entertain an intense urge for higher education.

Withdrawal of the Government support from the system of higher education would have been possible, if there were alternative sources of finance. The experience of non-aided applied courses like computer science, electronics and polymer chemistry, etc., shows that neither industry nor business is ready to extend its financial support to education. Raising fees will deprive the economically backward students of educational facilities, which is what is happening in the case of the non-aided courses. Professors Dandekar and Rath suggest that the students may be given educational loans. Prof. Bhave thought that the recovery of loans will be very difficult in most of the cases and Government will have to issue waivers of loans periodically.

Prof. Bhave's contention was that though the expanse of higher education appears enormous in absolute terms, less than 5.0 per cent of the relevant age group are enrolled for higher education. This percentage is even smaller in some sections, such as women, Scheduled Castes and Tribes. Therefore, placing a moratorium on expansion or freezing of outlays on higher education at the present level will amount to virtual denial of education to these strata of society and complete and unilateral reversal of Government's long standing policies.

Even in financial terms the burden of expenses on higher education is almost negligible; only slightly more than 3.0 per cent of the Gross National Product. The amount spent on higher education in arts, science and commerce is even smaller and inconsequential when compared with the total budget of the country. Thus in Prof. Bhave's opinion, the economic argument for throwing the system of higher education to the vagaries of the market mechanism does not stand scrutiny. But, he thought that the accountability argument appears prima facie more forceful and deserves closer examination.

Elaborating, Prof. Bhave said that there is provision for appraisal of the performance of teachers. The prescribed workload is 15 clock hrs., of classroom teaching which means 20+ lectures per week. Teachers are required to stay 20 clock hrs., on campus, but there are no common room, leave alone separate cabins or even cubicles. Understandably in these circumstances, university authorities do not have courage to undertake performance appraisal.

There is little autonomy even in the matter of admission of students because of pressures from staff, management and politicians; there is equal pressure in the matter of examination-pressures to give marks, permit copying, etc. Political pressure is all pervading. University is totally bound by the directives of the State Government—legally as well as illegally under the University Acts.

Prof. S.V. Kogekar

Prof. Kogekar, former Vice-Chancellor of the Maharashtra Tilak Vidyapeeth (a Deemed to be University), Pune, in his intervention, said that it needs to be admitted that there is wide-spread dissatisfaction with the present state of higher education; except for the leaders of the unions of college and university teachers, who do not think there is anything wrong with the system. Most of the others who have taken interest in this subject and/or expressed themselves publicly, have commented about allowances and lack of interest in academic pursuits; teachers' preoccupation with their emoluments and allowances and lack of interest in academic pursuits; standardization of syllabi and examinations; politicization of the managements of colleges and universities; and the commercialization of admissions to these institutions, have all contributed to this sorry state of affairs. Unless something is done seriously and urgently to stem the downward slide of the system, the country will suffer incalculable harm to its long-term prospects in the field of higher education.

Prof. Kogekar said that Prof. Dandekar has in his paper given a shock treatment, as it were, to this subject and emphasized the need for a radical reorganization of the system. With growing numbers of students seeking university degrees on the one hand and the prospect of government funds for higher education being progressively curtailed on the other, alternative ways of meeting the problem must be thought of and put into practice making due allowance for a certain transitional period for changing over to the new system.

Making students pay for the bulk, if not the whole, of the cost of their education; permitting teachers to charge fees for the courses they teach, much in the way other professionals, like doctors or architects do; making all colleges autonomous in respect of syllabi, examinations and even the grant of degrees, apart from being primarily responsible for providing the infrastructural facilities like, class-rooms, laboratories, and libraries and offering attachment to teachers who could utilize these facilities on payment of the colleges, are the main features of Prof. Dandekar's scheme with a number of other details mentioned. The objective is to ensure proper performance on the part of both teachers and students and to secure the accountability of teachers to their students by linking their incomes to the fees paid to them by their students.

Such a radical reorganization of the system cannot be brought about overnight. But steps can certainly be taken in the direction of bringing it about by agreed phases spread over the next twenty or twenty-five years. However, there will be great resistance to the change from those who have acquired a vested interest in the existing system. The initial agreement on the new system may not, therefore, be possible and without it, the scheme cannot make any headway.

It is, therefore, worth considering whether some steps which do not involve too drastic a departure from the existing system could not be initiated to start with. The grant of autonomy to colleges by which you remove the protective umbrella provided by the university would appear to be the first such step. It would make each college fully responsible for the quality of its academic programme and its rating in the public mind. Students would not be attracted to colleges which are below the expected standard and they would either close down or take steps to make up for their deficiency. Since there will be no standardized examination system even by a university, students would tend to pay due attention to their class work and assigned reading. It would not be possible for them to pass examinations by cramming a few ready-made answers to questions from a limited question bank prepared to suit the capacity of the worst-prepared of them, as happens at present.

Degrees may be awarded by autonomous colleges. Where they do not feel confident to do so the University might award the degree, making it quite clear in the degree certificate that the student belonged to a particular college (by name) and was certified by it as being fit to receive the degree on the basis of passing its examination for the same.

Teachers will also be put on their honour by providing for their assessment after every five years by their peers. Students's rating of their teachers should be an important element in such assessment along with the research/publications undertaken by the teacher. While automatic promotions to higher scales based only on the seniority of the teachers should not be permitted, increments within a scale should be advanced or withheld, as the case may be, on the basis of the five-yearly assessments.

If the grants from governments—Central and State—are not forthcoming to meet the salary bill of teachers and expenditure on infrastructural facilities, the fee structure should be rationalized and students made to pay an increasing proportion of the total cost. Older colleges can draw upon their past students for meeting a part of the expenditure or for subsidizing the fees payable by students who cannot pay them fully.

The problem of increasing numbers of students clamouring for admission to colleges and universities still remains. The number of institutions of the requisite standards cannot be increased in proportion, for want of finance and man-power. In this situation, external examinations by an independently constituted body; correspondence courses; part-time instruction given intensively during short periods and similar devices may have to be thought of. Delinking of degrees from employment in non-academic jobs may also help to reduce the rush of students to colleges. But with all these, the problem of numbers is still bound to prove intractable and may be our undoing.

Summing Up

Summing up Prof. Dandekar expressed the view that it was difficult to say that any consensus emerged from the discussions in the workshop. Nevertheless, the following points may be listed as the highest common denominator.

(i) On the whole, the quality of higher education was not up to mark; it did not help to develop either the intellectual potential of the students or to initiate them into a world of ideas; and even in the development of personality and character with a firm foundation of honesty and integrity, the system has fallen below expectations. Undoubtedly, there are some good institutions and some outstanding teachers and students: but this cannot exonerate the generally disappointing performance of the system;

(ii) Under the present dispensation, while the government almost unquestioningly underwrites nearly the entire expenditure on higher education, the management, teachers and the students, are making a pretence of teaching and studying. This can be improved only by establishing some correspondence between performance and rewards of teachers and students and parents paying a substantial portion of the cost of education. The teachers who undoubtedly play the crucial role, cannot legitimately demand public support without being accountable. A possible way of introducing performance based incentives to teachers would be to provide for a minimum retainer to everyone and envisaging further accruals of income on the basis of the quality and quantum of performance; and

(iii) In addition to taking hard-headed measures for improving the performance and enforcing the accountability of the conventional system of higher education, efforts should be made for strengthening and enlarging the alternative modes of imparting education such as the open universities and correspondence courses. In addition to these, considerable savings of public expenditure and a great deal of innovation and diversification could also be brought into by allowing the establishment of private universities and other institutions imparting higher education, without the recognition or support of government, with different objectives, contents, management patterns, personnel policies, etc.

List of Participants in the Workshop

1. Prof. S.M. Bhave, 33/20, Prabhat Road, 4th Lane, Pune-411004.
2. Dr. V.G. Bhide, University Campus, S.B. Road, Pune-411016.
3. A.P. Bhupatka, Director, Institute of Management Development Research, Ferguskhon College Campus, Deccan Gymana, Pune-411004.
4. Prof. V.M. Dandekar, President, Indian School of Political Economy, Arthabodh Pune-411016.
5. Dr.(Ms) Armaity S. Desai, Director, Tata Institute of Social Sciences, Sion-Trombay Road, Deonar, Bombay-400088.
6. Dr. P.K. Ghosh, Director, Jamna Lal Bajaj Institute of Management Studies, Dadabhai Nauroji House, 164, Back Bay Reclamation, Road No. 3, Church Gate, Bombay-400020.
7. Prof. A. Gnanam, Vice-Chancellor, Pondicherry University, R.V. Nagar, Kalapet, Pondicherry-605014.
8. Dr. S.C. Gupte, Vice-Chancellor, University of Poona, Poona-411007.
9. Dr. R.M. Honawar, Director, Indian School of Political Economy, Arthabodh, Pune-411016.
10. Shri S.K. Kakkar, President, DUTA, University of Delhi, Delhi-110007.

11. Prof. S.V. Kogekar, 1937, Sadashiv Peth. Pune-411030.
12. Prof. A.S. Nadkarni, Indian School of Political Economy, Arthbodh, Pune-411016.
13. Dr. K.B. Powar, Secretary; Association of Indian Universities, AIU House, 16 Kotla Marg, New Delhi-110002.
14. Shri T. Rajgopalan, Editor, Hindu, Mount Road, Madras.
15. Dr. N. Rath, Indian School of Political Economy, Arthabodh, Pune-411016.
16. Dr. G. Ram Reddy, U.G.C. Chairman, University Grants Commission, Bahadur Shah Zafar Marg, New Delhi-110002.
17. Dr. Anand Sarup, Honorary Editor, Journal of Higher Education, University Grants Commission, Bahadur Shah Zafar Marg, New Delhi-110002.
18. Dr. S.P. Sathe, Hon. Director, Institute of Advanced Legal Studies, ILS Lane College Road, Pune-411004.
19. Prof. M.I. Savadatti, Vice-Chancellor, Mangalore University, Mangalore, Mangalagangotri-574199.
20. Prof. B.M. Udgaonkar, 705, Vigyan, Plot No. 23 Sector, Vashi, New Bombay-400703.

4

Report of the National Advisory Committee on Learning Without Burden (1992-93)

Introduction

Concern regarding academic burden on students and unsatisfactory quality of learning has been voiced time and again in our country during the past two decades. The question has been discussed extensively by several committees and groups. The Ishwarbhai Patel Review Committee (1977), NCERT Working Group (1984) and NPE Review Committee (1990) made several recommendations to reduce the academic burden on students. The curriculum development agencies are generally in agreement with the recommendations of the committee and assure the public that these would be kept in view at the time of the forthcoming revision of curricula. But the problem, instead of being mitigated, becomes more acute when a new curriculum is introduced. This has happened in the case of new curriculum introduced in the wake of implementation of National Policy of Education (1986).

Terms of Reference

With a view to have a fresh look on the problems of education, particularly with regard to the problem of academic burden on students, the Ministry of Human Resource Development, Government of India, set up a National Advisory Committee in March 1992 with the following terms of reference :

> "to advise on the ways and means to reduce the load on school students at all levels, particularly the young students, while improving quality of learning including capability for life-long self-learning and skill formulation."

Learning Without Burden : Report of the National Advisory Committee appointed by the Ministry of Human Resource Development, to Suggest Ways and Means to Reduce the Academic Burden on School Students, Ministry of Human Resource Development, Department of Education, New Delhi, 1993.

The Committee at Work

Before starting its work, the Committee decided the parameters of its work and also the methodology for completing the task entrusted to it. With a view to keeping a national perspective in view, the Committee decided not to confine its work to the CBSE or NCERT syllabi and textbooks but to take into account the textbooks used in different States and Union Territories also. Secondly, the Committee decided to base its recommendations on the data obtained through perception surveys, wide ranging consultations with teachers and analysis of textbooks and other instructional materials. Thirdly, the Committee decided to look at the work of agencies/organisations doing innovative programmes.

The process of consultation was initiated by holding a meeting with a few faculty members of NCERT followed by meetings with teachers and principals working in different states at four places in the country viz. Delhi, Trivandrum, Pune and Calcutta. The consultation meetings were also held with voluntary organisations engaged in innovative programmes, syllabus and textbook writers, private publishers and Chairpersons of Boards of Secondary Education. Some members of the Committee organised meetings with parents, teachers and students at Bombay, Nasik, Baroda and Calcutta. Surveys to ascertain the opinions of teachers and parents were conducted with the help of questionnaires at Bombay and Delhi.

To involve the whole country in this exercise of looking at the problems of school education from the perspective of mechanical load of studies on children, views and suggestions were invited from the students, teachers, parents and general public through advertisements in the newspapers and special announcements by All India Radio and Doordarshan. The Committee received more than 600 memoranda, letters and write-ups from students, teachers, parents and professionals interested in children's education.

The wide-ranging consultations with knowledgeable people, analysis of the existing instructional materials and reactions of the teachers and students have enabled the Committee to understand the functioning of the present educational system which forms the basis of its recommendations.

In its work, the Committee received cooperation from a large number of teachers, principals, syllabus and textbook writers, organisations, associations and departments.

4.1 TEXT OF THE REPORT

The Problem

Preamble

Our Committee was concerned with one major flaw of our system of education. This flaw can be identified briefly by saying that 'a lot is taught but little is learnt or understood'. The problem manifests itself in a variety of ways. The most common and striking manifestation is the size of the school bag that children can be seen carrying from home to school and back to home everyday. A survey conducted in Delhi revealed that the weight of school bag, on an average, in primary classes in public schools is more than 4 kgs while it is around one kg in MCD schools. Nevertheless the load we want to discuss is not only the physical load but the load of learning which is there for all children irrespective of the category or type of schools where they study. Eminent write R.K. Narayan had drawn the country's attention to this daily sight by making a moving speech in the Rajya Sabha a few years ago. The situation has become worse over these years, with even pre-school children carrying a bag of books and notebooks. And the sight is not confined to metropolitan cities alone; it can be seen in small towns and the bigger villages too.

The weight of the school bag represents one dimension of the problem. Another dimension can be seen in the child's daily routine. Right from early childhood, many children specially those belonging to middle classes, are made to slog through home work, tuitions and coaching classes of different kinds. Leisure has become a highly scarce commodity in the child's especially the urban child's life. The child's innate nature and capacities have no opportunity to find expression in a daily routine which permits no time to play, to enjoy simple measures and to explore the world.

Joyless Learning

It is hard to reconcile the rigorous 'academic' regime that is imposed on children from an early age with the widespread complaint made about the declining norms and performance of the formal system of education. Teachers routinely complain that they do not have enough time to explain anything in detail, or to organize activities in the classroom. 'Covering' the syllabus seems to have become an end in itself, unrelated to the philosophical and social aims of education. The manner in which the syllabus is 'covered' in the average classroom is by means of reading the prescribed textbook aloud, with occasional noting of salient points on the blackboard. Opportunities for children to carry out experiments, excursions, or any kind of observations are scarce even in the best of schools. In the average school, especially the school located in a rural area, even routine teaching of the kind described above does not take place in many cases. In several states, school teachers encourage children to attend after school tuition given for a fee while regular classroom teaching has become a tenuous ritual.

One message of this situation is that both the teacher and the child have lost the sense of joy in being involved in an educational process. Teaching and learning have both become a chore for a great number of teachers and children. Barring those studying in reputed or exceptional institutions, the majority of our school-going children are made to view learning at school as a boring, even unpleasant and bitter experience. They are daily socialised to look upon education as mainly a process of preparing for examinations. No other motivation seems to have any legitimacy.

The contribution that teachers make towards this kind of socialisation is especially worrisome. Trained teachers are expected to be aware of the wider aims of education; indeed; aims like 'development of the childs' total personality' are the shibboleths of teacher training institutions everywhere in the country. It appears that teachers feel they can do little to pursue such lofty aims in any realistic sense under the harsh circumstances created by factors like excessively large classes, a heavy syllabus, difficult textbooks and so on. Moreover, majority of them neither know nor have the necessary skills to realise the goals of education. The recommended pupil-teacher ratio of forty to one is now more an exception that a norm and in many parts of the country it is customary to have sixty to eighty students in one class. The committee learnt that in many states senior secondary classes often have one hundred or more students, many of them spilling into the corridor. In the national capital, many 'model' secondary schools, Central schools and several elite 'public' schools have classes, including primary classes, with more than sixty students.

This kind of class-size understandably generates a feeling of helplessness among teachers, but why must teachers feel helpless in the face of curriculum-related problems such as heavy syllabi, poorly produced textbooks, etc.? Why don't they act in more vocal ways and involve themselves in curriculum reform? Apart from the fact that there are very few forums encouraging curriculum inquiry and reform in any systematic manner, it seems to be an entrenched attitude among teachers to regard all decisions about curriculum and textbooks as the responsibility of 'authorities'. The fact is that while the teachers' involvement in the preparation of syllabi and textbooks is verbalised as a matte of principle, in practice it takes the shape of token involvement of a handful of teachers. Most teachers have reason, therefore, to think that they have little to say about the changes made from time to time in syllabi and textbooks. Even in such extreme cases where a textbook has a factual mistake, no complaints are made by teachers asking for correction of error. There is no established procedure or official forum to mobilise teacher vigilance and participation in curriculum improvement. On the contrary, there are cases where an individual teacher complained about an error in a state-published textbook, was taken to task. Even if such cases can be described as rare or exceptionally unfortunate, they explain why the majority of teachers intuitively feel that it is not their business to critically examine the syllabus and texts they teach.

Examination System

Much has been written by various official committees on the ills of our examination system. The major, well understood defect of the examination system is that it focuses on children's ability to reproduce information to the exclusion of the ability to apply concepts and information on unfamiliar, new problems, or, simply to think. The public examinations taken after classes X and XII have assumed the importance of major events which have a set character or culture of their own. The awe they generate, the responses they trigger, and the kind of preparation they demand have all got so entrenched into the social lore that minor improvements in the style of question papers do not make difference to the dominant influence that the examination system has on the processes of learning and teaching. The influence is so strong that schools start holding a formal written examination several years prior to class X indeed, in the primary classes in many parts of the country. And children receive the message almost as soon as they start attending that the only thing which matters here is one's performance in the examination.

Both the teacher and the parents constantly reinforce the fear of examination and the need to prepare for it in the only manner that seems practical, namely, by memorising a whole lot of information from the textbooks and guidebooks. Educated parents, who have themselves gone through examinations and the uneducated parents, whose knowledge of the examination system is based on social lore, share the belief that what really matters in education is the score one gets in the final examination. This belief is undoubtedly rooted in social or market reality. Percentage of marks obtained in the high school, higher secondary or BA/B.Sc examinations is what ultimately matters in determining a student's chance of being called for an interview for admission to a university or for employment. Since the examination score is what a candidate carries with him or her as the key authoritative record of school or college performance, higher level institutions or employing agencies understandably rely on it. It is a process in which no beginning or end can be meaningfully established. Changing the system of examination in a structural or even in a merely procedural sense does not require that a source outcome or cause effect relationship be established; yet, the examination system goes on, apparently with the help of energies or rationales located in the system of education itself.

Textbook as the 'Truth'

The pervasive effects of the examination system can be seen in the style and content of textbooks and not just guidebooks which are specifically manufactured to help children pass an examination. If 'facts' or 'information' constitute the main burden of an examination, the same is true of textbooks. Barring exceptions, our textbooks appear to have been written primarily to convey information or 'facts', rather than to make children think and explore. Over the years some attempts have been made to incorporate a certain amount of reflective writing in textbooks. Such writing is so exceptional that its examples can be spotted and named without difficulty. 'How leaves are designed' in a class VIII textbook is one such piece of writing.* It stands out from among the thousands of pages of textbooks in different subjects that our teachers and children have to go through painstakingly so that they can retain the information recorded in those pages in a highly compressed, usually abstruse manner. The more common style used in the textbooks is exemplified by passages of the following kind :**

---

* Class VIII Science textbook prepared by the NCERT.

** We have decided to cite such examples without giving a reference in order to avoid the impression that we are criticising certain specific titles, authors, publishers or organisations. Our aim is to highlight certain common tendencies in the style of textbook writing.

The term pH is defined as the negative logarithm to the base 10 of the hydrogen ion concentration expressed in gramions per litre or moles per litre. (Class X)

Fatty acids are slowly hydrolysed during digestion in the small intestine to form glycerol and fatty acids through the enzyme action of lipase which is secreted by the pancreas. (Class X)

We find that while dividing a decimal by a multiple of 10,000 or 1,000 we first move the decimal point to the left as many places as there are zeros in the number and then divide the resulting decimal by the second factor of the divisor. (Class V)

The problem of readability in textbooks becomes grim in the context of a system which often leaves the child with no resource other than the prescribed textbook. The extent to which the child can rely on a teacher to elucidate tersely written text material is dependent on the quality of teachers, their training and their accountability. From what impression the Committee could form about these aspects of the system, it seems valid to say that the child is very often helpless in the face of a style of teaching that is far from being interactive, let alone the absence or irregular presence of teachers (And we are not saying that the teachers alone are responsible for the kind of teaching that takes place daily in lakhs of classrooms that have hardly any equipment and often even a proper means of ventilation or lighting). Under the circumstances that are widely prevalent in our country, a child is more likely than not to mug up the definition of 'pH' quoted above without grasping it. And mugging does get the child through the examination!

Textbooks and guidebooks form a tight nexus. In some parts of the country children are compelled to buy the guidebook (or 'key') alongwith the textbook. The economic and business aspects of this pairing apart, the academic function of the textbook has become quite dubious indeed. It is *not* perceived as one of the resources for learning about a subject, but as the *only* authoritative resource. This kind of sanctity distorts what useful purpose the textbook could serve. Teachers see it as a body of 'truths' which children must learn by heart. This perception and the urge to 'cover' the chapters of the prescribed textbook, turn all knowledge into a load to be borne by the child's memory.

The distance between the child's everyday life and the content of the textbook further accentuates the transformation of knowledge into a load. We are not talking here about advanced science or mathematics, but about elementary science, social studies, language and arithmetic. Textbooks treat these subjects in a manner that leads to alienation of knowledge from the child's world. This tragic phenomenon takes different forms in different subjects. In the natural sciences, it takes the form of esotricisation of the subject. In the social sciences it becomes manifest in the coating of every inquiry in didacticism, suggestive of one preferred answer to every question. A common source of alienation of subject matter from the children's perspective and life is the presentation of the life-style and world-view of the urban well-off class. This life style is characterised by access to concrete housing, modern kitchens, electrical gadgets and so on. Of course there is nothing 'wrong' with this life-style; but the symbolisation of this life-style in every illustration and description that concerns a child's home life alienates millions of children who live in houses with traditional kitchens, or with no separate kitchens. Objects of daily use in common Indian homes, such as a broom or clay pitcher, are seldom seen in textbooks. One wonders whether the common Indian broom, which could be a versatile resource for learning about the social and physical environment, is perceived by our textbook writers and illustrators with a sense of stigma or as a symbol of backwardness. Or could it be that it is simply too common to be seen as being of any use in an educational material? Neither of the two guesses is totally irrelevant in view of the complete absence of common objects of ordinary Indian life in the world depicted in textbooks.

The most common message that children get from the textbooks is that the life ordinary people live is 'wrong' or irrational. And this kind of didactic rejection does not apply to non-middle class life alone. All simple joys of childhood are also criticised. No better example of this can be given than the message conveyed in a Class V exercise which asks children to decide whether the statement 'Road is also a playground', is correct or wrong. The right response is that this statement is 'wrong', the message of the lesson being that playing on the street can be dangerous. This message is of course true in a normative sense, but it ignores the reality of the overwhelming majority of urban children who have no other space except the street to play. The moot point is not the scarcity of space, but rather the need to accept the universally valid fact that children enjoy play on the street. This joy must be respected in a text written from a child-centred point of view. To argue that a respectful acknowledgement of this joy will amount to sanctioning carelessness, or to say that children must be warned about the risks of playing on the street is to trivialise the issue. Every child who plays on the street fully knows the dangers involved in it. Science textbooks need not waste valuable pages on such trivial preaching which is precisely what they do throughout the elementary classes in place of using these golden years of childhood to arouse curiosity about things and ideas.

Language textbooks

We hardly need to assert that our textbooks are not written from the child's viewpoint. Neither the mode of communication, nor the selection of objects depicted, nor the language conveys the centrality of the child in the world constructed by the text. This last dimension of language deserves some elaboration. The vocabulary and syntax used in the textbooks in the Hindi region were critically referred to by a number of individuals and groups whom the committee met during the course of its deliberations. Not just the textbooks used for the teaching of the natural and the social sciences, but even the textbook used for the teaching of the mother tongue are written in such stylised diction and sentence-structure, that children cannot be expected to see the language used in them as their own. Words, expressions and nuances commonly used by children and others in their milieu are all absent from textbooks. So is humour. An artificial, sophisticated style dominates textbook lessons, reinforcing the tradition of distancing knowledge from life. The language used in textbooks, thus, deepens the sense of 'burden' attached to all school-related knowledge.

Observation discouraged

A highly disturbing tendency we discovered in text writing, which exacerbates the problem we are discussing, is that of treating pictures as substitutes for experience. We found textbooks asking children to observe a picture of the object under study rather than asking children and the teacher to go out and observe the object itself in nature. For example, a class V science text says : 'Look at the picture of a cactus plant'. Observe the thick green structure...'Such an instruction preempts what motivation there may be in a teacher or child to bring an actual cactus plant to the class or to grow one. The most painful example of this phenomenon brought to our attention was one in which a private publisher claimed that he had made the teacher's task 'easier' by turning an official 'Teacher's Guide', which suggests that the teacher should take children outside the school and identify some common birds, into a text where the pictures of all the common birds with their names were provided for ready use. This case is especially painful as it shows how even a specific instruction given in a Teacher's Guide. (Teacher's Guides are themselves rare; and in subjects in which they have been prepared in certain states, circulation has not been satisfactorily looked after) to encourage teachers to extend the lesson beyond the four walls of the classroom is co-opted within the dominant, traditional approach of teaching everything verbally from a textbook. Over the recent years, some textbooks have adopted the vocabulary of observation and exploration or discovery as a necessary part of science teaching, but even here virtually all commands for observation conclude with statements about what will be seen in an observation is actually made, thereby making it unnecessary for the teacher and children to find an object and actually observe it.

Structure of syllabus

The absence of the child's viewpoint is also reflected in the organisation of syllabi in different subjects. We received a large number of complaints from parents as well as teachers that the content of syllabi lacks an overall organization or coherence. Gaps in the syllabi between the lower and the higher secondary stages are as common as repetitions of the same content. These weaknesses of organisation apparently lead to memorisation and poor comprehension, both exacerbating the sense of curriculum load. Gaps between the secondary and the senior secondary stages seem to be glaring in the science syllabi. When students come to class XI, they often find themselves without a clue even if they have done in class X. The level of abstraction attempted in the senior secondary stage science syllabi and textbooks, especially the physics textbooks, represents a jump in many topics. Apparently, those preparing the senior secondary syllabi and texts lacked adequate familiarity with the syllabi and texts used in the earlier classes. In fact, they had no occasion to interact with the persons involved in the preparation of syllabi and textbooks for secondary classes (IX & X).

Repetitions of concepts and information also lead to boredom and a sense of load. The need to repeat is rooted in the flawed structure of syllabi. In the primary classes, ideas and information are presented in a synoptic manner, making the text look deceptively simple. In the later classes, the same ideas are repeated, with some elaboration which does not prevent the child from viewing the ideas as trivialised by repetition. In the study of nutrition and health, for example, virtually the same ideas and information are given in the syllabi and texts of classes III, IV, V, VII and X. Even the questions given at the end of the lessons in the texts are almost of the same kind. Apparently, the structure of syllabi is not carefully thought out. Indeed, our Committee was told by senior experts, who have been involved in syllabus and textbook preparation, that experts working on the syllabus of different levels (secondary and senior secondary) had no contact with each other. Reference to such procedural lapses, however, is not necessary to explain the tendency towards repetition that is embedded in the structure of the syllabus and has been reinforced by tradition.

History is the most clear case in point. Although it forms one part of the subject called social sciences, it offers a prime example of curriculum load. Despite many changes that have come about in the style of history texts, the history syllabus continues to be a frustrating and meaningless experience for children. The aim of teaching history is defeated because children are not enabled to relate to their own heritage. Traditionally, it requires children to form an overall picture of the 'whole' of India's known history, from ancient to modern times, during the three years from classes VI to VIII. Since the texts for these classes are required to cover such a vast span, the density of these texts becomes extremely high which means that historical time is greatly compressed, i.e., a few sentences are deemed to 'cover' several decades. The synoptic style forces the child into 'accepting' whatever is narrated. There aren't enough details that a child could use to work out some kind of argument or interpretation, but the sheer volume of text (which is supposed to 'cover' 'all' of India's history in three years) forces the child (and the teacher) to 'take in' as much text as possible without 'wasting' time in studying or constructing an argument.

This common problem of the history syllabus apart, we found that the content of the history syllabus in certain states was conceived as a densely packed box of informations. The syllabus of history in West Bengal illustrates this tendency in tragically exaggerated proportions. For example in class VIII, children are required to learn seventeen topics in all which are :

1. Modern age; 2. Renaissance in Europe; 3. Europeans widen the world; 4. Reformation in Europe; 5. The English Revolution in the 17th century; 6. India; 7. Foundation and growth of the British power in India till 1857 in short narrative form; 8. World in the 18th century; 9. Europe since 1815; 10 (a) Developments in China till 1911; (b) Rise of Japan as a great power till 1914; 11. India under the crown 1858-1914; 12. The first World War; 13. The Bolshevik Revolution; 14. Europe 1919-1939; 15. The Second World War; 16. India 1919-1947; 17. (a) Revolution in China

1911-1949; (b) Revolution in South East Asia after 1945; (c) Spread of nationalism and unrest in subject countries during World War II.

The entire syllabus is to be covered in 135 pages of a text, according to the instruction given in the syllabus itself. Apparently, the syllabus makers believe that compression of information in terms of page-space does not affect the readability, let alone comprehensibility, of a text.

Teaching Everything

The problem of densely packed syllabi like this one cuts across disciplines. In geography, it takes the form of all the continents being 'covered' under regional geography between classes VI and VIII. In mathematics and the natural sciences, the packing of details makes any kind of learning with understanding, leave alone enjoyment, virtually impossible. Numerous examples could be given from these disciplines to illustrate the problem. In *one* page of a class VII science textbook we find all these items 'covered': definition of time period, how to find the number of oscillations per second, definition of frequency, 'Hertz' unit of frequency, the idea that vibrations have amplitude and frequency, definitions of these, the concept of sound as vibration, loudness and pitch and finally frequency/pitch and its relation to speed of rotation and tension. We are not citing this example as a specific case to be looked into, but as evidence of a deeply rooted tendency, rather an ideology, which impels syllabus and textbook planners to include 'everything' without any regard for children's ability at different ages to learn and the time available in an average school for teaching a subject. Class XI and XII textbooks of science, prepared recently with a view apparently to implement the National Education Policy, have been widely critised on these scores. Children studying science subjects have been asked by their teachers to look for private tutors, the rationale being that there may not be enough time in the class to cover the syllabus and some of the syllabus being beyond the capacities of the teacher. The terse content of these texts was apparently edited and reviewed in some haste, we were informed, due to constraints of time while sending the manuscripts for publication. Perhaps it can be argued that these textbooks are liked by the highly motivated and the brightest among the students and teachers. If this indeed is the case, it gives all the more reason to worry about the fate of the overwhelming majority of children studying in ordinary schools.

In mathematics, the situation seems to be grim right from the start of the child's school career. Far too many abstractions are introduced all at once with scant attention paid to well-known facts about development of mathematical thinking in children. To begin with, children are expected to handle arithmetical operations on a very large numbers early. In class I, they are supposed to go upto 100 (compared to this a British child in this class spends the whole year working with numbers upto 20), in class II upto 1000, in class III, upto 10,000 in class IV upto a million and in class V upto a crore. Even though the conservation of volume and weight are known to emerge in the child's mind after the conservation of length is fully established, all three are introduced simultaneously (usually in one unit of study) at the young age of seven or eight years, with the expectation that children will compute with standard units. Concrete operational thought, which is characteristic of elementary school children, demands manipulation of objects and activities using a variety of materials (to enable 'elaboration' of a concept, i.e., its dissociation from any one material or object). Such activities become impossible to organise under a curriculum which 'progresses' so swiftly from concept to concept. Also, children of this stage find proportional reasoning difficult, yet percentage and ratio are introduced in classes IV and V. In the middle and higher classes, the tendency to follow the logic of the discipline of mathematics rather than psychology of learning as the basis of the curriculum becomes even more dominant. Mathematics, thus, acquires the image of an esoteric discipline which has little application in the real life of the child.

Starting early

The general problems of curriculum conceptualisation that we have discussed in this part of our report can all be seem reflected in the emerging pre-school sector of the education system. Despite official stipulations that no textbooks be used at this stage, pre-school teachers and parents in the urban centre are feeling 'compelled' to burden the young child with textbooks and the formal learning they represent. The sense of compulsion comes from a widespread feeling that unless academic training of a child starts early, he or she cannot cope with the fast-paced pedagogy and the competitive ethos of the later school years. The pernicious grip of this false argument manifests itself in absurd and of course deeply harmful, practices in preschools and primary schools, such as early emphasis on shapely drawing, writing and memorising information. Intrinsic motivation and the child's natural abilities are being smothered at a scale so vast that it cannot be correctly estimated. Our national commitment to the development of human resource is daily challenged in our nurseries and primary schools.

Not just an urban problem

The problem we have tried to identify in this part of the report is not confined to urban areas as some people think. It is deeply relevant to children's education in rural India although there, more basic problems—such as abysmally poor condition of schools, absenteeism among teachers, etc., may cloud the problem of curriculum load. In our view, the problem of a high drop-out rate, which has rightly preoccupied our policy-makers for a long time, has one of its origins in the curriculum scenario we have portrayed. A curriculum policy that takes away the elements of joy and inquiry from learning obviously contributes to the rate at which children leave school in the early years, undoubtedly under the force of economic and social circumstances. As we have indicated earlier, symbolic tilt towards an urban, middle class way of life in textbooks can also be expected to make the rural child's association with his or her experience at school thin and brittle. Quality of teachers and the equipment available to them also make an impact on the tenuous and fragile link that the first-generation learner in many parts of rural India tries to establish with the system of education.

4.2 ROOTS OF THE PROBLEM

Knowledge vs. information

In our discussions with people directly involved in syllabi and textbook preparation all over the country, we found one argument repeated over and over again as the main justification for the phenomenon we have described in Chapter II. The argument was that India has to catch up with the developed countries where an explosion of knowledge has occurred; therefore, our children must learn a lot more than they used to, which means that new topics, new concepts and information have to be added to the syllabi and textbooks. This argument seems to be so widespread and so tenacious that those who believe in it use it as an undebatable 'given'. When it is pointed out to them that children of the so-called developed countries learn certain concepts a lot later than our children do (for example, in chemistry, the concept of valency is not taught in our schools in class VII whereas European children do not hear about it till they are in class IX), supporters of the 'explosion of knowledge' argument simply say that the European societies are already way ahead of us, so they can afford to instruct their children at a relaxed pace. In geography, when it is pointed out that European and North American children do not have to study every continent (only selected countries are intensively studied instead), the answer given is that in Western societies children have access to many resources of learning outside the school whereas the majority of our children are dependent on the school for getting to know about the world. The idea entrenched in the 'explosion of knowledge' theory finds similar justifications for the present state of syllabi and texts in other school subjects.

The notion that there has been an explosion of knowledge apparently treats knowledge and information as synonymous. It is true that the twentieth century has been a period of massive expansion in human capacity to find new facts and to store them, but the concepts and theories that assist in the generation and organisation of information can hardly be said to have multiplied at an 'explosive' rate. (It is another matter that in an ex-colonial society it often looks as if all new 'knowledge' is being produced by 'others' and our job is simply to 'learn' and consume this knowledge). Also, the important thing in children's education ought to be concept-formation and growth of capacity for theory-building, rather than possession of vast amounts of information. The 'explosion of knowledge' idea prevents us from appreciating that learning in childhood is not the same thing as storing information about different subjects. If we say that a child has knowledge of phenomenon 'x', we can anticipate three possible ways in which this statement will be interpreted :

(i) the child has been given information about phenomenon 'x';
(ii) the child can reproduce information about phenomenon 'x';
(iii) the child has understood phenomenon 'x' and s/he can apply this understanding on other phenomena.

It is mostly the first two meanings that hold in the context of formal education in our country, the first being used as a basis for the second. 'Understanding' is often confused with 'acquisition of facts'.

Such a confusion leads to the neglect of 'understanding' as an aim of education. It would be correct to say that this neglect of understanding has gone so far and deep in our education system that a child can pass almost any examination without any understanding of the phenomena she has been told about in books or in the classroom. To a great extent, this paradoxical situation can be attributed to the excessive emphasis placed in our syllabi and textbooks on information or 'names' of things. Children have no choice but to memorise all the 'names' in order to 'prove' at an examination that they have 'understood' a phenomenon. Despite all kinds of claims that examinations have been reformed, they continue to focus on testing the possession of 'correct' information (i.e., the names of things, definitions, examples, etc.). Recall type questions outnumber the questions that test the child's capacity to speculate, evaluate or judge and to apply an idea in an unfamiliar context. Board examinations, taken at the end of class X and class XII, have remained rigid, bureaucratic and essentially uneducative (as the child never sees why s/he was marked in a certain way), and mainly a source of awe because of the amount of information they demand in a manner ready for instant recall. Such a system obviously influences the tests and annual examinations taken by students in earlier classes as well as the daily pedagogy practised in classrooms. The fact that entrance tests of prestigious institutions like the Indian Institutes of Technology have less focus on recall (although they put a premium on speed) is ignored and even these tests are cited for justifying the excessively large syllabi in certain subjects in the senior secondary classes.

Isolation of experts from classroom realities

The new topics and information put into the syllabus and textbooks at the time of each successive revision are usually added at the behest of experts of different subjects. These experts are university-level teachers, sometimes including individuals of high stature in the research world. Their involvement in the writing or revision of textbooks is indeed appreciable but they have little exposure to children in classroom situations. Their exposure to school teachers is also confined to interaction with the few teachers who are selected as members of syllabus and textbook committees. Several factors, such as the difference of social and official status, make it difficult for school teachers serving on these committees to freely put across their feelings and experiences regarding the teachability of a syllabus or the style of a textbook.

Teachability can be defined as the quotient of content that an average teacher can put across at a comfortable pace in a thirty-five minute school period. If our textbooks were to be judged in the light of this criterion, most of them, especially in the sciences, mathematics and the social sciences, would appear as unteachable. The amount of information and concept load they present are far in excess of the amount that can be put across in any meaningful way in thirty-five minute periods allocated for a school subject in one academic session.

It appears that no rigorous count, using the thirty-five minute period as a unit, of the total teaching time available for a subject in any year is used as a basis for determining syllabus and text content. Indeed, the syllabi and textbooks are evidence to say that the experts involved in preparing them have little knowledge of school and classroom realities. This limitation of the experts extends to their possible ignorance of children and of the processes that children use for learning new ideas. Text books simply do not reflect the versatile search of the ordinary child for clues to make sense of natural or social phenomena. Typically, school texts proceed in a linear fashion, adding bits of information in and concepts as they go along. The linear patterns they follow often spill across school years, i.e., something left off in class VII is picked up again in Class IX and so on. Very seldom is an effort made to construct knowledge-patterns in non-linear ways.

We feel that if experts involved in the preparation of syllabi and textbooks had the opportunity to work with children and their teachers, they would have a chance to develop some insight into children's learning strategies. This would have helped them to develop the ability to emulate such strategies in script-writing for textbooks. Interaction with children might enable experts to develop a certain amount of sensitivity towards the living and versatile approaches used by children. Also, in the course of such interaction, the experts might also perceive the need to equip themselves with knowledge of children's psychology, particularly the psychology of learning, before venturing out on the task of textbook preparation. This, of course, implies that the job of syllabus and textbook preparation be perceived as a serious professional activity, not as a part-time obligation.

Centralised character

In the specific context of the curriculum planning and textbook production, we feel, the system invites a number of problems upon itself on account of being unnecessarily centralised. It seems there is a wide-spread misconception which justifies centralisation in these matters. This misconception treats the content of syllabus and textbooks as synonymous with learning and testing norms. On the basis of this confusion, it is argued that syllabi and textbooks should be the same all over a state, even all over the country, in order to ensure uniformity of standards. This kind of argument completely overlooks the lopsided manner in which standards are set under the present system by an examination system which focuses on information rather than on skills and capacity to apply skills. Indeed, there is a 'catch 22' situation : the examination system ignores skills, concentrating on memorised information, definitions and descriptions; therefore, syllabus and textbooks, which cannot do justice to diversified milieux, varying needs and facilities, become necessary to ensure that all children 'know' the same 'facts'.

This circular argument has created a situation in which curriculum and textbook preparation is confined to the state capitals and New Delhi. At regional and local levels, teachers do not perceive curriculum development and preparation of educational materials as part of their job. And indeed, the way these tasks have been defined and traditionally carried out in our country, they are not the teacher's job. The teacher sees his or her role as one of elucidating whatever content of knowledge is prescribed in the syllabus. At the primary and lower secondary stages, teachers come to know the syllabus through the textbook which acts as the *de facto* syllabus. 'Covering' the syllabus means 'covering' or finishing the textbook. This kind of perception results in the confinement of classroom life to a narrow orbit. Classroom knowledge assumes total independence from the child's own experience and knowledge of the world. As a consequence of this de-coupling, children begin to compartmentalise knowledge into two categories: that which has currency in the school and classroom and the other which has uses and relevance outside the school. Necessarily, the knowledge in the first category ceases to have any 'life' and becomes increasingly ritualistic and burden-some. Teachers also carry the same kind of categorisation in their mind; very few of them are able to help the child make bridges between what is learnt at school and what is required to face real-life situations. One teacher who tried to make such a bridge in a lesson about letter-writing was asked by a class VI child: 'Madam, shall we write it the way we write at home or in the school way?'

While several factors, including those related to the training of teachers, can be held responsible for this aspect of the situation, we feel that the centralised structures of syllabus and textbook preparation set the tone. Howsoever 'good' a textbook produced at central level may be on professional standards, it cannot reflect the subtler nuances of life in a village of Kashmir or Assam. Adaptation to local conditions is indeed officially carried out to match the content of textbooks with local conditions, but it does not change the basic character of a textbook. Adaptation of syllabi to local conditions is even less effectively possible.

Convention of 'teaching the text'

Lack of adequate opportunities for teachers to participate in the processes of syllabus and textbook preparation is a major factor indirectly responsible for the problem of unrealistic syllabi or curriculum load. Teachers perform a more direct role in the context of this problem by perceiving the content of the textbook as a rigid boundary or definer of their work in the classroom. Boredom is the inevitable outcome when a tersely written textbook is taught in a rigid, mechanical manner. Poor grasp among teachers of their role as translators of the curriculum into classroom activity is a widely prevalent characteristic of our system. We are citing this as a relevant aspect of the phenomenon of curriculum load *without* suggesting that there is a vicious cycle here, i.e., teaching cannot improve unless there are better textbooks, etc. We feel that strategies to improve textbook writing and production must work parallel to strategies for improvement in teacher training and for creating an ethos in which teachers would feel motivated to take an academic interest in their work. The perception that a teacher can do little in the classroom that is different from what the textbook says is part of a historical legacy. This legacy must be transcended and the self-perception rooted in it must be changed. Teacher training institutions and the mass media both can assist in making this change possible.

In the context of constructing a new self-image of the teacher, preservice training is a key but elusive area of reform. Past attempts to improve teacher training programmes and institutions have met with rather limited success. By and large, teacher training continues to be isolated from mainstream academic areas related to education. Inservice training too in most of the places, has assumed the character of a ritual devoid of academic substance or the capacity to stimulate. The current efforts to provide statutory status to the National Council of Teacher Education (as envisaged in the National Education Policy) may perhaps make some impact on the weak training that is generally available in the country to people who want to work with children, especially young children.

Administrative and legal concern needs to be applied to several training programmes running as commercial success-stories, such as those offering a degree by correspondence. Similarly, there is need to examine existing policies with regard to nursery teacher training courses and institutions. Indeed, what is required is a review of the overall training policy which permits the traditional bifurcation of degree-programmes from non-degree programmes and their application to different stages of school education. We hope that after acquiring statutory status, the NCTE will work out a comprehensive training programme to cover all stages of schooling, ending the bifurcation we have mentioned above. Such a programme will have to be radically different from the present ones which are anchored in the culture of late-19th century Normal schools and are sadly lacking both in perspective and means to equip teachers with the capacity to understand children and their learning processes in a professional manner.

Competition based Social Ethos

Our social ethos, particularly in the urban areas, is now fully entrenched in the competitive spirit which is fast becoming our way of life. The desire to catch up with the industrially developed countries has given it further impetus. Rising aspirations of people in all sections of the society and the growing realisation that education is an important instrument to fulfil their aspirations have resulted in a craze for admission to English-medium schools which start imparting formal education too early in the child's life.

The educated sections of the society believe that command over English is the key to upward mobility in social life. This has led to unprecedented growth in the number of private schools where English is not only taught as a subject but is also used as medium of education in all subjects right from class I. It is a well known fact that young children studying in English medium schools mug up the content of science and social sciences without understanding. It is an accepted principle of pedagogy that whatever is memorised without understanding proves burdensome for children. Any language other than the mother tongue of the child, if used as medium of instruction, is a big source of academic burden on children. Most of the parents in urban and semi urban areas do not realise it, in fact they try to promote the use of English as a medium of education. Unfortunately, instead of resisting the pressure of the competitive spirit prevalent in the society or directing it in appropriate channels, our educational system has succumbed to it. The most conspicuous manifestations of this phenomenon in education are upgradation of content of syllabus by advancing introduction of many topics and subjects in utter disregard of the process of maturation. The entrance tests for admission to professional courses like engineering and medicine have influenced the objectives, content and methodology of education in many ways. The 'Quiz culture' which has taken roots in education, can be attributed to these tests.

With a view to provide incentives to 'high achievers' and 'talented' in different fields, high profile competitions are organised by different departments and institutions in the name of 'talent search' which at the most provide moments of brief glory to the winners but damage the 'ego strength' of numerous others who participate in the contests at the cost of leisurely pursuit of knowledge at their own pace and in their own ways. The experience of the ignominy of failure on the part of millions of children have long term deleterious effect on the personality of the individual and the matrix of society. It would be better to reward group performance so as to convey the message to everyone that excellence in group work rather than individual effort should be the target.

Absence of Academic Ethos

Adequate time, staff accommodation and its maintenance funds, pedagogical equipment, playgrounds are essential pre-requisites for effective curriculum transaction but, unfortunately, an overwhelming majority of schools do not have even the minimum essential facilities. It is a matter of great concern that the number of teachers with a sense of commitment is gradually shrinking while cynicism, feelings of helplessness and hopelessness are on the rise. Lack of adequate infrastructural facilities, rigid administrative structures and growing cynicism are responsible for the absence of academic ethos in majority of schools.

The methods of teaching used by majority of teachers are devoid of any type of challenge for the students. Transmission of information rather than experimentation or exploration or observation characterises the teaching learning process in most of the classrooms. We have no reason to believe that there is something wrong with our children, rural or urban. Luckily they have not compartmentalised knowledge; they are interested in seeking understanding rather than mere information. As they are educated by us, while they grow older, freshness goes away, as does romance and curiosity. Before anything is learnt they want to find out why they need to know. Must we, in the name of so-called 'proper education' go on committing the murder of their innate desire to discover and to learn on their own?

Children are not allowed to observe and explore natural phenomena, but at the same time they are also not provided opportunity to explore the world of books. The concept of a library as a readily available resource for learning simply does not exist in most schools. Even those rare schools that do happen to have a library stock little more than copies of prescribed textbooks, often stored behind locked doors. If children are to be prepared for experiencing the beauty and richness of nature and the fascination of ideas without feeling the curricular load, priority has to be given to developing school libraries and their adequate and appropriate utilisation.

Similarly, science laboratories even in the few cases where they are adequately equipped are not used for experimentation and discovery. A laboratory is not perceived as a place where children can conduct even those experiments which are not prescribed in their syllabi and come out with novel observations that need exploratory frameworks. The main purpose of a laboratory programme is to visualise children's natural talents and develop their ability to learn through observation and exploration. Over regimentation of prescribed experiments with the entire emphasis on getting the final result, is contrary to this spirit. Laboratories should be conceived as exploratories and schools should have the freedom to structure experiments to suit the needs of their children.

4.3 RECOMMENDATIONS

We have come to the conclusion that the problem of the load on school children does not arise only from over-enthusiastic curriculum designers, or poorly equipped teachers, or school administrators, or book publishers, or District, State or Central education authorities. Yes, what all these groups, agencies and administrations do can exacerbate or alleviate the problem. But, there is a deeper malaise in our society, which impacts our young children. If we continue to value a few elite qualifications far more than real competence for doing useful things in life and if the economic distance, between those who can manage to cross some academic hurdles and those who can't, continues to widen, we will probably continue to spend our effort in designing hurdles, instead of opportunities for children to learn with joy. As the body of the report analyses, a major problem is connected with the notions of "knowledge explosion" and the "catching up" syndrome. We believe that these problems cannot be fully addressed through easily manageable administrative actions. They need wider discussions because they are centrally connected with images of our civilization, self-esteem and societal goals. Such a wide discussion can come about through publication of this report and through a set of seminars, meetings and media discussions. Academics, thinkers, need to pour over this basic problem.

The question of medium of instruction, particularly in early life, will not be fully resolved till the time our dominant and externally connected sections of society continue to give more importance to elementary graces in a foreign language, than to intimate connections with the "vernacular" knowledge which our children gain during every week of their growing up before they go to school. It is because of this reason that we have restrained ourselves from repeating the recommendation that mother-tongue alone should be the medium of instruction at the primary stage.

1. A number of organisations and departments organise competitions at district, state and national level for students in various fields such as school subjects, exhibitions, essay writing, elocution etc. Perhaps the spirit behind these activities is to recognise and reward the talent in diverse fields. But, unfortunately this tends to produce somewhat unhealthy singling out of people for their brief moment of glory. Competitions where individual achievement is rewarded need to be discouraged since they deprive children of joyful learning. However, group activities and group achievements must be encouraged and rewarded to give a boost to cooperative learning in schools.

2. (a) The process of curriculum framing and preparation of textbooks be decentralised so as to increase teachers' involvement in these tasks. Decentralisation should mean greater autonomy, within state-level apparatus, to district-level boards or other relevant authority and to heads of schools and classroom teachers to develop curricular materials on their own best suited to the needs of local environment. All the schools be encouraged to innovate in all aspects of curriculum, including choice of textbooks and other materials.

(b) Voluntary organisations with a specific commitment to pedagogical innovations within the formal or non-formal system be provided greater freedom and support in development of curriculum, textbooks and teacher training. A suitable and adequate mechanism be evolved for wider dissemination of the experiences of such organisations.

(c) We endorse the idea of setting up education committees at village, block and district level to undertake planning and supervision of schools under their jurisdiction.

(d) Sufficient contingency amount (not less than 10% of the total salary bill of the school) be placed at the disposal of heads of schools for purchase, repair and replacement of pedagogical equipment.

3. The culture of writing textbooks be changed so as to involve a much large number of teachers in the preparation of textbooks. The scientists and experts in various disciplines may be associated with the preparation of textbooks as consultants and not as writers of the books. Initiative in this regard should rest with groups of enlightened and innovative teachers who should be provided training in book writing.

4. At least three parallel systems of school education (syllabus, textbooks and examination) are running concurrently in different states. In each state majority of schools are affiliated to the State Board of Education while a few are affiliated to either CBSE or ICSE. The schools affiliated to CBSE in the states other than Delhi enjoy the prestige of being elite schools. The CBSE curriculum becomes a trend setter for the State Boards leading to heavier curriculum for majority of children. Therefore, the committee recommends that jurisdiction of CBSE be restricted to Kendriya and Navodaya Vidyalayas and all other schools be affiliated to the respective State Boards.

5 (a) Appropriate legislative and administrative measures be adopted to regulate the opening and functioning of early childhood education institutions (pre schools). Norms regarding accommodation, staff, apparatuses, play materials be laid down for the recognition of these schools. It should be ensured that these institutions do not perpetrate violence on young children by inflicting a heavy dose of 'over education' in the form of formal teaching of Reading, Writing and Numbers. The practice of holding tests and interviews for admission to nursery class be abolished.

(b) Norms for granting recognition to private schools be made more stringent. This will prove conducive for improving the quality of learning on the one hand and arrest growing commercialisation on the other. The norms, thus developed, be made uniformly applicable to all schools including the state run institutions.

6. There is no justification for torturing the young children by compelling them to carry very heavy bags of books every day to schools. Textbooks should be treated as school property and thus, there should be no need for children to purchase the books individually and carry them daily to homes. A separate time table for the assignment of home work and for the use of textbooks and notebooks be prepared by the school and be made known to the children in advance.

7. The nature and character of homework needs a radical change. In the primary classes, children should not be given any homework save for extension of explorations in the home environment. In the upper primary and secondary classes, homework, where necessary, should be non-textual and textbooks, when needed for work at home should be made available on a rotation basis.

8. The existing norm for teacher-pupil ratio (i.e. 1:40) should be enforced and an attempt should be made to reduce this to 1:30, at least in the primary classes, as a basis for future educational planning.

9. Greater use of the electronic media be made for the creation of a child-centred social ethos in the country. A regular television programme addressed to students, teachers and parents and possibly called 'Shiksha Darshan' be launched, along the lines of the 'Krishi Darshan' programme.

10. (a) Inadequate programme of teacher preparation leads to unsatisfactory quality of learning in schools. The B.Ed., programme should offer the possibility of specialisation in secondary or elementary or nursery education. The duration of the programme should either be one year after graduation or 3-4 years after higher secondary. The content of the programme should be restructured to ensure its relevance to the changing needs of school education and to make it more practiced centred. The emphasis in these programmes should be on enabling the trainees to acquire the ability for self learning and independent thinking. Preservice teacher education programme, being a professional course, has to be a rigorous, thorough and intensive programme. Therefore, B.Ed degree courses by correspondence be derecognised.

(b) The continuing education of teachers must be institutionalised. The organisation of inservice education programmes and other activities aimed at professional growth of teachers be systematically designed and conducted imaginatively.

11. The public examinations taken at the end of class X and XII be reviewed with a view to ensure replacement of the prevailing text based and 'Quiz type' questioning by the concept-based questioning. This single reform is sufficient to improve the quality of learning and save the children from the tyranny of rote memorisation.

12. (a) A Project team with a number of sub-groups be set up in each state to examine the syllabi and textbooks for all school classes. The sub-groups be required to decide the following :

(i) the minimum number of topics required to be taught.

(ii) the minimum number of concepts to be introduced within each topic.

(iii) the total time needed for teaching this minimum number of concepts comfortably by a teacher in the total working days realistically available in a year.

(b) Mathematics curriculum for primary classes in all parts of the country be reviewed with a view to slowing down the pace at which children are required to learn basic mathematical concepts and broadening the scope of primary mathematics to include areas other than number worked (e.g., space and shape related concepts and problem solving). The tendency embedded in the syllabi and textbooks of primary mathematics to accelerate children's mathematical skills by teaching them mechanical rules at the expense of understanding and intelligent application ought to be discouraged in future syllabi and texts.

(c) Language textbooks should adequately reflect the spoken idiom. An attempt should be made in future textbooks to give adequate representation to children's life experiences, imaginary stories and poems and stories reflecting the lives of ordinary people in different parts of the country. Pedantic language and excessive didacticism ought to be avoided.

(d) Science syllabi and textbooks in the primary classes should provide greater room and necessity for experimentation than they do at present. In place of didacticism in areas like health and sanitation, the texts should emphasise analytical reflection on real-life situations. A great deal of trivial material included in primary-level science texts should be dropped.

(e) The syllabi of natural sciences throughout the secondary and senior secondary classes be revised in a manner so as to ensure that most of the topics included are actively linked to experiments or activities that can be performed by children and teachers.

(f) Besides imparting knowledge of history and geography, the social sciences curriculum for classes VI-VIII and IX-X should convey the philosophy and methodology of the functions of our socio-political and economic system and enable the students to analyse, understand and reflect on the problems and priorities of socio-economic development. The repetitious nature of history syllabus should be changed. The history of ancient times should be introduced for systematic study in secondary classes (IX and X). The history syllabus for classes VI-VIII should focus on the freedom struggle and post independence developments. The civics, as it is taught today, puts a great load on children's capacities to memorise. Therefore, it may be dropped in its present form and be replaced by 'contemporary studies'. The study of geography be related to contemporary reality.

5

Report of the Group to Examine the Recommendations of the National Advisory Committee on Learning Without Burden (1993)*

Introduction

A National Advisory Committee was set up on 1 March 1992 by the Ministry of Human Resource Development under the Chairmanship of Prof. Yash Pal, former Chairman of the University Grants Commission (UGC), to advise on the ways and means to reduce the academic burden on school students. The Committee submitted its Report to the Ministry on 15 July 1993.

On receipt of the Report of the National Advisory Committee, a decision was taken by the Ministry to set up a Group under the Chairmanship of Shri Y.N. Chaturvedi, Additional Secretary, Department of Education of the Ministry, to examine the recommendations of the Committee, give its views on the feasibility of implementing them and a time schedule of implementation. The Group was set up on 25 August 1993 and a copy of the Government Order giving the composition and terms of reference of the Group is given in Annex A.

The Group held two meetings on 23 and 25 September 1993 in which it examined the recommendations made in the Yash Pal Committee Report. The Group had the benefit of advice of Shri R.C. Tripathi, Adviser (Education), Planning Commission, also. The list of members who participated in the deliberations is given in Annex B. In addition

---

* Report of the Group to Examine the Feasibility of Implementing the Recommendations of the National Advisory Committee Set- up to Suggest Ways to Reduce Academic Burden on School Students. Department of Education, Ministry of Human Resource Development, Government of India, New Delhi, 1993.

to participation by two senior functionaries of the National Council of Educational Research and Training (NCERT), the Grof a detailed critique of the Yash Pal Committee Report prepared by the NCERT. This was a particularly useful input in view of the role the NCERT plays in curriculum development, textbook preparation and other aspects of school education.

5.1 TEXT OF THE REPORT

General Observations

The Group has observed with considerable appreciation the participative nature of the Yash Pal Committee Report about the load of curriculum on school students. While discussion on curriculum load has been extensive over the years in the mass media, it has been largely confined to the physical load of the school bag which a student has to carry. Many have felt that there has been a lot of generalisation in such discussions on the basis of the size of the school bag seen in metropolitan cities and particularly in regard to students studying in public schools even at the pre-school stage. The Report has taken note in the beginning itself that "a survey conducted in Delhi revealed that the weight of school bag, on an average, in primary classes in public schools is more than 4 kg, while it is around 1 kg in MCD schools". This finding of the Yash Pal Committee is in tune with the information with the educational managers that firstly, the load of the school bag is not a forbidding one in schools in villages and in small towns and secondly, even in big towns, the problem is in its most aggravated form in regard to students of public schools and children of pre-school classes. Luckily, there are signs recently of the more enlightened public schools de-emphasising subject-matter learning at pre-school stage as also de-emphasising the need to prescribe a lot of books and exercise books at pre-school stage. Since such schools are pace-setters, it is hoped that this example will soon influence other pre-primary schools. This Group is recommending subsequently some specific measures in pursuance of one of the recommendations of the Yash Pal Committee to accelerate this process.

The Yash Pal Committee has instead taken the problem at a more elevated plane by observing that in the present schools "a lot is taught but little is learnt or understood". It has, therefore, inferred that the load of non-learning or non-comprehension is the real load one should be concerned about. This approach of looking at the problem of academic burden has imparted to the Report of the Yash Pal Committee a great deal of significance.

Simultaneously, the Group noted that there are a few things to which the Yash Pal Committee could have given specific attention. The National Policy on Education (NPE) and the Programme Of Action (POA) enunciate the need to have a national core curriculum and have spelt out some of the features of this. The Policy also strongly enunciates a child-centred approach to education. It is in pursuance of this that the NCERT framed a curriculum framework for the school stage which has been accepted by all the states. The NCERT has also developed the levels of competencies to be attained at the end of primary stage. These exercises with a lot of validity in them have been the basis for developing syllabi and textbooks for different stages of school education. While there may be some flaws in the syllabi and the textbooks prepared by the NCERT, it does not seem that they can be accused of being grossly unsuitable or overloaded. In regard to curriculum load, the NCERT had carried out a study in mid-eighties which identified the physical overload of curriculum at some stages of school education and also pointed out that inadequate teacher competency, insufficient teaching days and inadequate classroom facilities, transfer the curriculum load to the students as well as indirectly to parents. The Yash Pal Committee has not referred to this work and the facts stated in the preceding statements. While the main argument forming the basis of the Yash Pal Committee Report is eminently sound, with regard to the main thrust of its recommendations, some of the statements in the Report do not indicate the data or basis on which the Committee has relied. Similarly, some of the recommendations like the one concerning affiliation of schools to the Central Board of Secondary Education (CBSE) are not accompanied by corresponding consideration in the main body of the Report. In a few cases like in regard to medium of instruction in schools, the Committee has noted in the main body of its Report: "the educated sections of the society believe that command over English is key to upward mobility in social life... It is a well-known fact that young children studying in English medium schools mug the content of science and social sciences without understanding. It is an accepted principle of pedagogy that whatever is memorised without understanding proves burdensome on children. Any language other than the mother tongue of the child, if used as medium of instruction, is a big source of academic burden on children". However, such strong statements do not have a corresponding recommendation. The Report also ignores the fact that for most of our students, medium of instruction is the mother tongue or regional language at all stages of school education. Overall it is an important Report which has brought to the fore an understanding about curriculum load which one does not frequently come across. For this it is bound to raise the level of debate about the curriculum load to a qualitatively higher level. It is expected that this report would lead to meaningful and adequate reform in curriculum formulation, textbook preparation, teacher training, etc. The Group feels that the nature of the problem is different for each stage of school education but the Committee has not specifically referred to the distinct problems of each stage and ways of dealing with them. The views of the Group in regard to individual recommendations made by the Yash Pal Committee are given below.

Recommendation No. 1

Comments

The Group is of the view that group activity and individual effort are not mutually exclusive or antagonistic. Rewarding individual achievement does not take away the joy of learning and is also a means to motivate towards higher achievement. In the view of the Group, the educational system should promote performance of the students both as an individual and as a member of the group.

Recommendation No. 2 (a)

Comments

The Group noted that the curriculum and syllabi are designed by the NCERT/CBSE at national level and by the State Boards of Secondary Education/SCERTs at state level by involving teachers and through teachers. However, the number of teachers associated with this exercise is limited to the number of members of the Committee or the Board. The Yash Pal Committee has rightly underlined the need to increase teachers' participation in curriculum development. The Group feels that while the size of committees at national or state level cannot be increased beyond a limit, a meaningful way of improving teachers' participation would be for either the NCERT/CBSE/State Boards/ SCERTs to prepare the draft syllabus and finalise it after subjecting it to regional or district level consideration by a large body of teachers or, in the alternative, to get multiple syllabi developed at regional and district levels on the basis of which the final syllabi could be prepared at the state/national level. The Group, however, does not recommend decentralisation in the preparation of syllabus or textbooks at the district or school level because it will be difficult to ensure adequate projection of national identity and of composite culture of India. Also, in such a situation, the adherence to even minimum standards in all parts of the country may become difficult.

In regard to textbooks, the Group agrees with the Yash Pal Committee that the primary responsibility for preparing textbooks, particularly for the lower classes should be that of teachers. It may, however, be remembered that the involvement of experts since the early 1960s led to qualitative improvement in school textbooks. They helped in weeding out dead wood, brought in new perspectives in tune with contemporary knowledge. The Group, however, shares the concern of the Yash Pal Committee that many textbooks presently tend to project predominantly the urban middle class life style. Therefore, the Group recommends that :

(a) The writing of textbooks, as far as possible, should be assigned to school teachers and to those who have developed professional expertise in the area. Subject-matter specialists should be engaged as consultants or advisers to vet the content and presentation of the subject-matter to ensure its accuracy.

(b) In states which have distinct socio-cultural geographical zones, different and parallel sets of textbooks with the same learning objectives should be prepared and used in schools for each such distinct socio-cultural geographical region.

(c) A conscious effort should be made by the textbook preparation agencies to take examples from rural areas for illustrating various points because a large majority of students are in rural areas.

(d) The textbook preparation agencies should undertake systematic review of all textbooks in a time-bound manner to ensure that any trivial matter which may have got included in the textbooks is weeded out. Similarly, such a review should also try to eliminate elements of repetitions of the topic covered in previous classes.

(e) The Group noted that, in some cases, the textbooks for subjects other than languages in some classes are written in a language which is considerably more complex and difficult than the language used in textbooks for that class. It, therefore, recommends that the group which writes a textbook should include one language teacher who should vet the manuscript to ensure that the degree of difficulty of the language used in the subject-matter is not more than the degree of difficulty designed for language competency for that class. In regard to curriculum transaction and teaching materials, the Group noted that there are no restrictions on schools and teachers to innovate. Indeed, the teacher training courses have consistently advocated this and many organisations have introduced special programmes to promote this. Needless to say that schools and teachers should be motivated to innovate to the fullest extent in regard to teaching methods and use of teaching materials.

Recommendation No. 2 (b)

Comments

The Group fully agrees that voluntary organisations with a commitment to education should be encouraged in all possible manners. The Group also noted that the governments, both at the national and the state levels have, in recent past, made a substantial move to expand such cooperation. The process needs to be continued. However, for reasons mentioned in 2 (a), the Group does not favour decentralisation in curriculum development and textbooks preparation to the extent of entrusting it to voluntary organisations because of the sensitivity of the matter.

Recommendation No. 2 (c)

Comments

This is acceptable in principle. This has been strongly advocated in para 10.8 of the NPE, 1986. Following the Constitutional Amendment for decentralisation at Panchayat level, the Central Advisory Board of Education (CABE) has already constituted a Committee on Decentralised Management of Education to examine and recommend measures for effectively carrying out the desired involvement of the local committees. Therefore, this recommendation should be implemented in the light of the recommendations of the CABE Committee.

Recommendation No. 2 (d)

Comments

This is acceptable. The State/UT Governments and autonomous bodies of the Central Government controlling their respective chain of schools (Kendriya Vidyalayas, Navodaya Vidyalayas, Central Tibetan Schools, Railway Schools and Sainik Schools and other schools run by the Defence establishments) should be urged to give this authority to the

Principals/Headmasters of the schools to make repairs to school buildings, purchase, repair and replace pedagogical equipment and books and also to carry out innovative projects, subject to the control of the local education committees. The organisations controlling the schools and the State Governments should categorically specify that the Head of the school does not require approval of any higher educational authority and the School Management/Advisory Committee for using the available money for these purposes.

Recommendation No. 3

Comments

The group agrees with the purport of this recommendation—greater involvement of teachers—and the views of the Group on this recommendation is included in the comments on 2 (a).

Recommendation No. 4

Comments

The Group has been unable to appreciate the arguments put forth by the Yash Pal Committee in this recommendation. The choice of educational boards that the schools have is already very limited—there is no free choice—and it can be exercised only with the approval of the State Government. Therefore, if a school in any part of the country has the choice of affiliating with one Board or the other, it should be generally good for education. As for CBSE, it relies heavily on the NCERT for developing syllabi and preparing textbooks. The NCERT, in turn, operates within the national policy framework and on the basis of guidelines contained in the National Curriculum Framework. Rightly the NCERT keeps in view the existing standards in the country, the capability of students and standards in developed countries because the syllabus and textbook must take note of all these. If there is unnecessary material in some of the NCERT books, it should be eliminated as the Group has suggested in the preceding recommendations. However, there is not adequate material on record to substantiate that CBSE syllabi or NCERT books *per se* are overloaded. Also, the Yash Pal Committee has recommended that affiliation to CBSE should be restricted to Kendriya and Navodaya Vidyalayas with all other schools being affiliated to respective State Boards. If affiliation to the CBSE is good for Kendriya and Navodaya Vidyalayas it cannot be bad for other schools.

Recommendation No. 5 (a) and 5 (b)

Comments

The Group is in agreement with the recommendations. While the NCERT has prepared some norms for the staff, nature of curriculum and educational material for pre-primary stage, this sector of education in the country is largely unsupervised and unregulated. It is also a known fact that most of these schools are loading the students with the burden of formal teaching of various subjects. The Group advised that an appropriate regulatory mechanism should be urgently set up in the country to ensure that learning at this stage is by playway method and formal teaching of subjects is scrupulously prevented. Similarly, the Group agrees that recognition and affiliation of both private and government schools should be made more stringent so that schools lacking in minimum essential facilities are not allowed to function because it really means punishment to the students. Although there is a well set arrangement for recognition and affiliation of schools but due to extraneous pressures the standards sometimes are not observed. The Group would like to suggest that the possibility of having a legislation to specify norms of facilities in schools and providing for powers to prevent opening of schools which do not have facilities should be seriously considered.

Recommendation No. 6 and 7

Comments

The Group has already agreed that there should be no formal teaching of subjects in the pre-school stage. The Group also feels that there should be no homework and project work at the primary stage (Classes I-V). However, it is an extreme point of observation that textbooks should be treated as school property. Besides the financial implications arising out of the burden on schools to purchase the textbooks and the concomitant responsibility on the schools to store the books when most of the schools of the country do not have either the financial resources or storage capacities, the children would be devoid of the opportunity to refer to the textbooks in their homes. For an overwhelming majority of school students of the country, the textbooks remain as the only source of reading material. The Group recommends that the class routine for the upper primary, secondary and higher secondary stages should be drawn up in such a way that every subject is not required to be taught everyday. This should be included in the norms for compliance by every school which the Group has suggested in para 5 (a) and 5 (b) above.

Recommendation No. 8

Comments

The Group agrees with a higher teacher-pupil ratio with improved teaching and standards of education. It understands that in reality the existing teacher-pupil ratio is around 1:40 in most parts of the country. Attempts should be made to bring it to 1:30 over a period of time. Such change in ratio would have a very large financial implication because of the need to induct a large number of extra teachers and therefore, this can be done only over a period of time. Efforts should be made to ensure that the class size does not exceed 40.

Recommendation No. 9

Comments

Greater use of electronic media for education is an essential part of modernising the educational system. A regular programme on TV addressed to students, teachers and parents would be very welcome. The Group took note of the fact that the Ministry of Human Resource Development, Department of Education, has already made a request for allocating one channel for education out of 15 or 16 channels which have recently become available with the commissioning of INSAT 2-A. The Group strongly suggests that an educational channel should be operationalised at the earliest and this channel should include a programme of the nature suggested by the Yash Pal Committee.

Recommendation No. 10 (a)

Comments

There is a lot of merit in the argument advanced by the Yash Pal Committee for having a programme of B.Ed., aimed at elementary or secondary education. In metropolitan cities, a large number of teachers are actually getting recruited for pre-school and elementary schools with B.Ed., qualifications. Recruitment in KVS and NVS is also, in practice, based on B.Ed., qualifications. Therefore, this reality needs to be taken cognizance of and the present practice of focussing on secondary education in B.Ed., needs to be given up by enabling B.Ed., to be pursued with either specialisation in secondary or in elementary or in pre-school education. In any case the existing arrangements, including the District Institutes of Education and Training (DIETs) for preparing primary school teachers need to be continued and strengthened.

The recommendation of the Yash Pal Committee for derecognising B.Ed., degree by correspondence course is more problematic, while the National Council for Teacher Education (NCTE) has earlier made recommendations on these lines and the UGC has been interacting with the concerned universities during the last ten years on that basis, such courses are continuing. A recent expert committee of the UGC has expressed that for women candidates and for people from rural areas, B.Ed., correspondence course opens up valuable career opportunities. Also, in a large number of countries, B.Ed., through correspondence course is one of the prominent courses in distance mode. These arguments cannot be totally ignored. The Group understands that the matter is at an advanced stage of consideration in the UGC. Also the NCTE as a statutory body is expected to become operational in the near future. The Group recommends that this matter should be referred to the UGC and the NCTE for appropriate decision.

Recommendation No. 10 (b)

Comments

The emphasis given by the Yash Pal Committee to continuing education of teachers is totally unexceptionable. Thus DIETs are being set up in the country primarily to meet this need. Distance education system also is coming up in the country which can be used to meet the needs of inservice education. However, the progress in this regard has been slow. The Group fully endorses the need to set up arrangements for regular and periodic inservice training of teachers and recommends that the DIETs should be operationalised as early as possible and the distance mode of education should be used extensively to strengthen inservice training of teachers.

Recommendation No. 11

Comments

The Group feels that the Yash Pal Committee's reference to the concept-based questioning perhaps advocates greater importance to questions of higher ability. The Group agrees with this but it should be remembered that assessment should test various kinds of abilities and not just of one kind. The Group also feels that the Boards of School Education should emphasise Continuous and Comprehensive Evaluation (CCE) that incorporates both scholastic and non-scholastic aspects of education, spread over the total span of instructional time as stipulated in para 8.24 (iii) of the NPE, 1986.

Recommendation No. 12 (a)

Comments

The Minimum Levels of Learning (MLLs) for language (mother tongue), mathematics and environmental studies for Classes I-V have already been prepared at the national level in 1990 and the NCERT, the Boards of School Education and the SCERTs have developed their resources to introduce the MLLs at the primary stage. Therefore, setting up another Project Team for the same purpose would amount to avoidable duplication. The Group feels that though in para 5.4.5 (vii) and para 21.3.1 (a), the POA, 1992 has called for laying down MLLs at the upper primary stage and in para 21.3.1 (b), the POA, 1992 has urged the Boards to lay down expected levels of attainment at Classes IX-XII, the reasonableness of laying down MLLs at the upper primary stage and above deserves a careful reconsideration since knowledge base is supposed to grow at a fast pace after the primary stage. Moreover, with emphasis shifting to subject-matter learning at the upper primary stage and above, the idea of laying down uniform MLLs after primary stage does not seem to be a viable proposition. However, at the time of curriculum renewal and preparation of textbooks, the curriculum/textbook designers should systematically check that those can be covered within the instructional time available to teachers. The NCERT at the national level and the State Boards/SCERTs/SIEs at the state level may consider the desirability of reviewing the school curricula/textbooks to ensure that non-essential matter and repetitive treatment of concepts in subjects in different classes is minimised as far as possible without sacrificing the requirements of cognitive development.

Recommendation No. 12 (b)

Comments

The Group endorses the recommendation that mathematics and syllabi for other subjects should be reviewed to assess whether they are overloaded . But it would not like to state at this stage that they indeed are overloaded. The MLLs adopted by the MHRD are now being tried out and the question of review should be considered only on the basis of the feedback. As has been referred to in the preceding recommendations, syllabi have to be designed keeping in view the existing standards, and capacity of students and standards in developed countries. However, the Group endorses the statement of the Yash Pal Committee that the syllabus should emphasise understanding and intelligent application rather than memorising without understanding.

Recommendation No. 12 (c)

Comments

These recommendations are acceptable. The NCERT and the Boards including CBSE and Council for the Indian School Certificate Examination (CISCE) should review their respective language textbooks from these angles.

Recommendation No. 12 (d)

Comments

The Group has already given its views that all the existing textbooks should be screened in a time-bound manner for eliminating trivial matter and repetition. The Group endorses the recommendation that there should be greater scope for experimentation at the primary stage. This should be systematically promoted through a large programme of inservice education of teachers.

Recommendation No. 12 (e)

Comments

The Group is of the view that while experiments and activities at all levels are important, the selection of topics in science curriculum at higher stages cannot be determined by the criterion that they are linked to experiment, etc. Every effort should, however, be made to see that experiments and activities, as much as possible, depending on the nature of the topic, are made a part of science teaching even at higher levels.

Recommendation No. 12 (f)

Comments

As regards the Committee's suggestion that history syllabus for Classes VI-VIII should focus on freedom struggle and post-independence developments, the Group holds the view that a large majority of children drop out at the end of Class VIII, which is also the last year of compulsory education and therefore, it would not be educationally sound to allow such a big section of our children to remain oblivious of the entire heritage of India before the freedom struggle. The Committee seems to have linked spiral approach (which is based on a well-established principle of curriculum construction) with repetition which 'leads to boredom and load and trivialisation of ideas'. The Group feels that in geography greater importance should be given to study of contemporary problems. The context or implications of the Committee's recommendation for replacing 'Civics' by 'Contemporary Studies' are not clear.

5.2 ADDITIONAL SUGGESTIONS OF THE GROUP

The Yash Pal Committee has made many thought-provoking recommendations which the Group has tried to recommend for implementation in a more specific manner. If these are implemented efficiently, the standards of school education will undoubtedly improve and as the Yash Pal Committee has envisaged alienation of students from education and the burden of 'non-understanding' on them would effectively diminish. However, in addition to the recommendations made by the Yash Pal Committee, there are a few more issues which immediately present themselves for consideration while considering any exercises for reducing the load of curriculum. The Group would like to suggest these also for implementation.

1. *Age of Entry*

It is a known fact that in India children join school at a rather early age than their counterparts do in most of the developed countries. At the age of 4 and 5, a difference of one year in age makes a lot of difference in the mental capability of a child. A more mature child can easily cope with the learning requirements. The effect of early admissions of children in schools, particularly at the pre-primary stage, is that she/he is unable to cope with the demands that the syllabus makes and consequently she/he starts in a situation of personal inadequacy. This contributed significantly to the load of non-learning. It is, therefore, desirable that the minimum age of admission to pre-primary classes and in primary classes should be reconsidered for being raised by one year.

2. *Teaching Days*

Kothari Commission recommended 210 teaching days but the actual number of school days are 125-150. Since the syllabi are framed on the basis that 210 days will be available, this only means that either a part of syllabus is not covered by the teacher or that she/he covers the syllabus in a hurried manner which creates difficulty for students for being able to cope with a lot of content in a limited time. Effective action to increase the number of teaching days to 210 in a year would undoubtedly very substantially reduce the daily learning load and would also improve standards.

3. *Classroom Facilities*

In large number of schools in the country not only the facilities in the classroom but the classroom themselves are grossly deficient. This inevitably affects the quality of teaching and therefore, of learning. The Yash Pal Committee has recommended and we have endorsed that recommendation earlier in this Report that norms for school facilities should be effectively and strictly enforced for recognition/affiliation. However, since government is the major funding agency for most schools, there should be a positive movement for improving availability of classrooms and improving availability of educational aids in schools. For primary schools, the Government of India is implementing a large programme of Operation Blackboard and in the Eighth Plan it is being extended to cover upper primary classes also. At secondary level, the Government of India is implementing a scheme for assisting schools for improving science equipment. However, a much large effort needs to be made. It would be imperative that the effort of the government is supplemented by individuals and philanthropic bodies because the requirement is large. It would be appropriate that the governments and the school systems consider how best they can encourage such individuals and philanthropic bodies to help schools to develop.

4. *Strengthening of the Professional Support System*

An area which needs to be looked into is the qualitative improvement of professional bodies like the SCERTs, Textbook Bureaus and Boards of School Education who are primarily responsible for curriculum, textbooks and examinations. It is these bodies which will ultimately have to reckon with the problem of load. Under the centrally sponsored scheme of teacher education, there is a component of strengthening of SCERTs which should be taken up on a priority basis.

5. "*...impact of examinations, admission to higher education institutions, including professional courses*"

This was one of the terms of reference of the Committee which has not been dealt with in the Report. The CABE may consider to refer this matter to a committee drawn from school and higher education. Another term of reference of the Committee related to "the measures such as formal recognition and weightage to sports and games and co-curricular and extra-curricular activities..." A CABE Committee is looking into this matter and its report is expected to be presented to the CABE shortly.

Time Schedule for Implementation

As regards laying down a time schedule for implementation of the recommendations found feasible, the Group felt that the recommendations are of long-term nature. Moreover, the report of the National Advisory Committee as well as this report of the Group would be placed before the CABE in its meeting scheduled to be held on 15.10.1993. As such, it would be advisable to wait for the CABE's approval to Committee's recommendations and then draw up a time schedule for implementation of the recommendations accepted by the CABE.

ANNEXURE A

No. F. 11-30/93-Sch. 4
Government of India
Ministry of Human Resource Development
Department of Education

New Delhi, Date 25.8.93

ORDER

Subject : Constitution of a Group to examine the recommendations made in the report of the National Advisory Committee set up on 1.3.92 to suggest ways to reduce academic burden on school students.

A National Advisory Committee was set up on 1.3.92 under the Chairmanship of Prof. Yash Pal, former Chairman of UGC to advise on the ways and means to reduce the academic burden on school students. The Committee has submitted its report on 15 July 1993. It has been decided to constitute a Group to examine the feasibility and implementation schedule of the recommendations made in the Report.

2. The Group shall consist of the following :

(i)	Shri Y.N. Chaturvedi Additional Secretary	*Chairman*
(ii)	Joint Secretary (School)	*Member*
(iii)	Dr. J.S. Rajput Joint Educational Adviser (EE)	*Member*
(iv)	Prof. A.K. Sharma Joint Director, NCERT	*Member*
(v)	Dr. (Smt.) R. Muralidharan Professor and Head Department of Pre-School and Elementary Education, NCERT	*Member*
(vi)	Shri V. Sankarasubbaiyan Education Secretary Tamil Nadu	*Member*

(vii)	Shri Abhimanyu Singh Education Secretary Rajasthan	*Member*
(viii)	Shri H.R. Sharma Director (Academic), CBSE	*Member*
(ix)	Shri D.V. Sharma Secretary, Council of Boards of School Education in India (COBSE)	*Member*
(x)	Shri A. Banerji Deputy Secretary (School)	*Member-Secretary*

3. The Group will analyse the recommendations made by the National Advisory Committee and give its views on the feasibility of implementing the recommendations and a time schedule in respect of the recommendations found feasible. The Group will give the views and the implementation schedule within a period of one month from the date of issue of order.

4. The Group shall devise its own procedures and methodology of work.

A. Banerji
Deputy Secretary

1. PS to AS
2. PS to JS (S)
3. PS to JEA (EE)
4. Prof. A.K. Sharma, Joint Director, NCERT
5. Dr. (Smt.) R. Muralidharan, Professor and Head, Department of Pre-School and Elementary Education, NCERT
6. Shri V. Sankarasubbaiyan, Education Secretary, Tamil Nadu
7. Shri Abhimanyu Singh, Education Secretary, Rajasthan
8. Shri H.R. Sharma, Director (Academic), CBSE
9. Shri D.V: Sharma, Secretary, Council of Boards of School Education in India (COBSE)
10. Shri A. Banerji, Deputy Secretary (S)

ANNEXURE B

LIST OF PARTICIPANTS IN THE MEETINGS OF THE GROUP HELD ON 23.9.93 AND 24.9.93

1. Shri Y.N. Chaturvedi — *Chairman*
   Additional Secretary
   Department of Education
2. Shri R.C. Tripathi
   Adviser (Education)
   Planning Commission
3. Shri Priyadarshi Thakur
   Joint Secretary (School)
   Department of Education
4. Prof. A.K. Sharma
   Joint Director
   NCERT
5. Dr. (Smt.) R. Muralidharan
   Professor and Head of the Department of
   Pre-School and Elementary Education
   NCERT
6. Shri Abhimanyu Singh
   Education Secretary
   Government of Rajasthan
7. Shri U.K. Sinha
   Director (Teacher Education)
   Department of Education
8. Shri H.R. Sharma
   Director (Academic)
   CBSE
9. Shri D.V. Sharma
   Secretary
   Council of Boards of School
   Education in India (COBSE)
10. Shri A. Banerji
    Deputy Secretary (School)
    Department of Education

6

Report of CABE Committee on Decentralised Management of Education (1993)

Introduction

With a view to suggest guidelines on decentralised management of education in the context of 73rd and 74th Constitutional Amendment Acts 1992, the Minister of Human Resource Development, in his capacity as the Chairman of the Central Advisory Board of Education, (CABE) set up a CABE Committee on February 2, 1993. The Committee held five meetings to deliberate upon the issues related to the decentralised management of education and thereafter submitted its report.

Terms of Reference

To formulate guidelines for the management of education on district, sub-district and village levels keeping in view the 72nd and 73rd Amendments of the Constitution of India.

Members and Permanent Invitees

Members

1. Shri M. Veerappa Moily Chairman
   Chief Minister
   Karnataka
2. Dr. (Smt.) Chitra Naik
   Member (Education)
   Planning Commission
   New Delhi
3. Shri E.T. Mohammed Basheer
   Education Minister
   Kerala

Report of Centre Advisory Board of Education Committee on Decentralised Management of Education, Government of India, Ministry of Human Resource Development, Department of Education, New Delhi, 1993.

4. Professor K. Ponnusamy*
Education Minister
Tamil Nadu
5. Shri S.S. Chakraborty
Education Minister
West Bengal
6. Shri Prafulla Chandra Ghadai**
Education Minister
Orissa
7. Shri G.C. Rajbanshi***
Education Minister
Assam
8. Shri Narhari Amin****
Education Minister
Gujarat
9. Dr. Sudhir Ray, MP
(Member CABE)
10. Dr. Syed Hasan
Director, Insan School/College
Kishanganj, Purnea (Bihar)
(Member, CABE)
11. Professor Mrinal Miri
Department of Philosophy
North Eastern Hill University, Shillong
(Member, CABE)
12. Shri P.K. Uma Shankar
Former Director, IIPA
New Delhi
(Chairman, Task Force on
Management of Education)
13. Shri S.R. Sankaran
Former Secretary
Department of Rural Development
14. Shri V.B.L. Mathur
Adviser to Governor of Rajasthan
Jaipur

---

* In place of Dr. C. Arranganayagam w.e.f. 30th July, 1993.

** In place of Shri Chaitanya Prasad Majhi w.e.f. 17th August, 1993.

*** In place of Dr. Karshandas Soneri w.e.f. 23rd April, 1993.

**** In place of Dr. Bhumi Dhar Barman w.e.f. 30th July, 1993.

15. Shri R.D. Sonkar
    Adviser to Governor of Utter Pradesh
    Lucknow
16. Secretary
    Department of Legal Affairs
    Ministry of Law, Justice
    and Company Affairs
    New Delhi
17. Secretary
    Ministry of Rural Development
    New Delhi
18. Secretary
    Ministry of Urban Development
    New Delhi
19. Secretary
    Ministry of Labour
    New Delhi
20. Dr. R.V. Vaidyanatha Ayyar — Member-Secretary
    Joint Secretary
    Department of Education
    Ministry of Human Resource Development
    New Delhi

Permanent Invitees

1. Dr. P.V. Ranga Rao
   Education Minister
   Andhra Pradesh
2. Secretary
   Department of Education
   Ministry of Human Resource Development
   New Delhi
3. Additional Secretary
   Department of Education
   Ministry of Human Resource Development
   New Delhi
4. Adviser (Education)
   Planning Commission
   New Delhi

5. Director
National Council of Educational
Research and Training
New Delhi
6. Joint Director
National Institute of Educational
Planning and Administration
New Delhi
7. Dr. S.C. Nuna
Fellow
National Institute of Educational
Planning and Administration
New Delhi

RECOMMENDATIONS (CHAPTER IV OF THE REPORT)

Constitutional Provisions

4.1 The Committee in its deliberations has been guided by the provisions of the Seventy-third and the Seventy-fourth Constitutional Amendment Acts, the National Policy on Education and Programme of Action (1992). The recommendations of the Committee are in the nature of guidelines, which may be considered as comprehensive though not exhaustive. The States may, after due consultations and deliberations choose a pattern and system suited to their needs and keeping in view the spirit of the Constitutional amendments and need to foster people's participation if educational goals are to be achieved. While the States which are delegating powers to the institutions of local self-government for the first time may prefer to proceed cautiously, those States which have already gained experiences in this sphere may decide to improve on these proposals and give higher levels of responsibilities to Panchayati Raj/Municipal bodies.

4.2 The Constitution makes a mandatory provision for establishment of Panchayats at the village, intermediate and district levels in each state. Keeping in view the three-tier structure (States with population below 20 lakhs need not have the intermediate tier) these proposals envisage delegation of responsibilities of educational management to the Panchayats, Panchayat Samitis and Zilla Parishads. A summary of the Committee's recommendations in this regard is presented in respect of

(a) Panchayats where jurisdiction is limited to one village, (b) Panchayats where jurisdiction extends to a group of villages, (c) Panchayat Samitis (intermediate level) and (d) Zilla Parishads (district level), in Statements IA, IB, II and III, respectively. Detailed description of the recommendations is contained in the subsequent paragraphs of this chapter.

Panchayat Level

4.3 For the purpose of defining the jurisdiction of the Panchayat, the village is to be specified by the Governor by a public notification and may include a group of villages so specified. A Panchayat area means a territorial area of a Panchayat. This implies that Panchayats at the Village level may comprise a village or a group of villages.

4.4 The Programme of Action approved by the CABE attaches considerable importance to Village Education Committees (VECs). The village normally represents a cohesive community and is ideally suited for promoting programmes, involving support of the community, such as, Early Childhood Care and Education, Primary Education, Non-formal Education and Adult Education. VEC may be considered the ideal organisation to mobilise and involve people in the educational efforts.

Panchayat Standing Committee on Education

4.5 The Education Committee at the Panchayat level where the panchayat comprises only one village can be named as the Panchayat Standing Committee on Education (PEC). It can be given statutory authority by bringing it under the Panchayati Raj legislation. The tenure of this Committee will be the same as the tenure of the Panchayat.

Composition

4.6 The Panchayat Standing Committee on Education may consist of not less than 7 and not more than 15 members. It may be headed by the Chairman of the Panchayat. At least one third of its members should be women. One member each representing Scheduled Castes, Scheduled Tribes, Backward Classes and minorities should also be on the Committee. A parent representative of the Parent-Teacher Association, the *Anganwadi* worker and an educationist or a person interested in education from the village may also be members of the Committee. Those members of the committee who are not elected members of the Panchayat may be nominated by the Panchayat. The Member-Secretary

TABLE 6.1 : Proposed Panchayatiraj Structures for Management of Education and their Responsibilities

STATEMENT-IA : PANCHAYAT LEVEL WHERE PANCHAYAT COMPRISES SINGLE VILLAGE

Proposed Structure for Management of Education and its Composition	Role and Function	Powers	Funds	Organisational and Administrative Support	Preparation and Training Requirements
Panchayat Standing commitee on Education (PEC) comprising not less than 7 and not more than 15 members, including Chairman of Panchayat One member of SC, ST, BC and Minorities A representative of PTA (Parent) An *Anganwadi* worker A person interested in education Member Secretary—Head-master of Primary/Upper Primary schools *Note* : 1. Members, other than elected Panchayat members will be nominated by the Panchayat 2. Of the total membership of the Committee, atleast one-third should be women	Supervision over adult education, early childhood care and education, non-formal and primary education Supervision over composite upper-primary schools under delegation of authority from Panchayat Samiti Generation and Sustenance of awareness among the village community ensuring participation of all segments of population Promote enrolment drives in primary schools and persuade parents of non-attending children to send their wards to schools Reduce drop outs in primary schools by initiating measures and services for retention Assist in smooth functioning of primary schools Seek support of teachers, youths and women and others for educational and other linked health and welfare programmes Mobilize resources and help schools to have water supply, urinals, play grounds and other facilities Prepare plans and proposals within their resources for development of education in the village and to attain total adult literacy and universal primary education Present reports and proposals to Panchayat Samities and make periodic self-assessment of progress of Committee's efforts Coordination with other social service departments and committees for mututal support	To visit educational institutions To check attendance and other registers to enquire and report to concerned authorities on educational deficiencies and requirements in the village To recommend annual budget of school to concerned authority To undertake construction and repair works entrusted to them To report on regularity of students, teachers attendance and school functioning To frame the school calendar under the guidance of the Zilla Parishad	Funds provided by State govts, Zilla Parishad and Panchayat Samiti Earmarked funds provided by concerned agencies of State government Funds locally raised from parents and public	Assistance of Head master and teachers in Government schools	Orientation/ training of PEC members, teachers and Headmasters

(*Contd.*)

TABLE 6.1 (*Contd.*)

STATEMENT-IB : VILLAGE LEVEL WHERE PANCHAYAT COMPRISES A GROUP OF VILLAGES

Proposed Structure for Management of Education and its Composition	Role and Function	Powers	Funds	Organisational and Administrative Support	Preparation and Training Requirements
Village Education Committee constituted by Panchayat as its sub-Committee constituted with not less than 7 and not more than 15 members Chairman of Panchayat or a member of Panchayat from the village concerned One member of SC, ST, BC and Minorities A representative of PTA (Parent) An *Anganwadi* worker A person interested in education from the village Member Secretary—Head-master of Primary/Upper Primary school *Note*: 1. Members other than elected Panchayat members will be nominated by the Panchayat from the Gram Sabha/institutions in the village 2. Of the total membership of the Committee, atleast one-third should be women	Supervision over adult education, early childhood care and education, non-formal and primary education Supervision over composite upper-primary schools under delegation of authority from Panchayat Samiti Generation and Sustenance of awareness among the village community ensuring participation of all segments of population Promote enrolment drives in primary schools and persuade parents of non-attending children to send their wards to schools Reduce drop outs in primary schools by initiating measures and services for retention Assist in smooth functioning of primary schools Seek support of teachers, youths and women and others for educational and other linked health and welfare programmes Mobilize resources and help schools to have water supply, urinals, play grounds and other facilities Prepare plans and proposals within their resources for development of education in the village and to attain total adult literacy and universal primary education Present reports and proposals to Panchayat Samities and make periodic self-assessment of progress of Committee's efforts Coordination with other social service departments and committees for mututal support	To visit educational institutions To check attendance and other registers to enquire and report to concerned authorities on educational deficiencies and requirements in the village To recommend annual budget of school to concerned authority To undertake construction and repair works entrusted to them To report on regularity of students, teachers attendance and school functioning To frame the school calendar under the guidance of the Zilla Parishad	Funds provided by State govts, Zilla Parishad and Panchayat Samiti Earmarked funds provided by concerned agencies of State government Funds locally raised from parents and public	Assistance of Head master and teachers in Government schools	Orientation/training of VEC members, teachers and Head-masters

(*Contd.*)

TABLE 6.1 (*Contd.*)

STATEMENT-II : PANCHAYAT SAMITI AT INTERMEDIATE LEVEL

Proposed Structure for Management of Education and its Composition	Role and Function	Powers	Funds	Organisational and Administrative Support	Preparation and Training Requirements
Panchayat Samiti Standing Committee on Education (PSEC) comprising not less than 11 and not more than 17 members This will include Chairman of Panchyat Samiti One member each of SC, ST, BC and Minorities One representative of PTA/NGO One or two representatives of VEC/PEC by rotation A Principal of Degree/Pre-degree College A Headmaster of school complex/secondary school A representative of teachers Member Secretary—Block Education Officer or its equivalent *Notes*: 1. Members other than elected members of the Committee will be nominated by the Panchayat Samiti 2. Of the total membership of the Committee, atleast one-third should be women	Management of Adult Education, Non-formal Education, Earily Childhood Care and Education and Govt. Primary and Upper Primary Schools under the supervision of Zilla Parishad Supervision and channelisation of grant to aided primary and upper primary schools in their jurisdiction under the guidance of Zilla Parishad Academic supervision of all primary and upper primary schools including private schools Preparation of plans for development of education upto upper primary level in their jurisdiction Development and coordination of school complexes Coordination with other social service departments and committees for mutual support	To recruit staff for Adult Education, Non-formal Education and Early Childhood Care and Education Programmes To appoint staff in schools from approved panels To transfer teachers within their jurisdiction subject to guidelines To perform academic supervision of all institutions upto upper-primary level To delegate the power of supervision over composite upper-primary schools to the PEC/VEC for purpose of continuity To prepare budget and to sanction plans and expenditure from the Panchayat Samiti Education Budget To channelise funds to aided institutions under supervision of Zilla Parishad To levy development fees and other fees to raise resources To raise public contributions and donations To propose measures to Panchayat Samiti to raise resources	Grants from Zilla Parishad Grants from state/centrally sponsored schemes through the state Earmarked funds by concerned agencies Voluntary donations, endowment trusts Funds raised through taxation by Panchyat Samiti	Services of the staff of education department at the level corresponding to the Panchayat Samiti will be placed with the Panchayat Samiti	Orientation/Training of non-official members of PSEC and officials working with them

(*Contd.*)

TABLE 6.1 *(Contd.)*

STATEMENT-III : ZILLA PARISHAD AT DISTRICT LEVEL

Proposed Structure for Management Education and its Composition	Role and Function	Powers	Funds	Organisational and Administrative Support	Preparation and Training Requirements
Zilla Parishad Standing Committee on Education (ZPEC) comprising not less than 15 and not more than 21 members which will include Chairman, Zilla Parishad A representative each of SC, ST, BC and Minorities A representative of PTA/NGO Two or more representatives of Panchayat Samiti and Panchayat/ Village Education Committees Principal of a College Professor of Education from University/College Principal of DIET A Head of school complex/secondary school A representative of teachers Member Secretary—Chief Education Officer or equivalent *Note* : 1 Members other than elected members of the Committee will be nominated by the Zilla Parishad 2 Of the total membership of the Committee, atleast one-third should be women	Overall supervision of all educational programmes in the district upto secondary level Preparation, implementation and review of plans for development of education upto secondary level in the district Formulation and operationalisation of programmes to achieve total literacy and universal elementary education Establish and manage schools upto secondary level Academic supervision of all institutions (Govt., aided, private) upto secondary level in the district including schools in Municipalities Preparation and coordination of plans for development of education upto secondary level including those of Municipalities To review progress and guide Panchayat Samiti and Panchayat Education Committees in their tasks Implementation of programmes for improvement of quality of education Coordination with other social service departments and committees for mutual support	To establish and maintain schools upto secondary level including recruitment, appointment and transfer of staff, payment of salaries and exercise control over the staff subject to govt. guidelines To exercise control and academic supervision of all schools including aided and private schools upto secondary level subject to govt. guidelines To lay down academic and administrative norms for better functioning of educational institutions To disburse grants to aided schools subject to govt. guidelines To supervise the work of Panchayat Samiti Education Committees and Panchayat Education Committees To prepare and sanction educational budget To administer district educational fund To prepare perspective plan for the district To propose measures including levy of cess, surcharge and taxes for mobilising additional resources for education to the Zilla Parishad	State Government grants, centrally sponsored schemes channelised through the state Earmarked funds by agencies Resources for education raised through taxation by Zilla Parishad Donations, voluntary contributions	Services of the staff of the education department at district level to be placed with the Zilla Parishad Services of the teachers working in Govt. schools will be placed with the Zilla Parishad. Their service conditions will be protected. The educational officers will continue to be under the department and will be deputed to work with the Zilla Parishad and Panchayat Samiti. Services of the subordinate staff will also be placed with the Zilla Parishad.	Orientation/training of non-official members of ZPEC and educational functionaries Programme orientation for members of ZPEC

of the Committee will be the Headmaster of a Panchayati Raj Primary or Upper Primary School in the village and will be nominated by the Panchayat.

Role

4.7 The role of the Panchayat Standing Committee on Education may include generation and sustenance of awareness among village community ensuring participation of all segments of population, developing teacher and community partnership to oversee and manage the effective and regular functioning of the schools and centres. It should be endeavour of this Committee that every child in every family participates in primary education.

4.8 The Committee will exercise supervision over early childhood care and education, non-formal education, primary education and adult education programmes in its jurisdiction. It will also exercise supervision over composite upper primary schools under delegation of powers from the Panchayat Samiti.

Functions

4.9 The Panchayat Standing Committee on Education will be required to visit institutions and centres periodically and promote enrolment drives. Persuading parents of non-attending children to send their wards to schools and enthusing adults for literacy programmes may form a significant agenda for its activities.

4.10 Steps to promote attendance and prevent drop-outs in the various educational programmes may also be one of the responsibilities of this Committee. It may also undertake supportive measures and services for retention of students and will assist in the smooth functioning of the primary schools, composite upper primary schools and other institutions. It should be the Committee's endeavour to encourage and support the teachers in their tasks. It may provide essential facilities like drinking water, urinals, play-ground, etc., in the schools. The Committee will present periodical reports and proposals to Panchayat Samiti on development of education and will assess progress of the programmes in their territorial jurisdiction. It may meet as many times as required but not less than once in a quarter.

Powers

4.11 The Panchayat Standing Committee on Education will have the authority to visit educational institutions and centres providing early childhood care and education, non-formal education, primary education and adult education and will check attendance and other registers. It would also have the authority to enquire and report to the concerned authorities on educational deficiencies and requirements of the village. The Committee would recommend the annual budget of the Panchayati Raj schools to the concerned authorities. It may report on irregularities of the attendance of students and teachers and functioning of the schools. It will prepare the school calendar indicating working days, holidays and vacation under the guidance of the Zilla Parishad.

Funds

4.12 The Committee will depend largely upon funds provided by the Zilla Parishad and Panchayat Samiti for various programmes to be undertaken in the village. It may also receive earmarked funds for specific programmes provided by concerned agencies of the State Government. The Committee may also raise funds locally from the parents and public.

Coordination

4.13 It will be desirable for VECs to hold joint meetings with similar bodies in the field of health and other subjects to seek their support in pursuance of its activities.

Administrative Support

4.14 The Village Education Committee will function largely on the basis of the Staff support provided by the Headmaster, staff and teachers in the Panchayati Raj schools and other educational programmes.

Training

4.15 The members of Village Education Committees would require orientation and training for discharging their functions effectively. The Headmasters may have to be given a special orientation to enable them to assist the Village Education Committees in their activities.

Village Education Committee as Sub-Committee of Panchayat

4.16 Where the Panchayat comprises more than one village, it may establish Village Education Committee (VEC) as the sub-Committee of the Panchayat for each village. It will have statutory authority as they will be established by the Panchayats under the powers conferred upon them by the State Panchayati Raj legislation. The Panchayat may be empowered statutorily to delegate powers to these committees.

Composition

4.17 The Village Education Committee may be presided over by the President of the Panchayat where he is elected from the village. In other villages a member of the Panchayat representing the village concerned may preside over the VEC. The number of members of the VEC may be the same as provided for the Panchayat Standing Committee on Education. The composition of the Committee may be the same, except that all the members must be drawn from the village.

4.18 The rest of the features of the Panchayat Standing Committee will also apply to the VECs (Sub-committees).

Panchayat Samiti

4.19 The Panchayat Samiti will be the Panchayati Raj body at the intermediate level in terms of the Constitutional amendment.

Panchayat Samiti Standing Committee on Education

4.20 The Panchayat Samiti may set up a Panchyat Samiti Standing Committee on Education (PSEC) for management of educational programmes in their territorial jurisdiction. This Committee will have the statutory recognition under the Panchayati Raj legislation and will have the same tenure as the Panchayat Samiti.

Composition

4.21 The Panchayat Samiti Standing Committee on Education may be headed by the Chairman of the Panchayat Samiti. The Committee may consist of not less than 11 and not more than 17 members with atleast one-third of the members being women. One member each representing the Scheduled Castes, Scheduled Tribes, backward classes and minority communities should be on the Committee.

4.22 A parent from the Parent-Teacher Association may also be on the Committee. Atleast two representatives of the Panchayat Standing Committees on Education/Village Education Committees may be nominated by rotation. A Principal of a degree/pre-degree college, Headmaster of a school complex/secondary school and a representative of teachers may also be on the Committee. The Member-Secretary of the Committee will be the block level Education Officer. The non-elected members of the Committee may be nominated by the Panchayat Samiti.

Role

4.23 The Panchayat Samiti Standing Committee on Education will be responsible for management of adult education, non-formal education, early childhood care and education and schools of the Panchayati Raj bodies upto upper primary level, under the overall supervision of the Zilla Parishad.

4.24 All existing government schools upto upper primary level with their staff will come under the control of Panchayat Samitis and schools in the state sector will in future be established only by the Panchayat Samitis. The Committee will also have supervisory power over aided upper primary schools and will channel grant to them under the guidance of Zilla Parishad. In this regard, the Committee will function in the same manner as the present departmental set-up at this level.

4.25 The Panchayat Samiti Standing Committee on Education will undertake academic supervision of all the educational institutions upto upper primary level including the private schools in its jurisdiction.

4.26 The Education Committee at this level will endeavour to promote school complexes in its jurisdiction. The Committee will periodically review progress of education in its area and actively pursue the programmes of total adult literacy and universalisation of elementary education.

Functions

4.27 The Committee will exercise control over all Panchayati Raj educational institutions upto upper primary level. Academic supervision of all the schools upto upper primary level, including private schools, will be one of its important functions. The Committee will be responsible for preparation of plans for development of education upto upper primary level in its jurisdiction and for their implementation. It will also prepare educational budget of the Panchayat Samiti and approve expenditure to be incurred. The Committee will coordinate with other bodies for social service programmes for mutual support.

Powers

4.28 The Panchayat Samiti Standing Committee on Education will exercise control over the staff in the government schools transferred to Panchayat Samiti including payment of salaries. It will appoint staff to schools under its control from the panel of names given by the appropriate body and transfer them within its jurisdiction subject to guidelines provided by the Zilla Parishad/Government. The Committee will be responsible for channelising grants to aided schools under the supervision of Zilla Parishad. It will have powers of academic supervision of all educational programmes in its jurisdiction upto upper primary level. The Committee will prepare the educational budget and plans of the Panchayat Samiti and sanction expenditure from the approved budget. It may raise its resources by levying development fees and other fees as well as by public contributions and donations. The Committee may propose measures to Panchayat Samiti and Zilla Parishad for mobilisation of additional resources. It may delegate its power of supervision over composite upper primary schools to the Panchayat Standing Committee on Education/Village Education Committee.

Funds

4.29 The Committee will receive grants from the Zilla Parishad and under various schemes for implementing different educational programmes in its jurisdiction. It may also receive earmarked funds from different agencies, voluntary donations and endowments and may raise funds on its own through the powers of taxation.

Organizational Support

4.30 The services of the staff of the education department at this level will be placed with the Panchayat Samiti. However, its control over the staff will be subject to guidelines laid down by the State Government and the academic norms adopted by the Panchayat Samiti Standing Committee on Education will be subject to over-all instructions issued by the department of education of the state.

4.31 The members of the Panchayat Samiti Standing Committee on Education will require orientation to prepare themselves for the effective discharge of the assigned tasks. They would also require to establish close rapport with officials at different levels and the state-level leadership for guidance in their work. The non-elected members of the Committee also will require orientation to enable them to work in harmony with others. Training for the officials and volunteers for effective implementation of various programmes may also be necessary.

Zilla Parishad Level

4.32 According to the Act, the Zilla Parishad will cover an entire district excluding municipal areas.

Zilla Parishad Standing Committee on Education

4.33 The Zilla Parishad may set up its Standing Committee on Education as a statutory body under the Panchayati Raj legislation for the management of educational institutions in its jurisdiction. The tenure of the Standing Committee will correspond with the tenure of the Zilla Parishad.

Composition

4.34 The Standing Committee may be headed by the Chairman of the Zilla Parishad. The Committee may consist of not less than 15 and not more than 21 members with atleast one-third members being women. These should include representatives of Scheduled Castes, Scheduled Tribes, backward classes and minorities. A parent from the Parent-Teacher Associations and one representative each of NGOs and teachers may also be on the Committee. Atleast two representatives of the Education Committees at Panchayat/Village level and Panchayat Samiti level may also be nominated to the Committee by rotation. A Principal of a College, a Professor of Education of a University or a College teacher, Principal of DIET and Headmaster of a School Complex or Secondary School may also be on the Committee. The Chief Education Officer of the Zilla Parishad may be the Member-Secretary of the Committee. The power of nomination of non-elected members will rest with Zilla Parishad.

Role

4.35 The role of the Zilla Parishad Standing Committee on Education will be the overall management and supervision of all educational programmes in the district upto secondary level. The Committee will prepare and implement plans for development of education upto secondary level in the entire district. It will review the progress of education upto secondary level in the district and will also have the specific responsibility for formulation and operationalisation of programmes to achieve total literacy and universal elementary education.

Functions

4.36 The Zilla Parishad may establish and manage schools upto secondary level. It will supervise and provide grant to aided schools upto secondary level and will exercise academic supervision of all institutions upto secondary level in the district. Preparation and coordination of plans for development of education upto secondary level may also be the responsibility of this Committee. It will review the progress of education upto secondary level in the district with particular reference to universalisation of elementary education and adult literacy.

4.37 One of the important functions of the Committee will be to oversee and guide Panchayat Samiti Standing Committees on Education and Education Committees at Panchayat/Village level in their tasks. The Committee will undertake implementation of academic programmes.

Powers

4.38 The powers of the Committee will include establishment and maintenance of schools upto secondary level including recruitment and appointment of staff and payment of salaries, subject to government guidelines. All existing schools upto secondary level will be transferred to the control of Zilla Parishad. In future all secondary schools in the state sector will be established only by the Zilla Parishad. The Committee will also channelize grants to aided schools subject to government rules. It will also exercise academic supervision of all schools including private schools upto secondary level. Laying down academic and administrative norms and procedures under the overall departmental and government supervision may also fall under the purview of the Committee. The Committee will guide the work of Panchayat Samitis and Panchayat/ Village Education Committees. It may recruit and appoint teachers in schools under its control subject to government guidelines. The Committee will also be responsible for preparation of education budget and plans for approval of the Zilla Parishad. The administration of the district education funds will be its responsibililty. Preparation of perspective plans for educational development of the district will be the responsibility of the Committee.

Funds

4.39 The resources of the Zilla Parishad will include grants from the State Government, the centrally assisted and sponsored schemes channelled through the State Government and funds provided by the other agencies. The Zilla Parishad may also raise resources through appropriate taxation measures as well as raise funds through voluntary donations and contributions.

Organizational Support

4.40 The services of the staff of the education department at the district level will be placed with the Zilla Parishad. The State Government, particularly the department of education, will provide necessary administrative and academic guidance to the Zilla Parishad for undertaking its educational responsibilities.

4.41 The Panchayati Raj bodies must take full benefit of the District Institute of Education and Training (DIET) in their efforts to improve the quality of education. The DIET must be fully involved in the functioning of the academic wings of the Panchayati Raj bodies through organisation of orientation and training programmes for the academic staff and by undertaking surveys, evaluation studies and innovative projects. Its support may also be enlisted for improved methods of learning and assessment procedures for attaining the minimum levels of learning.

Training Needs

4.42 The non-officials of the Zilla Parishad would require orientation to introduce them to the tasks of the Zilla Parishad. They may also receive adequate orientation in respect of various schemes in operation as well as programmes, such as, universalisation of elementary education, adult education and non-formal education. The officials working under the Zilla Parishads may also require training to enable them to establish effective working relationship with the members of the Committee and Zilla Parishad.

4.43 It is now well-recognized that both the non-officials and officials involved in the Panchayati Raj programmes relating to education require orientation, training and preparation for discharging their responsibilities effectively in the new set-up. They need advice, guidance and support to develop sound and efficient methods of functioning in the Panchayati Raj set-up. The state would need to consider setting up appropriate arrangements both at the state and district levels to ensure required training and orientation. The establishment of State Institutes of Educational Planning and Administration offers one such possibility.

Personnel Management

4.44 Democratic decentralisation implies placing the services of employees with the Panchayati Raj bodies. Therefore, it is necessary to ensure that this is done in a manner and with such safeguards which enable these employees to work in a congenial and cordial atmosphere.

4.45 Following this approach, services of the teaching staff working in government primary, middle and secondary schools at the time of transfer to Panchayati Raj Institutions may be placed with the Panchayati Raj bodies. It is necessary to protect their service conditions while doing so. In future all teaching staff in schools under the Panchayati Raj bodies, selected and allotted by an appropriate organisation, will be appointed by the Panchayati Raj bodies and will be under their exclusive control.

4.46 All the staff under the Panchayati Raj bodies, whether appointed by them or otherwise, should enjoy the same service conditions and benefits.

4.47 The non-teaching staff of the government schools and departmental officers whose services are placed with Panchayati Raj bodies may be treated on par with similar staff of other departments whose responsibilities and services would stand transferred to the Panchayati Raj bodies.

4.48 Educational officers, such as, District Inspectors of Schools, Headmasters of Secondary Schools, District Education Officers and Deputy Directors, who may come under the control of the Panchayati Raj bodies, may be treated as on deputation or on loan of services to these bodies. The Panchayati Raj bodies would have full control over them including discipline, subject to such guidelines as the State Government may lay down.

Recruitment of Teachers

4.49 Recruitment of teachers is a sensitive and responsible task. The State Government may develop appropriate recruitment system including involvement of the State Public Service Commission where ever necessary. The objective must be to decentralise recruitment of teachers at district level through appropriate bodies with suitable representation of the Zilla Parishad. The procedure must ensure impartial selection through well laid out procedures, with provision for reservation of posts for the prescribed categories. While allocating the candidates to various Panchayat Samitis, it may be ensured that local candidates are preferred. This may minimise the problem of subsequent transfers.

Disbursement of Salaries

4.50 The prompt and regular payment of salaries to staff is a matter of importance. The state government must stipulate that the Panchayati Raj bodies introduce mechanisms in their budgetary control to ensure that salary and service benefits flow to the teaching and non-teaching staff in schools in a regular and prompt manner.

4.51 The state governments may suitably adapt these recommendations to suit the local conditions.

Role of the State Government

4.52 While the Panchayati Raj bodies may perform the functions outlined above, the State Government or an appropriate state level body would exercise overall supervision and retain residuary powers, particularly in regard to the following issues :

1. Laying down academic standards and norms, including academic calendar, teacher-pupil ratio, etc.
2. Formulation of syllabi and curricula.
3. Preparation and prescription of text-books, supplementary reading materials.
4. Conduct of public, scholarship and other examinations.
5. Teachers' training and retraining.
6. Academic innovations, over-all supervision and assessment.
7. Administrative norms, scale of fees, fee concessions.
8. Norms for transfer of teachers and disciplinary control, etc.
9. Periodic monitoring of the educational activities of the Panchayati Raj bodies and preparation of guidelines for their efficient functioning.
10. Establishment and management of organisations and institutions intended to improve the academic standards and staff development, such as SCERT, SIE, DIETs, etc.

The state and these bodies may consider delegating authority in stages to the Panchayati Raj bodies at different levels for preparation of academic calendar, conduct of examinations, of academic supervision under the over-all guidance of the Department.

Financial Support

Non-Plan Grant

4.53 Pending constitution of the State Finance Commission, the grant to Panchayati Raj bodies may include the following non-plan grants :

1. Grant for salary and other benefits to teaching and non-teaching staff. This will include two components :

(a) The component for the government schools transferred to Zilla Parishad.

(b) The component for aided schools in the jurisdiction of Zilla Parishad.

2. Maintenance Grant : This may include financial assistance to meet the cost of maintenance of building, equipment, library, contingencies, etc. This may again have two components pertaining to :

(a) Government schools transferred to Zilla Parishads, and

(b) Aided schools, as per the norms laid down.

Development Grant (Plan)

4.54 This may include :

(i) Provision for opening of new schools including salary component for staff.

(ii) Provision for construction of building for existing and new schools.

(iii) Provision for purchase of equipment and teaching-learning aids for existing and new schools.

(iv) Assistance under the centrally sponsored schemes such as Operation Blackboard, etc.

(v) Assistance under state schemes to schools for improving libraries, science teaching, sports, etc.

(vi) Provision for scholarships, fellowships, etc.

4.55 The ultimate objective is to transfer all funds which are now operated at a district level to the Zilla Parishad for management of education. Notwithstanding the above provisions, the Government will have to equip Zilla Parishads with authority to raise additional resources to support their efforts.

Special Grants

4.56 Provision for special grants to Zilla Parishads which are educationally backward will have to be made for reducing disparities.

Incentive Grants

4.57 Provision for matching grants for those Zilla Parishads which perform well, according to norms to be laid down, may also need to be made.

Budget

4.58 The state budget document should be suitably redesigned to reflect the allocation of funds to Panchayati Raj bodies. The education budget should depict the allocations preferably districtwise under each appropriate head and if feasible, in accordance with different educational functions assigned to the Panchayati Raj bodies.

Mobilization of Additional Resources

4.59 The Zilla Parishad and Panchayat Samiti may suitably be empowered to raise additional resources for educational activities through :

1. Levy of cess on land revenues, sales tax, quarrying, etc.
2. Levy of surcharge on building tax, professional tax, etc.
3. Local contributions towards different schemes for extending benefits to students.
4. Voluntary contributions by parents and community towards supporting development of educational institutions.

4.60 The objective must be to encourage the local bodies to generate local resources and supplement the support provided by the State Government for undertaking development programmes. The Panchayati Raj bodies should be encouraged to develop cost effective programmes.

Financial Implications

4.61 It is an acknowledged fact that resource position of the local bodies is not too happy. Most of them depend upon grants from the State Government and other sources. Very few of them have been able to identify and develop sources of income within their own jurisdiction. It is also a fact that by tradition and practice they have not made efforts to generate their resources. Over a period of time they have developed an attitude and approach which essentially implies dependence on outside support. It would, therefore be necessary that the Panchayati Raj bodies inculcate a new approach which will favour generation of their own resources and gradual reduction in the dependence on external funding and support. There is also a need for building efficiency and cost effectiveness in their functioning.

4.62 These changes, however, can take place only over a period of time. Meanwhile, the transfer of management of education to Panchayati Raj bodies without providing adequate resources to them will be a harmful step. The State Government have to ensure sufficient financial support to the Panchayati Raj bodies for ensuring successful management of the educational programmes. Along with the transfer of responsibilities, the funds with which the State Government used to discharge such responsibilities, must be made available to the Panchayati Raj bodies.

4.63 Special measures are necessary to overcome the acute deficiencies of school infrastructure. The government may, therefore, consider setting up a financial institution exclusively for the development and maintenance of the schools managed by Panchayati Raj and Municipal bodies. This would provide a much needed financial incentive for devolution of powers to these bodies.

Management of Education in Municipal Areas

The Seventy-fourth Amendment Act to the Constitution of India provides for the establishment of the Municipalities in the urban area. It envisages to give the responsibility of "promotion of cultural, educational and aesthetic aspects" to Municipal bodies. The proposals of the Committee in this regard are described in the following paragraphs.

Jurisdiction

4.64 The area, population and resources of Municipalities vary significantly from state to state as well as within the State. The responsibilities of educational management to be assigned to the Municipalities will have to vary depending upon the specific circumstances of each Municipal body. It is difficult to lay down a broad pattern for this purpose as it has been done in the case of the Panchayati Raj bodies for rural areas. Broadly speaking, the States may categorise the Municipalities according to their jurisdiction, resources and capabilities into three categories. The first category may include Municipalities which may be given the responsibilities of managing education upto primary level, the second category may have responsibilities upto upper primary level and the third category may be those Municipalities which may be given the control of education upto secondary level.

Structure

4.65 The Municipalities may constitute standing committees on education for managing the educational institutions and other responsibilities entrusted to them. These committees may provide for representation of

Scheduled Castes, Scheduled Tribes, backward classes and minorities besides elected members of the Municipalities. The parent-teacher association may also be represented on the Committee. Educationists such as a Principal of a college, Headmaster of a secondary school or senior secondary school may also be members of the committee. Atleast one-third of the members of the committee must be women. The Member-Secretary of the Committee may be the Chief Education Officer of the Municipality or an officer nominated by it. These committees will be responsible for administering the educational programmes in their jurisdiction.

Functions

4.66 The government primary, upper primary and secondary schools in the municipal areas along with their staff may be transferred to different Municipalities. They will have control over the staff except in matters of recruitment which will be done by an organisation designated for this purpose by the State Government.

4.67 The channelisation of grant to aided schools in the municipal areas may be done through the Municipalities having adequate capabilities to undertake this task.

4.68 It is possible that some Municipalities have built up viable management structures which include academic wings. In such cases they may be entrusted with academic supervision of the institutions in the municipal areas subject to guidelines laid down by the Department of Education.

4.69 While the Municipalities may prepare plans and programmes for development of education in their jurisdiction, their plans will be coordinated by the District Planning Committee for the district as a whole. The Municipalities will be responsible for promoting universal elementary education and total literacy in their jurisdiction.

4.70 The State Government may periodically review the working of the Municipalities in the sphere of education and enlarge their areas of responsibilities with appropriate financial and staff support as they gradually gain experience.

Administrative Support

4.71 The staff of the schools transferred to the Municipalities and the headquarter staff provided by the Municipality would provide the administrative support.

Training

4.72 Orientation/training may be provided to the members of the Municipal Education Committee and the staff working with them to enable them to discharge their responsibilities successfully. The Municipalities may draw upon the resources of DIET to improve the quality of education. The State Government may also organise training programmes in various spheres of educational development for non-official and official members of the Municipalities who are assigned responsibility for education.

Funds

4.73 The State Government may provide adequate grants to these bodies for managing the institutions transferred to them. They may also provide development grants for plan programmes in municipal areas. Besides these grants, Municipalities may generate their own resources through appropriate taxation measures.

7

External and Internal Resource Mobilization for Education For All (1993)*

Introduction

Education For All Summit of Nine High Population Countries namely, Bangladesh, Brazil, China, Egypt, India, Indonesia, Mexico, Nigeria and Pakistan was held at New Delhi in December 1993. On this occasion several discussion papers were prepared. One of the papers prepared by the National Institute of Educational Planning and Administration, New Delhi was titled *External and Internal Resource Mobilization for Education For All.* Executive Summary prepared by Jandhyala B.G. Tilak of the NIEPA is reproduced below :

Executive Summary

Investment in basic education yields high economic returns to the society. More importantly, there are a multitude of externalities associated with primary education, including positive effects on health, reduction in infant mortality rate, reduction in infertility rate, etc. Primary education is also a 'public good'. All this necessitates a positive approach to financing education, and underscores the need to step up the levels of public expenditure on primary education substantially. But the present pattern of financing education and primary education in particular needs much improvement.

1. *A Few Stylized Facts (1) : Public Expenditure on Basic Education*

1.1 Total and per capita expenditure on education in the world increased in real prices rapidly during the last 2-3 decades. But the

* *Resouree Mobilisation for EFA* National Institute of Educational Planning and Administration, New Delhi, 1993.

growth in some of the developing economies has not been commensurate with the rates of economic growth. The requirements of the education systems are much higher than the levels of availability of resources.

1.2 While in many developed countries, about six per cent of GNP is allocated to education, in developing countries the corresponding figure is less than four per cent and in Asian and African countries it is further less.

1.3 As a proportion of GNP, very little amounts are being invested in primary education in several countries. But the intra-sectoral allocation of resources in education seems to be improving over time in some of the developing countries in favour of primary education.

1.4 Most education budgets are 'current' budgets, with insignificant proportions being allocated to items that lead to capital formation like buildings, furniture, etc. Scanty amounts are available for non-recurring items. The needed physical capital formation does not take place in education sector in general and primary education in specific.

1.5 Expenditure on libraries and books forms 'composite' capital : physical and human. Budget allocations seem to be unduly discriminating against such composite capital, which should have been given more attention. Teachers' salaries form the largest chunk of the recurrent budgets and virtually little is available for investment in those items such as text books, chalks, globes, maps and other necessary class room material, that is found to be yielding higher returns. The externalities associated with books are too important to be ignored. The parents and other children who do not go to schools may look at these books when carried home and the effects could be significant.

1.6 Expenditure on primary education per student is trivial in many developing countries (a) relative to the needs of the primary education system, (b) in comparison with other levels of education, and (c) compared to the developed countries. The present levels of spending per student in developing countries are hardly adequate to provide meaningful quality education for all. More importantly, in some of the countries the real expenditure per student has declined over the years.

1.7 Government has been the major financier of basic education in developing countries, the non-governmental sources dwindling rapidly.

1.8 Major systematic attempts to raise non-governmental finances need to be confined to higher education. But in case of basic education, the role of the community is believed to be potentially significant. At the same time there appears to be no case for fees, nor for increased role of the private sector in basic education.

2. *A Few Stylized Facts (2) : External Assistance for Education*

2.1 While there are several international agencies—bi-lateral and multi-lateral, the role of the World Bank has become very prominent both in terms of quantum of aid and in influence on planning and policies.

2.2 Only since the mid 1980s, when the attention of the international agencies shifted in favour of poverty alleviation, the importance of primary education was recognized and accordingly, the share of primary education has become significant in total education lending. A clear shift in favour of primary education can be noted after the Jomtien Conference.

2.3 Generally the external resources that flow into the education systems are expected to be additive to the domestic resources and that they would not substitute the national efforts. But it is not necessarily the case always.

2.4 Relative to the countries' domestic education budgets, the external assistance for education is generally very small.

2.5 The high population countries are at a disadvantage when it comes to external assistance. Almost as a rule the more the populous a country is the less is the education assistance per capita it receives and vice-versa.

2.6 During the periods of implementation of the stabilization and structural adjustment programmes primary education in many countries suffered.

3. *The Financial Requirements of EFA*

3.1 Simple, crude and quick calculations suggest that the global requirements for Education for All would be more than $400 billion (on 1985 prices) on the current account alone in 2000 AD, compared to the level of expenditure of about $160 billion in 1985. The real expenditure should increase by more than 2.5 times during this period.

3.2 The developing countries have to increase the public recurrent expenditure by 3.6 times from $23.4 billion in 1985 to $83.4 billion by the turn of the century. The share of the developing countries in the world expenditure on EFA will have to increase from 14.6 per cent in 1985 to 20.5 per cent in 2000 AD.

4. *Policy Issues (1) : On Mobilizing Domestic Resources*

4.1 Family investments in education are estimated to be as important and significant as public investments in quantum. The scope for raising families' contributions, voluntary, or compulsory like fees, to education seems to be limited.

4.2 Contributions from the communities should be treated as peripheral sources to supplement the levels of the funding by the government. The core educational activities should not critically depend upon such contributions and the state must ensure the smooth functioning of the core education activities though its own funding. Excessive reliance on parental and community contributions for basic education will produce serious adverse effects on equity, contributing to inequalities between several groups of population and between regions, thus finally contributing to under-optimum levels of social investment in education.

4.3 Private schools in general do not necessarily reduce the financial burden of the government. They might even work against financial, educational and other social considerations of the welfare state. Policies encouraging privatization in education need to be made with caution.

4.4 The evidence on decentralization and local financing of primary schools is not conclusive with regard to school effectiveness and funding. One has to be cautious in laying exclusive stress on decentralization as a panacea for all the problems in educational development in developing countries.

4.5 It may be desirable to have a national norm, applicable to all regions in a country, with regard to, say, the minimum share of the budget that should be allocated to education, and to basic education in particular. This will help in promoting balanced development of education in the country.

5. *Policy Issues (2) : On Mobilizing External Resources*

5.1 External assistance will play an important catalytic role in the development of education, but it is too much to expect that it will solve the financial problems of education in developing countries substantially.

5.2 Externally aided projects should become sustainable over time.

5.3 The shift in aid programmes in favour of education and more specifically in favour of basic education needs to be strengthened and sustained.

5.4 The undesirable trends in primary education during the process of stabilization and adjustment strongly suggest the need for necessary accompanying of compensatory programmes such as the Social Safety Net programme along with the adjustment loans. It may be better in fact, if the stabilization and adjustment programmes exclude human development sectors like education from general conditions of budget cuts and rather include conditions of strengthening education budgets.

5.5 There exists a threshold level of buildings and other hardware facilities for meaningful education activities to be carried on and external assistance should make appropriate investments in physical capital, apart from software.

5.6 The needs of the developing countries relating to the nature and type of external assistance vary and there cannot be a single pattern of external assistance to all developing countries.

- Countries with low levels of income and low levels of educational development need to be provided assistance in terms of technical assistance as well as physical (material and direct monetary) inputs.
- Countries with low levels of income and reasonably high levels of educational development do not require technical assistance; external aid may be concentrated on direct money inputs and material support.
- Countries with high levels of income and low levels of educational development need to be provided external aid in terms of technical assistance.
- Countries with high levels of income and high levels of educational development obviously do not require any kind of external assistance for education.

5.7 The efforts of donor agencies in all categories of countries should concentrate on building national capacities and long term development of education in the country concerned.

5.8 It may be advisable to look at the possibility of providing debt relief, or more clearly swapping the education debts of the poor countries as a means of funding education, like the debt-swaps relating to environment initiated in 1987.

5.9 The international donor community, including the bilateral and multilateral agencies should substantially raise their support for education in developing countries and may also fix a norm regarding the minimum level of the share of education in their development aid programmes and the share of basic education in their education aid programmes.

6. *In Conclusion*

6.1 The basic approach to financing education both by the national governments and international donor community needs to be changed. Expenditure on education should be viewed as 'investment' that yields benefits for a long time, some times even across generations and that this investment is "crucial for national development and survival".

8

Report of Expert Committee on Performance Appraisal System for Teachers of Technical and Management Institutions (1993)

Background

The Department of Education, Ministry of Human Resource Development, Government of India Constituted a Committee for developing a Performance Appraisal System of the Teachers of Technical and Management Institutions coming within the purview of the Department of Education. The Convener of the Committee was Dr. G.K. Valecha, Indian Institute of Management, Bangalore. The other members of the Committee were Prof. Ashok Chandra, Prof. Shri Handa, Prof. P.S. Satsangi, Prof. S.A. Balu, Prof. K.M. Bahauddin, Prof. N.J. Rao, Prof. Y.V.N. Rao, and Prof. M.H. Dhananjaya. The report presents a model of the P.A.S. delineating the various aspects and dimensions related to the faculty, Government and the Institute that have significant bearing on the operational functioning of a system of appraisal of performance.

TEXT OF THE REPORT

1. Introduction

The role of the teacher is widely recognised as crucial to the effective implementation of any educational programme. This is all the more so with technical management education of today and of the future due to changing economic, social, industrial and technological scenario and the consequent changes in programmes to meet the current and projected needs of industry/user systems. The contribution towards quality and

---

Report of Expert Committee for Developing a Performance Apprisal System ..., Ministry of Human Resource Development, Department of Education, Government of India, New Delhi, 1993; reproduced from *New Frontiers in Education* Octobar-December, 1993.

excellence of any amount of physical, technical and economic resources available in institutions will be limited by the level of competence and commitment of the teachers implementing the programmes. On the other hand, the ingenuity and innovativeness of the dedicated teacher can to a great extent overcome the deficiencies in physical resources, and other handicaps.

In the past the major role of teachers of most technical institutions was related to instruction. The curricula in operation and technologies were comparatively static. Curriculum development and staff development programmes were rather infrequent. The problems of administration of institutions were comparatively less complex. Research and development as well as innovations were considered as a prerogative of a selected few institutions and individuals. In comparison with the above picture, the current scenario is one of continuously changing curricula, rapidly changing technologies, a variety of programmes in different forms and modes, rapidly changing industry; students coming from diverse target groups, environments and social backgrounds with widely varying expectations, values and interests, contributing to complex administrative and other problems within campuses. Yet another factor in operation is disparity in salary scales between industry and technical institutions.

Teachers of today have to perform a variety of tasks pertaining to diverse roles. In addition to instruction, teachers need to innovate and conduct research for their own self-renewal, keep abreast with changes in technology, develop expertise for the effective implementation of curricula. They are also expected to provide services to the industry and community for understanding and contributing to the solution of real life problems in industry (to keep themselves up-to-date). Another role relates to the shouldering of administrative responsibilities in co-operation with other teachers, heads of departments and the head of institutions. The need for each teacher to perform such multiple roles has been recognised in the National Policy on Education not only from the point of view of encouraging the performance of individual teachers but also for promoting the quality of programmes and institutions as a whole.

An effective performance appraisal system for teachers is vital for optimizing the contributions of individual teachers to institutional performance. Such a system has to be considered mainly as one which would help the teacher to grow academically and professionally and to perform effectively in the multiple roles described above and not as one which would cause regimentation, curb innovativeness or exercise controls which would inhibit the creativity and ingenuity of the individual teacher.

The National Policy on Education has, therefore, recognised the need to formulate salary structures and service conditions which would attract and retain competent personnel to the technical education systems. The performance appraisal system is very much linked to these measures and also to the operation of a sound incentive-reward system which would keep the motivation of teachers at a high level, provide them opportunities for career and self-development and for performance of roles compatible with their aptitude, competence and interest.

In developing the above type of appraisal system the following aspects were kept in view:

—it needs to be as simple as possible,
—open,
—participative, and
—data based.

Other important factors which guided the development of the system as proposed in this document are the minimisation of subjectively, implementability, acceptability and adaptability to widely differing institutional structures and environments.

2. Present Position

The present system of teacher appraisal in many technical (and management) institutions, although widely varying, has deficiencies which are present in, by and large, most institutions. These deficiencies relate to (1) The lack of openness, and (2) objectivity, (3) inadequate participation, the near absence of data base, the data available being scanty for any rational decision making for rewards, promotions or the planning of career development and the rather vague statements made in the so-called confidential reports which are the only available record, if at all one considers these as appraisal/data information. The other important features of the existing situation are:

* the absence of a reward system of any kind for motivating a teacher to perform effectively or for even sustaining the level of motivation of those teachers who perform effectively;
* poor linkage with career/staff development programmes including QIP, continuing education of teachers and the respective programme structures;

* inadequate opportunity to teachers to perform in their own respective areas of competence due to lack of physical resources or poor work-distribution between teachers as a consequence of ineffective managerial processes or the location of institutions in non-industrial environments;
* very few instances in which teachers participate in the planning and development of curricula/staff development programmes and other institutional development programmes and projects;
* high percentage of vacancies and consequent understating of institutions compelling the teachers to take heavy work loads in terms of instruction, which adversely affect their quality of performance and also reduce the possibility of the teachers devoting time for innovative, developmental or extension activities; and
* In engineering colleges especially, due to the heavy proliferation in a short span of time, non-availability of well qualified teachers, taking below-par persons for academic (e.g. lecturers) positions.

2.1 *Deficiencies of Existing Teacher Appraisal Systems*

The issue of teacher appraisal in technical institutions has attracted attention of many national forums, although it was only last year (1992) that the need for formal action in this area was recognised at a national policy level through the National Policy on Education. A national workshop on optimizing faculty contribution in polytechnics jointly organised by the four IITs of the country in the seventies, identified the following major deficiencies in the existing system which, even today hold good in the present context of institutions, but for a few exceptions.

The main deficiencies relate to:

* absence of previously agreed standards of performance against which a teacher could be appraised;
* the lack of objectivity of the questions for which the heads of departments, institutions have to offer remarks, their memory often being the main source of data;
* very little meaningful discussion between the head of institution/ head of department and the concerned teacher/s on areas of activity and targets to be attained and the actual performance accomplished;
* very little attention to education, developmental or retraining activities for benefiting both the individual teacher as well as the institution, in relation to systematic needs assessment—a poor

linkage between appraisal system and staff development/training systems;

* a fear that appraisal data could and would be used by management for punitive purposes rather than for incentives and rewards, adversely affecting the trust between the management and the teacher in sharing performance data; and
* a value system in which appraisers (heads of departments, heads of institutions) prefer offering remarks having a central tendency; i.e., being non-committal.

3. Need for Change

The need for change of the existing system of teacher appraisal leading to the introduction of a new system which will enable individual teachers and institutions to improve quality and move towards better standards of performance is recognised by all concerned and the National Policy on Education. Such a system is expected to create conditions facilitating the teachers to perform the variety of roles expected of them more effectively. Two major considerations namely, the crucial role of the teacher and the expanding and changing roles of technical and management institutions, dictate urgent attention to the fulfilment of this need through introduction of performance appraisal system.

3.1 *Teacher's Role*

The crucial role of the teacher in making optimal contribution to the accomplishment of the institutional goals and objectives and the promotion of high standards of performance is of vital importance to the quality of performance of institutions and the system as a whole. Having accepted the crucial nature of the role of the teacher, the major questions are how to meaningfully and objectively appraise the performance of the multiple roles by the teacher and how to create conditions which will motivate most if not all teachers of an institution to perform at higher and better levels. In this regard there can be little doubt of the need of a reward system, which will effectively reward good performers and a staff development system which will provide development opportunities for improving the level of performance of not only of the low performers but of all teachers.

3.2 *Changing Roles of Institutions*

Technical and Management institutions can no longer be considered as merely responsible for the production of technical and managerial manpower for the organised sector; the National Policy on Education envisages and recognises the need for developing institutions to perform a variety of much-required additional roles.

1. Greater induction of improved technologies and a supply of technical and managerial manpower to the infrastructure and service sectors as well as the unorganised rural and underdeveloped sectors.
2. Institutions have to constantly plan for development and reorganisation with specific reference to the likely changes in the economy, social environment, production and management processes, the rapid expansion of knowledge, especially in science and technology.
3. The social relevance of programmes offered by institutions have also to be continuously reviewed and improved through a system of identification of needs and problems in the community. Target populations requiring technology/improved technology inputs and programmes for contributing to the solution of some of the problems and for causing socio-economic upliftment of the community around have to be identified.
4. Another role of institutions of vital importance is that of innovation, research, extension and development. Research, innovation and extension are integral to the totality of academic processes of technical and management institutions. Participation in research and innovative activities provides a continuous challenge and opportunity to the teachers and also creates a dynamic learning environment to both teachers and students; it also contributes to the development of new knowledge, new and improved technologies, extension/transfer to wider settings for solving problems concerning socio-economic realities and innovations for improving productivity or for enhancing production, both in industry as well as in technical education

Institutions will, therefore, have to plan not for survival through continuation and refinement of the existing programmes but also for improving their credibility through better and relevant performance and development of new programmes compatible with the additional roles described above. All these would mean a challenge to the teachers whose levels of motivation will have to be enhanced, opportunities provided for performance of the multiple roles and a system of appraisal installed which in conjunction with the reward and staff/ career development systems will result in enhanced contribution by all teachers.

3.3 *Need for Action*

Section 9.2 of the National Policy on Education states: "A system of teacher evaluation—open participative and data based—will be created and reasonable opportunities of promotion to higher grades provided. Norms of accountability will be laid down with incentives for good performance and disincentives for non-performances." This is all the more valid in the Technical and Management institutions in view of the two major considerations stated above. The introduction of a purposeful and meaningful appraisal system aimed at removing the existing deficiencies is vital to the promotion of quality and performance of Technical/Management institutions.

4. Factors Influencing Teacher Performance

The performance of the individual teacher within a department of an institution is dependent on many factors, some of which are attributable to the individual are his/her competence, abilities, knowledge, expertise, commitments and attitude towards work. Other institutional factors relate to the opportunity provided to the individual for demonstrating competence, the physical facilities and resource available, the institutional climate, staff development planning and implementation, recruitment, selection and promotion criteria and policies; system of incentives and rewards and system for handling grievances of individuals. Each one of these factors is dealt with in some detail in the following.

4.1 *Teacher Competence*

This relates not only to instructional competence in technical and pedagogy areas but also competence related to instructional resource development research, innovation, extension work and management/ administration. Deficiencies in competence can be removed through appropriate staff development programmes. It has to be recognised that competence in the requisite area is an essential prerequisite for performance the first foundation-step for expected performance.

4.2 *Attitude Towards Work*

While competence in a field is essential for performance, one who does not have any positive attitudes and willingness to work, can by no stretch of imagination contribute to performance. Although this is a factor mainly pertaining to the individual, the external factors like institutional climate, reward system, development opportunities, promotions, assignment to prestigious projects etc. do influence the motivational level of the individual and therefore his willingness and attitudes toward work.

4.3 *Opportunity*

A good match between competence (area of strength of individuals) and the opportunity available for performance is a factor which significantly contributes to the performance of individuals. A mismatch could adversely affect performance. Establishing a befitting match is an important issue in the management in institutions, (i.e., work-allocation between individuals which requires concerted consultations between department/teachers). There are instances in which a teacher after participation in a development programme and attaining competence finds himself in situations where opportunities are not available to him for demonstrating such competence. This not only defeats the very purpose of development, but also adversely affects the attitude and willingness of such individuals for work and better performance.

4.4 *Physical Facilities and Resources*

There are a large number of institutions which are ill-equipped in terms of physical facilities and equipment. There is a limit upto which teachers can enhance their performance through their innovativeness. Lack of attention to this factor may result in making adverse judgments on teachers who might otherwise have the potential for higher levels of performance, (give the right facilities and resources).

4.5 *Nature of Programmes*

One of the important factors which influence teacher's performance is the kind and nature of programmes that are offered by the educational institute. Programmes which are in keeping with the expertise, motivation and abilities of the teachers in the institute would contribute towards effective performance. Institutes with progressive and long range perspectives develop newer programmes and provide facilities and incentives for furthering of knowledge, skills and expertise of the teachers in an integrated manner. It becomes all the more necessary (during the last decade of the 20th Century) since many new areas of educational and academic input are felt to be needed by the society, for example in the field of computers, electronics, design and technology, courses related to environmental and ecological fields in which technological and scientific knowledge can play a very positive and significant role.

4.6 *Institutional Climate*

This is a factor which has vital implication for the performance of teachers, although the factor as such is rather intangible. The leadership style of the head of the department/institution, the existence of unhealthy rivalry between groups, inadequate attention to issues related to inter-personal relationship, decision making styles and a variety of other factors influence the performance of individual teachers. While a healthy institutional climate might itself be a motivating factor encouraging teachers to improve their own performance, and unhealthy climate adversely affect individual as well as institutional performance.

4.7 *Planning and Implementation of Staff Development*

The rational basis for staff development planning has to be teacher appraisal and needs-assessment, keeping in view institutional/ departmental development plans, in addition to individual's development needs. Career development is yet another factor to be considered in the planning of staff development. However, if ad hoc and improper decisions are made on staff development, no appraisal system can be expected to yield positive results. The deployment of staff after participating in a development programme is yet another aspect which could influence performance. It is, therefore, necessary to examine the linkage between appraisal, development and deployment as well as subsequent appraisal in the context of establishing an effective appraisal system.

4.8 *Recruitment, Selection and Promotion Criteria*

The dimensions against which staff are appraised and the method of using the appraisal data for decisions related to rewards have necessarily to influence the criteria for recruitment, selection and promotion. The absence of effective linkages between the above aspects would only have adverse affects on the operation of the system of appraisal.

4.9 *System of Incentives and Rewards*

The major reason for introducing effective appraisal systems in institutions is for improving the performance of individual teachers who ultimately would .contribute to the promotion of quality and excellence of the programmes and the institution as a whole. Incentives and rewards for good performance and development opportunities to all for improving their competence are essential for promoting the levels of motivation and the desire to improve performance of each individual. The kind of rewards and incentives that are functionally available in any educational institute consist of two sets of categories, one intrinsic and non-material, and the other extrinsic and material. It is expected that in the progressive educational institutes there would be significant amount of emphasis laid on providing intrinsic and non-material rewards in terms of recognition and appreciation of good performance, honouring of dedicated and high performing teachers, providing a congenial and positive climate and atmosphere wherein one finds it highly satisfying to function; there could also be provision of institutionalising extrinsic rewards which be in terms of research and study grants, best teacher awards, etc., in order to supplement and complement the intrinsic rewards.

4.10 *Grievance-handling system*

When there is vagueness and ambiguity in the operational functioning of any system (including Performance Appraisal System), it lends itself to dissatisfaction and grievances. The envisaged PAS is expected to be devoid of ambiguity and vagueness as far as possible; however, in any system there can be legitimate or perceived defects; since no system can be perfect. It is proposed that there will be a grievance handling machinery or system which would be an integral part of the PAS. Each educational institute would be expected to establish a speedy, fair and impartial grievance handling system which would deal with all grievances within a reasonable amount of time (say not more than 6 months at the maximum, preferably within a period of 3 months). The persons involved in handling of grievance would be expected to enjoy the confidence of the teaching community and to be persons of high repute and calibre.

4.11 *Factors to be Considered as an Integral Part of PAS*

Attention has been drawn to the above factors, the operation of each one of which would need serious consideration while making decisions based on appraisal data. The consideration of these factors has, therefore to be an integral part of the Performance Appraisal System (PAS).

5. The Proposed System: Objectives

The objectives of the PAS for the technical teachers are:

Enhancement and development of professional competence of the teacher which is expected to contribute towards better performance in the large interests of the teacher, the students as well as the institute. The thrust is towards rewarding of better performance; the whole outlook or framework being positive and development. It is expected that the Performance Appraisal System would be:

(i) simple
(ii) data-based
(iii) open and participative; and
(iv) development-oriented.

The proposed PAS is expected to be not only acceptable, but possible to be welcomed by the teachers themselves since it is meant to be as objective and data-based as possible, and to reduce as much of the subjective element as one systematically and humanly can.

5.1 *Formative, Summative and Development Roles*

The purpose of staff appraisal could be (1) formative, (2) summative and (3) development in nature. The proposed system is designed to accomplish all these purposes. The formative role of the PAS concerns itself with the individual's improvement and the provision of data, judgements and suggestions in this direction. This would help in providing opportunities for the individual's development. This might also help the individuals/departments/institute in identifying development needs and programmes in which the teachers need to participate. Improvements in many of the factors listed on section 4 might also be indicated by the PAS in which case needed action at the departmental/institutional level might be necessary.

The summative role of the PAS is concerned with the overall evaluation to help in decisions related to the identification of those teachers whose performance is at a very high level. The number of teachers so identified might constitute, say, 10 per cent of the teachers within the institute. These 10 per cent could be identified on two major consideration : (1) Five per cent who are adjudged best on the basis of absolute ratings and the other five percent who have shown the maximum improvement between successive years. Such a system would motivate the high level performers to maintain/excel in their subsequent performance and the low and average level performers to show the maximum improvement by applying the best efforts possible. The teachers so identified would be provided incentives/rewards in the form of grants for procurement of resources, opportunity to undertake/coordinate prestigious programmes or projects, recognition in the form of commendations and promotional opportunities and other viable rewards. The results of summative evaluation from time to time would also be available to authorities/committees considering promotions, fellowships, scholarships, study grants etc.

The developmental role of the PAS relates to the identification of areas for instructional development, requiring resources, and improvement in institutional policies and mechanisms.

The following paragraphs detail the steps involved in the introduction of the performance appraisal system within Technical/ Management institutions.

5.2 *Formulation of Long and Short Term Institute Development plans*

Institutes like IITs, IIMs and others with long range programmes would evolve strategic plans (10 years period) and perspective plans (15 year period) together with development of long term plans of 3 to 5 years duration. In case of Polytechnics and Engineering Colleges, they would need to develop their plans in keeping with the plans for technical education developed by the respective States in which the polytechnics or colleges are situated. Each institute will be expected to clearly spell out the Mission and goals of the Institute.

An operationally concrete plan of one year would be developed by each of the teaching institutes. In the formulation of long term plans, issues such as industry-academic-inter-actions; contributions the institute intends to make for the betterment of the community; starting of evening classes for working technicians and managers, development of newer and better teaching-training methodologies, enhancing qualitative aspects of teaching-learning processes; would be kept in view. Each institute works out an integrated frame-work of linking institutional goals to departmental objectives which in turn would be related to specific achievements of individual faculty members.

5.3 *Formulation of Individual Work Plan (Annual)*

The format for the individual work plan/job description is given in Appendix-A (i). This would be prepared through a consultative process involving the concerned heads of departments, the head of the institution which might require a series of departmental/inter-departmental meetings. The multiple roles which each teacher will have to perform are entered in the first column of the work plan. These roles are instructional resource development, research/innovations, extension services/con sultancy, management/administration and any other significant roles required to be performed for fulfilling the institutional objectives/ plan. Each of these roles would have to be further broken down into tasks and objectives with targets and the period of activity (i.e. dates from-to) entered against each task/objective. In the case of the instructional role, the task would include classroom teaching of theory subjects, laboratory instruction and other instructional activities, for a time period each expressed in hours per week. The teaching load would comply with the norms in this regard. The performance of the other roles would be the time in addition to that devoted for instructional purposes. In the sample work plan given in Appendix-A(ii) sample tasks and objectives are given. These may vary from institute to institute and between different types of institutes i.e. IIMS, IITs, Regional Engineering Colleges, Stage Engineering Colleges, Polytechnics, etc. In column 4, the individual from whom assistance is required is mentioned. After filling up all the tasks and objectives related to the performance of multiple roles, the weightage for each task would have to be assigned as a percentage of the total work. This weightage would very much depend on the time to be devoted for the performance of each task. The summation of the weightages assigned to each one of the tasks would be 100 per cent. In finalising the work plan by an individual, a number of consultations might be needed with the head of the department, other departments and possibly other teachers, Columns 6 and 7 are meant to be used during appraisal, and therefore would be left blank at the planning stage. A copy of the work plan would be available with each individual teacher, the head of the department as well as the head of the institution.

5.4 *Source of Evidence and Instrumentation*

For each one of the roles incorporated in the work plan (sometimes for each one of the tasks) a specific instrument will have to be used for gathering data from respondents/appraisers. While in respect of the instructional role, the instrument which has been provided may need only little modification, in respect of the other roles the instruments which are appended are suggestive. Depending on the nature of the task and objectives, the items within the instruments may need modification.

The work report of the teacher including courses conducted, laboratory work, regularity of classes and other details provided (by the teacher) would serve as an input for evaluation of the contribution of a teacher.

5.4.1 *The Instructional Role*

There would be ratings/evaluation of the teacher by the students at the end of the course (term-wise, semester-wise, or annually, as the case may be). Significant weightage would be attached to the student evaluation, together with evaluation by H.O.D. and to the self-assessment by the teacher.

Appendices B, C, D and E are relevant for the above.

5.4.2 *Other Roles*

For each one of the other roles related to developing learning-resource material, research/innovation, extension services/consultancy, management/administration, a specific instrument has been designed. Additional models that can be considered are given in Appendices-J and K. The appraisers for each of the tasks within these roles are also given the respective instruments. As already stated, the items within these instruments might need modification depending on the nature of the task/objective by the teacher.

5.5 *Departmental Appraisal Scheme*

Based on the work plans of all individual teachers within a department, each head of department will have to prepare a departmental appraisal scheme which indicates the appraisers in respect of each teacher, namely, the peers/experts who will be appraising the performance of a teacher in respect of a particular task/objective. This should indicate the name of the teacher, the name of the appraiser, the type of the instrument to be used, the date on which the observation is to be made and the date on which the completed data would be furnished to the respective head of the department. Simultaneously the self-ratings on each task by each individual teacher will also be gathered on a date to be shown on the departmental appraisal scheme. The head of department would have to play an important role in ensuring the implementation of the appraisal scheme. The provision of the requisite instrument/forms, the collection of data and analysis.

5.6 *Flowchart Depicting Operation of PAS*

The flowchart given in Appendix-L depicts the important stages in introduction of the Performance Appraisal System within an institution in the first cycle of one year. At the end of this stage the rating from the different appraisal instruments, i.e., the ratings in respect of each task will have to be transferred to the work plan of the individual. Here again it would be seen that in column 6 of the self-rating and in column 7 the average rating of all other appraisers are entered. After entering the rating in respect of all tasks the aggregated rating has to be arrived at by multiplying each rating by the weightage assigned to the particular task/objective and thereby computing weighted average which would be the rating assigned to the individual teacher for a particular year.

5.7 *Performance Appraisal of Individuals*

The interpretation of these aggregate ratings has to be done with a lot of care, especially in cases where the rating is average or low. Within each institution a PAS Committee will be constitutes which will be responsible for making decisions based on appraisal and advising the Head of Institution/Management on actions related to rewards/staff development planning etc. It would be an important function of the Performance Appraisal Committee within the institution to consider the extent of operation of the different factors enumerated in Section 4. Listening to the concerned individual on his view on the operation of such factors would also be necessary. A record of the same should be made in the workplan itself.

Relevant information would be elicited from the appropriate source related to performance of a teacher concerning research, consultancy, development of material. For example, the research work would be evaluated in terms of reputation and quality of the journal in which the research work has been published, if necessary a report on the same would also be obtained from the experts in the field concerned. As related to consultancy, the report received from the client would be taken into account. As related to development of teaching material, its utility for the students and also for others outside the institute would be taken into account. Similarly, when computer software is developed, it would be evaluated in terms of its contributions for better teaching and problem solving purposes.

5.8 *Identification of Best Teachers of the Institute*

The workplans of all teachers of the Institute with appraisal ratings and remarks about the level/rating of performance will be the basis for selecting the best teachers. Although this could be done annually, an annual review and biennial (once in two years) summative appraisal followed by decisions for reward and development would be appropriate.

The first appraisal would be given an opportunity to all teachers to get a feel of operation of the system and the subsequent appraisal would enable identification of high performers both on absolute and relative criteria.

5.9 *Appraisal of HOD*

The Evaluation of a Head of Department (HOD) would be done by the Principal plus two HODs. If there is a felt need to co-opt a subject matter expert, then the Principal, would do the same; in that case, there would be four persons.

6. Performance Appraisal of Heads of Institutions

The roles to be performed by the Heads of Institutions would be much different from those of individual teachers. This might be true to some extent in the case of heads of departments as well. The roles of heads of Departments could, however, be accommodated in the performance appraisal system meant for teachers by making adjustments in the weightages assigned to the different roles of the teacher and making additions in the type of managerial/administrative tasks to be performed by heads of departments.

In the case of heads of institutions such as adaptation of the suggested work plan for teachers cannot meet the requirements of delineation of the roles as well as the mode of appraisal of the different roles to be performed by Heads of Institutions. Also the appraisers for assessing the performance of the Head of Institutions would be different from those appraising individual teachers. The instruments to be used for data gathering would also differ considerably. However, a Performance Appraisal System for teachers which does not provide for the appraisal of the Head of the Institution would not only be considered inadequate but would also affect the acceptability of the concept itself.

An instrument for appraising the performance of the Heads of Institutions is given in Appendix-M. This instrument lists the major variables against which the Head of an Institution would need to be appraised and the indicators pertaining to these variables against which the actual performance of the Head of the Institution should be appraised. A rating scale or quantification of the performance against each indicator would only make the appraisal rather too simple and hence an open ended assessment of the position of each indicator by a committee constituted by the management (Governing Board/Government) is suggested in this regard.

The question of rewards for the Head of the Institution depending on his performance is yet another aspect which needs consideration. An annual appraisal of the type suggested and maintenance of the record would go a long way in assisting management in making decisions on tenures, on expansion of programmes/projects within institutions etc. and these should serve as rewards for Heads of Institutions performing at a high level.

7. Strategy for Implementation of Scheme

The stipulation regarding the introduction of a meaningful system of performance appraisal for teachers in the National Policy, the linking up of salary structures and service conditions with staff appraisal, the efforts being made for maintaining standards and for promoting quality and excellence of the system and the grant of statutory authority to the AICTE (All India Council for Technical Education) which has mainly this purpose in view, are all factors which not only emphasise the need but also facilitate the introduction of a new system of performance appraisal, a model for which has been delineated in the foregoing sections. Some of the significant contextual factors that need to be kept in mind while developing and implementing a viable Performance Appraisal System for teachers of Technical and Management Institutes are:

(i) *Resources*—availability, that is, of the funds available for upgradation of facilities and developmental work.

(ii) *Transfers*—the frequency, nature and basis of transfers which may have a bearing upon the long-range planning and commitment of faculty.

(iii) *Work-load*—the extent and nature of work-load; for example, in case of heavy teaching load there may very little time be available for teachers to do anything else, and even may be unable to do full justice to the quality of teaching.

(iv) *Procedure and Systems*— In case of cumbersome rules and procedures there would be demotivation towards initiating performance of high calibre or creative nature.

(v) The *Student Quality* in terms of their intellectual and academic calibre, and their interest in educational pursuits.

(vi) *Examination System* prevalent in the Institute and the concerned University.

(vii) The degree of autonomy available to the college and to the teacher.

(viii) The *Environmental Opportunities* in term of industrial organizations and academic institutes located in the same area of the institute.

However, this model would need validation and refinement to make it acceptable and adaptable to conditions and environments existing in the different types of technical/management institutions. In this context the following strategies are suggested for facilitating the implementation of the scheme.

7.1 *Validation/Refinement of the Scheme Through a National Workshop*

A National workshop in which Heads of the Institutions and identified senior teachers from a representative cross section of all types of technical and management institutions participate, would be held mainly with a view to validating the concepts as well as necessary mechanisms, forms/instruments required for installation of the scheme in institutions. It is expected that the deliberations and the outcome of the National Workshop would greatly enhance the acceptability and relevance of the proposed scheme with improvements wherever needed.

7.2 *Pilot Trial in Selected Institutions*

The scheme with the refinement effected through the National Workshop would be ready for implementation in selected institutions which would really be a pilot trial for the installation of the scheme. Orientation programmes for the staff of these institutions would provide adequate data on the likely problems and would enable the formulation of strategies/ solutions to such problems. It may not be necessary to wait for a period of whole cycle (of completion) for the pilot trial with a view to expediting the extension of the system to most institutions in the country. A pilot trial for a shorter duration might be preferable. The necessary modifications, improvements to the scheme on the basis of the pilot trial would be effected and the scheme would then be ready for implementation by all institutions. A system of conducting orientation on a very large scale would, however, have to be evolved.

7.3 *Actions by Management/Governments*

In addition to the stipulations in the National Policy and related documents, the Central and State Governments will have to undertake some more actions for the success in the introduction of the scheme. These would relate to the issue of necessary directives, substituting totally the present system and the provision of the needed budgets (a percentage of the total budget of an institution) for meeting the expenditure related to rewards for teachers performing at a higher level of achievement and for the conduct of staff development programmes.

7.4 *Action Research/Case Studies*

Professional institutions and organisations can help not only in disseminating the experiences and problems in the operation of the scheme (of PAS) but also in continuously undertaking action research in some typical institutions with a view to effecting continual improvements to the scheme. The publication of case studies based on such action research and their dissemination would go a long way in creating a proper understanding of the issues, problems and likely solutions for making this scheme a success.

7.5 *Conclusion*

The introduction of the scheme in the large number of institutions in the country and the development of models appropriate to the type and size of technical/management institutions is a complex task. This document only provides a broad framework with examples of work plans/instruments/forms of the operations of the scheme. The scheme has been kept adaptable to enable each institution to make marginal/ necessary modifications needed for the operation of the scheme. In implementing the scheme, however, it has to be ensured that the following pre-requisites are fulfilled:

- The system has the understanding and acceptability of people for whom it is operated and on whom it is applied.
- Appropriate skills and knowledge of the system are possessed by persons responsible for operating it, prior to its adoption through participation in properly designed orientation programmes.
- The scheme is supported by a system of rewards and a plan for staff development to meet the education and training needs of the teachers based on appraisal.

APPENDIX-A (I)

WORK PLAN/JOB DESCRIPTION

Name..................................Designation..............................Department..

Role	Tasks/Objectives	Period of activity	Assistance of Guidance	Weigh-tage	Appraisal rating Self	Appraiser	Aggre-gate
1	2	3	4	5	6	7	8
1. Instructional	1.1						
	1.2						
	1.3.................						
	1.4.................						
2. Resource Development	2.1						
	2.2						
	2.3.................						
3. Research Innovations	3.1						
	3.2						
4. Extension/Services/ Consultancy	4.1						
	4.2						
	4.3................						
5. Management Administration	5.1						
	5.2						
	5.3................						
6. Any other important/ significant work	6.1..................						
	6.2..................						

Remarks : Related to the existence of factors which have influenced the individual's performance—See Section IV of the paper.

Individual *Head of Department* *Head of Institution*

APPENDIX-A (II)

WORK PLAN/JOB DESCRIPTION

Name..............................Designation.............................Department.. year ....

Role		Tasks/Objectives	Period of activity	Assistance of / Guidance	Weightage	Apraisal rating Self	Appraiser	Aggregate ruling
1		2	3	4	5	6	7	8
1. Instructional	1.1	Teaching Engineering Mechanics course, second semester—Theory 2 2 hrs/week Practical 2 Hrs/week	Jan-April	—	20%			
	1.2	Teaching Mechanics of Structures course, First semester—Theory 2 Hrs/week Practical 2 Hrs/week	July-Nov.	—	20%			
	1.3	....						
	1.4	....						
2. Resource Development	2.1	Writing of six new experiments in Engineering Mechanics	July-Nov.	HOD	10%			
	2.2	Preparation of OHP transparency package for teaching the topic of BH & SF in Mechanics of structures	Jan.-April	Media Centre	10%			
	2.3	....						
3. Research Innovations	3.1	Conducting a survey maintenace tasks performed by Civil Diplomates	December	Guidance of HOD	5%			
	3.2	....						

(Contd.)

Appendix-A (ii) *(contd.)*

Role		Tasks/Objectives	Period of activity	Assistance of /Guidance	Weightage	Apraisal rating Self	Appraiser	Aggregate ruling
1		2	3	4	5	6	7	8
4. Extension/Services/ Consultancy	4.1	Conducting socio-economic survey for determining areas requiring induction/transfer of technology	April	Guidance from HOD	5%			
	4.2	Assistance in the planning of a local small scale industry	Jan.-April	Assistance from other project	5%			
	4.3	....						
5. Management/Aminis-tration	5.1	Guiuding cultural activities of students as in-charge of the cul-tural committee	Whole year	—	5%			
	5.2	Assisting HOD in purchase of stores, equipment for the depart-ment	Whole year	Guidance from HOD	5%			
	5.3	....						
6. Any other important/ significant work	6.1	....						
	6.2	....						

Remarks: Related to the existence of factors which have influenced the individual's performance—see Section IV of the paper.

Individual *Head of Department* *Head of Institution*

APPENDIX B

PERFORMANCE APPRAISAL OF CLASS ROOM TEACHING

To be *used for anonymous evaluation by students Frequency—End of a semester or End of an year*

0. Never 1. Rarely 2. Sometimes 3. Frequently 4. Always

Sl. No.	Item	Rating scale 0	1	2	3	4	Remarks
1.	Aims/Objectives of each lesson made clear						
2.	Teaching techniques are effective						
3.	Teaching done in small steps						
4.	Concept and principles illustrated with concrete examples						
5.	Active student participation ensured in classes						
6.	Question posed at proper levels						
7.	Students free to raise doubts/ask questions						
8.	Communication effective						
9.	Chalkboard work systematic						
10.	Student interest maintained						
11.	Proper link-up of main points at the end of each class						
12.	Planning and preparation for teaching evident						
13.	Confidence in subject matter evident						
14.	Homework/assignments, examined and returned within reasonable time						
15.	Engages class punctually						

Different. Forms for Undergraduates and Post-graduates may be prepared – Appendix C.

APPENDIX-C

PERFORMANCE APPRAISAL OF CLASS ROOM TEACHING

To be used by self/peers/experts Frequency—Twice a semester or Twice a year

0. Very poor 1. Poor 2. Satisfactory 3. Good 4. Excellent

Sl. No.	Item	Rating scale 0	1	2	3	4	Remarks
1.	Aims/objectives clear to the teacher and students						
2.	Content appropriate to the stated/unstated aims and level of students						
3.	Teaching techniques appropriated to the content						
4.	Introduction effective, caught students attention and established rapport						
5.	Content broken into small bits to enable students learn step by step						
6.	Learning of concepts and principles ensured through verbalised or concrete examples						
7.	Sequencing logical						
8.	Students active participation in learning						
9.	Teacher questions at proper level						
10.	Students free to raise doubts/ask questions						
11.	Positive reinforcement evident						
12.	Communication effective						
13.	Chalkboard work effective						
14.	Students interests sustained						
15.	Assessment of student attainment						
16.	Proper link-up of main points at the end of the lesson						
17.	Planning of the lesson evident						
18.	Confidence in content evident						

Remarks: (Please enter any factor in operation influencing performance—Refer Section 4) Different Forms for Under-graduate and Post-graduates to be prepared.

APPENDIX-D

PERFORMANCE APPRAISAL OF LABORATORY INSTRUCTION

To be used by students, anonymous Frequency—End of each semester or year

0. Never 1. Rarely 2. Sometimes 3. Frequently 4. Always

Sl. No.	Item	Rating scale 0 E	1 D	2 C	3 B	4 A	Remarks
1.	Lab. work was interesting						
2.	Laboratory work was relevant to the course/ programme						
3.	Laboratory work was well organised in terms of time, equipment and instructional material						
4.	Aims/objectives of laboratory work clearly stated						
5.	Initial instruction was adequate, for proceeding with lab work						
6.	Provides needed guidance at intermediate stages of the experiment						
7.	Ensures observance of safety precautions and care of equipment						
8.	Ensures quality laboratory reports of students on lab. work						
9.	Effectively examines lab. reports of students and returns within reasonable time						
10.	Demonstrates high degree of familiarity in handling/operating equipment						
11.	Communicates effectively with students						
12.	Encourages student question on lab. work						
13.	Responds adequately to student questions						
14.	Engages lab. sessions punctually						

APPENDIX-E

PERFORMANCE APPRAISAL OF LABORATORY INSTRUCTION

To be used by self/peers/experts Frequency—Twice a semester or Thrice a year

0. Very poor 1. Poor 2. Satisfactory 3. Good 4. Excellent

Sl. No.	Item	Rating scale					Remarks
		0 E	1 D	n C	3 B	4 A	
1.	Laboratory work was interesting						
2.	Laboratory work was relevant to the course/ programme						
3.	Laboratory work was well organised in terms of time, equipment						
4.	Aims/objectives of laboratory work clearly stated						
5.	Initial instruction was adequate for proceeding with laboratory work						
6.	Provides needed guidance at intermediate stages of the experiment						
7.	Ensures observance of safety precautions and care of equipment						
8.	Ensures quality laboratory reports of students on laboratory work						
9.	Effectively examines laboratory reports of students and returns within reasonable time						
10.	Demonstrates high degree of familiarity in handling/operating equipment						
11.	Communicates effectively with students						
12.	Encourages student questioning on laboratory work						
13.	Responds adequately to student questions						
14.	Engages laboratory session punctually						
15.	Demonstrated confidence in subject matter						
16.	Prepares and plans for conducting laboratory work						

Remarks : Please enter any factor in operation influencing performance—Refer Section (4).

APPENDIX-F

PERFORMANCE APPRAISAL IN RESPECT OF LEARNING RESOURCE DEVELOPMENT

To be used by self/peers/experts/users

Task Objectives : ---

N/A—Not applicable 0. Very poor 1. Poor 2. Satisfactory 3. Good 4. Excellent

Sl. No.	Criteria	N/A	Rating scale 0 E	1 D	2 C	3 B	4 A	Remarks
1.	Clarity and adequacy of directions for use							
2.	Relevance to the curricula							
3.	Clarity and adequacy of media, if any							
4.	Will this sustain the interest of students?							
5.	Appropriateness of time allocation							
6.	Correctness of subject matter							
7.	Potential for improvement of instruction							
8.	Originality of the resource							

Remarks: Please enter any factor in operation influencing performance—Refer Section (4)

APPENDIX-G

PERFORMANCE APPRAISAL IN RESPECT OF RESEARCH INNOVALATION

To be used by self/peers/experts/users

Task Objectives : (from work plan)--

N/A—Not applicable 0. Very poor 1. Poor 2. Satisfactory 3. Good 4. Excellent

Sl. No.	Criteria	Rating scale 0 E	1 D	2 C	3 B	4 A	Remarks
1.	Contribution to new knowledge						
2.	Applicability of findings in real situations						
3.	Potential for increasing efficiency of instruction/ industrial practice/process						
4.	Is this replication or original research						
5.	Potential for publishing in standard journals/magazines						
6.	Comments on utility and the needed follow-up						

Remarks: (Please enter any factor in operation influencing performance—Refer section 4.)

APPENDIX-H

PERFORMANCE APPRAISAL IN RESPECT OF EXTENSION SERVICES/CONSULTANCY

To be used by self//HOD/Users

Task Objectives : (from workplan)---

N/A—Not applicable 0. Very poor 1. Poor 2. Satisfactory 3. Good 4. Excellent

Sl. No.	Item	Rating scale 0 E	1 D	2 C	3 B	4 A	Remarks
1.	Relevance to institutional objectives						
2.	Relevance to curriculum/discipline in individual						
3.	The extent to which the problem has been solved/the need for services has been fulfilled						
4.	Extent of improvement in rapport with user/system						
5.	Cooperation extended by user/system						
6.	Contribution to individual development						
7.	Acceptability of services/consultancy report to the user system						
8.	Potential for continuing work in this area						
9.	Comments on scope for further work, extent to which this might strengthen institutional development/affect institutional work, availability of infrastructural facilities, resources etc.						

Remarks : (Please enter any factor in operation influencing performance—Refer to section 4).

APPENDIX-I

PERFORMANCE APPRAISAL IN RESPECT OF MANAGEMENT/ ADMINISTRATION OF INSTITUTE

To be used by self//HOD/Users

Task Objective : (from work plan)---

N/A—Not applicable 0. Very poor 1. Poor 2. Satisfactory 3. Good 4. Excellent

Sl. No.	Item	N/A	Rating scale
1.	Extent to which objectives are accomplished.		
2.	Availability of infrasctructural facilities		
3.	Demonstrated ability in taking administrative problems		
4.	Cooperation of other staff/students involved in this area		
5.	Cooperation/Rapport with external agencies		
6.	Comments on administrative competence, reasons for shortfall in the attainment of objective/targets, if applicable and necessary.		

Remarks: (Please enter any factor in operation influencing performance—Refer section 4).

APPENDIX-J

ABET PROFORMA FOR FACULTY INFORMATION

Institution_____________________________Date________________

Programme______________________________________

Information regarding Faculty Members

On separate pages, please furnish the following information for each member of the faculty of the department administering this programme. Use of format given below.

1. Name and date of birth
2. Academic rank (State whether full-time or part-time, and if part-time indicate non-academic activity and percent of time devoted to it.)
3. Degrees with fields, institutions and dates
4. Number of years of service in this faculty, including date of original appointment and dates of advancement in rank.
5. Other related experience—teaching, industrial, etc. (What capacity, where, when?)
6. Consulting
7. State in which registered
8. Principal publications of last five years. (Give title and reference)
9. Scientific and professional societies of which a member
10. Honours and awards
11. Subjects or courses taught this year by terms. (Give hours per week of lecture, recitation, and laboratory and number of sections if more than one. Designate day, evening, extension or graduate).
12. Other assigned duties performed during the academic year, with average hours per week. Indicate which carry extra compensation.
13. List any specific programmes in which faculty member has participated to improve teaching and professional competence.
14. Special duties of co-op faculty coordinators).

APPENDIX-K

PROFORMA FOR FACULTY INFORMATION AS PROPOSED BY "MANYATA"

Institution :

Department :

Name :

Please tick ( ) the appropriated box.

1. Highest academic qualification

   Bachelors ( ) Masters ( ) Doctoral ( )

2. Teaching Experience

   <1 Year ( ) >1 Year ( ) >2 Years ( )

   >3 Years ( ) > 4 Year ( ) >5 Years ( )

3. Project guidance (Number of B.E. level projects both completed and in progress)

   None ( ) One to Four ( ) Five to Nine ( ) Ten and More ( )

4. Technical papers published/patents registered

   None ( ) One ( ) Two ( )

   Three ( ) Four ( ) Five and more ( )

5. Monographs/Books published

   None ( ) one ( ) Two ( ) Three and more ( )

6. Industrial experience

   <1 Year ( ) >1 Year ( ) <2 Years ( )

   >3 Years ( ) <4 Years ( ) <5 Years ( )

7. Quantum of funds generated for the Institution through sponsored schemes, projects, consultancy, etc.

   Nil ( ) <Rs. 0.50 lakh ( ) <Rs. 0.50 lakh ( )

   —Rs. 1.00 lakh ( ) <Rs. 5.00 lakh ( ) <Rs. 20.00 lakh ( )

8. Continuing Education Received

   (a) Number of Intensive courses/workshops attended (up to 10 days duration)

   None ( ) One ( ) Two ( ) Three and more ( )

APPENDIX-K (II)

   (b) Number of short term courses attended (about 2-4 weeks duration)

   None ( ) One ( ) Two ( ) Three and more ( )

   (c) Number of semester/term long courses attended

   None ( ) One ( ) Two ( ) Three and more ( )

   (d) Programmes leading to recognised diplomas attended

   No ( ) Yes ( )

9. Professional activities

(a) Association (present and past) with professional societies/national or state level Advisory Bodies

None ( ) Member ( ) Officer Bearer ( )

(b) Your involvement in imparting Continuing Education has been as

None ( ) Faculty ( ) Organiser ( ) Organiser and faculty ( )

(c) Have you formally been involved in the organization of any conference, symposium or seminar?

No ( ) Yes ( )

(d) Have you reviewed papers for technical journals or served on their Editorial Boards?

No ( ) Yes ( )

10. Have you been a recipient of Awards/Honours

Not applicable ( ) University/Institute level ( )
State level ( ) National/International level ( )

APPENDIX-L

FLOW CHART DEPICTING THE OPERATION OF PERFORMANCE APPRAISAL SYSTEM WITHIN INSTITUTES

Previous years' goals/objectives/performance National/State/District Development Goals/Plans Interdepartmental meetings Survey conducted by Institute	Formulation of Institutional/Departmental Goals and objectives Beginning academic session
Departmental/Inter-departmental meetings/ consultations	Formulation of individual work- plan tasks/ objectives within multiple role Beginning of each academic session
Departmental/Inter-departmental individual Consultations/Meetings	Appraisal scheme for individual/department. Beginning of each academic session
Implementation of Appraisal Scheme by Each HOD-Administration of questionnaire/collection and Analysis of Data	Data on each individual's work-Appraisal MID semester/end of term
Intermediate/Formative feedback to individuals-Mid semester/term	Reviewed work-plans-staff Development decisions Mid semester/end of term
Continued administration of appraisal scheme by HODs. Collection and analysis of appraisal data	Identification of excellence-top 10% teachers staff development need and decisions—decisions on rewards/incentives End of each academic session

APPENDIX-M

PERFORMANCE APPRAISAL OF HEAD OF INSTITUTION

Sl.	Factors	Indicators*
1.	Planning, organization and control	1. Vision of the future/ability to anticipate future areas of work and role. 2. Clarity of goals and objectives. 3. Resource consideration 4. Faculty development and deployment 5. Monitoring and review mechanisms 6. Delegation of authority 7. Control of task attainment.
2.	Resource mobilisation	1. Financial status of the institution 2. The state of self-sufficiency 3. Acquisition of resources from private agencies 4. Acquisition of resources from government 5. Resource generation 6. National and international consultancies/ projects
3.	Environment linkages	1. Rapport with client groups/user systems/ community/industry 2. Promoting interaction of teachers with user systems 3. Feedback mechanisms.
4.	Institutional climate	1. Motivational level of faculty 2. Innovative work by faculty 3. Research/productive work other than routine instruction 4. New and beneficial ideas put into practice 5. Staff student relationship 6. Learning environment 7. Sense of belonging of faculty and students 8. Grievance handling mechanisms ++9. Inter-group rivalries ++10. Internal conflicts 11. Interpersonal relationship
5.	Communication	1. Effectiveness of communication channels-internal and external 2. Openness of information and information sharing
6.	Internal management	1. Resource allocation 2. Resource utilisation 3. Cost consciousness 4. Staff discipline 5. Professional ethics
7.	Staff development and training	1. Effectiveness of staff appraisal 2. Effectiveness of staff development 3. Effectiveness of staff deployment 4. Linkages between appraisal, development and deployment

Sl.	Factors	Indicators*
8.	Leadership and decision making	1. Issue and problem identification 2. Timely attention to issues and problems 3. Decision making style 4. Timeliness of decision and 5. Level of enthusiasm and team spirit in faculty 6. Respect commanded amongst faculty and staff 7. Dependability for task completion and target attainment.

Remarks:(See section 6 for method of appraisal)

Note: The position in respect of each indicator should be assessed through observation/ discussion with concerned people within the institution, significant clientele/audience connected with the institution.

++negative indicators

* See note on page (ii) of This report

9

Delhi Summit : UNICEF Background Paper—Education For All (1993)*

Introduction

UNICEF prepared a background Paper for a Panel Discussion for the Summit of Nine High Population Countries, held at New Delhi in December 1993. The Paper entitled 'Education For All, All For Education' discusses various aspects of Popular Participation, Mobilization and Decentralization for Education for All.

9.1. OPPORTUNITY AND CHALLENGE

Because basic learning needs are complex and diverse, meeting them requires multisectoral strategies and action which are integral to overall development efforts. Many partners must join with the education authorities, teachers and other educational personnel in developing basic education if it is to be seen, once again, as the responsibility of the entire society. This implies the active involvement of a wide range of partners—families, teachers, communities, private enterprises (including those involved in information and communication), government and non-governmental organizations, institutions etc.—in planning, managing and evaluating the many forms of basic education. (World Declaration on Education for All, Framework of Action, Principles of Action No. 11).

The 1990s are likely to be characterised as the decade in which a new global ethic for children began to emerge. An unprecendented period of activism in the international community in support of human development is beginning to be seen as the landmark of the decade.

The World Conference on Education for All (Jomtien, Thailand, March 1990) was the global platform of proclaiming the urgent need

* *Reproduced from Progressive Educational Herald* 8 (2) January 1994.

for action to redress the denial of basic education to intolerably large numbers of the world's children and adults. Access to basic education for all and achievement of a functional and sustainable level of learning and life skills by a large majority—at least 80 per cent was the suggested target—were regarded as the criteria for universalization.

The Convention on the Rights of the Child that made free and compulsory primary education an obligation of the state and the right of all children came into effect in September 1990. Since then, over 150 countries have ratified the Convention, more than for any other human rights treaty.

The World Summit for Children, the first truly global summit meeting, established a range of social development goals including universal access to primary education and completion of the primary cycle by at least 80 per cent of those enrolled. Over a hundred countries have been re-examining their national priorities and strategies for basic education in the wake of the Jometien Conference and the Summit for Children; most have prepared national programmes of action to accelerate progress. Regional forums of governments, several at the level of heads of state and government, have endorsed the global goals and some have adopted regional decade and mid-decade targets.

The World Summit for Social Development scheduled for 1995 will be another major occasion for world leaders to take stock of progress and constraints, to intensify the efforts to reach landmark social targets by the year 2000 and to maintain the momentum into the 21st Century.

The Education For All Summit of nine high population countries, representing over half of the global population, (held in Delhi from December 13-16,1993) is in keeping with the new consensus and activism at the international level by national leaders on social and human development priorities. The preparatory process had already helped to energize national efforts in EFA and to draw increased international attention to the need for accelerating the pace of progress. The Declaration of Principles and the Framework for Action expected to be adopted by the leaders of the nine countries will be a powerful instrument for advocacy and mobilization in the hands of national leaders and all activists in the cause of education for all in each country and internationally.

The increased worldwide attention now being paid to Education for All, presents a new opportunity and poses the challenge for broadening and deepening people's participation, mobilization of the whole society and bringing authority and decision-making closer to communities and families in each country in support of education goals.

9.2. INTER-RELATED AND OVERLAPPING CONCEPTS

The educational system should not be regarded as a branch of the bureaucracy. Instead, it should be a sub-system highly interactive with all other parts of the social whole. The point is to give pupils, parents and teacher's responsibility over their own affairs, to the point of enabling them to administer the educational system on their own within the context of natural or contractual communities. This assumption of responsibility must necessarily embrace three indispensable areas—participating in design and decision-making processes; regular, structured involvement in the processes of management and evaluation; and finally, financial accountability with regard of both income and contributions (Ki-Zerbo, 1990, p. 86).

The terms *participation*, *mobilization* and *decentralization* have become common in current education and development parlance all over the world. They all refer to the same general category of needs. In the context of education, these needs are to define educational development in terms of people's real priorities and demands, to unleash the energies and resources of people and society to make education a concern and a task of the whole society and to create conditions and institutional environments for people to articulate their goals and priorities in education and to make their contribution to educational development. These three terms together constitute the key elements of a framework for promoting and assessing progress in educational development.

People's participation is a *sine qua non* in Education For All. By definition, education for all must engage people widely and actively as beneficiaries and contributors. But even more, participation, in its various dimensions, has come to be recognized as a basic *principle of action, an overall development strategy*, in national development efforts including educational development. It is both a means and an end of development. As a principle that guides action, participation derives its rationale from values and goals that are important in most societies, such as :

* Accepting democratic practices and values as a way of organizing society;
* giving a prominent role to institutions of civil society in the nation's governance;

* giving people the chance to participate in events and processes that shape their life;
* liberating people's energy, creativity and entrepreneurial spirit; and
* equitable access to opportunities of life including essential social services such as basic education.

In the context of basic education, therefore, participation is an expression of the overall development strategy of recognizing the critical role of people's collective action in the broad range of political, social and economic arenas.

Participation

To participate literally means being part of something. But there are various ways and degrees of "being part of" or "taking part in" : (1) use of a particular service; (2) contribute resources, materials and/or labour; (3) attend; (4) be consulted on a particular issue; (5) get involved in the delivery of the service; (6) take part in the implementation of delegated powers; (7) take part in decision-making. On the other hand, it has been argued that "the participation issue is not so much a problem of degree or quantity but rather of the quality of such participation" (Coraggio, 1991:218). It is also stressed that participation is "not only an agreement to follow but an active decision to assume responsibility in considering the rationale, implications and potential outcomes" of any particular process (Benard, 1990, in Shaeffer, 1992, p. 8).

Participation, if understood as an empowering and formative experience, may enable people to : (a) gain knowledge, awareness and democratic experience, as well as self-confidence, self-reliance, pride and autonomy; (b) take action to solve their own problems; (c) gain control of their own lives; and (d) gain social and political power (Shaeffer, 1992).

Social Mobilization

Social mobilization is a broad-scale movement to engage large number of people in action for achieving a specific development goal through self-reliant efforts. It is a planned process that seeks to facilitate change and development. It takes into account the felt needs of the people, embraces the critical principle of community involvement and seeks to empower individuals for action...(Ling and Hewett, 1992, p.1).

Mobilization in the context of basic education refers to active involvement of all relevant sectors of society in promoting and supporting education. Social mobilization, therefore, is a manifestation of the principle of participation through organized and systematic actions.

The martial overtone of the term social mobilization is not accidental. It reflects a sense of urgency about overcoming a common problem or achieving a common purpose through expression of collective commitment of society, formulation of strategies to achieve results and engagement of large numbers of people in coordinated and goal-oriented group actions. The spread of participatory democratic values and new forms of social organization such as popular organizations of women, youth and workers; cooperatives; religious and cultural organizations; professional associations; non-governmental and voluntary organizations; and elected bodies of local government, has created new opportunities for social mobilization. At the same time, advances in communication technology—electronic and print media as well as new and traditional forms of cultural expression reaching large audiences—have expanded the potential reach of social mobilization to a degree unthinkable in the past.

Decentralization refers to the organization and structure of governance that make it possible for the participatory principle and its manifestation in action through social mobilization to be practised. The dominant connotation is of a shift of authority and decision-making from the central government and capital city to regions, districts, towns and villages that would allow participation, facilitate mobilization and promote efficiency. Along with the vertical shift to remedy over-centralization of political and economic structures, a redefining of roles and functions of governance at different levels is also necessary. It is not a matter of divesting central authorities of their responsibilities and obligations, but assigning authorities and tasks at levels where they can be handled most effectively, conforming to the principles of participation and requirements for effective social mobilization. For decentralization to function effectively, national leaders and the administrative and legislative organs of central governments, for example, must continue to define the overall objectives and priorities for educational development, ensure that adequate national resources are mobilized for and directed to human priorities, determine broad allocations of national resources among competing categories of needs, promote principles of universality and equality for all the people and foster a political culture including adoption of legislative and administrative measures for decentralization.

Decentralization

Decentralization can take three forms: deconcentration (passing down administrative functions with authority to review and overrule retained at the central level), delegation (passing down authority and decision-making powers with discretion to review and overrule retained at the central level) and devolution (granting decision-making powers to local authorities and allowing them to take full responsibility without reference back to central government with sharing of authority protected by legislative or statutory measures). In many developing countries, decentralization has not gone much beyond the deconcentration level. Decentralization also has a horizontal dimension, that is, the need to (re) distribute power among institutions at the same level (UNDP, 1993).

Speaking of decentralization in education means an attempt to re-structure the education system with three main objectives : (a) improving the finance, efficiency and quality of the system, (b) redistributing political power, and (c) promoting stability in the system (Prawda, 1993).

9.3. WHERE WE ARE—LESSONS FROM EXPERIENCE

The Conventional Educational Model

The conventional educational model has been characterized by highly centralized structures and decision-making in all spheres—legal, administrative, curricular, pedagogical, organizational. Typically, educational policies and reforms have been designed by political and technical elites, without systematic consultation with the larger society. A small group of individuals often decides what the learning needs are for all and now they are to be satisfied.

Although the rhetoric of participation has become commonplace, participation in education is still narrow in conception and limited in practice. Learners and communities are usually referred to as beneficiaries and teachers classified as inputs, together with textbooks and other instructional materials. Parents remain outsiders, requested to participate through "voluntary" contributions—cash or labour—to the (otherwise impossible to maintain) school system. Students are passive listeners in the classroom, teachers are passive executors of predetermined curricula, parents are passive receivers of complaints and results.

The tendency to consider education programmes as strictly sectoral Ministry of Education bureaucracy-controlled activity persists in most countries. Basic education does not figure high enough on political and development agendas and there is not enough opportunity for public debate and consensus-building around educational priorities, targets, strategies and performance. The extraordinary outreach capacity of mass media and communications technology to inform and involve people in burning social issues is not being exploited. The organizational and administrative structures that would allow people to participate effectively are still evolving in many countries.

Popular or community participation is to often understood in economic terms—participation viewed as "cheap labour" or "cost-sharing"' and from a one-way perspective; what the community can do for the school rather than what the school can do for the community. Parents may even be allowed to have a say in organizational and administrative matters, but are not to "interfere with technical matters"—that is, with the nuts and bolts of their children's learning process—as attested to by restrictive private and public school regulations, and even some national education laws. Paradoxically enough, while school-related activities, especially at the pre-school and primary level, are considered a female domain in many countries (in as much as they are considered a simple extension of mothers' responsibilities and housework), the role of women in their children's education is not valued and women's education is grossly neglected.

Teachers have become increasingly alienated from their work, constrained by structures and practices that do not favour professional advancement, updating of skills, teamwork and experience-sharing. Teachers are increasingly held responsible for their students' learning achievements, but are not given the professional autonomy that goes together with such a responsibility. Over and over again they are required to accommodate to policy changes and to implement educational reforms without proper information, much less participation. Given this background—over and above the important issue of inadequate remuneration—it is not difficult to understand teachers' skepticism about "innovation" and even opposition to proposals for decentralization and community participation.

Students, meanwhile, have very limited, if any, participation in decision-making on educational matters, including the most elementary ones (e.g., schedules, uniforms, etc.). It is taken for granted that children and youth have nothing pertinent to contribute to their own education. Even strong advocates of participation in education often ignore learners as legitimate educational partners.

Social mobilization for education has often taken the form of one-shot, short-term campaigns, around a particular action or goal. While social mobilization has been given greater attention in literacy, adult education and the non-formal education spheres, less common are social mobilization efforts in the context of the regular school system and the basic learning needs of children.

Decentralization in different forms is a subject of great interest in most developing countries at present. The prevailing mood in favour of "small government" and of divesting government of inefficient public services and enterprises has influenced ideas and action in the sphere of education. In some situations, central authorities have loosened control by allowing the private sector—including commercial profit-making enterprises—to play a greater role in the provision of services. This can be a positive development when society's needs are met effectively and equitably through harnessing the capacities and resources of the private sector. But it can also lead to a dereliction of public responsibility if the consequence is increased inequity in access and participation.

Shifting responsibilities for social services including basic education to local levels has been prompted in part by the resource crunch faced by central governments. To the extent that this is a major motivation and the resource base at the local level remains meager, decentralization becomes a cover for governmental neglect of fundamental obligations to the public.

Country Experiences

If one takes a retrospective view of the past few decades, there is no doubt educational systems are moving in the direction of greater adherence to particular norms, more effective social mobilization and increased decentralization of authority and responsibility. However, much still needs to be done to bridge the gap between theory and practice, rhetoric and action and where we are and where we want to be. For too many children do not have access to schooling or non-formal education for too many enroll only to drop out soon thereafter due to the incapacity of educational systems to offer learning that is relevant to the conditions of poor rural and penurban communities.

Participation as a political norm

Most developing countries, including the meagre population countries, recognize the importance of participatory norms and values. However, participation as a democratic value and a principle of organizing the institutions of society, including basic education services, is difficult to practice. As UNDP's Human Development Report 1993 put it, "Participation is a plant that does not grow easily in the human environment" (p. 28). The road is long and paved with difficulties, full of ups and downs and not without unexpected outcomes. Obstacles are numerous, including rigid legal systems, bureaucratic institutions and attitudes, outmoded social values and cultural norms, entrenched political interests and above all, inequity in the distribution of wealth and power. The starting point has to be the nurturing of a participatory culture and of participatory structures in a sustained participation-building process. Progress in developing the participatory culture, norms and practices, which cannot be applied in the sphere of education alone or in an isolated way, has been uneven among the nine countries. The urgent need to persist in this effort is clear in all of them.

Participation as access

Participation in terms of access to educational opportunities (including continuation until completion of basic schooling) is more specific, quantifiable and easier to assess. Several of the nine countries have been successful enough in expanding access and continuation in primary education to come close to the universalization target. A political priority supportive of universal access to basic education and the development of participatory structures allowing communities to be actively involved in the education of children have been important factors in this success. The community's involvement takes different forms in different societies, but effective participation always implies both enhancing the resources for education and taking part in defining and guiding the programme at the community level.

How Communities may Participate in Basic Education

* Parents and family members working with teachers to help and guide children;
* Community organisations encouraging all potential learners to participate in learning activities;
* Community organisations looking after upkeep of educational facilities and their contribution to establishing or adding to such facilities;
* Community organisations ensuring that schools function, teachers attend to classes, students do not play truant and so on;
* Helping identify people in the community to take up part-time teaching assignments in non-formal centres and encouraging them to perform better;

* Helping define learning needs in relation to developmental needs and prospects of the locality and make learning activities connect better with other development activities; and
* Helping different learning activities work in a mutually supportive way, responding to total learning needs of the community.

(M. Ahmed *et al.*, *Basic Education and National Development : Lessons from China and India*, pp. 127-128).

Social Mobilization Lessons : Attention to social and human development goals in the 1980s in the developing countries, including the nine populous countries, has generated useful lessons for social mobilization. The importance of the underpinning of participatory culture and values and strengthening of participatory social organisations for effective social mobilization has already been noted.

Five conditions stand out as critical in successful, large-scale social mobilization efforts in such areas as universal child immunization, adoption of new farming practices and literacy campaigns :

* Objectives and targets reflect important needs of society, are defined in clear and precise terms and are widely understood and accepted;
* Political goals and ideology are supportive of social mobilization and the ideological and political priority is forcefully and unambiguously expressed by national leaders;
* The programme supported by social mobilization is lifted out of the bureaucratic sectoral confines and implemented as a national endeavour with the contribution and involvement of all who are in a position to become involved;
* Emulation and competition within the country and among countries are encouraged with models and examples serving as the source of motivation for greater effort as well as useful practical lessons; and
* A systematic process of monitoring with a few well chosen indicators reported, reviewed and given wide publicity serves to keep public interest alive and maintain the momentum of the programme;

The Social Mobilizers : In the context of primary and basic education, of special significance are the roles of children, women, teachers and parents.

"The individual learners themselves constitute a vital human resource that needs to be mobilized" (WCEFA, 1990, p. 11). Students are obviously the key actors and partners in the educational process. Experience all over the world in such fields as adult literacy, health and environment has shown that youth are a resource that is all too often neglected and underutilized. Young people are not only open to new ideas and change, but are also enthusiastic and committed innovators when provided the right conditions and support. Youth can help revitalize and renovate education and revitalize themselves by getting involved in a socially relevant task (Torres, 1985, 1991).

Given the opportunity, children have proven to be good communicators and social mobilizers. Children are not only able to teach their families and neighbours what they learn in school, but they can help change parental and community perceptions and attitudes towards education. "Child-to-child" projects in various countries are living examples of children's active involvement in promoting health, education and children's rights (Hawes and Scotchman, 1993).

Empirical evidence and evaluation of programmes confirm that, despite cultural and economic barriers, girls and women all over the world are not only eager to learn but they do the most with what they learn. Women constitute the majority of learners in most adult literacy programmes, stay longer in the programmes and their learning results are often better than those of men. Women are the first and most important promoters of children's education. Mothers' expectations and attitudes towards their children's schooling are an important determinant of success or failure in children's performance. Women are effective programme organizers and implementers, are dominant in the ranks of primary teachers in many countries and have assumed key educational roles as both early childhood and adult educators. Employment of women teachers have been found to be a critical factor in overcoming gender disparity in primary and basic education programmes.

Despite all the remarkable progress that has been made in information and communication technology teachers obviously cannot be replaced as the main contact point of basic education programmes with their learners. Decentralization of authority and community ownership of primary education go hand-in-hand with teachers' and schools' responsiveness to the needs of learners and the community. This means, on the one hand, a less bureaucratic and hierachical administrative system with greater authority at the community level with the school made accountable to the community and on the other hand, a greater autonomy of individual institutions with teachers and headmasters being able to interact with the community. Teachers' unions and associations are legitimate partners in planning and implementing educational reforms. The antipathy sometimes demonstrated by professional organisations of teachers to community control of education would soften if the teachers' professional leadership was perceived as being linked to community accountability.

It is only reasonable that parents should be the most interested party among all those who are concerned with the education of children. Parents' and teacher-parents' associations are beginning to be seen as important beyond the material and financial contribution they may make. Parental and community involvement in the development of curriculum, an important new initiative in the formal school tradition, has been incorporated into the educational laws of Indonesia and is evolving less formally in several other countries. Parents' schools for orienting and preparing parents for their role in the school's affairs and in guiding their children's education is a feature of Chinese primary education.

Not all answers in decentralization : Various forms of decentralization, deconcentration, delegation and devolution of authority and functions—have been introduced or are being debated in most developing countries. Greater success in universalization of primary education and expansion of basic education opportunities in the nine high-population countries correlate with a higher degree of effective decentralization in planning, management and control of resources in educational programmes. At the same time, these countries also illustrate the problems and dilemmas that decentralization often generates. These shortcomings can defeat the very educational principles and social objectives that decentralization is expected to serve unless the practice of decentralization is adapted to specific circumstances and complemented by necessary countervailing measures.

For example, decentralised elaboration of curricula and production of instructional materials do not necessarily lead to relevance, flexibility and adaptation to the learners' and communities' needs. Without the required technical capacity and social sensitivity, locally designed curricula and textbooks may be even more rigid and prescriptive than those produced centrally. They may also be weak pedagogically and lack creativity.

Often, "decentralization" in practice consists of giving local governing units new responsibilities but little real authority, as observed in a study conducted in three Sub-Saharan African countries—Ghana, Ivory Coast and Nigeria—(*The Forum*, 1993). Analysis of four Latin American countries—Argentina, Chile, Colombia and Mexico—conclude that decentralization did not increase resources for education, that it was not an important factor in enrolment and internal efficiency and that the quality of education did not improve (Hevia, 1991; Prawda, 1993). In the specific case of Chile, the quality of education even deteriorated during—and partly as a result of—decentralization (Nunez, 1992; Lagos, 1993).

There is general agreement that decentralization (and more so privatization) may result in greater social inequities and regional imbalances. Growing economic and financial constraints have reinforced the trend of depending on local communities for financial resources for education. However, while community financial or labour contribution may encourage parents' interest in their children's education, empirical evidence also shows that community finance may have negative effects on equity, quality and social cohesion. Community schools often serve as instruments of social stratification and community finance may exacerbate inter-regional and intraregional disparities. The cases of China and Zimbabwe, while generally presented as overall positive examples, are also illustrative of such contradictory results. (Ahmed, *et al.*, 1991; Cheng, 1993; Chung, 1993).

In summing up, it can be said that centralization is neither the sole culprit for all the problems that educational systems face today, nor is decentralization the panacea that will solve all of them. On balance, the trend of decentralization has to be supported and encouraged; it has to be carried to communities and villages from the provincial and district levels and has to include real transfer of authority and meaningful decision-making so that people can actively participate and be involved. However, decentralization has to be implemented with sensitivity and countervailing measures are needed to compensate for unintended negative consequences.

Some Lessons on Decentralization and Participation

* Major decentralization with greatly enhanced local responsibility and popular involvement is crucial for creating a conducive environment for solving key problems of basic education;
* A political choice has to be made to adopt decentralization and devolution of authority as a key strategy for giving national development efforts a human development focus;

* Legislative measures will help establish structures of effective decentralization and participation, such as village education committees with statutory functions;
* A multi-level system of technical support is needed for capacity-building at local and sub-national levels;
* A competent cadre of basic education planners and managers at the local and regional/sub-national levels has to be built up; the total neglect of this critical need has to be remedied urgently.
* Voluntary organizations, social activists and the higher levels of the government have to serve as countervailing forces to entrenched local structures of domination and exploitation; and
* A norm of partnership between local government, voluntary organizations and the private sector has to be developed to meet the diverse basic learning needs of the entire community;

(M. Ahmed, *et al.*, *Basic Education and National Development : Lessons from China and India*, pp. 13-15).

9.4. FULFILLING THE POTENTIAL : WHAT SHOULD BE DONE

A substantial body of experience and knowledge has emerged on how the three related concepts of people's participation, social mobilization and decentralization of organizations and functions can be put to work to promote universal basic education. People, government and national leaders are readier than ever for decisive action. Fulfilling the potential that now exists requires building and acting on experience and major lessons that have accumulated, including :

1. A clearly articulated goal and vision : A clear definition of goals with time-bound objectives and programmes that people can understand and relate to will facilitate effective participation and social mobilization. For countries in which a large proportion of children are deprived of primary education, primary education for all children within the shortest possible time has to be the rallying cry for participation and mobilization. The internationally adopted target of access to primary education in a formal or an equivalent programme for all children by the year 2000, with at least 80 per cent of them completing the primary stage, provides an easily and widely understood focus for advocacy, participation, mobilization, programme planning and monitoring. Major strategies or sub-goals such as reducing gender disparity and preventing large-scale drop-outs would then fit under the over-arching goals. The children who should complete primary education by the year 2000 must enroll in school in the next two to three years. The class of 2000, consisting of all current primary entry-age children, deserves everything their societies can give them to ensure a successful outcome for them by the year 2000. Providing them with the support they need to stay in school and learn what they need to learn should become the pivot of a nationwide mobilization effort in each country.

2. High profile and frequent monitoring : An education programme of universal scope that aims to reach large numbers—all primary school age children in the case of primary education—within a specific time-table must develop an effective method of monitoring progress. A system of monitoring that includes a few clearly defined indicators; that reports results frequently, regularly and publicly; that is undertaken at national, regional and local levels; and that leads to quick remedial action when problems are detected, is an unmistakable signal of commitment and seriousness. Monitoring can be a powerful tool for promoting popular participation and social mobilization. National leaders at the highest level can use the monitoring system as an effective instrument for mobilization and action by personally leading public reviews of progress, deciding on necessary course-corrections and encouraging officials down the line to do the same.

3. Visibility on the national agenda : If the whole of society is expected to participate in and mobilize around universal primary education, it must be brought to the centre of national attention. In order for this to happen, it must be shown how primary education provides benefits across the board in major areas of societal concern, such as better health, labour productivity, greater democratic participation, enhanced competitiveness in the global market, protection of the environment and slowing of population growth. Obviously, the message is not that expansion of primary education will solve all these problems; it is that primary education is the linchpin of the nation's effort and of each individual's contribution to addressing these critical national concerns. National leaders have to take the lead in this nationwide dialogue and recruit opinion leaders in all sectors of society to the cause. The aim is to build public awareness and understanding leading to support and involvement of the whole society.

4. Building a national consensus : Participation and mobilization on an enduring basis can be promoted only on the foundation of a national consensus on the major goals and priorities and the main strategies for achieving them. Reaching a consensus on as critical and sensitive subject as education is difficult and it is not reached once and forever. Consensus-building is an ongoing process that needs to be nurtured. The national leaders, especially the government leaders in the ruling political parties, have a special responsibility to initiate and support open dialogue on key issues of policies and strategies and to ensure that the consensus on basic goals and strategies are non-partisan enough to survive changes of government and personalities in high places.

5. *Identifying, emulating and creating success stories* : Nothing succeeds better than success. The problems and constraints of universal primary education are largely known; so are the elements of the solution. It is essential to identify promising examples of success, creative and innovative combinations of action that have helped to move the system out of a rut and accelerate progress. These models have to be used for emulation and motivation and as sources of useful practical lessons both within a country and among countries. All of the nine countries and others as well have many examples of success which need to be studied and adapted for wider application.

6. *Decentralization based on shared responsibilities* : Decentralization of responsibility and functions must be introduced and implemented in such a way that it is not seen as an excuse for abdicating the state's responsibility for basic education or as a means of shifting the burden from the central authorities to the local level. Decentralization works when it is a means of redistributing functions and authority among different levels of government and of the civil society in order to make systems more efficient and democratic, allowing people to participate and contribute. The role of central organs of the state and national leadership in defining national purposes and priorities, setting national standards, compensating for disparities, creating conditions for local levels to function and maintaining a national overview is and will continue to be vital for the success of decentralization efforts. At the same time, a system of planning, management, monitoring and community mobilization has to function effectively at each local administrative unit in order to achieve genuine participation in education in each community and household.

7. Building on existing institutions and practices : The starting point for promoting popular participation, social mobilization and decentralization has to be the existing institutions, practices and norms in each society. Local government in one form or another has always existed. There are traditional structures for community efforts. Religious,

cultural, labour, professional and other types of organizations and collective entities exist. It is important to identify the potential and weaknesses of these institutions and practices, build on the strengths and find ways of overcoming the weaknesses so that they all can contribute at the local and national levels.

8. Effective use of the power of modern communication : Recent advances in information and communication technology have brought virtually every citizen within the effective reach of modern communication. Yet the potential of the communication media for expanding people's access to educational opportunities and for mobilizing people's support for and involvement in education is far from being fully exploited. Mass media cannot substitute for effective organization and leadership; but the possibility now exists for use of the media for interactive communication so that the vision of the leaders is widely shared and people's voices are expressed leading to a collective sense of mission and direction.

The last decade of the 20th century offers a rare window of opportunity for accelerating social progress and Education for All occupies a critical place on the world's agenda for priority action. Let us not allow this opportunity to slip through our fingers.

10

Report of the Expert Group on National Literacy Mission (1993-94)

Introduction

The Ministry of Human Resource Development constituted in 1993, a 6-member Expert Group consisting of the following Members to undertake a Status-cum-Impact Evaluation of Literacy Campaigns as a mid-term assessment of the National Literacy Mission which was launched in 1988.

1. Prof. Arun Ghosh, Ex-Member, Planning Commission.
2. Prof. Vina Mazumdar, Centre for Women's Development Studies.
3. Prof. Andre Beteille, Professor of Sociology, Delhi School of Economics.
4. Prof. U.R. Ananthamurty, President, Sahitya Akademi.
5. Prof. S.M. Kansal, Indian Statistical Institute, New Delhi.
6. Shri Achin Vanaik, Fellow, Nehru Memorial Museum and Library.

The report submitted in 1994 touched upon the importance of mass involvement and strong political commitment to make a success of NLM. It has been suggested by them that primers for teaching be reassessed and all materials that send negative messages to learners be removed. As far as evaluation is concerned, they think it is more important and practical to have high success rate than "total literacy". Apart from these, the Committee has dwelled at length on one major problem that today confronts the literacy campaign—Post-literacy/Continuing Education.

Literacy Mission, November-December 1994.

Major Recommendations on Literacy Campaigns

General

The Group has made recommendations on decentralisation of procedure for pre-appraisal and sanction of projects, constitution of state level core groups to guide, monitor and assess projects and also to recommend to the Central Government for release of grants, on the need to further improve the primers specially with regard to their content reflecting on the status/image of women and to ensure that the content does not lower the self esteem of the learners and made some special recommendation on implementation of the campaigns in the major Hindi-speaking States.

According to the Group, a strong political commitment to the cause of literacy, existence at the State and district level of a strong core group fully committed to the Literacy Campaign, village level mass involvement/popular enthusiasm, adequate pre-launch preparations and an atmosphere of a popular movement are the minimum pre-conditions of a Literacy Campaign. The Group, therefore, recommended as follows :

* *A State level core group of 4-5 persons* including some from outside the Government known for their full commitment to literacy campaigns must be constituted. This group *should provide an adequate framework for preparation/monitoring at the State level before District level Literacy Campaigns are launched.*
* There should be orientation courses for *Collectors and senior administrators* not only relating to the *nitty gritty of the programme but also on the conceptual aspects* of a literacy campaign.
* The present system of sanctioning literacy campaigns at the Centre should be replaced by the following procedure : On the basis of a preliminary proposal for Literacy Campaign in a district for environment building and preparatory activities some funds should be released for such activities. At the end of this phase, the State level core group should assess the adequacy of preparation for launching the teaching learning phase and they should recommend further release of grants by the Centre.
* *The Group has welcomed the NLM strategy of sanctioning a PLC when 25% of the learners or 50,000 learners, whichever is less, have completed primer-II.* The Group has recommended that *the concept of "total literacy" at 80% level of success be given up.* The target approach of achieving "total literacy" should be given

up and the objective should be to seek to achieve high success rates rather than "total literacy". *A success rate of 55-60% among identified non-literates should be considered to be a good success rate.*

* The resources should be utilised to make the 9-45 age group literate rather than higher age groups. There should be a graded range of learning outcomes such as outstanding, excellent, very good, good, mediocre and poor.
* There should be a second cycle of literacy campaign in low *literacy/difficult areas after another round of motivational campaigns* so as to reinforce the achievement of the first cycle of the literacy campaigns and also achieve substantial results.

Primers for Teaching/Learning

* The NLM in collaboration with SRCs should organise *reassessment of the content of primers to remove materials* which patronise learners and send messages that lower the self-esteem and those which have a general bias against women. The ZSSs will have to play a sensitive monitoring role in this.

Hindi-Speaking States

* Regarding the Hindi belt the Group has recommended that attention should be given to *ensure political commitment* particularly to Universal Primary Education and eradication of illiteracy;
* Stability of administration including *stability of tenure of Collectors has to be ensured in these States*; and
* Adequacy of preparation in districts in these States should include the following :

  (a) *Each village should have an identified activist as a key-organiser* who would have already distinguished himself/herself in the early part of the environment building phase; and

  (b) In States with low political commitment, *there is need to ensure such full timers* who would be available for the duration of the Literacy Campaigns and great care should be taken to *select only those with proven dedication and commitment;*

* It should be ensured that the *basic education projects in these States are coordinated with the Literacy Campaign projects.*

* Particular attention should be paid to integrate literacy and development even during the course of Literacy Campaigns in these States. *At least one government development scheme should be coordinated with the introduction of a full Literacy Campaign project*; and
* Programmes and resources of the government should be pooled right from the Literacy Campaign stage. This will ensure *linking of socio-economic development programmes with the literacy campaigns.*

Recommendations on Post Literacy Measures

The Group has suggested a framework for post literacy and continuing education programmes. They have specifically mentioned that carrying out successful PL/CE remains the single most difficult problem confronting the NLM and the whole of the literacy programme. Following recommendations have been made :

* The Group holds a strong view that *PL/CE should not be attempted in the 'campaign mode'*. New forms of institutionali-sation, new agencies of organisation, new attitudes towards the PL/CE phase fundamentally different from the literacy campaign phase are required;
* At least *one PL/CE centre per village* or even per Tola or for a cluster of Tolas is essential. The current policy of one JSN per 5,000 learners which tends to serve a cluster of villages has not been recommended;
* The literacy campaign and the PL/CE phases must be integrated and should be one continuum;
* Organisational control of the PL/CE should be different from the structure in the literacy campaign phase. *Mahila Mandals,* women members of Panchayats and staff of primary and secondary schools should play a more prominent role than the traditional village hierarchy in controlling PL/CE activity. Since the literacy campaign and PL/CE are to be integrated, the organisational structure for running the PL/CE must emerge and operate alongside the organisational structure for running the literacy campaign;
* To begin with, the *PL/CE centre could become an 'information window'* in the village. Information about various schemes e.g., for education, for training, for services rendered by different

cadres of functionaries is seldom available at the district level and hardly at the village level. Pooling and dissemination of such information is critical for both neo-literates and planners to widen their own choices, vision and courage for innovation, as well as for making literacy as a means of enhancing 'access' and 'capability'.

* The Group has strongly recommended that access to knowledge about *basic laws and legal procedures* should be an essential component of PL/CE. A great deal of experience and material already exists as a result of the activities of the Committee for Implementation of Legal Aid Schemes (CILAS) in 80's. The Committee has recommended simplified literature to be produced as in the case of literature for development schemes.
* The *library is critical* for the success/expansion of PL/CE activities. Support in the acquisition of material and a full time paid Prerak/librarian and caretaker for such PL/CE centres has been suggested. Necessary training for PL/CE librarians on a group basis could be arranged at the block/district levels.
* On the whole there should be a *structured and* an *unstructured part* of PL/CE. There should be both mopping up operation and an element of continuing education. The *structured part* of PL/CE *should be* the function of *information window* for all government/non-governmental programmes, legal literacy etc. The unstructured part of the programme should be left to each local community to fill in. Resource mapping may be first introduced in few areas and extended to become a part of the structured part of every PL/CE programme. This should be in the shape of "information system" and a motivating factor for education.

Monitoring and Evaluation of Campaigns

The Group has broadly endorsed the need for and utility of bringing out Status Reports on a regular basis at the national level as is being done now. These reports are, however, based on internal information being provided by the campaigns. Therefore, there is need to considerably tighten up the system and current practice of external evaluation about which strong reservations have been expressed. It has been emphasised that *proper internal evaluation is a must* in every case which *should be corroborated/validated by external evaluations.*

Approach to Evaluation

The approach to evaluation should be a participatory approach involving participants in programme implementation and should be non-threatening in nature. In this context, it has been recommended that *the concept of "total literacy" may be abandoned* so that a target centred approach does not lead to undesirable pressures leading to manipulation of figures. The Group has specifically mentioned that *increasing the literacy rate in a district from 15% to 50% would be deemed to be quite credit-worthy as compared to a progression from 50% to 85%.* This is so because the size of the literate population providing volunteers in the former case is much less than in the latter.

Design for External Evaluation

This has been suggested based on the basic principle to ensure that every member of the target population gets an equal chance of being included in the sample and also special groups of learners belonging to SCs, STs, minority community, other backward castes etc., get a fair representation. It is important to cover varying social demographic and regional characteristics of the district and different organisational features of the campaign.

Internal evaluation should be conducted for all learners on 100% basis and should conform, as closely as possible, to the standards set for external evaluation. This would also help to provide baseline information to chalk out all PL/CE strategies and activities. The internal evaluation data should be properly stored at appropriate levels.

Impact evaluation studies should be conducted after 1-2 years of the literacy campaign adopting a 'household survey' approach by selected social science institutes/departments of universities.

Strengths

Among the strengths highlighted by the Expert Group are :

(i) Literacy campaigns have been more of a movement than a programme; (ii) There has been a overwhelming impact on women who constitute between two-thirds to three-fourths of adult illiterates; (iii) Inter-mixing of social strata has had a positive impact on castes and communal relations; (iv) Greater demand had been generated for primary education and a new determination to enrol girls; (v) Direct interaction between the volunteers and the poor has resulted in generation of social activists with the concern for developing a just, humane society; (vi)

TLC has helped to sensitize the bureaucracy to the concern of ordinary village fold especially those who are the most deprived; and (vii) Literacy has been placed on the national agenda and the transparency of the programme has been greater than for any other government programme.

Weaknesses

Among the weaknesses the Group has pointed out the following :

(i) Owing to pre-occupation with "Total Literacy", quality of the programme has sometimes suffered; (ii) The levels of literacy attainment are fragile posing serious problems of relapse; (iii) Because of easy availability of funds there has been a tendency to meet "politically committed" targets that is total literacy by the year 2000 leading to sanction of projects which are not prepared to take up campaigns; (iv) Bureaucratisation or 'top-down' approach leading to 'volunteer fatigue' in some cases; (v) In the Hindi belt States, especially in UP and Bihar, progress achieved has been patchy and sometimes doubtful because of the problems of large size of illiterates, small size of the pool of literates, lack of literacy, traditional/movements, low political commitment, etc.; and (vi) Poor progress in urban areas where the problems are infinitely more difficult for diverse reasons.

11

45th All-India Adult Education Conference (1994)

Introduction

The 45th All-India Adult Education Conference of the Indian Adult Education Association organised in collaboration with Rajasthan Vidyapeeth Kul began its 4-day session in Ajmer (Rajasthan) on June 15, 1994. The theme was "Total Literacy in the context of Education for All by 2000".

Over 250 delegates from 18 States and UTs attended the Conference. Most of the affiliated organisations of IAEA, State Governments, State Resource Centres, Shramik Vidyapeeths, TLC Districts and the universities of Aligarh Muslim, Amravati, Annamalai, A.P.S. (Rewa), Dr. Baba Saheb Ambedkar (Aurangabad), Bangalore, Barkatullah (Bhopal), Bharthidasan, Bhavnagar, Calicut, Gurukul Kangri (Hardwar), Jiwaji (Gwalior), Kurukshetra, Magadh, Manipur, M.S. University of Baroda, Nagpur, Rajasthan Vidyapeeth, Rani Durgabai (Jabalpur), Saurashtra, Sri Venkateswara (Tirupati), South Gujarat, Poona, Vikram (Ujjain) and Viswa Bharti deputed their representatives. Inaugurating the conference, Prof. Kanta Ahuja, Vice-Chancellor, Maharishi Dayanand Saraswati University, Ajmer said that girls were being kept out of school because their parents did not appreciate the importance and value of education. The condition of the school and the quality of education specially in the government schools in the rural areas were other bottlenecks in attracting children towards the school. She feared that unless the gender gap which was widening was reduced, the illiterates between age group 15-35 would only be women.

Prof. Kanta Ahuja emphasised the need to provide education and awareness to the adult illiterates so that they send their children specially girls to schools. India, she said, was poised towards the phase of

---

Indian Journal of Adult Education 55 (2) April-June, 1994.

accelerated growth and progress and to continue with it, it was essential that there should be consensus on education and other national issues at the political level. Literacy, education, population and environment protection were areas that need to be kept free from politics along party lines, she emphasised.

Plenary Sessions

In the first plenary session, the working paper was presented by Prof. B.B. Mohanty, Resident Director, Indian Institute of Mass Communication, Dhenkanal, Orissa.

The delegates were divided into six groups to discuss the following sub-themes of the conference :

1. Resource Mobilization
2. Creation and Sustenance of Environment for Learning
3. Training of Functionaries
4. Media Support
5. Women's Literacy
6. Post Literacy and Continuing Education.

The Chairman of the groups were Dr. M.S. Talwar, Prof. R. Krishnamoorty, Dr. S.K. Kejariwal, Prof. Nanubhai Joshi, Smt. Kamala Rana and Dr. D.P. Mukherjee.

Zakir Husain Memorial Lecture

The Zakir Husain Memorial Lecture was delivered by Dr. Chitra Naik. She said that the goals of the literacy and Education For All need to be fixed in local context and in a disaggregated manner, for their effective pursuit.

Education For All, she said, was a comprehensive concept. It covers mass literacy, universal primary education and further education facilities. Learning to handle new information, analysing it and processing it for application to work, family life and social affairs, would henceforth require not only basic literacy skills, but skills involving a well-developed cognitive process at a much higher level, she said.

Stressing the need for continuing education, she said, that young and old men and women should be liberated and empowered not merely by literacy and basic education but by a clear realization of their cultural and intellectual potential.

Shri V.S. Mathur, President of the Labour Organisation of the Rural Poor presided.

Reports of Member Organisations and TLC Districts

The representatives of member organisations of IAEA and the TLC Districts presented their reports during the plenary sessions. Over 20 reports were presented.

Role of ASPBAE and ILSS

In another plenary session Dr. Om Shrivastava, Asain Regional Coordinator, ASPBAE spoke about the role of Asian South Pacific Bureau of Adult Education (ASPBAE) for promoting adult education in the Asian and Pacific region. He said that the ASPBAE was an organisation of NGOs. But in countries where there were no NGOs, the governmental agencies were enrolled as members.

Dr. Shrivastava said that ASPBAE was focussing on five issues :

1. Literacy, post literacy and universalization of elementary education.
2. Education for empowerment of women.
3. Education for sustainable development.
4. Education for peace and human rights; and
5. Education for the workers.

He said that 120 organisations from the Asian pacific region are members of the ASPBAE. It is not a funding agency and now believes in partnership concept, he stressed. It provides learning opportunities through arranging exchange visits, workshops and training programmes. It is providing access to information through newsletters and ASPBAE Courier.

The International Literacy Support Service (ILLS) was established by the International Council for Adult Education (ICAE) during the International Literacy Year 1990. It is confining its activities at present for promotion of women's literacy.

Thematic Workshops

Three thematic workshops were also held during the conference. The following three themes were discussed :

1. Adult Education and Communal Harmony—Chairman—Prof. Yashvant Shukla;
2. Monitoring and Evaluation—Chairman—Prof. B.B. Mohanty;

3. Empowerment and Education of Women and Weaker Sections—Chairman—Prof. K.K. Vashisht.

Cultural Programmes

Two cultural programmes were organised on the 15th and 16th June. The folk dances and folk music of Rajasthan were presented.

Recommendations

1. The 45th All India Adult Education Conference on "Total Literacy in the context of Education for All by 2000" which met in Ajmer on June 15-18, 1994 welcomes the initiative and efforts made by the Government of India and the State Governments to achieve total literacy through campaign approach, but it feels that there are several issues on which greater quality is needed.
2. The Conference notes that lot of efforts are being made to create environment through the Jathas, Street Plays (Nukkad Nataks) etc., but feels that one time effort is not sufficient to sustain the interest of learners and volunteers. It recommends that with the help of local voluntary organisations environment building should be a continuous process so that the motivation of volunteers and of the learners should continue till the completion of the six months programme. It further stresses that the local talent should be utilized to create need based environment.
3. The Conference recommends that each district in the country must be analysed in terms of its strengths and weaknesses. The strengths particularly should be highlighted so as to motivate others for this programme.
4. The Conference urges that school children must be involved by assigning them projects to make atleast two illiterates literate.
5. The Conference recommends that adult education functionaries should be trained not only in imparting 3 R's but also for mobilising the community support so that literacy really becomes people's own programme.
6. For promoting communal harmony through adult education, the Conference recommends that national integration should be invariably interwoven in the training programmes of all levels of functionaries. It further recommends that relevant materials on the subject should be produced which could go a long way in promoting communal harmony in the country.
7. The Conference recommends that there is an urgent need to prepare more and more success stories through the print and the

audio visual media so that both educated and uneducated get inspiration to participate in this national endeavour.

8. The Conference feels that for achieving total literacy by the year 2000 multi-pronged approach should be adopted and not restricted to the literacy campaigns only.
9. For JSNs, the Conference feels that no general prescribed criteria be fixed for the entire country. It should be designed according to the need of the area. It recommends that Prerak in the JSN should be given a minimum honorarium of Rs. 500 so that it commensurates with his/her duties and responsibilities.
10. The Conference feels that both print and electronic media have to play a meaningful role in making it a people's movement. For achieving this the electronic media should televise at the prime time success stories so that a learning environment is created. The traditional media has an equally important role and should be effectively utilized.
11. To make literacy programme a success, the Conference feels that it should be interwoven with the rural development programmes. This integration, it feels, would be beneficial for both.
12. The Conference recommends that monitoring in the context of Total Literacy Campaigns has to be a continuous on-going process so as to provide the necessary timely correctives; and evaluation has to be less mechanistic, participatory and more humane providing continuous feed-backs for overall improvement in the programme. The Conference further recommends that monitoring and evaluation should be built into the curriculum of the various training programmes organised in the context of Total Literacy Campaigns.

12

The New AICTE Regulations (1994)*

Introduction

To monitor the technical education in the country the All India Council for Technical Education here issued the following notification on October 31, 1994, making necessary changes in its rules and regulations.

The text of the notification is being reproduced verbatim;

NOTIFICATION

No.F. 304-4/CCE/REG/94-In exercise of the powers conferred by sub-section (1) of section 23 of the All India Council of Technical Education Act, 1987 (52 of 1987), the All India Council for Technical Education hereby makes the following regulations, namely :

Short Title and Commencement

(1) These regulations may be called the All India Council for Technical Education (Grant of approval for starting new technical institutions, introduction of courses or programmes and approval of intake capacity of seats for the courses or programmes) Regulations, 1994.

(2) They shall come into force on the date of their publication in the Official Gazette.

Applicability

These regulations shall be applicable to the proposals relating to,

(a) grant of approval of the Council for establishment of new technical institutions including Universities or University Departments and deemed Universities; and for technical institutions functioning on

---

* Reproduces from *Contemporary Academician*, December 15-31, 1994, 4 (19).

the date of commencement of these regulations at a Degree and Diploma levels;

(b) grant of approval of the Council for introduction of any course of programme in the technical institutions and technical departments of Universities or deemed Universities; and

(c) grant of approval of the Council for existing intake capacity of seats and for increase in the annual intake capacity of seats in courses and programmes.

Definitions

In these regulations, unless the context otherwise requires,

(a) "Act" means the All India Council for Technical Education Act, 1987 (52 of 1987);

(b) "Bureau BOS" means the Bureau of Board of Studies of the Council;

(c) "Bureau MPCD" means the Bureau of Manpower Planning and Career Development of the Council;

(d) "Bureau RA" means the Bureau of Recognition and Accreditation of the Council;

(e) "Bureau RC" means the Bureau of the Regional Committees of the Council;

(f) "Council" means the All India Council for Technical Education established under section 3 of the Act;

(g) "Deemed University" means any institution of higher education other than a University, declared as such under section 3 of the University Grants Commission Act, 1956 (3 of 1956);

(h) "Form" means a form appended to these regulations;

(i) "Regional Office" means the Regional office functioning as the secretariat of the Regional Committee of the Council;

(j) "University Technical Department" means the Department of the concerned University conducting 'Technical Education' courses or programmes;"

(k) All other words and expressions used herein and not defined but defined in the All India Council for Technical Education Act, 1987 (52 of 1987), shall have the meanings respectively assigned to them in the said Act.

Requirement of Grant of Approval

(1) After the commencement of these regulations,

a) no new technical institution or University Technical Department, shall be started; or

b) no course or programme shall be introduced by any technical institution, University including a deemed University or University Department or College; or programmes; and

d) no approved intake capacity of seats shall be increased or varied; except with the approval of the Council.

(2) Applications for grant of approval under sub-regulation (1) hall be made by any of the following, namely :

(i) Government institutions, Government aided institutions, deemed Universities and University Departments or Colleges; and

(ii) Registered Societies/Trusts in respect of professional colleges.

Forms for Applications

1) Every application for starting a technical institution, or for approval of institutions functioning on the date of commencement of these egulations or for introducing courses or programmes, or for increase n the intake capacity of seats in the courses shall be made in the form pecified in sub-regulation (2) and shall be accompanied by the documents called for therein.

(2) (a) An application for starting technical institution shall be in Form I.

(b) An application for approval of Degree level institution functioning on the date of commencement of these regulations shall be made in Form II.

(c) An application for approval of diploma level institution functioning on the date of commencement of these regulations shall be made in Form III.

(d) An application for introduction of additional courses or increase in the intake of seats in the degree level institution shall be made in Form IV.

(e) An application for introduction of additional courses or increase in the intake of seats in the diploma level institution shall be made in Form V.

Conditions for Grant of Approval

Every application under sub-regulation (1) of regulation 4 shall be considered subject of the fulfilment of the following conditions, namely, :

(i) The financial position of the applicant shall be sound for investment in developed land and in providing related infrastructural and instructional facilities as per the norms and standards laid down by he Council from time to time and for meeting the annual recurring expenditure;

(ii) the courses or programmes shall be conducted as per the assessed technical manpower demands;

(iii) the admissions shall be made according to the regulations and directions of the Council for such admissions in the respective technical institution or university;

(iv) the tuition and other fees shall be charged within the overall criteria as may be laid down by the Council;

(v) the staff shall be recruited as per the norms and standards specified by the Council from time to time;

(vi) the Governing Body in case of private technical institutions shall be as per the norms as specified by the Council;

(vii) any other conditions as may be specified by the Council from time to time.

Submission of Application

(1) Every application for approval of the Council shall be submitted with six spare copies of the same, complete in all respects, by 31st December in respect of the institutions or courses or programmes proposed to commence in the subsequent academic year.

(2) Every application for approval from the Government institutions and Government aided institutions shall be sent by the State Government concerned to the Bureau RC, alongwith the consent of affiliation by the University/State Board.

(3) Every application pertaining to a University, University Department or deemed University shall be submitted through the University Grants Commission.

(4) Every application from a registered Society or Trust for approval of intake capacity of seats shall be submitted to the Bureau RC and also simultaneously to the concerned State Government, the University or the State Board of Technical Education, whichever applicable and the Regional Office concerned by the Society or Trust, as the case may be.

Scrutiny of Applications

(1) The Bureau RC shall make a preliminary scrutiny of every application received by it.

(2) If the Bureau RC finds any application incomplete in any respect, it shall return the same, within fifteen days of its receipt, to the applicant specifying the defects.

(3) The application which has been found by the Bureau RC as complete in all respects shall be processed in the manner specified in these regulations.

(4) The Bureau RC shall invite comments/recommendations on the applications referred to in sub-regulation (3) from the following namely :

(i) the State Government concerned;
(ii) the affiliating University/State Board of Technical Education
(iii) Bureaus MPCD,
(iv) Bureau BOS,
(v) Bureau RA,
(vi) the Regional Office.

(5) The Regional Office shall arrange visit of an Expert Committee, constituted by the Council under sub-regulation, (2) of regulation 9, and forward the recommendations of the Regional Committee to the Council's Office ordinarily within a period of two months or such other period as may be granted by the Council.

(6) The State level Committee constituted under sub-regulation (4) of regulation 9 shall consider the recommendations of the State Government and others mentioned in sub-regulation (4) and shall make its recommendations to the Central Task Force.

(7) The Central Task Force constituted under sub-regulation (5) of regulation 9 shall consider the recommendations of the State level Committee and send its recommendations to the Member-Secretary of the Council.

(8) If there is a disagreement in the recommendations made by the State Government, University or the Regional Committee, the Central Task Force shall invite representatives of the respective agencies for further consultations before making final recommendation;

(9) On the recommendation of the Central Task Force, the Council shall decide the question of grant of approval as sought for in the application; Provided that the Council may, for reasons to be communicated to the applicant, allow the approval with such restrictions or modifications as it may deem necessary;

(10) The decision of the Council shall be communicated to the State Government concerned or the University Grants Commission, as

the case may be, the University or the State Board concerned, the Regional Office concerned and the applicant by 30th April in case the application was made before the preceding 31st December.

(11) If the Council has rejected an application the reasons for such rejection shall be communicated to the applicant.

(12) The rejection of an application shall not disentile an applicant to make fresh application for any subsequent academic year.

(13) The Council shall, in every year, before 31st December publish the names of approved technical institutions, University Departments or Deemed Universities conducting courses in technical education, the courses and programmes approved by the Council and the number of seats permitted (annual intake capacity) for each course or programme and communicate relevant extracts of the same communicated to the competent authorities in the month of December.

(14) The time schedule and sequences of processing applications for approved proposals shall be as given in the Schedule appended to these regulations.

Provided that the Council may, for good and sufficient reasons to be recorded in writing modify the time schedule in respect of any class or category of applications.

Committees

(1) For processing of applications under these regulations, the Council shall constitute the following Committees, namely :

(a) Expert Committee;
(b) State level Committee;
(c) Central Task Force.

(2) An Expert Committee which shall be constituted by the Council in consultation with the Chairman of the Regional Committee, shall consist of a representative of the concerned State Government, the Regional Officer or his nominee, a nominee of the University or Board concerned and Expert members.

(3) Notwithstanding anything contained in sub-regulation (2) in urgent or special circumstances, Chairman of the Council shall appoint an Expert Committee with an officer of the Council as Member-Secretary to consider any specific class or category of application.

(4) A state level Committee shall consist of the Chairman of the concerned Regional Committee, Secretary of the State Government concerned dealing with technical education and Director of Technical

Education of the state government concerned, two vice-chancellors, one Director of an Indian Institute of Technology, one member for the Executive Committee, nominee of the University Grants Commission and expert members from academic institutions and industry nominated by the Chairman of the Council, Adviser (BOS), Adviser (MPCD), Adviser (RA) and Adviser (RC), Regional Officer, Chief NTMIS Project, representative of MHRD.

Technical Bureau and any other member nominated by the Chairman of the Council. The State level Committee shall be chaired by an eminent educationist/industrialist nominated by the Chairman of the Council and Adviser of the Council shall be nominated as Member-Secretary of the State level Committee by the Council.

(5) Central Task Force—The Central Task Force shall consist of two members of the Executive Committee of the Council, an Educational Planner/Administrator, two expert members, one member from judiciary. The Central Task Force shall be chaired by the member of the Executive Committee nominated by the Chairman of Council and Adviser of the Council shall be nominated as Member-Secretary of the Central Task Forces by the Council. The expert members shall be nominated, provided they are not members of the State level Committee.

(6) Notwithstanding anything contained in these regulations, the Council may invite any person to be associated with any of the above Committees.

Interpretation

(1) If any question arises as to the interpretation of these regulations, the same shall be decided by the Council.

(2) The Council shall have the power to issue clarification to remove any doubt which may arise in regard to implementation of these regulations.

Power to relax

The Council may, for removal of any hardship or such other reasons to be recorded in writing, relax any of the provisions of these regulations in respect of any class or category of institutions.

Withdrawal of approval

If any technical institution including University, University Department or Deemed University or College contravenes any of the provisions of

these regulations, the Council may, after making such inquiry as it may consider appropriate and after giving the technical institution concerned an opportunity of being heard, withdraw the approval granted under these regulations.

Y.N.Chaturvedi
Member-Secretary
31 October, 1994
New Delhi

PART-THREE

EDUCATIONAL STATISTICS

13

Educational Statistics (1993-94)

13.1 ALL INDIA : GENERAL EDUCATION

1.Expansion of Educational Facilities

TABLE 13. 1 : Growth of Recognised Educational Institutions since 1951

Year	Primary Schools	Upper Primary Schools	High/Hr. Sec. Schools Inter/ Pre-Degree Jr. Colleges	Colleges for Gen. Edn.	Colleges for Prof. Edn.	Universities
1950-51	209671	13596	7416	370	208	27
1955-56	278135	21730	10838	466	218	31
1960-61	330399	49663	17329	967	852	45
1965-66	391064	75798	27614	1536	770	64
1970-71	408378	90621	37051	2285	992	82
1975-76	454270	106571	43054	3667	3276**	101
1980-81	494503	118555	51573	3421	3542**	110
1985-86	528872	134846	65837	4067	1533**	126
1990-91	560935	151456	79796	4862	886	184@
1991-92*	565786	152077	81747	5058	950	196@
1992-93*	572541	153921	84086	5334	989	207@
1993-94*	572923	155707	88411	5639	1125	213@

* Provisional

** Includes Institutions for Post-Matric Courses.

@ Includes Deemed to be Universities and Institutions of National Importance.

TABLE 13.2 : Comparative position of selected type of institutionsduring 1992-93 and 1993-94.

Type of Institutions	Number of Institutions 1992-93	1993-94
(a) Pre-Primary Schools	13662	17172
(b) Primary Schools	572541	572923
(c) Middle Schools	153921	155707
(d) High Schools	62984	65255
(e) Hr. Sec. Schools (New Pattern)	18880	20167

(Contd.)

TABLE 13.2 *(Contd.)*

Type of Institutions	Number of Institutions 1992-93	1993-94
(f) Inter/Jr./Pre Degree Colleges	2222	2989
(g) Arts. Sci. and Com. Colleges	5334	5639
(h) Engg./Tech. Colleges (Degree and above Level)	299	308
(i) Medical Colleges (Allopathy/Ayurvedic)	@ 133	233
(j) Teacher Training Colleges	557	584
(k) Polytechnics	1040	1021
(l) Universities*	207	213

* Includes Deemed to be Universities and Institutions of National Importance.

@ Excludes Ayurvedic Colleges.

Enrolment

Statement given below presents the progress of sex-wise enrolment figures for different stages of school education from 1950-51 to 1993-94:

TABLE 13.3 : Sex-wise Enrolment by Stages/Classes since 1951 - school level

(in millions)

Year	Primary			Middle/UpperPrimary			High/Hr. Sec.		
	Boys	Girls	Total	Boys	Girls	Total	Boys	Girls	Total
1950-51	13.8	5.4	19.2	2.6	0.5	3.1	1.3	0.2	1.5
1955-56	17.1	7.5	24.6	3.8	1.0	4.8	2.2	0.4	2.6
1960-61	23.6	11.4	35.0	5.1	1.6	6.7	2.7	0.7	3.4
1965-66	32.2	18.3	50.5	7.7	2.8	10.5	4.4	1.3	5.7
1970-71	35.7	21.3	57.0	9.4	3.9	13.3	5.7	1.9	7.6
1975-76	40.6	25.0	65.6	11.0	5.0	16.0	6.5	2.4	8.9
1980-81	45.3	28.5	73.8	13.9	6.8	20.7	7.6	3.4	11.0
1985-86	52.2	35.2	87.4	17.7	9.6	27.3	11.5	5.0	16.5
1990-91	57.0	40.4	97.4	21.5	12.5	34.0	12.8	6.3	19.1
1991-92*	59.2	42.4	101.6	21.4	13.0	34.4	14.2	7.0	21.2
1992-93*	60.5	44.9	105.4	23.7	15.0	38.7	15.0	7.7	22.7
1993-94*	61.8	46.4	108.2	24.2	15.7	39.9	15.3	8.0	23.3

* Provisional

The Participation of girls at all stages of education has been increasing steadilty over the time as may be seen from Table13.4. However, the percentages are still much below fifty per cent at all stages of education.

TABLE 13.4 : Girls Enrolment by Stages

(% to total enrolment)

Year	Primary I-V	Middle VI-VIII	Sec./Hr. Sec 10+2/Inter	Hr. Education (Degree and above level)
1950-51	28.1	16.1	13.3	10.0
1955-56	30.5	20.8	15.4	14.6
1960-61	32.6	23.9	20.5	16.0
1965-66	36.2	26.7	22.0	20.4
1970-71	37.4	29.3	25.0	20.0
1975-76	38.1	31.3	26.9	23.2
1980-81	38.6	32.9	29.6	26.7
1985-86	40.3	35.6	30.3	33.0
1990-91	41.5	36.7	32.9	33.3
1991-92*	41.7	37.8	33.0	32.3
1992-93*	42.6	38.8	33.9	33.2
1993-94*	42.9	39.3	34.3	33.5

* Provisional.

N.B. Some discrepancies have been observed in the data on enrolment received from some of the States relating to by Stage and by Type of Institutions at Primary, Middle, High/High Secondary levels.

Gross Enrolment Ratios

The gross enrolment ratio is defined as the percentage ratio of the enrolment in classes I-V and VI-VIII to the estimated child population in the age groups 6-11 years and 11-14 years. Enrolment at primary stage 6-11 years include under age and overage children. Hence the total percentage may be more than 100. The gross enrolment ratios for the age-group 6-11 years and 11-14 years are presented below in the statement:

TABLE 13.5 : Gross Enrolment Ratios

BOYS

Years	I-V Primary	VI-VIII Upper Primary	I-VIII Elementary
1950-51	60.6	20.6	46.4
1960-61	82.6	33.2	65.2
1970-71	95.5	46.5	75.5
1980-81	95.8	54.3	82.0
1990-91	114.0	76.6	100.0
1991-92	116.6	74.2	101.2
1992-93	118.1	80.5	104.2
1993-94	115.3	79.3	102.3

(Contd.)

TABLE 13.5 *(Contd.)*

GIRLS

Years	I-V Primary	VI-VIII Upper Primary	I-VIII Elementary
1950-51	24.8	4.6	17.7
1960-61	41.4	11.3	30.9
1970-71	60.5	20.8	44.4
1980-81	64.1	28.6	52.1
1990-91	85.5	47.0	70.8
1991-92	88.1	47.4	73.2
1992-93	92.7	53.8	75.5
1993-94	92.9	55.2	79.3

TOTALS

Years	I-V Primary	VI-VIII Upper Primary	I-VIII Elementary
1950-51	42.6	12.7	32.1
1960-61	62.4	22.5	48.7
1970-71	78.6	33.4	61.9
1980-81	80.5	41.9	67.5
1990-91	100.1	62.1	86.0
1991-92	102.7	61.2	87.7
1992-93	105.7	67.5	91.8
1993-94	104.5	67.7	91.2

TABLE 13.6 : Dropout Rates at Primary and Middle Stages

	1960-61	1970-71	1980-81	1990-91	1991-92
Classes I-V					
Boys	61.7	64.5	56.2	42.0	41.0
Girls	70.9	70.9	62.5	47.6	45.2
Total	64.9	67.0	58.7	44.3	42.8
Classes I-VIII					
Boys	75.0	74.6	68.0	60.6	54.3
Girls	85.0	83.4	79.4	67.6	62.0
Total	78.3	77.9	72.7	63.4	57.5

Teachers

In terms of teachers, a susbtantial increase has been registered from 1950-51 to 1992-93 at all types of schools except a slight decrease in upper primary schools due to decline in their number as reported by certain states (viz. Andhra Pradesh, Bihar, Goa, Punjab, Tamil Nadu, West Bengal and U T of Pondicherry) as may be seen in the table below:

TABLE 13.7 : Distribution of Teachers by Type of Schools Since 1951

(in 000's)

Year	Primary			Upper Primary			High/Hr Sec		
	M	F	T	M	F	T	M	F	T
1950-51	456	82	538	73	13	86	107	20	127
1955-56	574	117	691	132	19	151	155	35	190
1960-61	615	127	742	262	83	345	234	62	296
1965-66	764	180	944	389	139	528	368	111	479
1970-71	835	225	1060	463	175	638	474	111	479
1975-76	965	283	1248	554	224	778	559	200	759
1980-81	1021	342	1363	598	253	851	669	257	926
1985-86	1094	402	1496	663	305	968	793	339	1132
1990-91	1143	473	1616	717	356	1073	917	417	1334
1991-92*	1194	499	1693	718	354	1072	880	430	1310
1992-93*	1189	493	1682	736	346	1082	908	445	1353
1993-94*	1196	507	1703	710	370	1080	938	467	1405

* Provisional.

TABLE 13.8 : Gross Enrolment Ratios SC/ST

Classes and age group	Scheduled Castes			Scheduled Tribes		
	Boys	Girls	Total	Boys	Girls	Total
1980-81						
I-V (6-11 years)	105.4	57.8	82.2	94.2	45.9	70.0
VI-VIII (11-14 Years)	41.4	16.2	29.1	28.2	10.8	19.5
1985-86						
I-V (6-11 Years)	116.6	73.2	95.5	113.2	68.8	91.6
VI-VIII (11-14 Years)	57.8	26.2	42.5	41.3	19.2	30.6
1990-91						
I-V (6-11 Years)	122.68	80.60	102.21	126.78	78.60	103.35
VI-VIII (11-14 Years)	61.40	33.28	47.71	51.33	27.50	39.72
1991-92						
I-V (6-11 Years)	121.4	83.6	103.0	125.6	82.6	104.7
VI-VIII (11-14 Years)	68.9	36.0	52.9	54.1	27.3	41.1
1992-93						
I-V (6-11 Years)	127.99	92.18	110.58	126.71	88.64	108.19
VI-VIII (11-14 Years)	75.07	44.04	59.97	58.54	32.04	45.64
1993-94						
I-V (6-11 Years)	123.33	91.15	107.81	123.90	88.80	106.97
VI-VIII (11-14 Years)	74.21	45.01	60.13	60.17	34.91	47.99

13.2 PLAN OUTLAYS AND EXPENDITURE

TABLE 13.9 : The Sector-wise Plan Expenditure for Sixth Plan, Seventh Plan and Outlay for Eighth Plan are indicated in the statement

(Rs. in crores)

Sector	Sixth Plan Expenditure			Seventh Plan Expenditure		
	Centre	States/UTs	Total	Centre	States/UTs	Total
1. Elementary Education	72.40	768.99	841.39	723.80	2142.07	2865.87
2. Adult Education	61.75	91.61	153.36	309.15	300.65	609.80
3. Secondary Education	16.75	517.64	534.39	558.31	1093.59	1651.90
4. Higher Education	242.82	317.58	560.40	631.46	460.13	1091.59
5. Other	92.02	164.29	256.31	198.54	250.32	448.86
6. Technical Education	135.80	137.06	272.86	615.40	349.71	965.11
Total	621.54	1997.17	2618.71	3036.66	4596.47	7633.13

Eighth Plan Outlay for Education

(Rs. in crores)

	Sector	Centre	State	Total
1.	Elementary Education	2880.00	6056.46	8936.46
2.	Adult Education	1400.00	394.44	1794.44
3.	Secondary Education	1519.00		
4.	Higher Education	700.00	3743.45	6082.45
5.	Other	120.00		
6.	Technical Education	824.00	1962.38	2786.38
	Total Education	*7443.00	12156.73	19599.73

* Excludes Outlay for Sports and Youth Services and Arts and Culture.

Expenditure on Education

TABLE 13.10 : Growth in Educational Expenditure by Centre and States (Plan and Non-Plan)

Year	Expenditure on Edn. (Rs. in crores)		Growth rate in Exp. on Edn. (%)	
	Centre	States	Centre	States
1981-82	240.74	3549.37	7.5	12.7
1982-83	302.58	4459.21	25.7	25.6
1983-84	352.73	5101.74	16.6	14.4
1984-85	445.32	5908.46	26.2	15.8
1985-86	528.51	6928.47	18.7	17.3
1986-87	648.23	7802.09	22.7	12.6
1987-88	1201.75	9228.44	85.4	18.3
1988-89	1595.51	10813.21	32.8	17.2
1989-90	1512.15	13532.14	(-)5.2	25.1
1990-91	1643.21	15550.45	8.7	14.9
1991-92	1714.06	17043.52	4.3	9.6
1992-93 (RE)	1820.82	19549.07	6.2	14.7
1993-94 (BE)	2155.96	21752.97	18.4	11.3

II. STATES

13.3. EDUCATIONAL FACILITIES IN STATES

TABLE 13.11 : Different Types of Educational Institutes in State

State/Union Territory	Univer sities*	Institutions deemed as Universities*	Institutions of National importance*	Boards of Inter/ Secondary Education	Research Institutions
1	2	3	4	5	6
Andhra Pradesh	14	3	0	1	0
Arunachal Pradesh	1	0	0	0	0
Assam	5	0	0	2	0
Bihar	16	2	0	2	4
Goa	1	0	0	1	0
Gujarat	10	1	0	1	11
Haryana	3	1	0	1	0
Himachal Pradesh	3	0	0	2	1
Jammu and Kashmir	3	0	0	1	9
Karnataka	10	2	0	2	2
Kerala	5	5	1	1	0
Madhya Pradesh	15	0	0	2	0
Maharashtra	14	6	1	6	21
Manipur	2	0	0	1	0
Meghalaya	1	0	1	1	0
Mizoram	0	0	0	1	0
Nagaland	0	0	0	1	0
Orissa	5	0	0	1	0
Punjab	3	1	0	1	0
Rajasthan	6	4	0	2	0
Sikkim	5	0	0	3	0
Tamil Nadu	13	3	2	5	1
Tripura	1	0	0	1	0
Uttar Pradesh	23	5	1	1	8
West Bengal	9	1	2	2	6
A & N Islands	0	0	0	0	0
Chandigarh	1	0	1	0	0
D & N Haveli	0	0	0	0	0
Daman & Diu	0	0	0	0	0
Delhi	4	5	2	1	1
Lakshadweep	0	0	0	0	0
Pondicherry	1	0	0	0	0
India	169	34	10	41	55

* As per the UGC Association of Indian Universities (as on June 1993).

TABLE 13. 12 : Number of Institutions

State/Union Territory	Arts, Science and Commerce Colleges	Engineering & Technology Colleges	Medical Colleges (M.B.B.S.) Ayuv.	Teacher Training Colleges	Pre-degree Junior Colleges
1	7	8	9	10	11
Andhra Pradesh	483	29	10	49	1465
Arunachal Pradesh	4	0	0	0	0
Assam	231	3	5	13	63
Bihar	557	6	40	15	105
Goa	19	2	1	1	0
Gujarat	285	11	20	41	0
Haryana	140	3	5	18	0
Himachal Pradesh	45	1	2	6	0
Jammu & Kashmir	32	1	2	4	0
Karnataka	617	51	18	64	317
Kerala	172	8	5	19	84
Madhya Pradesh	448	13	6	20	0
Maharashtra	749	94	53	100	661
Manipur	29	0	1	2	29
Meghalaya	23	0	0	1	0
Mizoram	16	0	0	1	13
Nagaland	16	0	0	1	5
Orissa	433	6	12	11	244
Punjab	177	5	8	18	0
Rajasthan	171	6	5	39	0
Sikkim	1	0	0	0	0
Tamil Nadu	234	39	13	21	0
Tripura	14	1	0	1	0
Uttar Pradesh	436	12	9	13	0
West Bengal	303	9	10	43	0
A & N Islands	2	0	0	1	0
Chandigarh	12	4	0	0	0
D & N Haveli	0	0	0	0	0
Daman & Diu	1	0	0	1	0
Delhi	62	3	6	0	0
Lakshadweep	0	0	0	0	2
Pondicherry	7	1	2	1	1
India	5639	308	233	584	2989

TABLE 13.12 : (*Contd.*)

State/Union Territory	Higher Sec. Schools (10+2 New Pattern)	High/Post Basic Schools	Middle/Senior Basic School
1	2	3	4
Andhra Pradesh	86	7145	6341
Arunachal Pradesh	61	79	277
Assam	502	3072	6729
Bihar	211	3850	13330
Goa	61	339	117
Gujarat	1814	3753	18345
Haryana	510	2129	1425
Himachal Pradesh	186	968	1067
Jammu & Kashmir	239	1039	2669
Karnataka	938	4699	16756
Kerala	47	2475	2919
Madhya Pradesh	2508	2050	15145
Maharashtra	2298	9579	19685
Manipur	36	453	653
Meghalaya	6	365	725
Mizoram	0	281	609
Nagaland	4	233	418
Orissa	181	4921	11866
Punjab	707	2157	1430
Rajasthan	1088	3336	9567
Sikkim	22	64	118
Tamil Nadu	2221	3270	5593
Tripura	150	332	431
Uttar Pradesh	3902	2735	15546
West Bengal	1317	5411	3156
A & N Haveli	41	31	44
Chandigarh	30	61	33
D & N Haveli	5	8	43
Daman & Diu	3	17	16
Delhi	952	311	531
Lakshadweep	0	9	4
Pondicherry	41	83	119
India	20167	65255	15507

TABLE 13.12 : (Contd.)

State/Union Territory	Primary/Junior Basic Schools	Pre-Primary/ Pre-Basic Schools	Teacher Training Schools	Polytechnic Institutes	Technical Industrial Arts & Craft Schools
1	5	6	7	8	9
Andhra Pradesh	49247	18	25	87	450
Arunachal Pradesh	1205	299	0	2	0
Assam	38876	482	1	8	27
Bihar	53029	1	95	15	51
Goa	1024	0	1	4	14
Gujarat	14228	2380	79	29	102
Haryana	5659	27	7	22	133
Himachal Pradesh	7548	15	6	6	32
Jammu & Kashmir	9784	0	14	4	33
Karnataka	23600	5336	128	183	117
Kerala	6702	261	101	27	183
Madhya Pradesh	68949	634	52	37	69
Maharashtra	40142	2507	272	270	1120
Manipur	3076	1	2	1	19
Meghalaya	4175	0	10	1	3
Mizoram	1082	0	3	1	1
Nagaland	1409	0	3	2	3
Orissa	41604	0	71	5	26
Punjab	12486	2	10	12	101
Rajasthan	32878	33	42	21	91
Sikkim	531	723	1	1	1
Tamil Nadu	30229	22	70	135	177
Tripura	2063	3410	2	1	4
Uttar Pradesh	79522	45	121	89	122
West Bengal	51021	0	55	46	160
A & N Islands	188	23	1	2	1
Chandigarh	59	0	0	2	2
D & N Haveli	125	0	0	0	0
Daman & Diu	49	12	0	1	2
Delhi	2072	760	22	5	15
Lakshadweep	19	9	0	0	1
Pondicherry	342	172	0	3	1
India	57223	17172	1194	1021	3061

TABLE 13.13 : Enrolment by Stages/Classes

State/Union Territory	Ph.D./D.Sc./D.Phill.			M.A.		
	Boys	Girls	Total	Boys	Girls	Total
1	2	3	4	5	6	7
Andhra Pradesh	1330	366	1696	6222	2074	8296
Arunachal Pradesh	0	0	0	185	58	243
Assam	167	109	276	1520	1340	2860
Bihar	578	153	731	7910	2771	10681
Goa	1	2	3	115	204	319
Gujarat	800	500	1300	8700	7300	16000
Haryana	917	278	1195	2354	2219	4573
Himachal Pradesh	839	378	1217	349	384	733
Jammu & Kashmir	155	115	270	738	805	1543
Karnataka	0	0	0	27	113	140
Kerala	673	634	1307	1970	2381	4351
Madhya Pradesh	1396	903	2299	10004	7690	17694
Maharashtra	3026	1640	4666	26336	11894	38230
Manipur	58	20	78	319	325	644
Meghalaya	59	49	108	388	302	690
Mizoram	0	0	0	0	0	0
Nagaland	0	0	0	35	40	75
Orissa	271	76	347	3895	2272	6167
Punjab	261	461	722	2327	4064	6391
Rajasthan	11	6	17	2400	1233	3633
Sikkim	0	0	0	0	0	0
Tamil Nadu	8	8	16	1208	986	2194
Tripura	0	0	0	117	258	375
Uttar Pradesh	6006	2117	8123	46954	21357	68311
West Bengal	872	411	1283	5125	5642	10767
A & N Islands	0	0	0	22	32	54
Chandigarh	30	54	84	637	900	1537
D & N Haveli	0	0	0	0	0	0
Daman & Diu	0	0	0	0	0	0
Delhi	3120	1797	4917	3108	3370	6478
Lakshadweep	0	0	0	0	0	0
Pondicherry	29	20	49	94	92	186
India	20607	100967	30704	133059	80106	213165

TABLE 13.13 : (Contd.)

State/Union Territory	M.Sc. Boys	M.Sc. Girls	M.Sc. Total	M.Com. Boys	M.Com. Girls	M.Com. Total
1	8	9	10	11	12	13
Andhra Pradesh	3871	1442	5313	2442	393	2835
Arunachal Pradesh	0	0	0	0	0	0
Assam	923	430	1353	550	30	580
Bihar	2254	567	2821	10826	3372	14198
Goa	110	126	236	79	79	158
Gujarat	3000	1700	4700	5100	3300	8400
Haryana	1045	630	1675	379	405	784
Himachal Pradesh	222	132	354	87	53	148
Jammu & Kashmir	520	613	1133	132	73	205
Karnataka	45	178	223	0	44	44
Kerala	1293	2190	3483	671	546	1217
Madhya Pradesh	5862	2820	8682	8500	1510	10010
Maharashtra	9582	4386	13968	15189	4836	20025
Manipur	290	163	453	45	31	76
Meghalaya	110	80	190	21	9	30
Mizoram	0	0	0	0	0	0
Nagaland	16	3	19	13	3	16
Orissa	1722	761	2483	1222	82	1304
Punjab	484	723	1207	43	96	139
Rajasthan	1098	571	1669	970	173	1143
Sikkim	0	0	0	0	0	0
Tamil Nadu	1747	1645	3392	762	441	1203
Tripura	121	59	180	129	3	132
Uttar Pradesh	11904	3604	15508	8963	300	9263
West Bengal	2612	1302	3914	2145	205	2350
A & N Islands	13	12	25	0	0	0
Chandigarh	136	186	322	29	25	54
D & N Haveli	0	0	0	0	0	0
Daman & Diu	0	0	0	0	0	0
Delhi	990	965	1955	820	805	1625
Lakshadweep	0	0	0	0	0	0
Pondicherry	61	92	153	4	32	36
India	50031	25380	75411	59121	16846	75967

TABLE 13.13 : *(Contd.)*

State/Union Territory	B.A./B.A. (Hons.)			B.Sc./B.Sc. (Hons.)		
	Boys	Girls	Total	Boys	Girls	Total
1	14	15	16	17	18	19
Andhra Pradesh	53568	26749	80317	39207	19635	588420
Arunachal Pradesh	1779	467	2246	119	28	147
Assam	60599	36469	97068	19864	3825	23689
Bihar	121672	34648	156320	50089	7137	57226
Goa	1191	2559	3750	1228	1351	2579
Gujarat	92400	87700	180100	26700	15500	42200
Haryana	47627	26893	74520	6508	5514	12022
Himachal Pradesh	10000	5000	15000	4000	1500	5500
Jammu & Kashmir	6123	6782	12905	13748	5129	18877
Karnataka	86639	51913	138552	30359	20172	50531
Kerala	19512	24789	44301	18657	22038	40695
Madhya Pradesh	55240	37960	93200	38965	13900	52865
Maharashtra	171826	100919	272745	71396	34678	106074
Manipur	5908	6011	11919	4892	2708	7600
Meghalaya	2579	2155	4734	842	380	1222
Mizoram	2122	1338	3460	227	145	372
Nagaland	1497	899	2396	210	58	268
Orissa	42353	19690	62043	12410	3515	15924
Punjab	42838	52197	95035	59280	6141	12069
Rajasthan	37177	20200	57377	16460	6168	22628
Sikkim	473	227	700	180	77	257
Tamil Nadu	11150	10416	21566	62596	48767	111363
Tripura	3681	3242	6923	1450	540	1990
Uttar Pradesh	185381	69841	255222	54564	13148	67712
West Bengal	60033	92204	152237	48203	23206	71409
A & N Islands	559	518	1077	179	149	328
Chandigarh	3009	3285	6294	1260	854	2114
D & N Haveli	0	0	0	0	0	0
Daman & Diu	196	161	357	62	28	90
Delhi	33490	34973	68463	7977	6535	14512
Lakshadweep	0	0	0	0	0	0
Pondicherry	1024	1139	2163	944	893	1837
India	1161646	761344	1922990	539224	263719	802943

TABLE 13.13 : Enrolment by Stages/Classes *(Contd.)*

State/Union Territory	B.Com./B.Com (Hons)			B.E./B.Sc. (Engg.) B. Arch.		
	Boys	Girls	Total	Boys	Girls	Total
1	20	21	22	23	24	25
Andhra Pradesh	52598	19664	72262	18312	2527	20839
Arunachal Pradesh	132	14	146	0	0	0
Assam	10437	1665	12102	2590	229	2819
Bihar	197952	43424	241376	5937	326	6263
Goa	3535	3118	6653	541	191	732
Gujarat	71400	44300	115700	12500	1500	14000
Haryana	8671	4645	43316	2708	264	2972
Himachal Pradesh	1450	500	1950	188	18	206
Jammu & Kashmir	2543	697	3240	502	21	523
Karanataka	32420	23885	56305	60302	6724	67026
Kerala	7714	5819	13533	6858	1992	8850
Madhya Pradesh	43060	4100	47160	8604	998	9602
Maharashtra	128180	81541	209721	61234	8020	69254
Manipur	407	125	532	0	0	0
Meghalaya	552	96	648	0	0	0
Mizoram	144	43	187	187	0	187
Nagaland	396	78	474	0	0	0
Orissa	9212	1205	10417	2462	99	2561
Punjab	8448	4804	13252	2831	359	3190
Rajasthan	13501	3872	17373	4425	126	4551
Sikkim	65	14	79	0	0	0
Tamil Nadu	23858	15896	39754	23037	4250	27287
Tripura	1316	40	1356	398	50	448
Uttar Pradesh	37989	1692	39681	13714	515	14229
West Bengal	62915	6712	69627	7292	395	7687
A & N Islands	118	44	162	0	0	0
Chandigarh	724	324	1048	1260	854	2114
D & N Haveli	0	0	0	0	0	0
Daman & Diu	229	89	318	0	0	0
Delhi	26901	8611	35512	3532	415	3947
Lakshadweep	0	0	0	0	0	0
Pondicherry	394	374	768	539	212	751
India	747261	277391	1024652	239953	30085	270038

TABLE 13.13 : (*Contd.*)

State/Union Territory	B.Ed./B.T. Boys	Girls	Total	M.B.B.S. Boys	Girls	Total
1	26	27	28	29	30	31
Andhra Pradesh	3924	3050	6974	2866	2141	5007
Arunachal Pradesh	26	6	32	0	0	0
Assam	937	603	1540	1596	626	2222
Bihar	1324	897	2221	3190	899	4089
Goa	30	73	103	191	167	358
Gujarat	2800	1950	4750	4300	2200	6500
Haryana	1269	2227	3496	601	655	1256
Himachal Pradesh	146	33	179	261	81	342
Jammu & Kashmir	457	443	900	695	542	1237
Karnataka	4410	2770	7180	5324	1964	7288
Kerala	1458	3311	4769	2108	1259	3367
Madhya Pradesh	3066	2459	5525	3165	1390	4555
Maharashtra	14857	7347	22204	10931	8903	19834
Manipur	140	121	261	308	100	408
Meghalaya	278	200	478	0	0	0
Mizoram	111	41	152	0	0	0
Nagaland	42	29	71	0	0	0
Orissa	1068	560	1628	1285	541	1826
Punjab	712	2357	3069	1536	1444	2980
Rajasthan	3838	2646	6484	2607	1410	4017
Sikkim	11	9	20	0	0	0
Tamil Nadu	404	1635	2039	4223	3312	7535
Tripura	166	46	212	0	0	0
Uttar Pradesh	9495	7328	16823	5318	1592	6910
West Bengal	5020	4213	9233	2812	958	3770
A & N Islands	12	29	41	0	0	0
Chandigarh	44	437	481	0	0	0
D & N Haveli	0	0	0	0	0	0
Daman & Diu	26	34	60	0	0	0
Delhi	279	541	820	2245	1853	4098
Lakshadweep	0	0	0	0	0	0
Pondicherry	138	7	145	428	154	582
India	56488	45402	101890	55990	32191	88181

TABLE 13.13 : (*Contd.*)

State/Union Territory	Intermediate/Jr. Colleges/ Pre-Degree/Pre-Univ.			Hr. Sec. (10+2)New Pattern, XI-XII Classes		
	Boys	Girls	Total	Boys	Girls	Total
1	32	33	34	35	36	37
Andhra Pradesh	441253	209509	650762	5022	3172	8194
Arunachal Pradesh	0	0	0	4395	2187	6582
Assam	89930	55830	145760	68529	36308	104837
Bihar	330714	62984	393698	16042	7460	23502
Goa	0	0	0	11872	10711	22583
Gujarat	0	0	0	308100	212100	520200
Haryana	0	0	0	111339	48858	160197
Himachal Pradesh	0	0	0	35890	18370	54260
Jammu & Kashmir	0	0	0	35020	17665	52685
Karnataka	213678	89054	302732	156045	79529	235574
Kerala	83442	86525	169967	6483	5957	12440
Madhya Pradesh	0	0	0	215240	79923	295163
Maharashtra	332807	185105	517912	332093	187171	519264
Manipur	9384	6920	16304	3610	1840	5450
Meghalaya	5995	5200	11195	273	213	486
Mizoram	1279	959	2238	0	0	0
Nagaland	3387	2235	5622	42	25	67
Orissa	163000	60500	223500	5000	2500	7500
Punjab	(	0	0	117753	88486	206239
Rajasthan	0	0	0	387000	90000	477000
Sikkim	0	0	0	2040	1488	3528
Tamil Nadu	0	0	0	332567	237042	569609
Tripura	0	0	0	11967	6564	18531
Uttar Pradesh	2944	915	3859	848708	297362	1146070
West Bengal	0	0	0	302793	188528	491321
A & N Islands	0	0	0	2177	1907	4084
Chandigarh	0	0	0	5822	6909	12731
D & N Haveli	0	0	0	607	433	1040
Daman & Diu	0	0	0	923	546	1469
Delhi	0	0	0	81900	65896	147796
Lakshadweep	258	143	401	0	0	0
Pondicherry	470	409	879	5878	5294	11172
India	1678541	766288	2444829	3415130	1704444	5119574

TABLE 13.13 : Enrolment By Stages/Classes(*Contd.*)

State/Union Territory	High/Post Basic (IX-X Classes)		
	Boys	Girls	Total
1	38	39	40
Andhra Pradesh	582678	345936	928614
Aruanchal Pradesh	8324	5073	13397
Assam	273968	214144	488112
Bihar	687378	201591	888969
Goa	22612	20295	42907
Gujarat	558900	362100	921000
Haryana	229851	128660	358511
Himachal Pradesh	100450	64380	164830
Jammu & Kashmir	82416	39895	122311
Karnataka	543109	342669	885778
Kerala	491317	515257	1006574
Madhya Pradesh	484935	181607	666542
Maharashtra	1213730	777159	1990889
Manipur	26980	22320	49300
Meghalaya	13341	11794	25135
Mizoram	10334	10185	20519
Nagaland	11726	9436	21162
Orissa	517000	281000	798000
Punjab	268964	203909	472873
Rajasthan	447000	102000	549000
Sikkim	4019	3600	7619
Tamil Nadu	786167	527128	1313295
Tripura	30212	25480	55692
Uttar Pradesh	1754060	532422	2286482
West Bengal	851333	538572	1389905
A & N Islands	4833	4053	8886
Chandigarh	8964	8275	17239
D & N Haveli	1206	730	1936
Daman & Diu	1764	1454	3218
Delhi	146150	109510	255660
Lakshadweep	825	602	1427
Pondicherry	14826	12633	27459
India	10179372	5603869	15783241

TABLE 13.13 : (*Contd.*)

State/Union Territory	Middle/Sr. Basic (Classes VI-VIII)			Primary/Jr. Basic (Classes I-V)		
	Boys	Girls	Total	Boys	Girls	Total
1	41	42	43	44	45	46
Andhra Pradesh	1631000	1128000	2759000	467000	3840000	8510000
Arunachal Pradesh	19514	14139	33653	74222	56199	130421
Assam	747208	519478	1266686	1987299	1764596	3751895
Bihar	1576661	644058	2220719	5854713	3045027	8899740
Goa	42039	35913	77952	69000	63372	132372
Gujarat	1224325	770906	1995231	3406339	2576579	5982918
Haryana	516000	347000	863000	1260000	1023000	2283000
Himachal Pradesh	219720	171680	391400	378900	333580	712480
Jammu & Kashmir	210115	121392	331507	480039	319414	799453
Karnataka	1106714	830594	1937308	3266851	2852807	6119658
Kerala	976737	929962	1906699	1549805	1469380	3019185
Madhya Pradesh	2049000	1154000	3203000	5242000	3798000	9040000
Maharashtra	2392087	1810166	4202253	5854301	5102918	10957219
Manipur	53150	45250	98400	127740	113760	241500
Meghalaya	28558	26233	54791	91269	84385	175654
Mizoram	30063	26734	56797	60874	54795	115669
Nagaland	31829	30136	61965	83779	74321	158100
Orissa	730000	529000	1259000	2267000	1575000	3842000
Punjab	509397	401315	910712	1110047	956687	2066734
Rajasthan	1340000	464000	1804000	3683000	1775000	5458000
Sikkim	10737	10023	20760	40018	35135	75153
Tamil Nadu	1986075	1548711	3534786	4229731	3791219	8020950
Tripura	81112	60119	141231	219088	180991	400079
Uttar Pradesh	3859216	1668192	5527408	9853898	6130820	15984718
West Bengal	2481000	2122000	4603000	5302000	4815000	10117000
A & N Islands	10307	8875	19182	23257	21054	44311
Chandigarh	17479	15270	32749	31449	27786	59235
D & N Haveli	3036	1766	4802	11189	7501	18690
Daman & Diu	3637	3042	6679	6845	6047	12892
Delhi	292350	233063	525413	509247	447845	957092
Lakshadweep	2129	1544	3673	4763	4010	8773
Pondicherry	32204	28622	60826	55646	50002	105648
India	24213399	15701183	39914582	61804309	46396230	108200539

TABLE 13.13 : (*Contd.*)

State/Union Territory	Pre-Primary/Pre-Basic Stage			Teacher Training Schools		
	Boys	Girls	Total	Boys	Girls	Total
1	47	48	49	50	51	52
Andhra Pradesh	33693	25221	58914	2701	1460	4161
Arunachal Pradesh	9510	7132	16642	0	0	0
Assam	10678	8617	19295	62	28	90
Bihar	20920	11347	32267	4738	5842	10580
Goa	0	0	0	3	90	93
Gujarat	90506	65781	156287	4984	5757	10741
Haryana	5864	4156	10020	196	131	327
Himachal Pradesh	3300	2740	6040	596	414	1010
Jammu & Kashmir	10828	7625	18453	254	145	399
Karnataka	184674	159192	343866	7435	8670	16105
Kerala	7870	7120	14990	1731	6317	8048
Madhya Pradesh	68903	49428	118331	6279	1229	7508
Maharashtra	191965	168248	360213	16095	13475	29570
Manipur	48510	43490	92000	0	0	0
Meghalaya	70728	62899	133627	350	322	672
Mizoram	0	0	0	227	132	359
Nagaland	36913	33547	70460	32	6	38
Orissa	0	0	0	3262	3235	6497
Punjab	13136	9706	22842	288	1296	1584
Rajasthan	81000	59000	140000	2976	2814	5790
Sikkim	9263	7866	17129	40	29	69
Tamil Nadu	2176	2481	4657	1831	7992	9823
Tripura	82311	81485	163796	236	0	236
Uttar Pradesh	22854	14683	37537	3248	2063	5311
West Bengal	0	0	0	4175	4698	8873
A & N Islands	2403	1977	4380	14	25	39
Chandigarh	7004	5555	12559	0	0	0
D & N Haveli	129	100	229	0	0	0
Daman & Diu	410	303	713	0	0	0
Delhi	34810	37519	72329	150	2050	2200
Lakshadweep	520	536	1056	0	0	0
Pondicherry	6928	5132	12060	0	0	0
India	1057806	882886	1940692	61903	68220	130123

TABLE 13.13 : (*Contd.*)

State/Union Territory	Polytechnic Institute Boys	Polytechnic Institute Girls	Polytechnic Institute Total	Tech. Indus., Arts & Crafts Schools Boys	Tech. Indus., Arts & Crafts Schools Girls	Tech. Indus., Arts & Crafts Schools Total
1	53	54	55	56	57	58
Andhra Pradesh	28162	7345	35507	74218	3113	77331
Arunachal Pradesh	157	19	176	0	0	0
Assam	3897	494	4391	3465	668	4133
Bihar	3986	90	4076	11436	1122	12558
Goa	1251	234	1485	3035	411	3446
Gujarat	17702	4163	21865	5220	451	5671
Haryana	5351	1023	6374	21094	2469	23563
Himachal Pradesh	919	196	1115	2231	1226	3457
Jammu & Kashmir	393	146	539	2433	798	3231
Karnataka	38774	6931	45705	3163	455	3618
Kerala	9865	2994	12859	21189	5422	26611
Madhya Pradesh	9745	1087	10832	10871	1674	12545
Maharashtra	50526	7965	58491	199522	22812	222334
Manipur	157	38	195	172	543	715
Meghalaya	248	25	273	158	114	272
Mizoram	219	65	284	105	44	149
Nagaland	302	3	305	297	164	461
Orissa	285	380	665	5782	29	5811
Punjab	4556	767	5323	12560	4263	16823
Rajasthan	3957	2658	6615	8358	812	9170
Sikkim	0	0	0	60	4	64
Tamil Nadu	52022	7682	59704	16591	4582	21173
Tripura	215	5	220	332	127	459
Uttar Pradesh	22997	1076	24073	47803	2341	50144
West Bengal	18925	418	19343	5503	7052	12555
A & N Islands	135	59	194	114	25	139
Chandigarh	772	470	1242	609	459	1068
D & N Haveli	0	0	0	0	0	0
Daman & Diu	207	45	252	546	72	618
Delhi	2459	1435	3894	6490	1853	8343
Lakshadweep	0	0	0	9	7	16
Pondicherry	592	372	964	0	313	313
India	278776	48185	326961	463366	63425	526791

TABLE 13.14 : Enrolment Ratio in Classes I-V and VI-VIII of Schools for General Education

State/Union Territory	Classes 1-5 (6-11 Yr.)			Classes 6-8 (11-14 Yr.)		
	Boys	Girls	Total	Boys	Girls	Total
1	2	3	4	5	6	7
Andhra Pradesh	116.4	100.1	108.4	73.9	53.1	63.7
Arunachal Pradesh	132.5	99.2	11.58	62.5	46.3	54.5
Assam	134.4	125.3	130.0	89.3	65.5	77.7
Bihar	95.9	54.4	76.1	47.4	21.0	34.7
Goa	102.3	93.7	98.0	104.3	88.6	96.4
Gujarat	131.4	106.0	119.1	82.8	55.5	69.6
Haryana	109.7	95.4	102.8	81.8	59.2	70.9
Himachal Pradesh	126.8	111.5	119.1	124.4	97.9	111.2
Jammu & Kashmir	104.3	72.6	88.8	79.7	48.8	64.7
Karnataka	124.3	115.2	119.9	72.4	57.2	65.0
Kerala	103.8	100.8	102.3	108.3	105.7	107.0
Madhya Pradesh	116.7	91.3	104.5	82.5	50.0	66.9
Maharashtra	123.6	115.0	119.4	89.0	71.9	80.7
Manipur	100.3	96.0	98.2	77.9	68.4	73.2
Meghalaya	77.8	71.8	74.8	42.7	38.3	40.5
Mizoram	138.6	132.3	135.6	111.7	103.2	107.5
Nagaland	110.9	101.6	106.3	70.1	68.9	69.5
Orissa	116.8	77.6	96.8	67.5	46.9	57.0
Punjab	92.9	88.1	90.6	71.8	63.4	67.8
Rajasthan	119.5	60.9	91.0	76.8	28.9	53.9
Sikkim	123.8	111.1	117.6	59.9	59.3	59.6
Tamil Nadu	149.0	140.8	145.0	111.3	91.0	101.4
Tripura	141.3	119.1	130.3	92.9	72.2	82.8
Uttar Pradesh	103.9	72.8	89.3	72.2	354.	55.0
West Bengal	124.7	123.0	123.9	98.2	89.1	93.8
A & N Islands	101.5	85.5	93.2	84.4	75.2	79.9
Chandigarh	65.5	64.0	64.8	62.2	63.3	62.7
D & N Haveli	125.7	92.6	109.9	58.3	36.7	48.0
Daman & Diu	—	—	—	—	—	—
Delhi	86.3	87.4	86.8	81.6	78.0	79.9
Lakshadweep	153.6	129.3	141.5	125.2	96.5	111.3
Pondicherry	146.4	133.7	140.1	138.8	125.5	132.2
India	115.3	92.9	104.5	79.3	55.2	67.7

TABLE13.15 : Number of Teachers and Percentage of Trained Teachers at Higher Secondary Schools/Junior Colleges (10+2 New Pattern).

State/Union Territory	Number of Teachers			Percentage of Trained Teachers
	Men	Women	Total	
1	2	3	4	5
Andhra Pradesh	11314	5266	16580	100
Arunachal Pradesh	1086	261	1347	65
Assam	12178	3933	16111	30
Bihar	3729	1552	5281	95
Goa	556	457	1013	69
Gujarat	31197	11333	42530	99
Haryana	8955	7576	16531	96
Himachal Pradesh	3129	1670	4799	98
Jammu & Kashmir	4255	1576	5831	79
Karnataka	16415	4578	20997	100
Kerala	839	1728	2567	99
Madhya Pradesh	31641	11222	42863	0
Maharashtra	76720	27049	103769	93
Manipur	1653	766	2419	44
Meghalaya	108	120	228	98
Mizoram	48	12	60	26
Nagaland	105	32	137	31
Orissa	2221	648	2869	50
Punjab	11055	11211	22266	99
Rajasthan	23066	7168	30234	97
Sikkim	483	406	889	50
Tamil Nadu	43883	30613	74496	99
Tripura	3763	1715	5478	62
Uttar Pradesh	49394	10180	59574	97
West Bengal	29094	8945	38039	72
A & N Islands	892	715	1607	98
Chandigarh	367	1266	1633	100
D & N Haveli	96	50	140	99
Daman & Diu	23	7	30	90
Delhi	15329	22411	37740	99
Lakshadweep	0	0	0	0
Pondicherry	962	546	1500	100
India	384560	175012	559570	91

TABLE 13.16: Enrolment and Teacher Pupil Ratio at Higher Secondary Schools/Junior Colleges (10+2 New Pattern)

State/Union Territory	Enrolment			Teacher-Pupil Ratio
	Boys	Girls	Total	
1	2	3	4	5
Andhra Pradesh	497471	248201	745672	45
Arunachal Pradesh	18760	12044	30804	23
Assam	388309	219027	607336	36
Bihar	485136	111295	596431	113
Goa	14243	13352	27595	27
Gujarat	845500	581300	1426800	34
Haryana	327276	181650	508926	31
Himachal Pradesh	108110	57100	165210	34
Jammu & Kashmir	67767	31306	99073	17
Karnataka	581586	264922	846508	40
Kerala	114897	112512	227409	89
Madhya Pradesh	489073	168662	657735	15
Maharashtra	664900	372276	1037176	9
Manipur	20754	12810	33564	14
Meghalaya	8707	6544	15251	67
Mizoram	1279	959	2238	16
Nagaland	5713	3994	9707	71
Orissa	175000	56000	231000	40
Punjab	419705	307140	726845	33
Rajasthan	697000	233000	930000	31
Sikkim	10455	9602	20057	23
Tamil Nadu	1564719	1164630	2729349	37
Tripura	74128	53340	127468	23
Uttar Pradesh	2349392	919979	3269371	55
West Bengal	833390	646764	1480154	39
A & N Islands	16902	14968	31870	20
Chandigarh	21064	21924	42988	26
D & N Haveli	2237	1488	3725	26
Daman & Diu	923	546	1469	49
Delhi	436859	348898	785757	21
Lakshadweep	258	143	401	12
Pondicherry	27211	20678	47889	31
India	11268724	6197054	17465778	31

TABLE 13.17: Number of Teachers and Percentage of Trained Teachers at High/Post Basic school by Type of High/Post Basic Schools

State/Union Territory	Number of Teachers			Percentage of Trained Teachers
	Men	Women	Total	
1	2	3	4	5
Andhra Pradesh	62790	33728	96518	97
Arunachal Pradesh	912	290	1202	54
Assam	24576	6832	31408	33
Bihar	36377	5209	41586	93
Goa	2020	1714	3734	97
Gujarat	19123	3910	23033	98
Haryana	21291	14495	35786	95
Himachal Pradesh	6675	2417	9092	97
Jammu & Kashmir	10970	5224	16194	72
Karnataka	26894	9542	36436	97
Kerala	33383	57595	90978	99
Madhya Pradesh	12277	3549	15826	0
Maharashtra	84942	42030	126965	96
Manipur	5326	2731	8057	29
Meghalaya	1825	1642	3467	33
Mizoram	1477	362	1839	88
Nagaland	3159	1501	4660	25
Orissa	34990	9315	44305	98
Punjab	16749	14493	31242	99
Rajasthan	29658	8748	38406	98
Sikkim	783	542	1325	43
Tamil Nadu	24524	17805	42329	100
Tripura	4227	1410	5637	38
Uttar Pradesh	32939	7093	40032	97
West Bengal	49453	32821	82274	73
A & N Islands	352	320	672	97
Chandigarh	268	1300	1568	100
D & N Haveli	29	4	33	98
Daman & Diu	114	46	160	100
Delhi	3647	4608	8255	99
Lakshadweep	251	69	320	97
Pondicherry	984	885	1869	99
India	552985	292223	845208	90

TABLE 13.18 : Enrolment and Teacher-Pupil Ratio at High/Post Basic Schools

State/Union Territory	Enrolment			Teacher Pupil Ratio
	Boys	Girls	Total	
1	2	3	4	5
Andhra Pradesh	1810453	1268636	3079089	32
Arunachal Pradesh	15556	12716	28272	24
Assam	452303	440559	892862	28
Bihar	1154463	377197	1531660	37
Goa	91931	80071	172002	46
Gujarat	382900	220400	603300	26
Haryana	823961	518412	1342373	38
Himachal Pradesh	190320	146060	336380	37
Jammu & Kashmir	208732	123173	331905	20
Karnataka	642292	430742	1073034	29
Kerala	1357287	1357925	2715212	30
Madhya Pradesh	339582	226388	565970	36
Maharashtra	1213730	777159	1990889	16
Manipur	83670	72770	156440	19
Meghalaya	40850	36875	77725	22
Mizoram	10334	10185	20519	11
Nagaland	55045	49009	104054	22
Orissa	517000	281000	798000	18
Punjab	506485	415045	921530	29
Rajasthan	724000	256000	980000	26
Sikkim	15236	13726	28962	22
Tamil Nadu	989850	825106	1814956	43
Tripura	70363	57608	127971	23
Uttar Pradesh	1530713	672907	2203620	55
West Bengal	2222144	1667450	3889594	47
A & N Islands	7915	6725	14640	22
Chandigarh	25898	22261	48159	31
D & N Haveli	464	198	662	20
Daman & Diu	3119	2456	5575	35
Delhi	92841	90482	183323	22
Lakshadweep	3117	2039	5156	16
Pondicherry	31778	28103	59881	32
India	15614332	10489383	26103715	30

TABLE 13.19 : Number of Teachers and Percentage of Trained Teachers at Middle/Senior Basic Schools

State/Union Territory	Number of Teachers			Percentage of Trained Teachers
	Men	Women	Total	
1	2	3	4	5
Andhra Pradesh	24386	14516	38902	96
Arunachal Pradesh	1454	400	1854	41
Assam	35012	7753	42765	33
Bihar	77521	20199	97720	93
Goa	198	233	431	97
Gujarat	77376	63526	140902	96
Haryana	7358	5462	12820	96
Himachal Pradesh	4210	1213	5423	99
Jammu & Kashmir	11948	6457	18405	32
Karanataka	56779	36043	92822	96
Kerala	18377	33102	51479	92
Madhya Pradesh	61466	21593	83059	0
Maharashtra	94260	61269	155529	95
Manipur	4736	2186	6922	29
Meghalaya	2075	1350	3425	36
Mizoram	2932	806	3738	75
Nagaland	3276	904	4180	26
Orissa	33515	5616	39331	98
Punjab	4871	4117	8988	98
Rajasthan	54642	20302	74944	98
Sikkim	1092	516	1608	41
Tamil Nadu	32299	29893	62192	100
Tripura	3764	1016	4780	35
Uttar Pradesh	77191	19181	96372	95
West Bengal	16091	5137	21228	0
A & N Islands	362	374	736	98
Chandigarh	48	509	557	100
D & N Haveli	180	255	435	94
Daman & Diu	155	91	246	100
Delhi	2342	4436	6778	99
Lakshadweep	79	46	125	100
Pondicherry	864	818	1682	94
India	710859	369519	1080378	90

TABLE 13.20 : Enrolment and Teacher-Pupil Ratio at the Middle/Senior Basic Schools

State/Union Territory	Enrolment			Teacher Pupil Ratio
	Boys	Girls	Total	
1	2	3	4	5
Andhra Pradesh	963814	744571	1708385	44
Arunachal Pradesh	25189	17876	43065	23
Assam	755599	524656	1280255	30
Bihar	2889515	1376061	4265576	44
Goa	8795	7941	16736	39
Gujarat	3383591	2495288	5878879	42
Haryana	267853	228166	496019	39
Himachal Pradesh	72090	57090	129180	24
Jammu & Kashmir	273604	164009	437613	24
Karnataka	2938837	2499777	5438614	59
Kerala	823137	760692	1583829	31
Madhya Pradesh	1854600	1236400	3091000	37
Maharashtra	2392087	1810166	4202253	27
Manipur	60374	50572	110946	16
Meghalaya	32287	29090	61377	18
Mizoram	30063	26734	56797	15
Nagaland	42062	35716	77778	19
Orissa	803000	452000	1255000	32
Punjab	111966	87246	199212	22
Rajasthan	1832000	742000	2574000	34
Sikkim	16157	14656	30813	19
Tamil Nadu	1740028	1434060	3174088	51
Tripura	64097	52006	116103	24
Uttar Pradesh	2686741	1096701	3783442	39
West Bengal	683956	616701	1300657	61
A & N Islands	8341	7510	15851	22
Chandigarh	7224	5856	13080	23
D & N Haveli	8495	5668	14163	33
Daman & Diu	3717	3218	6935	28
Delhi	80428	60123	140551	21
Lakshadweep	1437	1627	3064	25
Pondicherry	25800	24495	50295	30
India	24886884	16668672	41555556	38

Table 13.21 : Number of Teachers and Percentage of Trained Teachers at Primary/Junior Basic Schools

State/Union Territory	Number of Teachers			Percentage of Trained Teachers
	Men	Women	Total	
1	2	3	4	5
Andhra Pradesh	73173	32967	106140	97
Arunachal Pradesh	2043	670	2713	43
Assam	59685	17827	77512	67
Bihar	91947	22137	114084	91
Goa	1040	1826	2866	97
Gujarat	23384	13294	36678	96
Haryana	10392	8239	18631	99
Himachal Pradesh	4260	1286	5546	86
Jammu & Kashmir	12103	6384	18487	64
Karnataka	34901	14876	49777	95
Kerala	16082	31930	48012	96
Madhya Pradesh	150444	47509	197953	0
Maharashtra	78462	57820	136282	94
Manipur	7744	3488	11232	46
Meghalaya	4253	2497	6750	42
Mizoram	2034	1810	3844	48
Nagaland	4702	1783	6485	48
Orissa	78775	26565	105340	100
Punjab	21784	26419	48203	99
Rajasthan	60786	22602	83388	98
Sikkim	1858	1424	3282	49
Tamil Nadu	68677	47846	116523	100
Tripura	8649	2318	10967	34
Uttar Pradesh	218576	49378	267954	98
West Bengal	148124	45511	193635	0
A & N Islands	461	360	821	91
Chandigarh	40	714	754	100
D & N Haveli	126	71	197	95
Daman & Diu	131	174	305	100
Delhi	10505	16028	26533	99
Lakshadweep	151	67	218	100
Pondicherry	959	1093	2052	92
India	1196251	506913	1703164	92

TABLE 13.22 : Enrolment and Teacher-Pupil Ratio at Primary/Junior Basic Schools

State/Union Territory	Enrolment			Teacher Pupil Ratio
	Boys	Girls	Total	
1	2	3	4	5
Andhra Pradesh	2898154	2439437	5337591	50
Arunachal Pradesh	56460	42094	98554	36
Assam	1581401	1414731	2996132	39
Bihar	3956603	2108625	6065228	53
Goa	30554	28927	59481	21
Gujarat	952972	686071	1639043	45
Haryana	455535	455810	911345	49
Himachal Pradesh	367740	330500	698240	126
Jammu & Kashmir	268315	187503	455818	24
Karnataka	1310229	1156531	2466760	50
Kerala	778935	.742587	1521522	32
Madhya Pradesh	5302903	3705428	9008331	46
Maharashtra	6046266	5271166	11317432	83
Manipur	104586	97418	202004	18
Meghalaya	128320	118215	246535	37
Mizoram	60874	54795	115669	30
Nagaland	64856	60981	125837	19
Orissa	2231000	1561000	3792000	36
Punjab	981141	850672	1831813	38
Rajasthan	2685000	1259000	3944000	47
Sikkim	24229	20128	44357	14
Tamil Nadu	3057119	2667785	5724904	49
Tripura	216102	191685	407787	37
Uttar Pradesh	9774834	5954807	15729641	59
West Bengal	5205102	4725719	9930821	51
A & N Islands	9819	8663	18482	23
Chandigarh	19112	11174	30286	40
D & N Haveli	4971	3176	8147	41
Daman & Diu	5820	5172	10992	36
Delhi	454329	394330	848659	32
Lakshadweep	3565	3144	6709	31
Pondicherry	31163	28816	59979	29
India	49068009	36586090	85654099	50

TABLE 13.23 : Dropout Rates in Classes I-V for the Year 1993-94

S.No.	State/Union Territory	Boys	Girls	Total
1	2	3	4	5
1.	Andhra Pradesh	42.48	41.78	42.18
2.	Arunachal Pradesh	60.09	61.09	60.52
3.	Assam	38.65	39.55	39.05
4.	Bihar	61.85	66.20	63.36
5.	Goa	-7.94	3.09	-2.57
6.	Gujarat	42.05	51.39	46.25
7.	Haryana	1.60	6.81	3.93
8.	Himachal Pradesh	24.64	28.16	26.28
9.	Jammu & Kashmir	53.12	42.35	48.66
10.	Karnataka	37.50	44.42	40.78
11.	Kerala	-5.35	-3.05	-4.23
12.	Madhya Pradesh	23.43	34.96	28.36
13.	Maharashtra	24.10	31.63	27.62
14.	Manipur	68.02	68.53	68.26
15.	Meghalaya	29.96	34.43	32.06
16.	Mizoram	56.73	58.54	57.58
17.	Nagaland	37.56	24.13	31.65
18.	Orissa	52.78	52.23	52.54
19.	Punjab	20.69	22.94	21.74
20.	Rajasthan	45.70	55.63	48.93
21.	Sikkim	63.18	61.19	62.27
22.	Tamil Nadu	16.39	18.35	17.30
23.	Tripura	60.57	66.95	63.49
24.	Uttar Pradesh	19.86	20.08	19.94
25.	West Bengal	36.17	45.76	40.43
26.	A & N Islands	9.26	10.34	9.77
27.	Chandigarh	-20.31	-9.04	-14.90
28.	D & N Haveli	40.50	55.19	47.00
29.	Daman & Diu	-7.32	-2.97	-5.32
30.	Delhi	19.25	28.83	25.74
31.	Lakshadweep	12.55	18.75	15.51
32.	Pondicherry	-7.86	-8.20	-8.02
	India	35.05	38.57	36.32

TABLE 13.24 : Dropout Rates in Classes I-VIII for the Year 1993-94

S.No.	State/Union Territory	Boys	Girls	Total
1	2	3	4	5
1.	Andhra Pradesh	59.94	66.46	62.82
2.	Arunachal Pradesh	69.62	67.45	68.72
3.	Assam	63.81	71.80	67.55
4.	Bihar	76.70	82.73	78.74
5.	Goa	8.57	16.34	12.28
6.	Gujarat	54.65	66.46	59.97
7.	Haryana	17.57	32.05	23.91
8.	Himachal Pradesh	13.11	27.39	19.74
9.	Jammu & Kashmir	45.25	72.73	56.46
10.	Karnataka	56.83	69.72	62.98
11.	Kerala	1.24	.57	.91
12.	Madhya Pradesh	38.12	54.15	44.68
13.	Maharashtra	44.02	56.30	49.79
14.	Manipur	72.41	72.26	72.34
15.	Meghalaya	58.14	57.11	57.65
16.	Mizoram	54.05	50.60	52.44
17.	Nagaland	36.71	39.58	38.13
18.	Orissa	62.64	59.04	61.21
19.	Punjab	36.15	42.78	39.22
20.	Rajasthan	62.34	72.34	65.43
21.	Sikkim	78.83	77.93	78.43
22.	Tamil Nadu	32.15	41.20	36.34
23.	Tripura	66.28	70.92	68.39
24.	Uttar Pradesh	31.99	47.63	37.51
25.	West Bengal	48.82	43.96	46.67
26.	A & N Islands	25.25	29.62	27.32
27.	Chandigarh	-5.96	-12.79	-9.09
28.	D & N Haveli	57.77	67.93	62.21
29.	Daman & Diu*	.00	.00	.00
30.	Delhi	19.89	31.24	25.35
31.	Lakshadweep	47.18	57.43	52.16
32.	Pondicherry	7.71	7.23	7.49
	India	49.95	56.78	52.80

* Included in Goa.

TABLE 13.25 : Dropout Rates in Classes I-X for the Year 1993-94

S.No.	State/Union Territory	Boys	Girls	Total
1	2	3	4	5
1.	Andhra Pradesh	76.70	82.13	79.04
2.	Arunachal Pradesh	77.99	80.11	78.82
3.	Assam	78.37	75.80	77.26
4.	Bihar	83.83	90.96	86.21
5.	Goa	42.06	42.89	42.46
6.	Gujarat	64.74	71.10	67.57
7.	Haryana	45.80	58.81	51.19
8.	Himachal Pradesh	41.00	56.91	48.29
9.	Jammu & Kashmir	66.12	78.30	70.97
10.	Karnataka	65.58	76.23	70.62
11.	Kerala	33.42	24.51	29.07
12.	Madhya Pradesh	75.46	85.24	79.31
13.	Maharashtra	58.60	70.70	64.25
14.	Manipur	75.17	79.84	77.32
15.	Meghalaya	67.28	67.57	67.42
16.	Mizoram	73.45	71.12	72.33
17.	Nagaland	75.01	78.92	76.87
18.	Orissa	53.43	63.53	57.49
19.	Punjab	44.87	52.80	48.54
20.	Rajasthan	77.87	88.02	80.89
21.	Sikkim	87.37	86.21	86.82
22.	Tamil Nadu	62.98	69.85	66.17
23.	Tripura	79.12	78.49	78.84
24.	Uttar Pradesh	61.78	75.40	66.02
25.	West Bengal	75.68	76.53	76.05
26.	A & N Islands	49.12	55.27	52.10
27.	Chandigarh	-.50	-1.99	-1.21
28.	D & N Haveli	73.21	76.54	74.52
29.	Daman & Diu*	.00	.00	.00
30.	Delhi	33.59	46.44	39.91
31.	Lakshadweep	55.65	64.65	50.78
32.	Pondicherry	38.39	41.22	39.74
	India	68.41	74.74	70.90

* Included in Goa.

TABLE 13.26 : Drop-out Rates of Scheduled Castes—(1989-90)

State/Union Territory	Primary Stage			Middle Stage			Secondary Stage		
	Boys	Girls	Total	Boys	Girls	Total	Boys	Girls	Total
	*								
Andhra Pradesh	60.53	65.83	62.80	77.41	85.44	80.85	84.17	88.74	86.15
Arunachal Pradesh	—	—	—	—	—	—	—	—	—
Assam	46.88	55.89	50.80	64.91	63.47	64.30	62.54	62.02	62.33
Bihar	67.69	73.50	69.33	83.37	89.79	85.04	87.98	94.20	89.50
Goa	39.27	32.06	36.02	55.52	65.68	60.28	79.26	85.57	82.27
Gujarat	24.95	45.55	34.13	50.40	70.34	59.11	66.50	79.78	72.21
Haryana	33.90	43.18	38.00	59.19	75.36	65.71	64.64	80.72	69.84
Himachal Pradesh	36.29	36.50	36.39	32.27	41.88	36.44	67.02	76.82	71.12
Jammu & Kashmir	39.27	30.39	35.84	50.11	52.73	51.10	77.86	82.32	79.52
Karnataka	51.05	59.59	54.90	62.11	73.77	67.08	73.63	84.60	78.45
Kerala	0	1.78	0.50	19.04	15.60	17.37	54.47	47.76	51.20
Madhya Pradesh	36.31	52.37	42.41	62.34	79.40	67.78	75.11	86.91	78.48
Maharashtra	38.54	51.58	44.60	52.90	69.77	60.54	67.91	81.16	73.82
Manipur	79.86	82.21	81.03	84.89	86.07	85.48	82.14	82.69	82.42
Meghalaya	33.13	41.88	37.46	27.86	51.85	39.64	34.62	66.39	50.00
Mizoram	—	—	—	—	—	—	—	—	—

(Contd.)

Table 13.26 : (Contd.)

State/Union Territory	Primary Stage			Middle Stage			Secondary Stage		
	Boys	Girls	Total	Boys	Girls	Total	Boys	Girls	Total
Nagaland	—	—	—	—	—	—	—	—	—
Orissa	* 55.16	59.22	56.77	75.97	83.19	78.76	77.86	86.42	81.22
Punjab	36.53	41.59	38.79	63.36	70.56	66.52	78.88	85.96	82.12
Rajasthan	60.42	74.37	63.89	69.53	83.53	72.18	80.82	92.39	82.96
Sikkim	70.00	67.85	69.04	84.96	83.67	84.37	91.62	93.60	92.51
Tamil Nadu	22.56	29.68	25.92	51.04	53.14	51.97	74.75	82.69	78.31
Tripura	58.21	63.09	60.47	75.87	81.84	78.60	86.88	90.20	88.39
Uttar Pradesh	32.89	51.69	38.86	57.92	69.52	60.87	66.97	84.97	71.57
West Bengal	* 58.54	66.71	61.92	74.18	84.88	79.02	89.74	90.12	89.88
A & N Islands	—	—	—	—	—	—	—	—	—
Chandigarh	0	0	0	0	0	0	27.17	14.23	21.03
D & N Haveli	18.60	39.96	28.09	0	0	0	45.28	70.27	55.56
Daman & Diu @	—	—	—	—	—	—	—	—	—
Delhi	33.74	35.74	34.63	47.68	58.61	52.79	54.06	74.25	63.71
Lakshadweep	—	—	—	—	—	—	—	—	—
Pondicherry	0	0	0	0	11.96	5.45	69.92	75.32	72.42
India	45.93	53.74	49.03	64.29	73.10	67.62	76.61	84.20	79.42

* Relates to 1988-89.

@ Included in Goa.

TABLE 13.27 : Drop-out Rates of Scheduled Tribes (1989-90)

State/Union Territory	Primary Stage			Middle Stage			Secondary Stage		
	Boys	Girls	Total	Boys	Girls	Total	Boys	Girls	Total
	*								
Andhra Pradesh	65.24	70.54	67.22	84.16	89.92	86.28	89.59	92.95	90.84
Arunachal Pradesh	63.47	59.43	61.98	78.52	77.90	78.30	81.97	88.10	84.06
Assam	65.15	65.87	65.46	71.78	75.67	73.44	70.80	75.82	72.93
Bihar	70.78	70.93	70.83	85.67	87.57	86.33	90.89	92.72	91.51
Goa	28.99	19.80	24.72	63.50	71.88	67.36	73.58	87.32	79.57
Gujarat	54.03	66.62	59.48	76.17	82.62	78.88	85.34	89.14	86.90
Haryana	—	—	—	—	—	—	—	—	—
Himachal Pradesh	30.59	34.53	32.23	36.58	45.89	40.03	67.93	70.41	68.79
Jammu & Kashmir	—	—	—	—	—	—	—	—	—
Karnataka	47.97	50.69	49.13	56.82	66.68	61.09	72.70	77.23	74.46
Kerala	18.88	15.88	17.44	36.02	35.30	35.68	70.14	65.86	68.12
Madhya Pradesh	48.38	60.36	52.82	75.57	85.14	78.61	83.74	91.81	86.14
Maharashtra	56.99	66.52	61.07	73.14	82.44	76.98	81.56	89.50	84.74
Manipur	77.54	78.43	77.95	84.76	85.79	85.23	85.44	87.24	86.26
Meghalaya	40.07	55.34	47.24	72.78	72.98	72.87	91.47	93.14	92.28
Mizoram	49.56	49.20	49.39	61.99	59.78	60.92	52.47	52.63	52.55

(Contd.)

TABLE 13.27 : (Contd.)

State/Union Territory	Primary Stage			Middle Stage		Secondary Stage			
	Boys	Girls	Total	Boys	Girls	Total	Boys	Girls	Total
Nagaland	34.75	43.54	39.00	70.71	64.85	68.15	75.97	73.87	75.10
Orissa	*77.66	78.66	77.98	84.33	86.92	85.26	87.49	92.84	89.38
Punjab	—	—	—	—	—	—	—	—	—
Rajasthan	69.76	83.15	73.08	74.74	90.17	77.65	84.93	94.30	86.45
Sikkim	62.87	50.46	57.73	71.26	65.41	68.70	85.52	86.81	86.07
Tamil Nadu	38.35	49.10	43.29	57.65	66.11	61.31	57.52	60.30	58.60
Tripura	71.97	76.53	73.91	85.55	88.19	86.64	90.47	93.24	91.56
Uttar Pradesh	17.22	59.64	34.11	47.73	74.11	55.59	33.49	78.84	46.31
West Bengal	*64.45	69.96	66.38	81.42	88.50	83.87	92.51	92.88	92.62
A & N Islands	5.73	19.77	12.36	49.44	47.88	48.73	55.23	62.58	58.57
Chandigarh	—	—	—	—	—	—	—	—	—
D & N Haveli	37.97	64.90	50.34	68.29	77.04	71.75	84.32	89.28	86.45
Daman & Diu @	—	—	—	—	—	—	—	—	—
Delhi	0	0	0	0	0	0	0	0	0
Lakshadweep	0	0	0	41.03	50.62	45.53	75.15	81.85	78.34
Pondicherry	—	—	—	—	—	—	—	—	—
India	61.86	66.98	63.81	77.42	82.67	79.35	84.83	88.90	86.28

* Relates to 1988-89.

@ Included in Goa.

TABLE 13.28 : Number of Teachers (1993-94)

SN.	State/U. Ts.	Primary			Middle			Sec./Hr. Secondary Schools		
		Male	Female	Total	Male	Female	Total	Male	Female	Total
	1	2	3	4	5	6	7	8	9	10
1.	Andhra Pradesh	71173	32967	106140	24386	14516	38902	74104	38994	113098
2.	Arunachal Pradesh	2043	670	2713	1454	400	1854	1998	551	2549
3.	Assam	59685	17827	77512	35012	7753	42765	36754	10765	47519
4.	Bihar	91947	22137	114084	77521	20199	97720	40106	6761	46867
5.	Goa	1040	1826	2866	198	233	431	2576	2171	4747
6.	Gujarat	23384	13294	36678	77376	63526	140902	50320	15243	65563
7.	Haryana	10392	8239	18631	7358	5462	12820	30246	22071	52317
8.	Himachal Pradesh	4260	1286	5546	4210	1213	5423	9804	4087	13891
9.	Jammu & Kashmir	12103	6384	18487	11948	6457	18405	15225	6800	22025
10.	Karnataka	34901	14876	49777	56779	36043	92822	43313	14120	57433
11.	Kerala	16082	31930	48012	18377	33102	51479	34222	59323	93545
12.	Madhya Pradesh	150444	47509	197953	61466	21593	83059	43918	14771	58689
13.	Maharashtra	78462	57820	136282	94260	61269	155529	161662	69072	230734
14.	Manipur	7744	3488	11232	4736	2186	6922	6979	3497	10476
15.	Meghalaya	4253	2497	6750	2075	1350	3425	1933	1762	3695
16.	Mizoram	2034	1810	3844	2932	806	3738	1525	374	1899
17.	Nagaland	4702	1783	6485	3276	904	4180	3264	1533	4797

(Contd.)

Table 13.28 : (Contd.)

1	2	3	4	5	6	7	8	9	10
18. Orissa	78775	26565	105340	33515	5816	39331	37211	9963	47174
19. Punjab	21784	26419	48203	4871	4117	8988	27804	25704	53508
20. Rajasthan	60786	22602	83388	54642	20302	74944	52724	15916	68640
21. Sikkim	1858	1424	3282	1092	516	1608	1266	948	2214
22. Tamil Nadu	68677	47846	116523	32299	29893	62192	68407	48418	116825
23. Tripura	8649	2318	10967	3764	1016	4780	7990	3125	11115
24. Uttar Pradesh	218576	49378	267954	77191	19181	96372	82333	17273	99606
25. West Bengal	148124	45511	193635	16091	5137	21228	78547	41766	120313
26. A & N Islands	461	360	821	362	374	736	1244	1035	2279
27. Chandigarh	40	714	754	48	509	557	635	2566	3201
28. D & N Haveli	126	71	197	180	255	435	125	54	179
29. Daman & Diu	131	174	305	155	91	246	137	53	190
30. Delhi	10505	16028	26533	2342	4436	6778	18976	27019	45995
31. Lakshadweep	151	67	218	79	46	125	251	69	320
32. Pondicherry	959	1093	2052	864	818	1682	1946	1431	3377
India	1196251	506913	1703164	710859	369519	1080378	937545	467235	1404780

13.4 SCHEDULED CASTES AND SCHEDULED TRIBES

TABLE 13.29 : Scheduled Castes/Scheduled Tribes Students Studying in Ph.D./D.Sc./ D.Phill. (1993-94)

State/Union Territory	Number of Students Belonging to					
	Scheduled Caste			Scheduled Tribe		
	Boys	Girls	Total	Boys	Girls	Total
1	2	3	4	5	6	7
Andhra Pradesh	55	17	72	5	6	11
Arunachal Pradesh	0	0	0	0	0	0
Assam	5	2	7	10	6	16
Bihar	0	0	0	0	0	0
Goa	0	0	0	0	0	0
Gujarat	30	10	40	15	10	25
Haryana	190	46	236	0	0	0
Himachal Pradesh	42	12	54	21	5	26
Jammu & Kashmir	0	0	0	0	0	0
Karnataka	0	0	0	0	0	0
Kerala	10	7	17	9	5	14
Madhya Pradesh	20	9	29	6	1	7
Maharashtra	137	43	180	15	10	25
Manipur	0	0	0	4	3	7
Meghalaya	1	0	1	40	24	64
Mizoram	0	0	0	0	0	0
Nagaland	0	0	0	0	0	0
Orissa	18	5	23	18	3	21
Punjab	18	7	25	0	0	0
Rajasthan	5	1	6	3	0	3
Sikkim	0	0	0	0	0	0
Tamil Nadu	5	1	6	0	0	0
Tripura	0	0	0	0	0	0
Uttar Pradesh	290	37	327	9	1	10
West Bengal	36	19	55	3	0	3
A & N Islands	0	0	0	0	0	0
Chandigarh	0	0	0	0	0	0
D & N Haveli	0	0	0	0	0	0
Daman & Diu	0	0	0	0	0	0
Delhi	98	31	129	30	19	49
Lakshadweep	0	0	0	0	0	0
Pondicherry	3	4	7	0	0	0
India	963	251	1214	188	93	281

TABLE 13.30 : Scheduled Castes/Scheduled Tribes Studying in M. A.

State/Union Territory	Number of Students Belonging to					
	Scheduled Caste			Scheduled Tribe		
	Boys	Girls	Total	Boys	Girls	Total
1	2	3	4	5	6	7
Andhra Pradesh	1210	235	1445	203	39	242
Arunachal Pradesh	1	2	3	131	27	158
Assam	112	70	182	145	90	235
Bihar	0	0	0	0	0	0
Goa	3	1	4	0	0	0
Gujarat	1350	650	2000	1100	650	1750
Haryana	513	78	591	0	0	0
Himachal Pradesh	53	18	71	28	15	43
Jammu & Kashmir	41	17	58	0	0	0
Karnataka	1	2	3	0	1	1
Kerala	225	187	412	16	7	23
Madhya Pradesh	1285	373	1658	882	195	1077
Maharashtra	5126	1533	6659	691	185	876
Manipur	3	2	5	18	11	29
Meghalaya	11	4	15	228	127	355
Mizoram	0	0	0	0	0	0
Nagaland	0	0	0	34	33	67
Orissa	305	91	396	139	39	178
Punjab	325	254	579	0	0	0
Rajasthan	255	0	263	326	0	326
Sikkim	0	0	0	0	0	0
Tamil Nadu	366	114	480	17	2	19
Tripura	27	18	45	2	1	3
Uttar Pradesh	8989	743	9732	340	158	498
West Bengal	302	175	477	13	2	15
A & N Islands	0	0	0	0	0	0
Chandigarh	90	39	129	0	0	0
D & N Haveli	0	0	0	0	0	0
Daman & Diu	0	0	0	0	0	0
Delhi	289	193	482	86	38	124
Lakshadweep	0	0	0	0	0	0
Pondicherry	13	6	19	0	0	0
India	20895	4813	25708	4399	1620	6019

TABLE 13.31 : Scheduled Castes/Scheduled Tribes Studying in M. Sc.

State/Union Territory	Number of Students Belonging to					
	Scheduled Caste			Scheduled Tribe		
	Boys	Girls	Total	Boys	Girls	Total
1	2	3	4	5	6	7
Andhra Pradesh	470	151	621	54	0	62
Arunachal Pradesh	0	0	0	0	0	0
Assam	76	22	98	60	20	80
Bihar	0	0	0	0	0	0
Goa	2	0	2	0	0	0
Gujarat	100	50	150	175	50	225
Haryana	49	10	59	0	0	0
Himachal Pradesh	47	14	61	11	4	15
Jammu & Kashmir	30	3	33	0	0	0
Karnataka	0	0	0	0	0	0
Kerala	144	170	314	6	6	12
Madhya Pradesh	190	90	280	125	45	170
Maharashtra	671	192	863	63	47	110
Manipur	1	1	2	9	8	17
Meghalaya	2	1	3	53	35	88
Mizoram	0	0	0	0	0	0
Nagaland	0	0	0	10	2	12
Orissa	99	31	130	42	7	49
Punjab	22	14	36	0	0	0
Rajasthan	27	0	27	7	0	7
Sikkim	0	0	0	0	0	0
Tamil Nadu	186	120	306	6	2	8
Tripura	6	2	8	0	0	0
Uttar Pradesh	636	92	728	29	9	38
West Bengal	148	15	163	7	2	9
A & N Islands	0	0	0	0	0	0
Chandigarh	14	6	20	2	3	5
D & N Haveli	0	0	0	0	0	0
Daman & Diu	0	0	0	0	0	0
Delhi	32	10	42	5	3	8
Lakshadweep	0	0	0	0	0	0
Pondicherry	4	3	7	0	0	0
India	2956	997	3953	664	251	915

TABLE 13.32 : Scheduled Caste/Scheduled Tribes Studying in M. Com.

State/Union Territory	Number of Students Belonging to					
	Scheduled Caste			Scheduled Tribe		
	Boys	Girls	Total	Boys	Girls	Total
1	2	3	4	5	6	7
Andhra Pradesh	324	50	374	67	3	70
Arunachal Pradesh	0	0	0	0	0	0
Assam	60	10	70	45	8	53
Bihar	0	0	0	0	0	0
Goa	5	3	8	0	0	0
Gujarat	625	225	850	370	50	420
Haryana	90	54	144	0	0	0
Himachal Pradesh	10	13	23	6	8	14
Jammu & Kashmir	6	1	7	0	0	0
Karnataka	0	0	0	0	0	0
Kerala	78	45	123	2	2	4
Madhya Pradesh	533	30	563	266	27	293
Maharashtra	2668	537	3205	366	81	447
Manipur	1	1	2	1	3	4
Meghalaya	0	0	0	13	6	19
Mizoram	0	0	0	0	0	0
Nagaland	0	0	0	10	2	12
Orissa	16	3	19	9	7	16
Punjab	2	6	8	0	0	0
Rajasthan	122	0	122	53	0	53
Sikkim	0	0	0	0	0	0
Tamil Nadu	134	32	166	2	0	2
Tripura	24	0	24	1	1	2
Uttar Pradesh	596	44	640	34	2	36
West Bengal	22	3	25	1	0	1
A & N Islands	0	0	0	0	0	0
Chandigarh	4	1	5	2	0	2
D & N Haveli	0	0	0	0	0	0
Daman & Diu	0	0	0	0	0	0
Delhi	79	13	92	11	3	14
Lakshadweep	0	0	0	0	0	0
Pondicherry	1	1	2	0	0	0
India	5400	1072	6472	1259	203	1462

TABLE 13.33 : Scheduled Castes/Scheduled Tribes Stuyding in B. A./B. A. (Hons.)

State/Union Territory	Number of Students Belonging to					
	Scheduled Caste			Scheduled Tribe		
	Boys	Girls	Total	Boys	Girls	Total
1	2	3	4	5	6	7
Andhra Pradesh	9615	3735	13350	1077	296	1373
Arunachal Pradesh	4	4	8	1465	308	1773
Assam	5166	3470	8636	10672	5136	15808
Bihar	0	0	0	0	0	0
Goa	11	10	21	3	0	3
Gujarat	13000	7000	20000	13500	9200	22700
Haryana	6169	802	6971	0	0	0
Himachal Pradesh	1000	413	1413	340	140	480
Jammu & Kashmir	208	185	393	0	0	0
Karnataka	14561	5058	19619	4516	1296	5812
Kerala	1696	1854	3550	78	72	150
Madhya Pradesh	8302	1657	9959	6260	1394	7654
Maharashtra	29112	11951	41063	6358	2250	8608
Manipur	427	524	951	1317	844	2161
Meghalaya	33	30	63	1716	1629	3345
Mizoram	0	0	0	2122	1338	3460
Nagaland	0	0	0	1367	826	2193
Orissa	3388	591	3979	2118	551	2669
Punjab	6577	4944	11521	0	0	0
Rajasthan	3708	214	3922	2829	90	2919
Sikkim	16	14	30	98	83	181
Tamil Nadu	2761	1491	4252	50	15	65
Tripura	493	294	787	178	119	297
Uttar Pradesh	35066	2649	37715	520	282	802
West Bengal	6002	4161	10163	332	212	544
A & N Islands	0	0	0	24	18	42
Chandigarh	128	61	189	37	10	47
D & N Haveli	0	0	0	0	0	0
Daman & Diu	14	11	25	88	16	104
Delhi	2210	2063	4273	153	142	295
Lakshadweep	0	0	0	0	0	0
Pondicherry	144	94	238	0	0	0
India	149811	53280	203091	57218	26267	83485

TABLE 13.34 : Scheduled Castes/Scheduled Tribes Studying in B. Sc./B. Sc. (Hons.)

State/Union Territory	Number of Students Belonging To					
	Scheduled Caste			Scheduled Tribe		
	Boys	Girls	Total	Boys	Girls	Total
1	2	3	4	5	6	7
Andhra Pradesh	3645	1426	5071	463	142	605
Arunachal Pradesh	0	0	0	87	17	104
Assam	1230	346	1576	1242	345	1587
Bihar	0	0	0	0	0	0
Goa	9	2	11	3	0	3
Gujarat	950	300	1250	430	170	600
Haryana	307	72	379	0	0	0
Himachal Pradesh	300	100	400	112	45	157
Jammu & Kashmir	424	117	541	0	0	0
Karnataka	2257	921	3178	467	241	708
Kerala	1444	1639	3083	42	31	73
Madhya Pradesh	1763	389	2152	910	205	1115
Maharashtra	9001	2469	11470	1921	432	2353
Manipur	301	249	550	264	187	451
Meghalaya	35	32	67	385	243	628
Mizoram	0	0	0	227	145	372
Nagaland	0	0	0	191	35	226
Orissa	685	172	857	642	78	720
Punjab	421	218	639	0	0	0
Rajasthan	621	58	679	331	15	346
Sikkim	3	7	10	19	10	29
Tamil Nadu	8565	4822	13387	124	124	248
Tripura	158	39	197	55	15	70
Uttar Pradesh	4781	274	5055	134	40	174
West Bengal	3895	3172	7067	111	41	152
A & N Islands	0	0	0	0	0	0
Chandigarh	20	4	24	7	3	10
D & N Haveli	0	0	0	0	0	0
Daman & Diu	1	0	1	0	0	0
Delhi	335	115	450	13	15	28
Lakshadweep	0	0	0	0	0	0
Pondicherry	116	121	237	0	0	0
India	41267	17064	58331	8180	2579	10759

TABLE 13.35 : Scheduled Castes/Scheduled Tribes Studying in B. Com./B. Com. (Hons.)

State/Union Territory	Number of Students Belonging to					
	Scheduled Caste			Scheduled Tribe		
	Boys	Girls	Total	Boys	Girls	Total
1	2	3	4	5	6	7
Andhra Pradesh	4664	1175	5839	630	140	770
Arunachal Pradesh	0	0	0	97	8	105
Assam	981	188	1169	747	235	982
Bihar	0	0	0	0	0	0
Goa	36	17	53	1	0	1
Gujarat	4100	1600	5700	2600	900	3500
Haryana	593	262	855	0	0	0
Himachal Pradesh	101	53	154	57	17	74
Jammu & Kashmir	60	8	68	0	0	0
Karnataka	2533	1345	3876	674	318	992
Kerala	754	563	1317	12	12	24
Madhya Pradesh	2622	184	2806	1450	72	1522
Maharashtra	15725	6022	21747	3214	1075	4289
Manipur	26	13	39	40	35	75
Meghalaya	19	13	32	317	86	403
Mizoram	0	0	0	144	43	187
Nagaland	0	0	0	216	37	253
Orissa	435	86	521	402	91	403
Punjab	346	106	452	0	0	0
Rajasthan	333	19	352	129	6	135
Sikkim	3	1	4	9	1	10
Tamil Nadu	3185	1698	4883	56	42	98
Tripura	119	14	133	20	5	25
Uttar Pradesh	2757	26	2783	74	2	76
West Bengal	5892	138	6030	218	12	230
A & N Islands	0	0	0	0	0	0
Chandigarh	1	2	3	0	0	0
D & N Haveli	0	0	0	0	0	0
Daman & Diu	13	3	16	16	1	17
Delhi	1670	307	1977	58	19	77
Lakshadweep	0	0	0	0	0	0
Pondicherry	51	35	86	0	0	0
India	47019	13878	60897	11181	3157	14338

TABLE 13.36 : Scheduled Castes/Scheduled Tribes Studying in B. E./B. Sc. (Engg.)/B. Arch.

State/Union Territory	Number of Students Belonging to					
	Scheduled Caste			Scheduled Tribe		
	Boys	Girls	Total	Boys	Girls	Total
1	2	3	4	5	6	7
Andhra Pradesh	2627	300	2927	461	39	500
Arunachal Pradesh	0	0	0	0	0	0
Assam	215	14	229	289	27	316
Bihar	0	0	0	0	0	0
Goa	0	0	0	0	0	0
Gujarat	0	0	0	0	0	0
Haryana	405	19	424	0	0	0
Himachal Pradesh	27	0	27	13	1	14
Jammu & Kashmir	34	2	36	0	0	0
Karnataka	2652	489	3141	577	142	719
Kerala	639	505	1144	34	5	39
Madhya Pradesh	982	47	1029	1395	54	1449
Maharashtra	2666	293	2959	287	28	315
Manipur	0	0	0	0	0	0
Meghalaya	0	0	0	0	0	0
Mizoram	0	0	0	0	0	0
Nagaland	0	0	0	0	0	0
Orissa	225	11	236	285	18	303
Punjab	504	25	529	6	0	6
Rajasthan	0	0	0	0	0	0
Sikkim	0	0	0	0	0	0
Tamil Nadu	2449	570	3019	115	12	127
Tripura	69	6	75	96	2	98
Uttar Pradesh	86	3	89	64	0	64
West Bengal	320	12	332	50	3	53
A & N Islands	0	0	0	0	0	0
Chandigarh	192	4	196	38	1	39
D & N Haveli	0	0	0	0	0	0
Daman & Diu	0	0	0	0	0	0
Delhi	405	33	438	73	4	77
Lakshadweep	0	0	0	0	0	0
Pondicherry	83	40	123	0	0	0
India	14580	2373	16953	3783	336	4119

TABLE 13.37 : Scheduled Castes/Scheduled Tribes Studying in B. Ed./B. T.

State/Union Territory	Number of Students Belonging to Scheduled Caste			Scheduled Tribe		
	Boys	Girls	Total	Boys	Girls	Total
1	2	3	4	5	6	7
Andhra Pradesh	555	411	966	127	26	153
Arunachal Pradesh	0	0	0	21	3	24
Assam	130	94	224	143	104	247
Bihar	0	0	0	0	0	0
Goa	1	0	1	0	0	0
Gujarat	325	135	460	270	160	430
Haryana	303	94	397	0	0	0
Himachal Pradesh	5	1	6	0	0	0
Jammu & Kashmir	19	7	26	0	0	0
Karnataka	325	105	430	41	20	61
Kerala	220	307	527	12	8	20
Madhya Pradesh	2	1	3	102	44	146
Maharashtra	1641	598	2239	476	182	658
Manipur	2	1	3	40	5	45
Meghalaya	1	1	2	79	85	164
Mizoram	0	0	0	110	32	142
Nagaland	0	0	0	31	21	52
Orissa	146	68	214	128	42	170
Punjab	165	217	382	0	0	0
Rajasthan	776	74	850	444	19	463
Sikkim	0	0	0	0	0	0
Tamil Nadu	92	253	345	0	3	3
Tripura	34	3	37	48	17	65
Uttar Pradesh	1288	264	1552	23	16	39
West Bengal	470	42	512	31	9	40
A & N Islands	0	0	0	1	0	1
Chandigarh	21	47	68	1	0	1
D & N Haveli	0	0	0	0	0	0
Daman & Diu	3	3	6	6	8	14
Delhi	21	54	75	10	2	12
Lakshadweep	0	0	0	0	0	0
Pondicherry	22	9	31	0	0	0
India	6567	2789	9356	2144	806	2950

TABLE 13.38 : Scheduled Castes/Scheduled Tribes Studying in M. B. B. S./Ayurved

State/Union Territory	Number of Students Belonging to					
	Scheduled Caste			Scheduled Tribe		
	Boys	Girls	Total	Boys	Girls	Total
1	2	3	4	5	6	7
Andhra Pradesh	393	359	752	238	758	996
Arunachal Pradesh	0	0	0	0	0	0
Assam	112	42	154	209	87	296
Bihar	0	0	0	0	0	0
Goa	13	9	22	0	0	0
Gujarat	0	0	0	0	0	0
Haryana	77	38	115	0	0	0
Himachal Pradesh	38	8	46	19	2	21
Jammu & Kashmir	50	34	84	0	0	0
Karnataka	0	0	0	22	7	29
Kerala	139	129	268	20	22	42
Madhya Pradesh	369	107	476	236	90	326
Maharashtra	1231	938	2169	307	129	436
Manipur	12	0	12	166	65	231
Meghalaya	0	0	0	0	0	0
Mizoram	0	0	0	0	0	0
Nagaland	0	0	0	0	0	0
Orissa	137	55	192	117	63	180
Punjab	327	184	511	2	1	3
Rajasthan	0	0	0	0	0	0
Sikkim	0	0	0	0	0	0
Tamil Nadu	692	492	1184	38	18	56
Tripura	0	0	0	0	0	0
Uttar Pradesh	159	22	181	40	1	41
West Bengal	313	35	348	12	3	15
A & N Islands	0	0	0	0	0	0
Chandigarh	0	0	0	0	0	0
D & N Haveli	0	0	0	0	0	0
Daman & Diu	0	0	0	0	0	0
Delhi	245	224	469	12	26	38
Lakshadweep	0	0	0	0	0	0
Pondicherry	115	50	165	0	0	0
India	4422	2726	7148	1438	1272	2710

TABLE 13.39 : Scheduled Castes/Scheduled Tribes Studying in Inter/Jr. Colleges/ Pre-Univ. (2 Yrs.)/Pre-Deg. (1 Yrs.)

State/Union Territory	Number of Students Belonging to					
	Scheduled Caste			Scheduled Tribe		
	Boys	Girls	Total	Boys	Girls	Total
1	2	3	4	5	6	7
Andhra Pradesh	21160	7823	28983	4803	970	5773
Arunachal Pradesh	0	0	0	0	0	0
Assam	9542	5856	15398	16374	8904	25278
Bihar	0	0	0	0	0	0
Goa	0	0	0	0	0	0
Gujarat	0	0	0	0	0	0
Haryana	0	0	0	0	0	0
Himachal Pradesh	0	0	0	0	0	0
Jammu & Kashmir	0	0	0	0	0	0
Karnataka	24448	8124	32564	4332	1391	5723
Kerala	12823	13951	26774	921	643	1564
Madhya Pradesh	0	0	0	0	0	0
Maharashtra	48478	17679	66157	8617	2461	11078
Manipur	592	818	1410	2145	1497	3642
Meghalaya	316	138	454	4219	3981	8200
Mizoram	0	0	0	1279	959	2238
Nagaland	0	0	0	3059	1910	4969
Orissa	9750	4000	13750	5800	2000	7800
Punjab	0	0	0	0	0	0
Rajasthan	0	0	0	0	0	0
Sikkim	0	0	0	0	0	0
Tamil Nadu	0	0	0	0	0	0
Tripura	0	0	0	0	0	0
Uttar Pradesh	189	77	266	18	6	24
West Bengal	0	0	0	0	0	0
A & N Islands	0	0	0	0	0	0
Chandigarh	0	0	0	0	0	0
D & N Haveli	0	0	0	0	0	0
Daman & Diu	0	0	0	0	0	0
Delhi	0	0	0	0	0	0
Lakshadweep	0	0	0	226	115	341
Pondicherry	35	24	59	0	0	0
India	127325	58490	185815	51793	24837	76630

TABLE 13.40 : Scheduled Castes/Scheduled Tribes Studying in Hr. Secondary (10+2 New Pattern, XI-XII Classes)

State/Union Territory	Number of Students Belonging to					
	Scheduled Caste			Scheduled Tribe		
	Boys	Girls	Total	Boys	Girls	Total
1	2	3	4	5	6	7
Andhra Pradesh	429	213	642	116	49	165
Arunachal Pradesh	6	6	12	2957	1281	4238
Assam	7980	4700	12680	10325	6218	16543
Bihar	1397	534	1931	1001	468	1469
Goa	95	56	151	7	3	10
Gujarat	30719	17007	47726	28395	16409	44804
Haryana	13741	3843	17584	0	0	0
Himachal Pradesh	4260	1440	5700	1410	370	1780
Jammu & Kashmir	2279	972	3251	0	0	0
Karanataka	34275	13043	47318	5406	2329	7735
Kerala	245	284	529	20	13	33
Madhya Pradesh	39634	8898	48532	36476	6180	42656
Maharashtra	42455	21761	64216	18070	7527	25597
Manipur	30	30	60	600	550	1150
Meghalaya	14	7	21	33	15	48
Mizoram	0	0	0	0	0	0
Nagaland	0	0	0	42	25	67
Orissa	200	150	350	210	90	300
Punjab	18929	9751	28680	0	0	0
Rajasthan	44000	4000	48000	17000	2000	19000
Sikkim	84	70	154	396	261	657
Tamil Nadu	49054	23846	72900	1928	1256	3184
Tripura	1481	699	2180	1612	535	2147
Uttar Pradesh	117406	22665	140071	1173	628	1801
West Bengal	28765	11359	40124	5972	3528	9500
A & N Islands	0	0	0	104	83	187
Chandigarh	443	558	1001	4	3	7
D & N Haveli	43	28	71	342	151	493
Daman & Diu	56	19	75	49	15	64
Delhi	12796	10199	22995	116	61	177
Lakshadweep	0	0	0	0	0	0
Pondicherry	730	591	1321	0	0	0
India	451546	156729	608275	133764	50048	183812

TABLE 13.41 : Scheduled Castes/Scheduled Tribes Studying in High/Post Basic (Classes IX-X)

State/Union Territory	Number of Students Belonging to					
	Scheduled Caste			Scheduled Tribe		
	Boys	Girls	Total	Boys	Girls	Total
1	2	3	4	5	6	7
Andhra Pradesh	93252	46089	139341	21757	6228	27985
Arunachal Pradesh	8	4	12	6140	3387	9527
Assam	37477	33208	70685	54150	39457	93607
Bihar	61714	10618	72332	38128	16261	54389
Goa	348	218	566	19	3	22
Gujarat	59356	32348	91704	56815	33370	90185
Haryana	33102	13317	46419	0	0	0
Himachal Pradesh	18730	10270	29000	3000	2040	5040
Jammu & Kashmir	6432	2803	9235	0	0	0
Karnataka	69101	34973	104074	17850	8919	26769
Kerala	49485	52923	102408	3303	3580	6883
Madhya Pradesh	64271	17614	81885	53481	13242	66723
Maharashtra	168086	96802	264888	72323	36491	108814
Manipur	490	450	940	6280	4920	11200
Meghalaya	351	210	561	10745	9351	20096
Mizoram	0	0	0	10334	10185	20519
Nagaland	0	0	0	9410	8388	17798
Orissa	53000	19000	72000	33000	21000	54000
Punjab	59770	40747	100517	0	0	0
Rajasthan	83500	8500	92000	65000	4000	69000
Sikkim	181	154	335	890	749	1639
Tamil Nadu	140645	79227	219872	5503	3532	9035
Tripura	5222	3195	8417	7824	3941	11765
Uttar Pradesh	275057	45375	320432	2432	758	3190
West Bengal	96351	42516	138867	16312	8635	24947
A & N Islands	0	0	0	388	400	788
Chandigarh	1652	1355	3007	0	3	3
D & N Haveli	60	36	96	751	378	1129
Daman & Diu	80	88	168	134	118	252
Delhi	22416	17155	39571	156	97	253
Lakshadweep	0	0	0	780	572	1352
Pondicherry	2233	1959	4192	0	0	0
India	1402370	611154	2013524	496905	240005	736910

TABLE 13.42 : Scheduled Castes/Scheduled Tribes Studyingin Middle/Senior Basic (Classes VI-VIII)

State/Union Territory	Number of Students Belonging to					
	Scheduled Caste			Scheduled Tribe		
	Boys	Girls	Total	Boys	Girls	Total
1	2	3	4	5	6	7
Andhra Pradesh	207924	120878	328802	57416	20485	77901
Arunachal Pradesh	37	19	56	12803	8903	21706
Assam	94425	77761	172186	121270	93518	214788
Bihar	170506	50132	220638	97106	47206	144312
Goa	671	490	1161	57	25	82
Gujarat	121440	73731	195171	135895	80909	216804
Haryana	80980	47512	128492	0	0	0
Himachal Pradesh	43280	29430	72710	7640	4180	11820
Jammu & Kashmir	19073	13206	32279	0	0	0
Karnataka	175505	114396	289901	54236	35599	89835
Kerala	108799	104097	212896	9302	8467	17769
Madhra Pradesh	298860	83692	382552	234112	74845	308957
Maharashtra	342332	234967	577299	164671	99227	263898
Manipur	870	810	1680	15170	12250	27420
Meghalaya	568	403	971	21183	19771	40954
Mizoram	0	0	0	30063	26734	56797
Nagaland	0	0	0	27791	24769	52560
Orissa	134300	78300	212600	127200	57900	185100
Punjab	138459	96742	235201	0	0	0
Rajasthan	210000	45000	255000	143000	32000	175000
Sikkim	501	462	963	2158	1943	4101
Tamil Nadu	367522	273347	640869	14498	9912	24410
Tripura	13098	9242	22340	24488	12271	36759
Uttar Pradesh	591194	155935	747129	6291	2279	8570
West Bengal	382175	352211	734386	112115	92730	204845
A & N Islands	0	0	0	849	733	1582
Chandigarh	3471	2780	6251	1	2	3
D & N Haveli	99	85	184	2260	1118	3378
Daman & Diu	163	135	298	473	352	825
Delhi	53840	42841	96681	262	160	422
Lakshadweep	0	0	0	2064	1472	3536
Pondichery	5674	5687	11361	0	0	0
India	3565766	2014291	5580057	1424374	769760	2194134

TABLE 13.43 : Scheduled Castes/Scheduled Tribes Studying in Primary/Junior Basic (Classes I-V)

State/Union Territory	Number of Students Belonging to					
	Schedules Caste			Scheduled Tribe		
	Boys	Girls	Total	Boys	Girls	Total
1	2	3	4	5	6	7
Andhra Pradesh	808974	645811	1454785	320466	205245	525711
Arunachal Pradesh	94	64	158	55034	42881	97915
Assam	233928	207594	441522	375211	311701	686912
Bihar	857300	362057	1219357	481706	293910	775616
Goa	1613	1443	3056	79	54	133
Gujarat	340355	268726	609081	546112	388783	934895
Haryana	254353	215259	469612	0	0	0
Himachal Pradesh	99010	83660	182670	16940	13000	29940
Jammu & Kashmir	42902	31279	74181	0	0	0
Karnataka	599535	489543	1089078	194503	151579	346082
Kerala	171154	163814	334968	18905	18394	37299
Madhya Pradesh	700661	475886	1176547	875031	518729	1393760
Maharashtra	885079	760350	1645429	587811	463262	1051073
Manipur	2100	1950	4050	46060	39390	85450
Meghalaya	1293	1031	2324	78864	73564	152428
Mizoram	0	0	0	60874	54795	115669
Nagaland	0	0	0	75728	67229	142957
Orissa	441100	280800	721900	545100	264200	809300
Punjab	416981	338873	755854	0	0	0
Rajasthan	605000	204000	809000	425000	143000	568000
Sikkim	2482	2187	4669	8954	7611	16565
Tamil Nadu	854406	738150	1592556	41451	32604	74055
Tripura	39674	33410	73084	76311	55484	131795
Uttar Pradesh	1744149	737375	2481524	19497	11307	30804
West Bengal	1176675	1012271	2188946	286712	271767	558479
A & N Islands	0	0	0	1877	1710	3587
Chandigarh	8555	6915	15470	4	10	14
D & N Haveli	214	175	389	9299	5881	15180
Daman & Diu	272	280	552	990	810	1800
Delhi	113125	95154	208279	371	315	686
Lakshadweep	0	0	0	4665	3912	8577
Pondicherry	10754	10995	21749	0	0	0
India	10411738	7169052	17580790	5153555	3441127	8594682

TABLE 13.44 : Scheduled Castes/Scheduled Tribes Studying at Pre-Primary/Pre-Basic Stage

State/Union Territory	Number of Students Belonging to					
	Scheduled Caste			Scheduled Tribe		
	Boys	Girls	Total	Boys	Girls	Total
1	2	3	4	5	6	7
Andhra Pradesh	2691	1972	4663	762	479	1241
Arunachal Pradesh	17	6	23	6950	5613	12563
Assam	1209	727	1936	1450	910	2368
Bihar	603	498	1101	6206	4874	11080
Goa	0	0	0	0	0	0
Gujarat	8849	5950	14799	3663	3018	6681
Haryana	215	158	373	0	0	0
Himachal Pradesh	280	250	530	70	50	120
Jammu & Kashmir	0	0	0	0	0	0
Karnataka	13673	11184	24857	2400	1900	4300
Kerala	1115	1015	2130	179	132	311
Madhya Pradesh	4320	2584	6904	3281	1865	5146
Maharashtra	25476	21947	47423	16415	14629	31044
Manipur	1010	960	1970	21950	18950	40900
Meghalaya	861	732	1593	53600	51373	104973
Mizoram	0	0	0	0	0	0
Nagaland	0	0	0	34122	30667	64789
Orissa	0	0	0	0	0	0
Punjab	373	251	624	0	0	0
Rajasthan	13000	8000	21000	7000	4000	11000
Sikkim	640	545	1185	1889	1620	3509
Tamil Nadu	0	0	0	0	0	0
Tripura	22367	21745	44112	34427	34645	69072
Uttar Pradesh	533	235	768	0	0	0
West Bengal	0	0	0	0	0	0
A & N Islands	0	0	0	90	105	195
Chandigarh	820	784	1604	1	0	1
D & N Haveli	8	6	14	18	12	30
Daman & Diu	24	7	31	15	9	24
Delhi	6716	6314	13030	36	35	71
Lakshadweep	0	0	0	512	529	1041
Pondicherry	547	454	1001	0	0	0
India	105347	86324	191671	195036	175415	370451

TABLE 13.45 : Scheduled Castes/Scheduled Tribes Studying in Teacher Training Schools

State/Union Territory	Number of Students Belonging to					
	Scheduled Caste			Scheduled Tribe		
	Boys	Girls	Total	Boys	Girls	Total
1	2	3	4	5	6	7
Andhra Pradesh	367	184	551	499	217	716
Arunachal Pradesh	0	0	0	0	0	0
Assam	5	4	9	15	11	26
Bihar	636	798	1434	698	996	1694
Goa	0	0	0	0	0	0
Gujarat	542	610	1152	704	606	1310
Haryana	23	14	37	0	0	0
Himachal Pradesh	0	0	0	85	46	131
Jammu & Kashmir	17	3	20	12	0	12
Karnataka	665	578	1243	114	92	206
Kerala	118	332	450	34	67	101
Madhya Pradesh	1100	177	1277	1192	274	1466
Maharashtra	2297	1395	3692	1340	731	2071
Manipur	0	0	0	0	0	0
Meghalaya	0	0	0	350	322	672
Mizoram	0	0	0	220	130	350
Nagaland	0	0	0	32	6	38
Orissa	315	312	627	235	175	410
Punjab	82	273	355	0	0	0
Rajashtan	850	427	1277	512	225	737
Sikkim	1	2	3	3	3	6
Tamil Nadu	327	1448	1775	18	79	97
Tripura	35	0	35	95	0	95
Uttar Pradesh	407	215	622	25	11	36
West Bengal	612	319	931	186	192	378
A & N Islands	0	0	0	3	4	7
Chandigarh	0	0	0	0	0	0
D & N Haveli	0	0	0	0	0	0
Daman & Diu	0	0	0	0	0	0
Delhi	50	150	200	0	0	0
Lakshadweep	0	0	0	0	0	0
Pondicherry	0	0	0	0	0	0
India	8449	7241	15690	6372	4195	10567

TABLE 13.46 : Scheduled Castes/Scheduled Tribes Studying in Polytechnic Institutes

State/Union Territory	Number of Students Belonging to					
	Scheduled Caste			Scheduled Tribe		
	Boys	Girls	Total	Boys	Girls	Total
1	2	3	4	5	6	7
Andhra Pradesh	5404	1255	6659	1837	293	2130
Arunachal Pradesh	0	0	0	71	3	74
Assam	282	50	332	261	28	289
Bihar	534	10	544	226	40	266
Goa	2	0	2	1	0	1
Gujarat	1200	199	1399	1896	225	2121
Haryana	962	83	1045	0	0	0
Himachal Pradesh	212	29	241	50	9	59
Jammu & Kashmir	26	5	31	0	0	0
Karnataka	2455	602	3057	602	95	697
Kerala	579	216	795	71	18	89
Madhya Pradesh	1358	118	1476	1227	75	1302
Maharashtra	3735	454	4189	1052	101	1153
Manipur	7	3	10	49	3	52
Meghalaya	17	0	17	105	15	120
Mizoram	0	0	0	219	65	284
Nagaland	0	0	0	297	3	300
Orissa	31	37	68	25	15	40
Punjab	919	136	1055	0	0	0
Rajasthan	503	90	593	410	26	436
Sikkim	0	0	0	0	0	0
Tamil Nadu	6156	1174	7330	108	11	119
Tripura	27	1	28	55	1	56
Uttar Pradesh	1761	48	1805	34	2	36
West Bengal	1820	42	1862	136	17	153
A & N Islands	0	0	0	4	1	5
Chandigarh	126	59	185	13	3	16
D.& N Haveli	0	0	0	0	0	0
Daman & Diu	21	0	21	11	0	11
Delhi	994	173	1167	104	16	120
Lakshadweep	0	0	0	0	0	0
Pondicherry	82	48	130	0	0	0
India	29213	4832	34045	8864	1065	9929

TABLE 13.47 : Scheduled Castes/Scheduled Tribes Studying in Technical Industrial. Arts and Craft School

State/Union Territory	Number of Students Belonging to					
	Scheduled Caste			Scheduled Tribe		
	Boys	Girls	Total	Boys	Girls	Total
1	2	3	4	5	6	7
Andhra Pradesh	11809	506	12315	2920	199	3119
Arunachal Pradesh	0	0	0	0	0	0
Assam	311	113	424	432	290	722
Bihar	1925	159	2084	1341	88	1429
Goa	5	2	7	7	0	7
Gujarat	445	38	483	469	89	558
Haryana	4652	830	5482	0	0	0
Himachal Pradesh	630	280	910	130	70	200
Jammu & Kashmir	142	73	215	62	6	68
Karnataka	0	0	0	27	2	29
Kerala	1888	1091	2979	161	52	213
Madhya Pradesh	1164	152	1316	2175	162	2337
Maharashtra	15012	1866	16878	5292	634	5926
Manipur	0	22	22	58	349	407
Meghalaya	16	5	21	50	25	75
Mizoram	0	0	0	105	44	149
Nagaland	0	0	0	0290	152	442
Orissa	385	19	404	197	5	202
Punjab	2843	771	3614	0	0	0
Rajasthan	1461	53	1514	1474	24	1498
Sikkim	3	1	4	5	3	8
Tamil Nadu	2791	531	3322	135	43	178
Tripura	51	23	74	93	19	112
Uttar Pradesh	838	37	875	69	10	79
West Bengal	242	315	557	34	3	37
A & N Islands	0	0	0	3	0	3
Chandigarh	110	67	177	5	4	9
D & N Haveli	0	0	0	0	0	0
Daman & Diu	30	5	35	58	3	61
Delhi	1823	535	2358	159	26	185
Lakshadweep	0	0	0	9	7	16
Pondicherry	0	50	50	0	0	0
India	48576	7544	56120	15760	2309	18069

TABLE 13.48 : Enrolment Ratio of Students Belonging to Scheduled Caste in Classes I, V, and VI-VIII

State/Union Territory	Classes I-V (6-11 Years)			Classes VI-VIII (11-14 Years)		
	Boys	Girls	Total	Boys	Girls	Total
1	2	3	4	5	6	7
Andhra Pradesh	135.62	113.26	124.69	63.40	38.33	51.11
Arunachal Pradesh	40.94	27.58	34.22	28.92	15.19	22.14
Assam	259.34	241.81	250.79	185.12	160.81	173.29
Bihar	96.86	44.61	71.86	35.38	11.27	23.81
Goa	109.28	97.47	103.37	76.03	55.25	65.61
Gujarat	183.45	154.51	169.45	114.72	74.25	95.13
Haryana	116.12	105.33	110.91	67.53	42.51	55.37
Himachal Pradesh	134.59	113.61	124.09	99.54	68.23	83.95
Jammu & Kashmir	112.18	85.60	99.20	87.07	63.90	75.82
Karnataka	151.42	131.21	141.62	76.25	52.30	64.58
Kerala	114.48	112.22	113.36	120.47	118.18	119.34
Madhya Pradesh	110.64	81.21	96.49	85.35	25.76	56.68
Maharashtra	261.90	240.00	251.30	178.42	130.77	155.37
Manipur	130.92	130.60	130.77	101.24	97.26	99.28
Meghalaya	290.08	230.91	260.47	223.76	154.82	188.86
Mizoram	.00	.00	.00	.00	.00	.00
Nagaland	.00	.00	.00	.00	.00	.00
Orissa	155.03	94.46	124.08	84.71	47.44	65.70
Punjab	129.92	116.30	123.44	72.69	56.92	65.25
Rajasthan	112.88	40.22	77.55	69.24	16.15	43.82
Sikkim	132.49	119.33	125.98	48.26	47.13	47.71
Tamil Nadu	164.08	149.47	156.97	112.25	87.59	100.21
Tripura	169.06	145.28	157.29	99.10	73.37	86.54
Uttar Pradesh	86.96	41.40	65.54	52.33	15.65	35.14
West Bengal	125.85	117.64	121.92	68.82	67.31	68.09
A & N Islands	.00	.00	.00	.00	.00	.00
Chandigarh	127.22	113.73	120.81	88.17	82.34	85.48
D & N Haveli	97.35	87.47	92.64	77.08	71.69	74.49
Daman & Diu	.00	.00	.00	.00	.00	.00
Delhi	106.38	103.09	104.86	83.41	79.59	81.67
Lakshadweep	.00	.00	.00	.00	.00	.00
Pondicherry	176.88	183.74	180.28	152.86	155.89	154.36
India	123.33	91.15	107.81	74.21	45.01	60.13

TABLE 13.49 : Enrolment Ratio of Students Belonging to Scheduled Tribe in Classes I, V and VI-VIII

State/Union Territory	Classes I-V (6-11 Years) Boys	Girls	Total	Classes VI-VIII (11-14 Years) Boys	Girls	Total
1	2	3	4	5	6	7
Andhra Pradesh	134.72	90.26	112.99	43.90	16.29	30.37
Arunachal Pradesh	140.71	108.48	124.51	58.76	41.80	50.37
Assam	198.24	173.03	185.94	113.30	92.17	103.02
Bihar	95.03	63.23	79.82	35.18	18.53	27.19
Goa	12.47	8.50	10.48	15.05	6.57	10.80
Gujarat	148.00	112.40	130.77	64.55	40.97	53.14
Haryana	.00	.00	.00	.00	.00	.00
Himachal Pradesh	123.25	94.49	108.86	94.05	51.87	73.04
Jammu & Kashmir	.00	.00	.00	.00	.00	.00
Karnataka	150.78	124.70	138.12	72.32	49.95	61.42
Kerala	123.01	122.59	122.80	100.20	93.51	96.90
Madhya Pradesh	84.82	54.34	70.17	41.04	14.14	28.10
Maharashtra	135.13	113.61	124.72	66.68	42.90	55.18
Manipur	132.97	122.16	127.76	81.75	68.11	75.03
Meghalaya	83.43	77.69	80.55	39.35	35.81	37.56
Mizoram	148.26	141.51	144.98	119.49	110.36	115.01
Nagaland	119.41	109.49	114.53	72.87	67.48	70.23
Orissa	125.22	58.09	90.92	52.44	22.93	37.39
Punjab	.00	.00	.00	.00	.00	.00
Rajasthan	113.00	40.18	77.59	67.19	16.36	42.85
Sikkim	119.49	103.82	111.74	51.96	49.56	50.80
Tamil Nadu	136.52	113.22	125.18	75.94	54.47	65.46
Tripura	173.29	128.57	151.16	98.73	51.91	75.89
Uttar Pradesh	97.95	63.97	81.97	56.11	23.05	40.61
West Bengal	119.78	123.36	121.49	78.86	69.22	74.18
A & N Islands	67.52	57.26	62.20	57.32	51.17	54.30
Chandigarh	.00	.00	.00	.00	.00	.00
D & N Haveli	133.29	92.62	113.91	55.44	29.71	43.09
Daman & Diu	.00	.00	.00	.00	.00	.00
Delhi	.00	.00	.00	.00	.00	.00
Lakshadweep	168.14	141.00	154.57	135.66	102.79	119.72
Pondicherryh	.00	.00	.00	.00	.00	.00
India	123.90	88.80	106.97	60.17	34.91	47.99

13.5 EDUCATIONAL OUTLAYS IN STATES

TABLE 13.50 : Budgeted Expenditure (Revenue Account) on Education and Other Department 1992-93

State/Union Territory	Budgeted Expenditure (Revenue Accounts) Plan	Non-Plan	Total (Rs. in Crores)	Population As on 01-03-93 (in Hundreds)	Percapita Budgeted Expenditure (In Rs.)	% of Budgeted Expdt. On Edn. to total Budget (Revenue Account)
1	2	3	4	5	6	7
Andhra Pradesh	190.67	1563.81	1754.48	677080	259.12	24.60
Arunachal Pradesh	19.15	31.35	50.50	8811	573.15	12.85
Assam	251.19	471.05	722.24	259199	278.64	27.62
Bihar	193.30	1401.25	1594.55	922607	172.83	24.65
Goa	16.05	66.06	82.11	13228	620.73	21.86
Gujarat	86.75	1154.81	1241.56	437352	283.88	23.24
Harayana	108.13	405.25	513.18	175118	293.16	20.07
Himachal Pradesh	58.69	191.17	249.86	55620	449.23	20.50
Jammu & Kashmir	29.48	139.30	168.78	81084	208.15	13.85
Karnataka	282.50	1043.86	1326.36	463071	286.43	23.36
Kerala	68.48	1033.57	1102.05	309292	356.31	29.94
Madhya Pradesh	326.70	1191.45	1518.15	681121	222.89	24.71
Maharashtra	101.00	2237.23	2338.23	809462	288.86	21.19
Manipur	19.31	77.29	96.60	19434	497.07	24.85
Meghalaya	27.27	61.33	88.60	18227	486.09	20.31
Mizoram	12.39	43.93	56.32	7417	759.34	17.20
Nagaland	12.82	50.26	63.08	11715	538.45	13.45
Orissa	211.48	549.10	760.58	331888	229.17	23.41
Punjab	139.64	622.16	761.80	209764	363.17	20.47
Rajasthan	214.85	930.05	1144.90	456583	250.75	24.01
Sikkim	12.12	20.73	32.85	4854	676.76	19.55
Tamil Nadu	108.07	1554.74	1662.81	568840	292.32	22.92
Tripura	40.35	112.69	15304	28009	546.40	23.27
Uttar Pradesh	254.56	2065.58	2320.14	1402792	165.39	20.35
West Bengal	234.65	1734.87	1969.52	686274	286.99	30.38
A & N Islands	5.16	20.64	25.80	3031	851.20	14.06
Chandigarh	7.78	45.24	53.02	7641	693.89	23.77
D & N Haveli	1.35	3.61	4.96	1506	329.35	13.60
Daman & Diu	1.16	3.72	4.88	1039	469.68	18.59
Delhi	70.66	294.35	365.01	97405	374.73	32.14
Lakshadweep	1.45	5.03	6.48	565	1146.90	12.88
Pondicherry	15.40	35.88	51.28	8023	639.16	19.93
States/ UTs	3122.56	19161.36	22283.92	8758052	254.44	23.44
Centre	1735.17	1137.18	2872.35	—	—	3.21
India	4857.73	20298.54	25156.17	8758052	287.24	13.62

TABLE 13.51 : Budgeted Expenditure on Education by Education Departments for 1993-94 Ranked in Order of Percentage of Education Budget to Total Budget

(Rs. in Crores)

S.No.	State/Union Territory	Budget of Education Department			Total State Budget	% of Edn. Budget to Total State Budget
		Plan	Non-Plan	Total		
1	2	3	4	5	6	7
1.	Delhi	78.91	307.98	386.89	1308.44	29.57
2.	West Bengal	121.38	1811.72	1933.10	7195.97	26.86
3.	Kerala	38.73	1091.96	1130.69	4306.75	26.25
4.	Assam	217.49	465.26	682.75	2774.50	24.61
5.	Manipur	13.42	80.08	93.50	388.84	24.05
6.	Karnataka	341.10	1068.41	1409.51	6588.49	21.39
7.	Tamil Nadu	67.90	1702.97	1770.87	8300.88	21.33
8.	Himachal Pradesh	62.68	232.27	294.95	1393.81	21.16
9.	Andhra Pradesh	140.29	1520.86	1661.15	7924.66	20.96
10.	Rajasthan	183.71	945.67	1129.38	5404.70	20.90
11.	Gujarat	44.70	1192.41	1237.11	5947.72	20.80
12.	Chandigarh	6.30	46.59	52.89	261.47	20.23
13.	Tripura	25.80	107.88	133.68	662.84	20.17
14.	Bihar	133.06	1327.16	1460.22	7266.19	20.10
15.	Orissa	133.81	584.45	718.26	3626.00	19.81
16.	Goa	13.75	70.17	83.92	429.58	19.54
17.	Uttar Pradesh	253.46	2221.13	2474.59	13172.80	18.79
18.	Madhya Pradesh	168.09	1034.89	1202.98	6595.04	18.24
19.	Maharashtra	106.47	2123.99	2230.46	12500.64	17.84
20.	Meghalaya	26.58	64.50	91.08	516.59	17.63
21.	Punjab	98.16	588.76	686.92	4001.11	17.17
22.	Sikkim	9.70	21.92	31.62	186.42	16.96
23.	Daman & Diu	0.79	4.48	5.27	32.34	16.30
24.	Haryana	75.82	379.76	455.58	2829.32	16.10
25.	Pondicherry	10.44	35.37	45.81	296.70	15.44
26.	Mizoram	10.79	44.39	55.18	364.88	15.12
27.	Nagaland	8.63	51.36	59.99	501.30	11.97
28.	Dadra & Nagar Haveli	1.20	3.86	5.06	42.96	11.78
29.	Arunachal Pradesh	25.76	32.22	57.98	498.75	11.63
30.	A & N Islands	3.51	21.33	24.84	206.16	12.05
31.	Jammu & Kashmir	23.95	114.15	138.10	1219.05	11.33
32.	Lakshadweep	1.05	7.59	8.64	78.09	11.06
All States/Uts		2447.43	19305.54	21752.97	106822.99	20.36
Central Sector		1308.78	847.18	2155.96	101839.00	2.12
Total (Centre & States)		3756.21	20152.72	23908.93	208661.99	11.46

TABLE 13.52 : Approved Outlays for Eighth Five Year Plan Period (1992-97)

(Rs. in Crores)

S.No.	State/Union Territory	Elementary Education	Adult Education	General Education	Technical Education	Total Education (Col. 5+Col. 6)
1	2	3	4	5	6	7
1.	Andhra Pradesh	176.13	17.12	222.95	56.50	279.45
2.	Arunachal Pradesh	113.92	2.79	151.90	0.00	151.90
3.	Assam	568.35	18.36	874.38	45.33	919.71
4.	Bihar	588.83	60.34	726.95	185.22	912.17
5.	Goa	27.30	1.11	65.00	13.00	78.00
6.	Gujarat	149.82	22.47	227.00	90.00	317.00
7.	Haryana	202.44	6.40	407.04	106.30	513.34
8.	Himachal Pradesh	98.90	1.77	230.00	42.00	272.00
9.	Jammu & Kashmir	157.65	7.16	315.30	19.00	334.30
10.	Karnataka	409.50	18.70	905.55	50.00	955.55
11.	Kerala	22.21	0.77	82.25	94.00	176.25
12.	Madhya Pradesh	432.68	19.84	618.12	85.38	703.50
13.	Maharashtra	350.00	22.00	730.07	225.18	955.25
14.	Manipur	40.80	2.05	68.00	5.50	73.50
15.	Meghalaya	64.33	3.37	90.60	1.37	91.97
16.	Mizoram	23,02	1.25	41.85	3.50	45.35
17.	Nagaland	18.47	0.72	42.95	4.50	47.45
18.	Orissa	242.66	44.91	527.52	82.86	610.38
19.	Punjab	47.15	10.80	216.78	196.00	412.78
20.	Rajasthan	567.75	30.50	860.23	100.18	960.41
21.	Sikkim	36.40	0.68	55.00	2.80	57.80
22.	Tamil Nadu	252.47	40.00	440.00	37.14	477.14
23.	Tripura	69.60	2.34	120.00	1.50	121.50
24.	Uttar Pradesh	663.53	24.26	1087.75	257.40	1345.15
25.	West Bengal	350.00	26.72	500.00	100.00	600.00
26.	A & N Islands	20.74	0.34	42.22	13.20	55.42
27.	Chandigarh	10.62	0.53	35.00	9.24	44.24
28.	Dadra & Nagar Haveli	7.00	0.06	10.78	2.00	12.78
29.	Daman & Diu	2.67	0.15	5.04	3.50	8.54
30.	Delhi	321.80	6.37	450.00	110.00	560.00
31.	Lakshadweep	1.68	0.16	7.02	0.00	7.02
32.	Pondicherry	18.04	0.40	37.10	19.78	56.88
All States/Uts		6056.46	394.44	10194.35	1962.38	12156.73
Centre		2880.00	1400.00	6619.00	824.00	7443.00
Total (Centre & States)		8936.46	1794.44	16813.35	2786.38	19599.73

Source : Analysis of Annual Plan 1992-93 (Education Sector) - Planning Commission.

TABLE 13.53 : Percentage of Sectorwise Approved Outlays to Total Outlays on Education during Eighth Plan Period

S.No.	State/Union Territory	Elementary Education	Adult Education	General Education	Technical Education	Total Education (Col. 5+Col. 6)
1	2	3	4	5	6	7
1.	Andhra Pradesh	63.03	61.3	79.78	20.22	100.00
2.	Arunachal Pradesh	75.00	1.84	100.00	0.00	100.00
3.	Assam	61.80	2.00	95.07	4.93	100.00
4.	Bihar	64.55	6.61	79.69	20.31	100.00
5.	Goa	35.00	1.42	83.33	16.67	100.00
6.	Gujarat	37.26	7.09	71.61	28.39	100.00
7.	Haryana	39.44	1.25	79.29	20.71	100.00
8.	Himachal Pradesh	36.36	0.65	84.56	15.44	100.00
9.	Jammu & Kashmir	47.16	2.14	94.32	5.68	100.00
10.	Karnataka	42.85	1.96	94.77	5.23	100.00
11.	Kerala	12.60	0.44	46.67	53.33	100.00
12.	Madhya Pradesh	61:50	2.82	87.86	12.14	100.00
13.	Maharashtra	36.64	2.30	76.43	23.57	100.00
14.	Manipur	55.51	2.79	92.52	7.48	100.00
15.	Meghalaya	69.95	3.66	98.51	1.49	100.00
16.	Mizoram	50.76	2.76	92.28	7.72	100.00
17.	Nagaland	38.93	1.52	90.52	9.48	100.00
18.	Orissa	39.76	7.36	86.42	13.58	100.00
19.	Punjab	11.42	2.62	52.52	47.48	100.00
20.	Rajasthan	59.12	3.18	89.57	10.43	100.00
21.	Sikkim	62.98	1.18	95.16	4.84	100.00
22.	Tamil Nadu	52.91	8.38	92.22	7.78	100.00
23.	Tripura	57.28	1.93	98.77	1.23	100.00
24.	Uttar Pradesh	49.33	1.80	80.86	19.14	100.00
25.	West Bengal	58.33	4.45	83.33	16.67	100.00
26.	A & N Islands	37.42	0.61	76.18	23.82	100.00
27.	Chandigarh	24.01	1.20	79.11	20.89	100.00
28.	Dadra & Nagar Haveli	54.77	0.47	84.35	15.65	100.00
29.	Daman & Diu	31.26	1.76	59.02	40.98	100.00
30.	Delhi	57.46	1.14	80.36	19.64	100.00
31.	Lakshadweep	23.93	2.28	100.00	0.0	100.00
32.	Pondicherry	31.72	0.70	65.23	34.77	100.00
	All States/Uts	49.82	3.24	83.86	16.14	100.00
	Centre	38.69	18.81	88.93	11.07	100.00
	Total (Centre & States)	45.59	9.16	85.78	14.22	100.00

TABLE 13.54 : Sectorwise Approved Plan Outlays for 1994-95

(Rs. in Crores)

S.No.	State/Union Territory	Elementary Education	Adult Education	General Education	Technical Education	Total Education (Col. 5+Col. 6)
1	2	3	4	5	6	7
1.	Andhra Pradesh	26.49	11.00	46.45	11.80	58.25
2.	Arunachal Pradesh	30.07	1.00	42.87	0.00	42.87
3.	Assam	116.26	3.49	201.71	12.81	214.52
4.	Bihar	92.99	10.00	118.99	32.87	151.86
5.	Goa	4.09	0.38	13.74	8.20	21.94
6.	Gujarat	14.51	3.95	34.35	24.00	58.35
7.	Haryana	34.24	2.00	74.40	38.97	113.37
8.	Himachal Pradesh	29.24	0.60	67.47	11.37	78.84
9.	Jammu & Kashmir	34.49	1.03	76.49	4.91	81.40
10.	Karnataka	129.04	9.12	247.59	18.94	266.53
11.	Kerala	0.00	0.00	25.75	25.00	50.75
12.	Madhya Pradesh	101.65	6.80	193.63	49.90	243.53
13.	Maharashtra	52.65	7.35	129.75	61.00	190.75
14.	Manipur	4.49	0.53	13.57	0.89	14.46
15.	Meghalaya	19.50	1.00	25.75	0.56	26.31
16.	Mizoram	5.75	0.18	9.81	0.75	10.56
17.	Nagaland	4.87	0.07	8.93	1.10	10.03
18.	Orissa	43.52	7.84	97.97	28.45	126.42
19.	Punjab	12.33	1.50	54.28	41.90	96.18
20.	Rajasthan	110.00	4.10	211.94	28.81	240.75
21.	Sikkim	6.60	0.12	10.25	0.25	10.50
22.	Tamil Nadu	42.57	19.24	81.60	15.03	96.63
23.	Tripura	17.00	0.80	27.50	0.15	27.65
24.	Uttar Pradesh	211.52	4.40	255.27	62.41	317.68
25.	West Bengal	29.49	5.26	78.94	21.70	100.64
26.	A & N Islands	6.55	0.06	13.96	2.07	16.03
27.	Chandigarh	3.14	0.00	9.87	2.16	12.03
28.	Dadra & Nagar Haveli	1.50	0.05	2.75	0.85	3.60
29.	Daman & Diu	0.90	0.03	1.70	1.30	3.00
30.	Delhi	76.66	0.52	127.50	29.00	156.50
31.	Lakshadweep	0.54	0.03	1.48	0.00	1.48
32.	Pondicherry	5.27	0.00	12.76	3.24	16.00
All States/UTs		1267.86	102.45	2319.02	540.39	2859.41
Centre		523.00	214.00	1318.46	231.00	1549.46
Total (Centre & States)		1790.86	316.45	3637.48	771.39	4408.87

Source: Planning Commission.

TABLE 13.55 : Percentage of Sectorwise Approved Plan Outlays for 1994-95

S.No.	State/Union Territory	Elementary Education	Adult Education	General Education	Technical Education	Total Education (Col. 5+Col. 6)
1	2	3	4	5	6	7
1.	Andhra Pradesh	45.48	18.88	79.74	20.26	100.00
2.	Arunachal Pradesh	70.14	2.33	100.00	0.00	100.00
3.	Assam	54.20	1.63	94.03	5.97	100.00
4.	Bihar	61.23	6.59	78.36	21.64	100.00
5.	Goa	18.64	1.73	62.63	37.37	100.00
6.	Gujarat	24.87	6.77	58.87	41.13	100.00
7.	Haryana	30.20	1.76	65.63	34.37	100.00
8.	Himachal Pradesh	37.09	0.76	85.58	14.42	100.00
9.	Jammu & Kashmir	42.37	1.27	93.97	6.03	100.00
10.	Karnataka	48.41	3.42	92.89	7.11	100.00
11.	Kerala	0.00	0.00	50.74	49.26	100.00
12.	Madhya Pradesh	41.74	2.79	79.51	20.49	100.00
13.	Maharashtra	27.60	3.85	68.02	31.98	100.00
14.	Manipur	31.05	3.67	93.85	6.15	100.00
15.	Meghalaya	74.12	3.80	97.87	2.13	100.00
16.	Mizoram	54.45	1.70	92.90	7.10	100.00
17.	Nagaland	48.55	0.70	89.03	10.97	100.00
18.	Orissa	34.42	6.20	77.50	22.50	100.00
19.	Punjab	12.82	1.56	56.44	43.56	100.00
20.	Rajasthan	45.69	1.70	88.03	11.97	100.00
21.	Sikkim	62.86	1.14	97.62	2.38	100.00
22.	Tamil Nadu	44.05	19.91	84.45	15.55	100.00
23.	Tripura	61.48	2.89	99.46	0.54	100.00
24.	Uttar Pradesh	66.58	1.39	80.35	19.65	100.00
25.	West Bengal	29.30	5.23	78.44	21.56	100.00
26.	A & N Islands	40.86	0.37	87.09	12.91	100.00
27.	Chandigarh	26.10	0.00	82.04	17.96	100.00
28.	Dadra & Nagar Haveli	41.67	1.39	76.39	23.61	100.00
29.	Daman & Diu	30.00	1.00	56.67	43.33	100.00
30.	Delhi	48.98	0.33	81.47	18.53	100.00
31.	Lakshadweep	36.49	2.03	100.00	0.00	100.00
32.	Pondicherry	32.94	0.00	79.75	20.25	100.00
All States/UTs		44.34	3.58	81.10	18.90	100.00
Centre		33.75	13.81	85.09	14.91	100.00
Total (Centre & States)		40.62	7.18	82.50	17.50	100.00

TABLE 13.56 : Relationship Between Budgeted Expenditure on Education and Net Domestic Products of States/UTs

S. No.	State/Union Territory	Year	Expenditure on Education by Education Departments	Estimates of NDP at current prices	% of Budget of Edn. Deptt. (Rev) to Net Domestic Product *(Rs. in Crores)*
1	2	3	4	5	6
1.	Andhra Pradesh	1992.93	1355.31	39704.10	3.4
2.	Arunachal Pradesh	1992-93	50.67	571.70	8.9
3.	Assam	1992-93	680.01	11735.60	5.8
4.	Bihar	1992-93	1323.41	29341.50	4.5
5.	Goa	1992-93	82.29	1222.00	6.7
6.	Gujarat	1992-93	1100.63	32239.80	3.4
7.	Haryana	1992-93	431.02	16391.80	2.6
8.	Himachal Pradesh	1991-92	196.15	2797.90	7.0
9.	Jammu & Kashmir	1992-93	138.10	3368.10	4.1
10.	Karnataka	1992-93	1151.51	29121.50	4.0
11.	Kerala	1993-94	1130.69	16944.60	6.7
12.	Madhya Pradesh	1992-93	1118.89	32306.60	3.5
13.	Maharashtra	1992-93	2305.12	75481.30	3.1
14.	Manipur	1991-92	85.23	760.50	11.2
15.	Meghalaya	1992-93	77.17	1070.70	7.2
16.	Mizoram	1990-91	42.51	304.00	14.0
17.	Nagaland	1991-92	49.46	680.50	7.3
18.	Orissa	1992-93	698.07	12922.20	5.4
19.	Punjab	1992-93	657.93	22499.20	2.9
20.	Rajasthan	1993-94	1129.38	23302.20	4.8
21.	Sikkim	1991-92	26.71	223.80	11.9
22.	Tamil Nadu	1992-93	1546.19	35224.50	4.4
23.	Tripura	1990.91	103.37	930.60	11.1
24.	Uttar Pradesh	1992-93	2267.67	61266.90	3.7
25.	West Bengal	1992-93	1515.11	41603.50	3.6
26.	A & N Islands	1992-93	24.31	207.90	11.7
27.	Chandigarh				
28.	Dadra & Nagar Haveli				
29.	Daman & Diu				
30.	Delhi	1991-92	306.08	11201.30	2.7
31.	Lakshadweep				
32.	Pondicherry	1992-93	42.08	792.80	5.3
All India (Centre+States/UTs)		1992-93	21369.90	556344.00	3.8

TABLE 13.57 : Technical Education
State-Wise Available PG Seats in Different Types of Institutions (1994)

S.No.	State	No. of Colleges	Number of seats in: IITs, IISc	Univ. & Dept.	RECs	State colleges		Total seats	Qualified in Gate '94
			Type A	Type B	Type C	Type D	Type E		
1.	Andhra Pradesh	7	—	130	120	—	260	510	3042
2.	Arunachal Pradesh	—	—	—	—	—	—	—	12
3.	Assam	—	—	—	—	—	—	—	54
4.	Bihar	6	—	—	40	100	360	500	627
5.	Chandigarh	2	—	—	—	—	80	80	405
6.	Delhi	5	310	—	—	90	150	550	513
7.	Gujarat	6	—	270	70	—	140	480	313
8.	Haryana	2	—	—	80	—	30	110	133
9.	Karnataka	26	200	—	80	160	510	950	1051
10.	Kerala	5	—	120	90	—	130	340	789
11.	Madhya Pradesh	7	—	—	90	60	190	340	771
12.	Maharashtra	13	320	—	70	200	400	990	2140
13.	Orissa	2	—	—	80	—	30	110	398

(Contd)

TABLE 13.57 *(Contd)*

S.No.	State	No. of Colleges	Number of seats in IITs, IISc	Univ. & Dept.	RECs	State colleges		Total seats	Qualified in Gate '94
			Type A	Type B	Type C	Type D	Type E		
14.	Punjab	3	—	—	—	60	140	200	101
15.	Rajasthan	4	—	—	40	400	250	690	489
16.	Tamil Nadu	12	350	300	130	510	100	1390	1169
17.	Uttar Pradesh	10	250	690	90	—	310	1340	1178
18.	West Bengal	6	490	650	80	60	60	1340	1279
	Grand Total	116	1920	2160	1060	1640	3140	9920	14464
	% Total Seat	15*	20%	22%	10%	17%	31%		

* 15 Colleges have zero out-turn since 1990, their seats are included here

Legend:

Type A : All IITs and IISc, Bangalore.
Type B : Universities/University faculties.
Type C : Regional Engineering Colleges (RECs).
Type D : Bigger size Engineering Colleges (AV out-turn during 1990-92 more than 50).
Type E : Small size Engineering Colleges (AV out-turn during 1990-92 less than 50).

TABLE 13.58 : Discipline-wise Available PG Seats and Gate Qualified Candidates (1992-94)

S.No.	Discipline	Seats Available			Candidates Qualified		
		1992	1993	1994	1992	1993	1994
1.	Agricultural	230	230	230	69	69	103
2.	Architecture	170	195	195	90	90	168
3.	Civil	1930	2010	2130	1610	2057	2700
4.	Chemical	660	660	660	221	314	397
5.	Computer	160	185	280	417	599	1289
6.	Electronics	650	690	690	1177	1668	2458
7.	Electrical	1380	1410	1410	741	1093	1572
8.	Instrumentation	190	200	200	103	135	265
9.	Industrial & Production	460	460	460	228	331	515
10.	Mechanical	1200	1285	1300	1153	1948	2551
11.	Pharmaceutical	500	520	520	217	324	398
12.	Textile	100	110	130	35	35	72
13.	Others	1170	1230	1715	2118	2571	1976
Grand Total		8800	9185	9920	8179	11289	14464
Percentage Increase		—	4.32%	8%	—	38%	28%

Source: J.P. Shrivastava. A Critical Review of Present and Future Post-Graduate Technical Education in India. *The Indian Journal of Technical Education,* Vol. 18, No. 2, April-June 1995.

TABLE 13.59 : Outlays and Expenditure on Education Total Plan and Non-Plan Budgetary Expenditure of Centre and States/UTs

	State/UT	1993-94 (Actual)			1994-95 (RE)			1995-96 (BE)		
		Plan	Non-Plan	Total	Plan	Non-Plan	Total	Plan	Non-Plan	Total
	1	2	3	4	5	6	7	8	9	10
1.	Andhra Pradesh	1392.18	6625.99	8018.17	1341.31	7980.86	9322.17	1518.17	9369.99	10888.16
2.	Arunachal Pradesh	126.65	272.23	398.88	151.53	284.12	435.65	171.24	310.91	482.15
3.	Assam	732.40	2168.78	2901.18	987.10	2254.78	3241.88	1330.02	2387.14	3717.16
4.	Bihar	1401.50	5917.14	7318.64	1221.35	6509.87	7731.22	1330.03	6880.09	8410.12
5.	Goa	66.29	364.25	430.54	73.60	431.91	505.51	77.87	539.80	617.67
6.	Gujarat	662.36	6271.43	6933.79	812.89	6516.73	7329.62	1139.23	7056.12	8195.35
7.	Haryana	434.89	2966.11	3401.00	636.95	6652.43	7289.38	718.36	4330.14	5048.50
8.	Himachal Pradesh	407.17	944.33	1351.50	442.33	1132.87	1575.20	517.63	1334.69	1852.32
9.	Jammu & Kashmir	246.87	1521.48	1768.35	307.92	2016.48	2324.40	267.47	2028.09	2295.56
10.	Karnataka	1546.87	4661.38	6208.25	2029.18	5622.53	7651.71	2587.04	6506.59	9093.63
11.	Kerala	629.83	3663.53	4293.36	835.09	4348.78	5183.87	930.23	4930.96	5861.19
12.	Madhya Pradesh	1710.55	5807.38	7517.93	2200.78	6093.74	8294.52	2785.31	6891.72	9677.03
13.	Maharashtra	1808.99	11299.70	13108.69	2054.37	12613.98	14668.35	2769.34	13996.36	16765.70
14.	Manipur	93.88	343.78	437.66	121.17	399.59	520.76	120.70	388.24	508.94
15.	Meghalaya	126.76	356.09	482.85	175.31	377.34	552.65	204.09	396.26	600.35
16.	Mizoram	136.59	282.21	418.80	156.17	331.61	487.78	90.50	339.55	430.05
17.	Nagaland	126.82	552.77	679.59	155.88	365.92	521.80	140.65	626.76	767.41
18.	Orissa	904.58	2577.63	3482.21	1329.66	3252.39	4582.05	1433.43	3675.83	5115.26

(Contd)

TABLE 13.59 : *(Contd)*

1	2	3	4	5	6	7	8	9	10
19. Punjab	594.28	3449.28	4043.56	591.81	5399.38	5991.19	674.02	6833.62	5707.64
20. Rajasthan	1072.08	4825.53	5897.61	1444.28	5408.38	6852.66	1624.27	6163.92	7988.19
21. Sikkim	52.96	135.95	188.91	75.04	461.01	536.05	98.44	466.99	565.43
22. Tamil Nadu	1706.79	7051.21	8758.00	1531.23	7655.93	9187.16	1648.52	8412.09	10060.61
23. Tripura	176.38	466.61	642.99	221.76	487.80	709.56	309.93	587.18	897.11
24. Uttar Pradesh	2285.72	10994.41	13280.13	2763.54	12660.12	15423.66	3205.16	14835.84	18041.00
25. West Bengal	1022.90	5882.85	6905.75	1706.36	6734.58	8440.94	1941.18	7692.72	9633.90
26. A & N Islands	24.45	178.05	202.50	32.70	205.24	237.94	44.15	252.44	296.59
27. Chandigarh	17.56	280.50	298.06	24.21	304.72	328.93	33.28	315.41	348.69
28. D & N Haveli	9.52	35.24	44.76	10.73	38.55	49.28	10.86	53.67	64.53
29. Daman & Diu	4.88	33.50	38.38	6.37	37.67	44.04	8.14	48.58	56.72
30. Delhi	255.77	252.08	507.85	406.22	1047.89	1454.11	676.24	1208.45	1884.69
31. Lakshadweep	17.89	64.08	81.97	17.99	82.48	100.47	22.70	92.34	115.04
32. Pondicherry	72.60	240.61	313.21	100.46	259.51	359.97	113.14	278.12	391.26
State/UTs	19868.96	90486.11	110355.07	23965.29	107969.19	131934.48	28947.34	119230.61	148177.95
Centre	24624.00	83545.00	108169.00	28937.00	93965.00	122902.00	29330.00	106998.00	136328.00
Grand Total	44492.96	174031.11	218524.07	52902.29	201934.19	254836.48	58277.34	226228.61	284505.95

Source: Annual Financial Statistics of Education Sector 1996-97. Ministry of Human Resource Development, Department of Education, Planning & Monitoring.

13.6. MISCELLANEOUS DATA—BRAIN DRAIN

TABLE 13.60 : Indian Students Going Abroad-Annual Outflow State- wise and Sex-wise 1992-93

Sl.No.	State/UTs	Male	Female	Total
1	2	3	4	5
1.	Andhra Pradesh	1810	188	1998
2.	Arunachal Pradesh	1	—	1
3.	Assam	15	3	18
4.	Bihar	37	4	41
5.	Goa	2	3	5
6.	Gujarat	184	19	203
7.	Haryana	34	4	38
8.	Himachal Pradesh	1	—	1
9.	Jammu & Kashmir	12	1	13
10.	Karnataka	647	116	763
11.	Kerala	81	15	96
12.	Madhya Pradesh	15	2	17
13.	Maharashtra	773	192	965
14.	Manipur	2	—	2
15.	Meghalaya	1	—	1
16.	Mizoram	—	—	—
17.	Nagaland	—	—	—
18.	Orissa	4	1	5
19.	Punjab	42	19	61
20.	Rajasthan	29	6	35
21.	Sikkim	2	—	2
22.	Tamil Nadu	955	173	1128
23.	Tripura	—	—	—
24.	Uttar Pradesh	101	10	111
25.	West Bengal	286	64	350
26.	A & N Islands	1	—	1
27.	Chandigarh	18	3	21
28.	Dadra & Nagar Haveli	—	—	—
29.	Daman & Diu	—	—	—
30.	Delhi	491	130	621
31.	Lakshadweep	—	—	—
32.	Pondicherry	2	—	2
	Total	5546	953	6499

Source: Department of Education, Ministry of Human Resource Development, Government of India, 1994.

BRAIN DRAIN

TABLE 13.61 : Indian Students Going Abroad-Annual Outflow Country-wise and Sex-wise 1992-93

Sl.No.	State/UTs	Male	Female	Total
1	2	3	4	5
1.	Afghanistan	1	—	1
2.	Australia	160	17	177
3.	Austria	6	—	6
4.	Belgium	10	2	12
5.	Canada	48	13	61
6.	China	3	2	5
7.	France	15	7	22
8.	Germancy	10	5	15
9.	Hungary	1	—	1
10.	Indonesia	1	—	1
11.	Italy	5	2	7
12.	Jorden	14	2	16
13.	Korea	1	—	1
14.	Laos	1	—	1
15.	Nepal	1	—	1
16.	Netherlands	2	—	2
17.	New Zealand	2	—	2
18.	Others	3	—	3
19.	Pakistan	2	—	2
20.	Philippines	4	—	4
21.	Singapore	1	—	1
22.	Sri Lanka	3	—	3
23.	Sweden	2	1	3
24.	Thailand	3	—	3
25.	U.K.	131	40	171
26.	U.S.A.	4910	816	5726
27.	USSR	158	39	197
28.	Others	48	7	55
	Total	5546	953	6499

TABLE 13.62 : Annual Outflow of Students to Different Continents

	Continent	1991-92		1992-93	
1.	America	5954	(92.1)	5787	(89.0)
2.	Europe	248	(3.8)	240	(3.7)
3.	Asia	35	(0.5)	39	(0.6)
4.	Oceania	180	(2.8)	376	(5.8)
5.	Others	49	(0.8)	57	(0.9)
	Total	6466	(100.0)	6499	(100.0)

Note: Figures in parenthesis indicate the percentage share for different continents.

BRAIN DRAIN

TABLE 13.63 Indian Students Going Abroad—Annual Outflow State-Wise, Sex- Wise & Subject-Wise—1992-93

S.No.	State/UTs	Arts		Science		Education		Engineering		Arch. & Design.		Tech. & Ind.		Med./Pharmacy		Den. & Vet Sci.		Agr. & Forsy.	
		Male	Female	Male	Female	Male	Female	Male	Female	Male	Female	Male	Female	Male	Female	Male	Female	Male	Female
1	2	3	4	5	6	7	8	9	10	11	12	13	14	15	16	17	18	19	20
1.	Andhra Pradesh	11	7	451	52	—	—	840	76	5	5	30	3	48	11	—	—	28	3
2.	Arunachal Pradesh	—	—	—	—	1	—	—	—	—	—	—	—	—	—	—	—		
3.	Assam	—	1	2	—	—	—	4	1	—	—	—	—	4	1	—	—	—	—
4.	Bihar	—	—	—	—	—	—	15	1	1	—	1	—	13	2	—	—	—	—
5.	Goa	—	—	—	—	—	—	—	—	—	—	—	—	—	—	—	—	—	—
6.	Gujarat	1	2	20	1	—	—	77	4	1	1	4	2	20	2	—	—	—	1
7.	Haryana	2	—	4	1	—	—	9	—	—	—	1	—	6	3	—	—	—	—
8.	Himachal Pradesh	—	—	—	—	—	—	—	—	—	—	—	—	1	—	—	—	—	—
9.	Jammu & Kashmir	1	—	—	—	—	—	4	—	1	—	1	—	1	—	—	—	—	—
10.	Karnataka	5	12	147	38	—	—	366	31	10	4	10	4	31	1	1	—	6	2
11.	Kerala	—	1	23	5	—	—	40	5	2	—	1	—	2	1	—	—	—	—
12.	Madhya Pradesh	—	—	5	1	—	—	5	—	—	—	—	—	3	—	—	—	—	—
13.	Maharashtra	22	20	222	54	—	—	270	23	14	9	24	3	67	32	—	—	5	1
14.	Meghalaya	—	—	1	—	—	—	—	—	—	—	—	—	—	—	—	—	—	—
15.	Meghalaya	—	—	—	—	—	—	—	—	—	—	—	—	—	—	—	—	—	—
16.	Mizoram	—	—	—	—	—	—	—	—	—	—	—	—	—	—	—	—	—	—
17.	Nagaland	—	—	—	—	—	—	—	—	—	—	—	—	—	—	—	—	—	—

(Contd.)

TABLE 13.63 (*Contd.*)

1	2	3	4	5	6	7	8	9	10	11	12	13	14	15	16	17	18	19	20
18.	Orissa	—	1	1	—	—	—	3	—	—	—	—	—	—	—	—	—	—	—
19.	Punjab	3	1	4	3	—	—	15	2	—	2	—	—	10	9	—	—	—	—
20.	Rajasthan	1	4	8	—	—	—	6	—	—	1	—	—	7	—	—	—	—	—
21.	Sikkim	—	—	—	—	—	—	1	—	—	—	—	—	—	—	—	—	—	—
22.	Tamil Nadu	15	13	172	33	—	—	310	27	8	1	12	1	56	18	—	—	10	1
23.	Tripura	—	—	—	—	—	—	—	—	—	—	—	—	—	—	—	—	—	—
24.	Uttar Pradesh	2	—	14	5	—	—	42	1	1	—	5	—	9	3	—	—	1	—
25.	West Bengal	20	11	54	23	—	—	72	4	1	1	5	2	19	5	—	—	1	1
26.	A & N Island	—	—	—	—	—	—	—	—	—	—	—	—	—	—	—	—	—	—
27.	Chandigarh	—	—	2	—	—	—	6	—	2	—	—	1	2	—	—	—	—	—
28.	Dadra & Nagar Haveli	—	—	—	—	—	—	—	—	—	—	—	—	—	—	—	—	—	—
29.	Daman & Diu	—	—	—	—	—	—	—	—	—	—	—	—	—	—	—	—	—	—
30.	Delhi	17	18	79	22	—	—	105	15	7	3	4	1	43	18	—	—	6	—
31.	Lakshadweep	—	—	—	—	—	—	—	—	—	—	—	—	—	—	—	—	—	—
32.	Pondicherry	—	—	—	—	—	—	—	—	—	—	—	—	—	—	—	—	—	—
	Total	100	91	1209	238	1	—	2190	190	53	27	98	17	342	106	1	—	57	9

Source: Department of Education, Ministry of Human Resource Development, Govt. of India, 1994.

Table 13.64 : Brain Drain: Indian Students Going Abroad—Outflow State-Wise, Sex-Wise & Subject-Wise—1992-93

S.No.	State/UTs	Arts		Com/B.Ed/B.MGT		Bank & Ins		Fine Arts		Nursing		Lib.Science		Other Subjects		Total	
		Male	Female	Male	Female	Male	Female	Male	Female	Male	Female	Male	Female	Male	Female	Male	Female
1	2	21	22	23	24	25	26	27	28	29	30	31	32	33	34	35	36
1.	Andhra Pradesh	3	—	141	24	6	—	2	—	1	—	—	—	244	7	1810	188
2.	Arunachal Pradesh	—	—	—	—	—	—	—	—	—	—	—	—	—	—	1	—
3.	Assam	—	—	5	—	—	—	—	—	—	—	—	—	—	—	15	3
4.	Bihar	—	—	3	—	—	—	—	—	—	—	—	—	4	1	37	4
5.	Goa	—	—	—	—	—	—	—	—	—	—	—	—	2	3	2	3
6.	Gujarat	—	1	14	2	—	—	1	2	—	—	—	—	46	1	184	19
7.	Haryana	—	—	10	—	—	—	—	—	1	—	—	—	1	—	34	4
8.	Himachal Pradesh	—	—	—	—	—	—	—	—	—	—	—	—	—	—	1	—
9.	Jammu & Kashmir	—	—	4	—	—	—	—	—	—	—	—	—	—	1	—	1
10.	Karnataka	—	—	56	11	—	—	1	9	—	—	—	—	14	4	647	116
11.	Kerala	1	—	11	2	—	—	—	—	—	—	—	—	1	1	81	15
12.	Madhya Pradesh	—	—	—	—	—	—	—	—	—	—	—	—	2	1	15	2
13.	Maharashtra	2	—	111	29	—	—	15	8	—	—	—	—	21	13	773	192
14.	Manipur	—	—	—	—	—	—	—	—	—	—	—	—	1	—	2	—
15.	Meghalaya	—	—	—	—	—	—	—	—	—	—	—	—	1	—	1	—
16.	MIzoram	—	—	—	—	—	—	—	—	—	—	—	—	—	—	—	—
17.	Nagaland	—	—	—	—	—	—	—	—	—	—	—	—	—	—	—	—
18.	Orissa	—	—	—	—	—	—	—	—	—	—	—	—	—	—	4	1
19.	Punjab	—	—	10	2	—	—	—	—	—	—	—	—	—	—	42	19

(Contd.)

Table 13.64 : *(Contd.)*

1	2	21	22	23	24	25	26	27	28	29	30	31	32	33	34	35	36
20.	Rajasthan	—	—	5	—	—	—	—	—	—	—	—	—	2	1	29	6
21.	Sikkim	—	—	—	—	—	—	—	—	—	—	—	—	1	—	2	—
22.	Tamil Nadu	1	1	113	19	—	—	2	4	—	—	—	—	256	55	955	173
23.	Tripura	—	—	—	—	—	—	—	—	—	—	—	—	—	—	—	—
24.	Uttar Pradesh	—	—	17	—	—	—	—	—	—	—	—	—	10	1	101	10
25.	West Bengal	4	—	54	2	—	—	3	2	—	—	—	—	53	13	286	64
26.	A & N Islands	—	—	—	—	—	—	—	—	—	—	—	—	1	—	1	—
27.	Chandigarh	—	—	3	2	—	—	—	—	—	—	—	—	3	—	18	3
28.	Dadra & Nagar Haveli	—	—	—	—	—	—	—	—	—	—	—	—	—	—	—	—
29.	Daman & Diu	—	—	—	—	—	—	—	—	—	—	—	—	—	—	—	—
30.	Delhi	5	3	129	14	—	—	12	8	—	—	—	—	84	28	491	130
31.	Lakshadweep	—	—	—	—	—	—	—	—	—	—	—	—	—	—	—	—
32.	Pondicherry	—	—	2	—	—	—	—	—	—	—	—	—	—	—	2	—
	Total	16	5	688	107	6	—	36	33	2	—	—	—	747	130	5546	953

Source: **Department of Education, Ministry of Human Resource Development, Govt. of India, 1994.**

TABLE 13.65—Foreign Students of Indian Universities Countrywise Data (1993-94)

Country	Number	Country	Number
1. Afghanistan	111	51. Nepal	909
2. Africa	4	52. Netherlands	2
3. Angola	7	53. New Zealand	1
4. Australia	10	54. Nigeria	84
5. Austria	2	55. Norway	3
6. Bangladesh	736	56. Oman	9
7. Bahrain	134	57. Pakistan	21
8. Belgium	2	58. Palestine	229
9. Bhutan	123	59. Peru	1
10. Botswana	1	60. Philippines	16
11. Bulgaria	6	61. Poland	5
12. Canada	46	62. Portugal	3
13. China	14	63. Qatar	5
14. China Taipei (Taiwan)	1	64. Saudi Arabia	38
15. Cambodia	1	65. Seychelles	3
16. Colombia	1	66. Singapore	20
17. Djibouti	3	67. Somalia	132
18. Egypt	36	68. Spain	5
19. Ethiopia	685	69. Sri Lanka	420
20. Fiji	24	70. Sudan	1294
21. France	35	71. South Africa	86
22. Gambia	8	72. Sweden	1
23. Germany	18	73. Senegal	2
24. Ghana	4	74. Switzerland	7
25. Greek	5	75. Syria	40
26. Guyana	2	76. Tanzania	82
27. Gaza	1	77. Thailand	152
28. Hong Kong	2	78. Tibetan Refugee Students	23
29. Indonesia	64	79. Trinidad & Tobago	8
30. Iran	338	80. Tunisia	2
31. Iraq	26	81. Turkey	3
32. Israel	9	82. Tonga	1
33. Italy	6	83. U.A.E.	39
34. Japan	34	84. U.K.	62
35. Jordan	860	85. U.S.A.	200
36. Kenya	4268	86. Ukraine	1
37. Korea (Demo Repub.)	34	87. U.S.S.R. (CIS)	20
38. Korea (Fed. Repub.)	20	88. Uganda	98
39. Kuwait	28	89. Venezuela	2
40. Laos	2	90. Vietnam	27
41. Lebanon	5	91. West Indies	1
42. Libya	9	92. Yemen	184
43. Malaysia	1421	93. Yugoslavia	1
44. Maldives	9	94. Zambia	4
45. Malta	2	95. Zaire	3
46. Mongolia	11	96. Zimbabwe	6
47. Mauritius	296	97. Miscellaneous	136
48. Mynamar	9	Total	13,866
49. Mozambique	1		
50. Namibia	1		

Source: SIS Unit, Association of Indian Universities, New Delhi.

TABLE 13.66 : Foreign Students of Indian Universities : University wise Data (1993-94)

	University	*Number*
1.	Agra Univ.	442
2.	Univ. of Agril. Sciences, Bangalore	9
3.	Univ. of Agril. Sci., Dharwad	1
4.	Alagappa Univ.	5
5.	Aligarh Muslim Univ.	440
6.	Univ. of Allahabad	26
7.	AIIMS, New Delhi	26
8.	Amravati Univ.	4
9.	Andhra University	52
10.	Andhra Pradesh Agril. Univ.	13
11.	Anna Univ.	6
12.	Annamalai Univ.	14
13.	Assam Agril. Univ.	2
14.	Avinashilingam Instt for Home Sci. & Hr. Edn. for Women, Copimbatore	3
15.	Babasaheb Bhimrao Ambedkar Bihar University, Muzaffarpur	185
16.	Banaras Hindu Univ.	202
17.	Banasthali Vidyapith	3
18.	Bangalore University	206
19.	Barkatullah Vishwavidyalaya, Bhopal	56
20.	Bharathiar University, Coimbatore	31
21.	Bharathidasan University, Tiruchirapalli	42
22.	Bidhan Chandra Krishi Vish., Distt. Nadia	3
23.	Birsa Instt. of Tech., Mesra, Ranchi	60
24.	BITS, Pilani	3
25.	Birsa Agril. Univ., Ranchi	2
26.	Univ. of Bombay	400
27.	Univ. of Bundelkhand, Jhansi	21
28.	Univ. of Burdwan	90
29.	Univ. of Calcutta	5
30.	Univ. of Calicut	65
31.	CIEFL Hyderabad	2
32.	Central Instt. of Hr. Tibetan Studies, Varanasi	8
33.	Central Instt of Fisheries Education	2
34.	Ch. Charan Singh Haryana Agril. Univ., Hisar	9
35.	Ch. Charan Singh Univ., Meerut	4
36.	C S Azad Univ. of Agri. & Tech., Kanpur	1
37.	Deccan College PG & Research Instt., Pune	32

TABLE 13.66 (*Contd.*)

	University	Number
38.	Univ. of Delhi	1011
39.	Devi Ahilya Vishwavidyalaya Indore	442
40.	Dr. Babasaheb Ambedkar Marathwada Univ.	867
41.	Dr. Ram Manohra Lohia Univ.	35
42.	Dr. Y.S. Parmar Univ. of Horti. & Forestry, Solan	1
43.	Gandhigram Rural Institute	47
44.	Goa University	63
45.	University of Gorakhpur	6
46.	GB Pant Univ. of Agri. & Tech., Nainital	15
47.	Gujarat Agril. Univ.	3
48.	Gujarat Ayurved Univ.	19
49.	Gujarat University	25
50.	Gulbarga University	1
51.	Gurukula Kangri Vishwavidyalaya	3
52.	Guru Nanak Dev Univ., Amritsar	15
53.	Univ. of Health Sciences, Vijayawada	1
54.	Hemwati Nandan Bahuguna Garhwal Univ.	4
55.	Univ. of Hyderabad	10
56.	IARI, New Delhi	10
57.	IIS Bangalore	10
58.	IIT Bombay	92
59.	IIT Delhi	74
60.	IIT Kanpur	53
61.	IIT Kharagpur	48
62.	IIT Madras	51
63.	ISM Dhanbad	3
64.	ISI Calcutta	15
65.	IVRI, Izatnagar	4
66.	IGNOU, New Delhi	3
67.	Indira Kala Sangit Vishwavidyalaya	4
68.	International Instt. for Population Sciences, Bombay	28
69.	Jadavpur Univ., Calcutta	46
70.	Jai Narain Vyas Univ.	56
71.	Jamia Hamdard, New Delhi	10
72.	Jamia Millia Islamia	108
73.	JKNV, Jabalpur	2
74.	Jawaharlal Nehru University	85
75.	Kakatiya University	59
76.	Univ. of Kalyani	35
77.	Karnataka Univ.	267
78.	Univ. of Kashmir	1

TABLE 13.66 (*Contd.*)

	University	*Number*
79.	Univ. of Kerala	43
80.	Kerala Agril. Univ.	3
81.	Konkan Krishi Vidyapeeth	4
82.	Kuvempu Univ.	34
83.	Kurukshetra Univ.	44
84.	LN Mithila University	66
85.	Univ. of Madras	92
86.	Madurai Kamaraj Univ.	101
87.	Magadh Univ.	1
88.	MS Univ. of Baroda	321
89.	Maharishi Dayanand Saraswati Univ. , Ajmer	5
90.	Maharshi Dayanand Univ., Rohtak	85
91.	Mahatma Gandhi Univ.	13
92.	MPKV, Rahuri	1
93.	Mangalore Univ.	192
94.	Manipal Academy of Hr. Edn.	1477
95.	Manonmaniam Sundaranar Univ.	7
96.	Marathwada Krishi Vidyapeeth	1
97.	Mohanlal Sukhadia Univ.	571
98.	Univ. of Mysore	187
99.	Nagpur University	334
100.	National Law School of India Univ.	8
101.	National Museum Instt. of History of Art, Conservation & Museology, New Delhi	6
102.	North Bengal Univ.	4
103.	NEHU, Shillong	1
104.	Orissa Univ. of Agri. & Tech., Bhubaneswar	6
105.	Osmania University	93
106.	Punjab Univ.	426
107.	Patna Univ.	12
108.	Pondicherry Univ.	53
109.	Univ. of Poona	1715
110.	PG Instt. of Medical Edn. & Research, Chandigarh	29
111.	Punjabi Univ.	95
112.	Punjabrao Krishi Vidyapeeth	3
113.	Rabindra Bharati Univ.	38
114.	Univ. of Rajasthan	80
115.	Rajasthan Vidyapeeth	114
116.	Rajendra Agril. Univ.	4
117.	Rani Durgavati Vishwavidyalaya	488
118.	Univ. of Roorkee	167

TABLE 13.66 (*Contd.*)

	University	*Number*
119.	Sambalpur Univ.	9
120.	Sampurnanand Sanskrit Vishwavidyalaya	29
121.	Sardar Patel Univ.	9
122.	Saurashtra Univ.	3
123.	School of Planning & Architecture	41
124.	Shivaji Univ.	304
125.	SNDT Women's Univ.	14
126.	South Gujarat Univ.	86
127.	Sri Sathya Sai Instt. of Higher Learning, Anantapur	10
128.	Sri Venkateswara Univ.	10
129.	Tamil Nadu Agril. Univ.	30
130.	Tamil Nadu Dr. MGR Medical Univ, Madras	179
131.	Tamil Nadu Vet. & Animal Sci. Univ.	3
132.	Tata Instt. of Social Sci., Bombay	1
133.	Telugu University	1
134.	Tilak Maharashtra Vidyapeeth, Pune	12
135.	Utkal University	1
136.	Vikram University	4
137.	Visva Bharati	89
	Total	13,866

PART-FOUR

APPENDICES
SIGNIFICANT DOCUMENTS NOT INCLUDED IN THE PREVIOUS SURVEYS

APPENDIX-1

REPORT OF THE COMMITTEE ON MINIMUM LEVELS OF LEARNING AT PRIMARY STAGE (1991)

Introduction

The National Policy on Education (NPE), 1986 emphasized the need for laying down Minimum Levels of Learning (MLLs) for each stage of school education as a prerequisite for setting performance goals for the teachers. This was visualized so that these could serve as effective guides for organizing teaching-learning experiences and evaluating pupil achievement.

Recognizing this, thie Ministry of Human Resource Development (MHRD), Department of Education, set up a committee in January 1990, under the chairmanship of Prof. R.H. Dave, formerly of the Unesco Institute for Education, Hamburg, Germany to study afresh the learning outcomes defined in the existing curriculum and to lay down Minimum Levels of learning (MLLs) that all children who pass the primary stage of education must achieve. The need to lay down Minimum Levels of Learning (MLLs) arises from the need for provision of equal access and conditions for success to all children irrespective of caste, creed, location or sex. This committee examined the existing curriculum of the primary stage of education in a series of workshops and meetings involving primary school teachers, non-formal education (NFE) instructors, eminent educationists and the State Councils of Educational Research and Training (SCERTs).

Terms of Reference

The terms of reference of the committee were as under :

1. Draw up minimum levels of learning for Classes III and V.

---

* *Minimum Levels of Learning : Report of the Committee set up by the Ministry of Human Resource Development Department of Education Government of India*, National Council of Educational Research and Training, New Delhi, 1991.

2. Recommend a procedure for comprehensive learner evaluation and assessment.
3. Look into the non-cognitive areas of learning and suggest concrete ways in which teaching in these areas can be improved.

The committee was further informed that the terms of reference related to both formal and non-formal systems of education.

Members of the Committee

The Committee consisted of the following members :

1. Dr. R.H. Dave, Director (Retd.), Unesco Institute for Education, Walterstrasse 120,2000 Hamburg 61, Germany.
2. Shri S.C. Behar, Principal Secretary and Chairman, Professional Education Board, Government of Madhya Pradesh, Bhopal.
3. Dr. C.J. Daswani, Head, Department of Non-Formal Education and Education of SC/ST, NCERT, New Delhi.
4. Dr. R. Govinda, Head, School and Non-Formal Education Unit, NIEPA, New Delhi.
5. Dr. John Kurrien, Director, Centre for Learning Resources, B-210, Gera Park, 15, Boat Club Road, Pune.
6. Professor J.S. Rajput, Joint Educational Adviser (EE), Ministry of HRD, Department of Education, New Delhi.
7. Smt. Kiran Dhingra, Director (EE), Ministry of HRD, Department of Education, New Delhi.
8. Dr. J.N. Joshi, Professor, Department of Education, Punjab University, Chandigarh.
9. Shri N.J. Bhatt, Gujarat State Council of Educational Research and Training, Ahmedabad.
10. Smt. Marwah, Teacher, N.D.M.C. School, New Delhi.
11. Dr. Pritam Singh, Professor and Head, Navodaya Vidyalaya Cell, NCERT, New Delhi, *Member Convener.*

In addition, the following persons were associated with the work of the committee and participated in its deliberations :

1. Shri Prabhakar Singh (Retd. Field Adviser, NCERT), 574 Mumfordganj, Allahabad.
2. Professor H.S. Srivastava, Head, DMES&DP, NCERT, New Delhi.
3. Dr. H.K. Dewan, Ekalavya, Bhopal.

Meaning of Minimum Levels of Learning (Extracts from Chapter 2).

Minimum levels of learning can, perhaps, be specified in a variety of ways. For instance, MLLs can be stated as expected learning outcomes defined as observable terminal behaviours. One may also go for a taxonomic analysis of learning objectives such as knowledge, comprehension, application, analysis, synthesis, evaluation and so on and accordingly indicate the expected learning outcomes. One can also state the MLLs in terms of learning competencies expected to be mastered by every child by the end of a particular class or stage of education. These different approaches for stating the MLLs are not mutually exclusive. Of the various alternatives available, the committee has chosen to state the MLLs in terms of terminal competencies. Each competency can be further delineated in terms of sub-competencies while specifying the content inputs or while designing specific measures of learning.

It may be noted that the set of MLLs would actually represent the *rational criteria* adopted for judging the adequacy of the curricular inputs provided and the learning outcomes to be expected. There can be no finality with respect to any set of MLLs. This applies to the set of MLLs developed by the committee also. Two basic considerations kept in view while formulating the MLLs are : (i) the cognitive capabilities of the children at different classes or grades corresponding to different stage of development; and (ii) the empirical reality in terms of enabling environmental conditions that characterise the primary education programme.

ACTION PLAN FOR IMPLEMENTATION

(Text of Chapter 8)

1. Introduction of MLLs in primary schools and NFE centres in the country will require a carefully worked out strategy with necessary phasing. The overall implementation plan may be divided into three or more phases. In the first phase this curriculum plan may be introduced in only a few selected districts or blocks in two or three states after making a thorough preparation. In this phase, a few innovative centres and ongoing reform projects may also be encouraged to follow the MLL approach in order to raise the standard of achievement. Even some individual specialists working in places like teachers' colleges and universities may be encouraged by the Ministry of Human Resource Development to introduce MLLs in selected schools and NFE centres.

2. The chief purpose of this phase should be to understand how the proposed MLLs function in both formal and non-formal delivery systems, what kind of orientation and aids are needed for the teacher in order to achieve the desired level of mastery by the students, what kind of modifications and adaptations are needed in the existing textbooks, how exactly should the system of evaluation and monitoring be evolved and made genuinely functional in different settings and what other administrative and academic measues would be required to succeed in attaining the ultimate goal of enhancing the quality of learner achievement. The second and third phases should aim at further refinement of MLLs and other related aspects and systematic expansion of the implementation programme.

3. It is proposed that in the first phase the number of blocks of different districts and states be kept as small as possible, say, about 4 to 6. However, all schools and NFE centres in the block concerned should be selected for implementation. For comparison purposes, matching samples from neighbouring blocks or districts may be taken. In any case, pre-testing must be carried out to establish benchmark data. Appropriate preparatory steps for making this phase most effective should be taken with full participation of local authorities including teachers, headmasters, supervisors and community members. The district level authorities including the office of DEO, DIET (where established) and other concerned agencies should take the responsibility of organizing, coordinating, implementing and evaluating the programme together with local agencies in charge of both formal education and NFE centres. The district should ultimately be treated as a unit of operation for this innovation and for carrying out various tasks involved at the stages of preparation, implementation, monitoring, evaluation and further expansion in cooperation with local authorities on the one hand, and state agencies including SCERT and State Education Department as well as national authorities on the other.

4. In the ultimate analysis, every district should ensure that the minimum essential standards of achievement laid down at the national level in terms of MLLs as a basic and common criterion of reference should be attained by all as early as possible and even go beyond. Different districts and schools within them may need different time frame and resources for obvious reasons and may set their own intermediate phases for moving towards the standards set by the MLLs. However, within the time span of a few years, to be determined locally, all districts in a given state and all states of the country must ensure the

achievement of atleast the minimum levels of learning for almost all children. In certain special programmes and projects such as those launched or being planned in Andhra Pradesh, Bihar, Orissa, Rajasthan and Uttar Pradesh, entire districts may be selected to introduce the MLL approach and intensive efforts be made to produce transactional and evaluation materials, etc., from the resources available for these programmes.

5. In order to assist the teacher, who will play the most central role in this programme, it will be necessary to prepare teachers' handbooks in different curriculum areas. The handbooks should provide all explanatory notes and illustrative material relating to MLLs and their effective use in teaching and testing. The handbooks should also indicate how existing textbooks could be used to achieve MLLs until such time that the textbooks are revised, if necessary, in relation to this approach. Suggestions for the use of supplementary textual materials, teaching-learning aids and activity-based methods should be made in the handbooks such that student learning becomes meaningful, effective and cheerful. Besides the handbooks for teachers of primary schools and instructors of NFE centres, those for supervisors and other local functionaries should also be prepared to improve the efficiency of their respective tasks in the context of the MLL approach.

6. While the draft MLLs are laid down nationally, they allow full flexibility for the use of local illustrations, materials and environment for the purpose of establishing their relevance and functionality in the local context. This particular aspect should be clearly shown in the handbooks so that the process of decentralization operates maximally within the national curricular framework. Moreover, this aspect should be sufficiently stressed in the training and retraining of teachers organized on the basis of MLLs. In course of time, integrated instructional materials may be produced which would include textual material, pupils, worksheets, unitwise evaluation exercises and reinforcement materials, on the basis of specific competencies indicated in the MLLs. It should be worthwhile to examine, in this context, the primers produced under the IPCL programme of adult education.

7. As proposed separately, a continuous and comprehensive scheme of evaluation should be made an integral part of the MLL approach to quality control right from the first phase of implementation. Teaching and evaluation should be intertwined in various ways including the incorporation of diagnostic testing, remedial teaching, mastery learning and criterion-referenced evaluation including pre-testing and post-testing

for monitoring the progress. For these purposes, a large pool of test items, units tests and other evaluation instruments such as those for vocabulary tests, dictation exercises, mental mathematics and application tests should be prepared and thereby teachers should be given further concrete help in making her/his work optimally efficient and effective. Supervisors can also use this pool of test materials for spot check of student achievement and district level agencies can utilize them for conducting criterion-referenced testing for the comparison of standards and other such purposes.

8. Based on MLLs handbooks, textual materials and items pools, and appropriate orientation of teachers should be organized before Phase I begins and should likewise be repeated before launching Phases II and III under the expansion programme. Similar orientation should be provided to supervisors and other concerned personnel in relation to their respective responsibilities. For all these functionaries a systematic plan of recurrent orientation during the entire implementation porgramme should be meticulously followed. The recurrent training should be of short duration and should be functional and task-oriented.

9. Efforts should be made to involve the local community in a variety of ways. Where local education committees exist, their cooperation and active participation should be sought, cooperation of those parents (among others) whose children do not attend school regularly should be sought by establishing contact with them and regular attendance of their children ascertained so that they do not lag behind in attaining the expected mastery of MLLs. If there are voluntary agencies or individual volunteers in the community or neighbouring communities who can provide guidance and support to the school especially in regard to raising the qualilty of education, their involvement and participation should also be explored. Such agencies and individuals may include, among others, retired educators or other professionals, personnel from a primary or secondary training college nearby, and officials of health department and other such agencies in a village who are motivated enough to extend a helping hand to the school or the NFE centre from time to time. In brief, full utilization of human, physical and even financial resources available in the local environment (whether village, town or city) should be made for effective implementation of MLLs.

10. Similarly, for the purposes of getting internal support and mutual reinforcement, networking of neighbouring schools may be introdued where feasible. Such school-clusters or complexes, as proposed by the Education Commission in the sixties, could work cooperatively

for sharing experiences and materials, solving certain problems of instruction, evaluation and monitoring among themselves, reducing time and cost by producing tests, remedical materials, etc., cooperatively and thus helping one another in improving the quality of the learning process. If the networking or clustering approach is followed, it should be seen that the size of these groups is kept manageable, say, clusters of some 5 to 10 schools in a compact area within a block. Teachers and headmasters may form their councils to run the networks and set agenda and targets for their cooperative work in the light of their felt needs.

11. The implementation strategy, to be effective, will need a sound monitoring system accompanied by a rersource support system. This should be established at the district level. Sufficient preparatory work should be carried out at the initial stage, a detailed design of implementation charted out and necessary financial provision made so that the implementation programme once started moves further with full steam and necessary help in the form of training, materials, evaluation instruments for pre-testing and stagewise assessment surveys, etc., the motivation and enthusiasm of all concerned is sustained and any unforeseen obstacles and bottlenecks are removed in time. This system should also be responsible for the review of MLLs, etc., at the end of Phase I of the implementation programme.

12. At the national level, the Department of Education of the Ministry of Human Resource Development (MHRD), Government of India, should continue to play a leading role at the implementation stage together with NCERT, NIEPA and NEO (National Evaluation Organisation, when established). It is recommended that the MHRD may undertake the following responsibilities, among others :

(i) It should coordinate the task of ensuring quality with equity in close cooperation with the state and district level authorities as part of the national programme of universalizing elementary education and providing 'Basic Education for All'. The MHRD should mobilize resources in cooperation with various agencies, motivate the people concerned and ensure political will for implementing the initial and subsequent phases of MLLs in all primary schools and NFE centres in the country as a time-bound programme;

(ii) It should periodically review and monitor progress of implementing this programme at the national level and introduce modifications so that eventually the ultimate goal of quality education for all children is accomplished. Towards this end, it should conduct achievement surveys, especially in the languages, mathematics and basic concepts of general or environmental studies (social, civic and scientific aspects) and take follow-up action on their findings leading to a drastic reduction, if not elimination, of unjustifiable disparities in the standard of achievement at the primary stage that exist between states, among districts within states, between urban and rural areas, and between boys and girls. For carrying out this work NEO may be established as early as possible;

(iii) Once the task of laying down MLLs for the primary stage takes shape, the MHRD should immediately undertake a similar exercise for the upper primary stage comprising Classes VI to VIII without which the work done for the first five classes will remain incomplete and will have less chances of success. In fact, this exercise should be extended in course of time up to the end of general education which includes Classes IX and X as well; and

(iv) The NCERT, NIEPA and pertinent agencies in the states should be involved in the implementation of MLLs while the MHRD should continue to play its vital role as an initiator, catalyst and cooperator with regard to resource mobilization and monitoring of results. The NCERT may set up a special unit for organizing different phases of implementation, for orienting teachers and other educators, for developing handbooks and other instructional materials aligned with MLLs, for producing pools of test materials and remedial exercises, and for several other such purposes. The task of achieving quality coupled with equity for millions and millions of children who are expected to receive primary education through formal or non-formal delivery systems is by no means easy. Keeping in view the magnitude and complexity of the task, MLLs Implementation Unit should have a sufficient number of competent and dedicated people representing subject specialities such as language, mathematics and general studies as well as pedagogical specialities such as teacher training, preparation of handbooks and other materials, instructional processes, evaluation and monitoring.

13. After examining the experience of Phase I and introducing necessary changes in MLLs and other related aspects, Phase II may be launched to include the whole district or clusters of districts for implementation of MLLs in selected places. If the experience is positive

and resources are available, this programme may be introduced in about 50 districts chosen from different states. All important steps such as those indicated in the previous paragraphs of this chapter should be taken in order to ensure that the ultimate goal of raising the quality of learning to the mastery level for practically all children in these basic subjects of study is in no way compromised. Again, after analysing the experiences and outcomes of the second phase and making necessary modifications in the MLLs as well as the implementation strategy, Phase III may be launched to extend the programme to all districts in every state/UT in the country. Needless to state that on the basis of the experience thus gained improving quality and enhancing equity in primary education, further cycles of reform should be undertaken periodically in the light of new needs and developments at the local, national and international levels.

14. A comparative analysis of competencies included in the curricula of literacy and post-literacy programmes of adults may also be carried out to understand the extent to which basic parity exists between different delivery modes all of which are aimed at basic education. Such an analysis may ultimately lead to establishing a common or comparable set of minimum learning competencies for all adults and children in the perspective of life-long learning.

APPENDIX-II

REPORT OF THE CONFERENCE OF CHAIRMEN OF BOARDS OF SCHOOL EDUCATION ON SEMESTERISATION AND EXAMINATION REFORM (1992)

Introduction

The National Conference of the Chairmen of Boards of School Education and Directors of selected SCERTs was organised by the NCERT in collaboration with the Council of Board of School Education (COBSE) on 6-8 July 1992, at the Mussori International School (MIS), Mussori, Uttar Pradesh. In all, 13 Charimen of the Boards and 4 Directors of SCERTs, besides some consultants of the COBSE and academic members of the NCERT participated in this conference.

Objectives of the Conference

(i) To clarify the various aspects of restructuring the curriculum from the point of view of semesterisation at the secondary stage.

(ii) To discuss the various academic and administrative problems that could arise as a result of semesterisation being implemented by the Boards of School Education and to suggest solutions to those problems.

(iii) To suggest a suitable strategy for learners' evaluation as a necessary element of adopting semesterisation.

(iv) To suggest and plan for the immediate follow-up action for the Boards to be taken up in this connection.

Major Outcomes of the Conference

Some of the major recommendations needing immediate attention and highlighted by all the participants are being summarised here :

(i) The main objectives of semesterisation should be to improve the quality of education as well as introduction of flexibility in the transaction of the curriculum, besides examination reform.

National Council of Educational Research and Training, New Delhi, 1992.

(ii) Semesterisation at the school level is a new concept for all those who are going to impelment it. Semesterisation is a major departure from the traditional approach to assessment and it needs carefully planned and designed strategy. If it is to succeed, a valid, reliable objective assessment of the competencies achieved by students at various levels is necessary.

(iii) Modified semester system will include both internal and external assessment. Since the emphasis in both types of semesters are different, the internal and external assessment may have to be separately reflected.

(iv) The Boards will need to play a much greater role in the curriculum transaction than what they have been doing so far.

(v) Coursewise, subjectwise restructuring of the syllabi will have to be taken up so as to identify the areas for external and internal evaluation. The curriculum will also have to be appropriately graded. A modular approach will have to be taken up in restructuring the curriculum.

(vi) It is necessary to consider the management issues carefully and evolve solutions before implementing this programme in this reform. The problems relate to examination work and its management and increased burden on administrators and teachers.

(vii) There is need for strengthening in-service and pre-service training programmes of teachers from this point of view.

(viii) The role of the Boards may require to be reviewed in the light of these reforms. Consequently, the Boards may have to reorganise their functions to fulfil their new role.

(ix) For effective implementation of these changes, the Government of India will have to provide financial support to the Boards of School Education and higher secondary schools in addition to academic and administrative support.

(x) The public examinations are still occupying a prominent position in the educational system more particularly at the school stage. In view of this situation, semesterisation has to be linked with the public examination system.

(xi) It is presumed that there will be two semesters every year and four semesters for the total duration of the Boards, i.e., Classes XI and XII. The end of each semester should mark a definite stage of evaluation. The end of two years' course should end with a final examination to be conducted by the Board.

(xii) There should be four criterion-referenced tests, initial and final comprehensive normative evaluation by the State Board. All the participants felt very strongly that there is a need for orientation of administrators, Board members, principals and teachers to enable them to appreciate the programme of semesterisation. It was particularly suggested that the academic staff, members of the Boards and some selected SCERTs and other resource persons may be trained in systematic training programmes to be organised at the zonal level by the NCERT with the support of the COBSE.

APPENDIX-III

SUPREME COURT OF INDIA JUDGEMENT (1992)

WRIT PETITION (CIVIL) NO. 456 OF 1991

Miss Mohini Jain ...Petitioner

Versus

State of Karnataka & ...Respondents

JUDGEMENT

KULDIP SINGH, J.

The Karnataka State Legislature, with the object of eliminating the practice of collecting capitation fee for admitting students into educational institutions, enacted the Karnataka Educational Institutions (Prohibition of Capitation Fee) Act, 1984 (the Act). The Act which replaces the Karnataka Ordinance No. 14 of 1983 came into force with effect from July 11, 1983, purporting to regulate the tuition fee to be charged by the private Medical Colleges in the State. The Karnataka Government issued a notification dated June 5, 1989 under Section 5 (1) of the Act thereby fixing the tuition fee, other fees and deposits to be charged from the students by the private Medical Colleges in the State. Under the notification the candidates admitted against "Government seats" are to pay Rs. 2,000 per year as tuition fee. The Karnataka students (other than those admitted against "Government seats") are to be charged tuition fee not exceeding Rs. 25,000 per annum. The third category is of "Indian students from outside Karnataka", from whom tuition fee not exceeding Rs. 60,000 per annum is permitted to be charged.

Miss Mohini Jain, a resident of Meerut, was informed by the Management of Sri Siddharatha Medical College, Agalokote, Tumkur, in the State of Karnataka that she could be admitted to the MBBS course in the session commencing February/March 1991. According to the management she was asked to deposit Rs. 60,000 as the tuition fee for the first year and furnish a bank guarantee in respect of the fees for the remaining years of the MBBS course. The petitioner's father informed the management that it was beyond his means to pay the exorbitant annual fee of Rs. 60,000 and as a consequence she was denied admission to the medical college. Mohini Jain has alleged that the management demanded a further capitation fee of rupees four and a half lakhs but the management has vehemently denied the same.

In this petition, under Article 32 of the Constitution of India, Miss Mohini Jain has challenged the notification of the Karnataka Government permitting the private medical colleges in the State of Karnataka to charge exorbitant tuition fees from the students other than those admitted to the "Government seats".

Mr. Santosh Hegde learned counsel appearing for the medical college, respondent No. 3, has contended that the students from whom higher tuition fee is charged belong to a different class. According to him those who are admitted to the "Government seats" are meritorious and the remaining non-meritorious. He stated that classification of candidates into those who possess merit and those who do not possess merit is a valid classification and as such the college management is within its right to charge more fee from those who do not possess merit. He further states that the object sought to be achieved by the said classification is to collect money to meet the expenses incurred by the college in providing medical education to the students. Mr. C.B. Vaidyanathan, learned counsel appearing for the intervener, Karnataka Private Medical Colleges Association, has argued that the private medical colleges in the State of Karnataka do not receive any financial aid from either the Central; or the State Government. According to him the private medical colleges incur about Rs. 5 lakhs per student as expenditure for a 5-year MBBS course. 40% of the seats in these colleges are set apart as "Government seats" to be filled by the Government. The students selected and admitted against Government seats pay only Rs. 2000 per annum, as such the rest of the burden falls on those who are admitted against management quota. He, therefore, contended that the tuition fee is not excessive and as such there is no question of making any profit by the private medical colleges in the State of Karnataka. Mr. Hedge and Mr. Vaidyanathan have vehemently contended that in order to run the medical colleges the managements are justified in charging the capitation fee. According to them, apart from the Act, there is no provision under the Constitution or under any other law which forbids the charging of capitation fee. Finally they have relied upon the judgement of this Court in *D.P. Joshi* vs. *The State of Madhya Bharat and Another* 1955 SCR 1215.

After hearing learned counsel for the parties and also perusing the written arguments submitted by them the following points arise for our consideration in this writ petition :

(1) Is there a 'right to education' guaranteed to the people of India under the Constitution? If so, does the concept of 'capitation fee' infract the same?

(2) Whether the charging of capitation fee in consideration of admissions to educational institutions is arbitrary, unfair, unjust and as such violates the equality clause contained in Article 14 of the Constitution?

(3) Whether the impugned notification permits the private medical colleges to charge capitation fee in the guise of regulating fees under the Act?

(4) Whether the notification is violative of the provisions of the Act which in specific terms prohibits the charging of capitation fee by any educational institution in the State of Karnataka?

In order to appreciate the first point posed by us it is necessary to refer to various provisions of the Constitution of India. The preamble promises to secure to all citizens of India "justice, social, economic and political", "liberty of thought, expression, belief, faith and worship". It further provides "equality of status and of opportunity" and assures dignity of the individual. Articles 21, 38, 39(a) and (f), 41 and 45 of the Constitution are reproduced hereunder :

> "21. Protection of life and personal liberty : No person shall be deprived of his life or personal liberty except according to procedure established by law".
>
> "38. State to secure a social order for the promotion of welfare of the people—(1) The State shall strive to promote the welfare of the people by securing and protecting as effectively as it may a social order in which justice, social, economic and political, shall inform all the institutions of the national life.
>
> (2) The State shall, in particular, strive to minimise the inequalities in income and endeavour to eliminate inequalities in status, facilities and opportunities, not only amongst individuals but also amongst groups of people residing in different areas or engaged in different vocations".
>
> "39. Certain principles of policy to be followed by the State : The State shall, in particular, direct its policy towards securing—
>
> (a) that the citizens, men and women equally, have the right to an adequate means to livelihood;
>
> (f) that children are given opportunities and facilities to develop in a healthy manner and in conditions of freedom and dignity and that childhood and youth are protected against exploitation and

against moral and material abandonment".

"41. Right to work, to education and to public assistance in certain cases : The State shall, within the limits of its economic capacity and development, make effective provision for securing the right to work, to education and to public assistance in cases of unemployment, old age, sickness and disablement and in other cases of undeserved want".

"45. Provision for free and compulsory education for children : The State shall endeavour to provide, within a period of ten years from the commencement of its Constitution, for free and compulsory education for all children until they complete the age of fourteen years".

It is no doubt correct that "right to education" as such has not been guaranteed as fundamental right under Part III of the Constitution but reading the above quoted provisions cumulatively it becomes clear that the framers of the Constitution made it obligatory for the State to provide education for its citizens.

The preamble promises to secure justice "social, economic and political" for the citizens. A peculiar feature of the Indian Constitution is that it combines social and economic rights along with political and justiciable legal rights. The preamble embodies the goal which the State has to achieve in order to establish social justice and to make the masses free in the positive sense. The securing of social justice has been specifically enjoined an object of the State under Article 38 of the Constitution. Can the objective which has been so prominently pronounced in the preamble and Article 38 of the Constitution be achieved without providing education to the large majority of citizens who are illiterate. The objectives flowing from the preamble cannot be achieved and shall remain on paper unless the people in this country are educated. The three pronged justice promised by the preamble is only an illusion to the teeming millions who are illiterate. It is only education which equips a citizen to participate in achieving the objectives enshrined in the preamble. The preamble further assures the dignity of the individual. The Constitution seeks to achieve this object by guaranteeing fundamental rights to each individual which he can enforce through court of law if necessary. The directive principles in Part IV of the Constitution are also with the same objective. The dignity of man is inviolable. It is the duty of the State to respect and protect the same. It is primarily education which brings forth the dignity of a man. The framers of the Constitution were aware that more than seventy per cent of the people, to whom they were giving the Constitution of India, were illiterate. They were also hopeful that within a period of 20 years illiteracy would be wiped out from the country. It was with that hope that Articles 41 and 45 were brought in Chapter IV of the Constitution. An individual cannot be assured of human dignity unless his personality is developed and the only way to do that is to educate him. This is why the Uiversal Declaration of Human Rights, 1948 emphasises "Education shall be directed to the full development of the human personality..." Article 41 in Chapter IV of the Constitution recognises an individual's right "to education". It says that "the State shall, within the limits of its economic capacity and development, make effective provision for securing the right...to education...". Although a citizen cannot enforce the directive principles contained in Chapter IV of the Constitution but these were not intended to be mere pious declarations. We may quote the words of Dr. Ambedkar in that respect :

> "In enacting this Part of the Constitution, the Assembly is giving certain directions to the future legislature and the future executive to show in what manner they are to exercise the legislative and the executive power they will have. Surely it is not the intention to introduce in this part these principles as mere pious declarations. It is the intention of the Assembly that in future both the legislature and the executive should not merely pay lip service to these principles but that they should be made the basis of all legislative and executive action that they may be taking hereafter in the matter of the governance of the country". (C.A.D. Vol VII p. 476)

The directive principles which are fundamental in the governance of the country cannot be isolated from the fundamental rights guaranteed under Part III. These principles have to be read into the fundamental rights. Both are supplementary to each other. The State is under a constitutional mandate to create conditions in which the fundamental rights guaranteed to the individuals under Part III could be enjoyed by all. Without making "right to education" under Article 41 of the Constitution a reality the fundamental rights under Chapter II shall remain beyond the reach of the large majority which is illiterate.

This Court has interpreted Article 21 of the Constitution of India to include the right to live with human dignity and all that goes alongwith it. In *Francis Coralie Mullin* vs. *The Administrator, Union Territory of Delhi* (1981) 2 SCR 516, this Court elaborating the right guaranteed under Article 21 of the Constitution of India held as under :

> "But the question which arises is whether the right to life is limited only to protection of limb or faculty or does it go further and embrace something more. We think that the right to life includes the right to live with human dignity and all that goes along with it, namely the bare necessaries of life such as adequate nutrition, clothing and shelter and facilities for reading, writing and expressing oneself in diverse forms, freely moving about and mixing and commingling with fellow human beings. Of course, the magnitude and content of the components of this right would depend upon the extent of the economic development of the country, but it must, in any view of the matter, include the right to the basic necessities of life and also the right to carry on such functions and activities as constitute the bare minimum expression of the human-self".

In *Bandhua Mukti Morcha* vs. *Union of India and Ors.* (1984) 2 SCR 67, this Court held as under :

> "This right to live with human dignity enshrined in Article 21 derives its life breath from the Directive Principles of State Policy and particularly clauses (e) and (f) of Article 39 and Articles 41 and 42 and at the least, therefore, it must include protection of the health and strength of workers men and women and of the tender age of children against abuse, opportunities and facilities for children to develop in a healthy manner and in conditions of freedom and dignity, educational facilities, just and humane conditions of work and maternity relief. These are the minimum requirements which must exist in order to enable a person to live with human dignity and so State, neither the Central Government or any State Government—has the right to take any action which will deprive a person of the enjoyment of these basic essentials".

"Right to life" is the compendious expression for all those rights which the Courts must enforce because they are basic to the dignified enjoyment of life. It extends to the full range of conduct which the individual is free to pursue. The right to education flows directly from right to life. The right to life under Article 21 and the dignity of an individual cannot be assured unless it is accompanied by the right of education. The State Government is under an obligation to make endeavour to provide educational facilities at all levels to its citizens.

The fundamental rights guaranteed under Part III of the Constitution of India including the right to freedom of speech and expression and other rights under Article 19 cannot be appreciated and fully enjoyed unless a citizen is educated and is conscious of his individualistic dignity.

The "right to education", therefore, is concomitant to the fundamental rights enshrined under Part III of the Constitution. The State is under a constitutional mandate to provide educational institutions at all levels for the benefit of the citizens. The educational institutions must function to the best advantage of the citizens. Opportunity to acquire education cannot be confined to the richer sections of the society. Increasing demand for medical education had led to the opening of large number of medical colleges by private persons, groups and trusts with the permission and recognition of State Governments. The Karnataka State has permitted the opening of several new medical colleges under various private bodies and organisations. These institutions are charging capitation fee as a consideration for admission. Capitation fee is nothing but a price for selling education. The concept of "teaching shops" is contrary to the constitutional scheme and is wholly abhorrent to the Indian culture and heritage. As back as December 1980 the Indian Medical Association in its 56th All India Medical Conference held at Cuttack on December 28-30, 1980 passed the following resolution :

> "The 56th All India Medical Conference views with great concern the attitude of state Governments particularly the State Government of Karnataka in permitting the opening of new Medical Colleges under various bodies and organisations in utter disregard to the recommendations of Medical Council of India and urges upon the authorities and the Government of Karnataka not to permit the opening of any new medical college by private bodies.
>
> It further condemns the policy of admission on the basis of capitation fees. This commercialisation of medical education endangers the lowering of standards of medical education and encourages bad practices".

Dr. K.S. Chugh, Chairman, Department of Medicine and Head Department of Nephrology Postgraduate Institute of Medical Education and Research, Chandigarh, recipient of Dr. B.C. Roy National Award as 'eminent medical man for 1991', in his Presidential Address delivered on January 17, 1992 at the 47th Annual Conference of the Association of Physicians in India held at Patna observed as under :

"In the recent past, there has been a mushroom growth of medical colleges in our country. At the time of independence we had 25 medical colleges which turned out less than 2000 graduates every year. At the present time, there are 172 (150 already functioning and 22 are being established) medical colleges with an annual turn over of over 20,000 graduates. The Mudaliar Commission had recommended a doctor-population ratio of 1:3500. We have already achieved a ratio of 1:2500. If we take into account the practitioners of other systems of medicine who enjoy pay scales and privileges comparable to those of allopathic doctors, India will soon have a doctor population ratio of 1:500. Such over production of technical man-power from our medical colleges is bound to lead to unemployment and frustration. Indeed the unabated exodus of our professional colleagues to other countries is a direct consequence of these lop-sided policies".

"According to some estimates, India has exported human capital worth over 51 billion dollars to USA alone during 1966-88. Currently about 8000 skilled youngmen and women are leaving the country every-year. It is high time a blanket ban is imposed on any further expansion of medical colleges in our country and a well thought out plan to reduce the intake into existing institutions is prepared. This will help to improve the standard of medical education and health care in our country".

"It is common knowledge that many of the newly started medical colleges charge huge capitation fees. Besides, most of these are poorly equipped and provide scanty facilities for training of students. At best such institutions can be termed as "Teaching Shops". Experience has shown that these colleges admit students who have been unable to gain admission in recognised medical colleges. The result is a back door entry into medical training obtained solely by the ability to pay one's way through. Even the advice of the Medical Council of India is sidelined in many such cases. The Government must resist all pressures to allow this practice to continue. Admission to medical colleges bought by paying capitation fees must be stopped forthwith and all such existing institutions required to strictly adhere to the Medical Council of Indian rules".

"In the words of my predecessor Dr. V. Parameshvara, "The need of the hour is better doctors than more doctors, better health education than more education, better health care than more health care delivery"."

The Indian Medical Association, the Association of Physicians of India and various other bodies and organisations representing the medical profession in this country have unanimously condemned the practice of charging capitation fee as a consideration for admission to the medical college.

We hold that every citizen has a 'right to education' under the Constitution. The State is under an obligation to establish educational institutions to enable the citizens to enjoy the said right. The State may discharge its obligation through state-owned or state-recognised educational institutions. When the State Government grants recognition to the private educational institutions it creates an agency to fulfil its obligation under the Constitution. The students are given admission to the educational institutions—whether state-owned or state-recognised—in recognition of their 'right to education' under the Constitution. Charging capitation fee as consideration for admission to educational institutions, is a patent denial of citizen's right to education under the Constitution.

Indian civilisation recognises education as one of the pious obligations of the human society. To establish and administer educational institutions is considered a religious and charitable object. Education in India has never been a commodity for sale. Looking at the economic front, even forty five years after achieving independence, thirty per cent of the population is living below poverty-line and the bulk of the remaining population is struggling for existence under poverty-conditions. The preamble promises and the directive principles are a mandate to the state to eradicate poverty so that the poor of this country can enjoy the right to life guaranteed under the Constitution. The State action or inaction which defeats the constitutional-mandate is per se arbitrary and cannot be sustained. Capitation fee makes the availability of education beyond the reach of the poor. The state action in permitting capitation fee to be charged by state-recognised educational institutions is wholly arbitrary and as such violative of Article 14 of the Constitution of India. During the last two decades the horizon of equality clause has been widened as a result of this Court's judgements. Earlier the violation of Article 14 was judged on the twin tests of classification and nexus. This Court in *E.P. Royappa* vs. *State of Tamil Nadu and Anr.* (1974) 2 SCR 348 gave new dimension to Article 14 in the following words :

> "Equality is a dynamic concept with many aspects and dimensions and it cannot be "cribbed, cabined and confined" within traditional and doctrinaire limits. From a positivistic point of view, equality is antithetic to arbitrariness. In fact equality and arbitrariness are sworn enemies; one belongs to the rule of law in a republic while the other, to the whim and caprice of an absolute monarch. Where an act is arbitrary it is implicit in it that it is unequal both according to political logic and constitutional law and is, therefore, violative

of Article 14".

This Court in *Maneka Gandhi* vs. *Union of India* (1978) 2 SCR 621, *Ramana Dayaram Shetty* vs. *The International Airport Authority of India and Ors.* (1979), 3 SCR 1014 and *Ajay Hasia etc.* vs. *Khalid Mujib Sehravardi and Ors. etc.* (1981) 2 SCR 79 following *E.P. Royappa* authoritatively held that equality is directly opposed to arbitrariness. In *Ajay Hasia* this Court observed as under :

> "Unfortunately, in the early stages of the evolution of our constitutional law, Article 14 came to be identified with the doctrine of classification...In *Royappa* vs. *State of Tamil Nadu* this Court laid bare a new dimension of Article 14 and pointed out that Article has highly activist magnitude and it embodies a guarantee against arbitrariness..."

The capitation fee brings to the fore a clear class bias. It enables the rich to take admission whereas the poor has to withdraw due to financial inability. A poor student with better merit cannot get admission because he has no money whereas the rich can purchase the admission. Such a treatment is patently unreasonable, unfair and unjust. There is, therefore, no escape from the conclusion that charging of capitation fee in consideration of admissions to educational institutions is wholly arbitrary and as such infracts Article 14 of the Constitution.

We do not agree with Mr. Hegde that the management has a right to admit non-meritorious candidates by charging capitation fee as a consideration. This practice strikes at the very root of the constitutional scheme and our educational system. Restricting admission to non-meritorious candidates belonging to the richer section of society and denying the same to poor meritorious is wholly arbitrary against the constitutional scheme and as such cannot be legally permitted. Capitation fee in any form cannot be sustained in the eyes of law. The only method of admission to the medical colleges in consonance with fair play and equity is by ways of merit and merit alone.

We, therefore, hold and declare that charging of capitation fee by the private educational institutions as a consideration for admission is wholly illegal and cannot be permitted.

Mr. Santosh Hegde and Mr. Vaidyanathan, learned counsels for respondent 3 and the intervener respectively, have relied upon *D.P. Joshi* vs. *The State of Madhya Bharat and Anr.* (supra) for the proposition that classification of candidates for admission to medical colleges on the basis of residence is permissible. In *D.P. Joshi's* case a resident of Delhi was admitted as a student of Mahatma Gandhi Memorial Medical College, Indore which was run by the State of Madhya Bharat. His complaint was that the rules in force in the said institution discriminated in the matter of fees between students who were residents of Madhya Bharat and those who were not and that the latter had to pay in addition to the tuition fee and charges payable by all the students a sum of Rs. 1500 per annum as capitation fee and that the charging of such a fee from the students coming out of Madhya Bharat was in contravention of Article 14 and 15(1) of the Constitution of India. In *D.P. Joshi's* case the only point for decision before this Court was whether the classification on the ground of residence was justified. This court while dealing with the question observed as under :

> "The impugned rule divides, as already stated, self-nominess into two groups, those who are bona fide residents of Madhya Bharat and those who are not and while it imposes a capitation fee on the latter, it exampts the former from the payment thereof. It thus proceeds on a classification based on residence within the State and the only point for decision is whether the ground of classification has a fair and substantial relation to the purpose of the law, or whether it is purely arbitrary and fanciful.
>
> The object of the classification underlying the impugned rule was clearly to help, to some extent, students who are residents of Madhya Bharat in the prosecution of their studies and it cannot be disputed that it is quite a legitimate and laudable objective for a State to encourage education within its borders. Education is a State subject and one of the directive principles declared in Part IV of the Constitution is that the State should make effective provisions for education within the limits of its economy. (Vide article 41). The State has to contribute for the upkeep and the running of its educational institutions. We are in this petition concerned with a Medical College and it is well-known that it requires considerable finance to maintain such an institution. If the State has to spend money on it, is it unreasonable that it should so order the educational system that the advantage of it would be some extent at least ensure the benefit of the State? A concession given to the residents of the State in the matter of fees is obviously calculated to serve that end, as presumably some of them might, after passing out of the College, settle down as doctors and serve the needs of the locality. The classification is thus based on a ground which has a reasonable relation to the subject-matter of the

legislation and is in consequence not open to attack. It has been held in The State of Punjab V. Ajaib Singh Anr., that a classification might validly be made on a geographical basis. Such a classification would be eminently just and reasonable, where it relates to education which is the concern primarily of the State. The contention, therefore, that the rule imposing capitation fee is in contravention of article 14 must be rejected".

D.P. Joshi's case is an authority for the proposition that classification on the ground of residence is a justificable classification under Articles 14 and 15(1) of the Constitution of India. The question that capitation fee as a consideration for admission is not permissible under the scheme of the Constitution, was neither raised nor adverted to by this court. The imposition of capitation fee was also not questioned on the ground of arbitrariness. The only question raised before the Court was that the Madhya Bharat students could not be exempted from the payment of the capitation fee. It is settled by this Court that classification on the ground of residence is a valid classification. Subsequently this Court in *Dr. Pradeep Jain etc.* vs. *Union of India and Ors. etc.* (1984) 3 SCR 942 reiterated the legal position on this point. We are, therefore, of the view that *D.P. Joshi's* case does not give us any guidance on the points before us.

To appreciate the third point it is necessary to notice the relevant provisions of the Act and the notification. Sections 2(b), (e), 3, 4 and 5 of the Act are as under :

"2(b). "Capitation fee" means any amount, by whatever name called, paid or collected directly or indirectly in excess of the fee prescribed under section 5, but does not include the deposit specified under the proviso to Section 3.

(e) "Government Seats" means such number of seats in such educational institution or class or classes of such institutions in the state as the Governnment may, from time to time, specify for being filled up by it in such manner as may be specified by it by general or special order on the basis of merit and reservation for Scheduled Castes, Scheduled Tribes, Backward Classes and such other categories, as may by specified, by the Government from time to time, without the requirement of payment of capitation fee or cash deposit.

(3) Collection of capitation fee prohibited—Notwithstanding anything contained in any law for the time being in force, no capitation fee shall be collected by or on behalf of any educational institution or

by any person who is incharge of or is responsible for the management of such institution :

Provided . . .

4. Regulation of admission to educational institutions etc.—Subject to such rules, or general or special orders, as may be made by the Government in this behalf and any other law for the time being in force.

(1) (a) the minimum qualification for admission to any course of study in and educational institution shall be such as may be specified by :

(i) the University, in the case of any course of study in an educational institution maintained by or affiliated to such University :

Provided that the Government may, in the interest of excellence of education, fix any 'higher minimum qualification for any course of study'.

(ii) the Government in the case of other courses of study in any other educational institution;

(b) the maximum number of students that could be admitted to a course of study in an educational institution shall be such as may be fixed by the Government from time to time;

(2) in order to regulate the capitation fee charged or collected during the period specified under the proviso to section 3, the Government may, from time to time, by general or special order, specify in respect of each private educational institution or class or classes of such institutions.

(a) the number of seats set apart as Government seats :

(b) the number of seats that may be filled up by the management of such institution.

(i) from among Karnataka students on the basis of merit, on payment of such cash deposits refundable after such number of years, with or without interest as may be specified therein, but without the payment of capitation fee; or

(ii) at the discretion;

Provided that such number of seats as may be specified by the Government but not less than fifty per cent of the total number of seats referred to in clauses (a) and (b) shall be filled from among Karnataka students.

Explanation—For the purpose of this section Karnataka students means persons who have studied in such educational institutions in the State of Karnataka run or recognised by the Government and for such number of years as the Government may specify.

(3) an educational institution required to fill seats in accordance with item (i) of sub-clause (b) of clause (2) shall form a committee to select candidates for such seats. A nominee each of the Government and the University to which such educational institution is affiliated shall be included as members in such committee.

5. Regulation of fees, etc. (1) It shall be competent for the Government, by notification, to regulate the tuition fee or any other fee or deposit or other amount that may be received or collected by any educational institution or class of such institutions in respect of any or all class or classes of students.

(2) No educational institution shall collect any fees or amount or accept deposits in excess of the amounts notified under sub-section (1) or permitted under the proviso to section 3.

(3) Every educational institution shall issue an official receipt for the fee or capitation fee or deposits or other amount collected by it.

(4) All monies received by any educational institution by way of fee or capitation fee or deposits or other amount shall be deposited in the account of the institution, in any Scheduled Bank and shall be applied and expended for the improvement of the institution and the development of the educational facilities and for such other related purpose and to such extent and in such manner as may be specified by order by the Government.

(5) In order to carry out the purposes of sub-section (4), the Government may require any educational institution to submit their programmes or plans of improvement and development of the institution for the approval of the Government.

The relevant part of the notification dated June 5, 1989 issued by the Karnataka Government under Section 5 of the Act is reproduced hereunder :

"In exercise of the powers conferred by sub-section (1) of Section 5 of the Karnataka Educational Institutions (Prohibition of Capitation Fee) Act, 1984, the Government of Karnataka hereby fix the Tuition Fee and other fees and deposits that may be collected by the Private Medical Colleges in the State with effect from the academic year 1989-90 and until further orders as follows :

(a) Candidates admitted to seats in Government Medical Colleges shall be charged a tuition fee of Rs. 2,000 each per annum (Rupees two thousand only);

(b) Candidates admitted against Government seats in Private Medical Colleges shall be charged a tuition fee of Rs. 2,000 each per annum (Rupees two thousand only). For this purpose "Government seats" shall mean Government seats as defined by section 2 (e) of the Karnataka Educational Institutions (Prohibition of Capitation Fee) Act, 1984.

(c) Karnataka Students (other than students admitted against Government seats as at (b) above) admitted by Private Medical Colleges shall be charged tuition fee not exceeding Rs. 25,000 each per annum (Rupees Twenty-five thousand only).

(d) Indian Students from outside Karnataka admitted by Private Medical Colleges shall be charged tuition fee not exceeding Rs. 60,000 each per annum (Rupees Sixty thousand only);"

The Act has been brought into existence by the Karnataka State Legislature with the object of effectively curbing the evil practice of collecting capitation fee for admitting students into the educational institutions in the State of Karnataka. The preamble to the Act which makes the object clear is reproduced hereunder :

"An Act to prohibit the collection of capitation fee for admission to educational institutions in the State of Karnataka and matters relating thereto :

"Whereas the practice of collecting capitation fee for admitting students into educational institutions is widespread in the State;

"And whereas this undersirable practice beside contributing to large scale commercialisation of education has not been conducive to the maintenance of educational standards;

"And whereas it is considered necessary to effectively curb this evil practice in public interest by providing for prohibition of collection of capitation fee and matters relating thereto :

"Be it enacted by the Karnataka State Legislature in the Thirty-fourth Year of the Republic of India as follows :"

Section 3 of the Act prohibits the collection of capitation fee by any educational institution or by any person who is in charge of or is responsible for the management of such institutions. Contravention of the provisions of the Act has been made punishable under Section 7 of the Act with imprisonment for a term which shall not be less than three years but shall not exceed seven years and with fine which may extend to five thousand rupees. Section 5 of the Act authorises the Government to regulate the tuition fees by way of a notification. The Karnataka Government have issued a notification under Section 5(1) of the Act wherein the fee charged from Indian students from outside Karnataka has been fixed not exceeding Rs. 60,000 per annum. Whether

Rs. 60,000 per annum can be considered a tuition fee or it is a capitation fee is the question for our determination.

The notification fixes Rs. 2000 per annum as the tuition fee for candidates admitted to the seats in Government medical colleges and for the candidates admitted against "Government Seats" in private medical colleges. All these seats are filled purely on the merit of the candidates. It is thus obvious that the State Government, in fulfilling its obligation under the Constitution to provide medical education to the citizens, has fixed Rs. 2000 per annum as tuition fee for the students selected on merit for admission to the medical colleges and also against "Government seats" in private medical colleges. Therefore, the tuition fee by a student admitted to the private medical college is only Rs. 2000 per annum. The seats other than the "Government seats" which are to be filled from outside Karnataka the management has been given free hand where the criteria of merit is not applicable and those who can afford to pay Rs. 60,000 per annum are considered at the discretion of the management. Whatever name one may give to this type of extraction of money in the name of medical education it is nothing but the capitation fee. If the State Government fixes Rs. 2000 per annum as the tuition fee in government colleges and for "Government Seats" in private medical colleges then it is the state responsibility to see that any private college which has been set up with Government permission and is being run with Government recognition is prohibited from charging more than Rs. 2000 from any student who may be resident of any part of India. When the State Government permits a private medical college to be set-up and recognises its curriculum and degrees then the said college is performing a function which under the Constitution has been assigned to the State Government. We are, therefore of the view that Rs. 60,000 per annum permitted to be charged from Indian students from outside Karnataka in Para 1(d) of the notification is not tuition fee but in fact a capitation fee and as such cannot be sustained and is liable to be struck down. Whatever we have said about para 1(d) is also applicable to para 1(c) of the notification.

Since we have held that what is provided in para 1(d) and 1(c) of the impugned notification dated June 5, 1989 is capitation fee and not a tuition fee it has to be held that the notification is beyond the scope of the Act, rather goes contrary to Section 3 of the Act and as such has to be set aside. We, therefore, hold and declare that it is not permissible in law for any educational institution to charge capitation fee as a consideration for admission to the said institution.

For the reasons given above we allow this writ petition and quash para 1(d) and 1(c) of the Karnataka State Government notification dated June 5, 1989. As a consequence paragraph 5 of the said notification automatically becomes redundant. We make it clear that nothing contained in this judgement shall be applicable to the case of foreign students and students who are non-resident Indians. We further hold that this judgement shall be operative prospectively. All those students who have already been admitted to the private medical colleges in the State of Karnataka in terms of the Karnataka State Notification dated June 5, 1989 shall not be entitled to the advantage of this judgement and they shall continue their studies on the same terms and condititons on which they were admitted to the consolidated MBBS course.

Although we have struck down the capitation fee and allowed the writ petition to that extent, we are not inclined to grant any relief regarding admission to the petitioner. She was not admitted to the college on merit and secondly the course commenced in March-April, 1991 and we see no justification to direct respondent 3, the medical college, to admit the petitioner. The writ petition is allowed in the above terms with no order as to costs.

......................J.
(Kuldip Singh)

......................J.
(R.M. Sahai)

New Delhi,
July 30, 1992.

APPENDIX-IV

REPORT OF NATIONAL COLLOQUIUM ON RIGHT TO EDUCATION AS A FUNDAMENTAL RIGHT (1992)*

Introduction

The National Colloquium was sponsored by the University Grants Commission and Association of Indian Universities in September 1992. Twenty-eight eminent educationists participated in the debate. The report includes the following:

Introductory Note from Secretry, AIU

Right to Education

The Context

Excerpts from the Judgement

The Issues

The Debate

  The Opening Statements

  The Constitutional/Legal Issues

  Issues for Education

  Levy of Fees

  Matters of Policy

The Agenda for Action

  The Private Sector—A New Role

  Deregulating Education

  Text of Supreme Court Judgement in Mohini Jain vs. State of Karnataka and Others

  List of Participants.

INTRODUCTORY NOTE FROM SECRETARY, AIU*

Report on National Colloquium on Right to Education as a Fundamental Rights, sponsored by University Grants Commission and Association of Indian Universities, September 1992, Association of Indian Universities, New Delhi, (1993), Published from the *Journal Higher Education, Autumn 1992.*

* *Not included.*

RIGHT TO EDUCATION

"Right to work, to education and to public assistance in certain cases—The State shall, within the limits of its economic capacity and development, make effective provision for securing the right to work, to education and to public assistance in cases of unemployment, old age, sickness and disablement and in other cases of undeserved want."

—*Article 41 of the Constitution of India*

"Provision for fee and compulsory education for children—The State shall endeavour to provide, within a period of ten years from the commencement of this constitution, for free and compulsory education for all children until they complete the age of fourteen years."

—*Article 45 of the Constitution of India*

"The Right to Education should be examined for inclusion amongst the fundamental rights guaranteed under the Constitution of India. All the socio-economic measures, without which realisation of this right will not be possible, should be taken."

—*Report of the Committee for Review of National Policy on Education, 1986.*

The Context

A National Policy on Education was formulated in 1968 following the submission of the report of the Education Commission (Kothari Commission) in 1966. The adoption of the National Policy was a major step in the development of education in post-independence India since then there has been considerable expansion of education at all levels. Besides, greater attention has been paid to the improvement of the quality of education; a national system of education with a common pattern and structure has come into being because of these and other measures taken by the government and the nation has been enabled to meet its need of educated manpower.

While taking note of these positive features of educational developments, it is equally necessary to take cognizance of the failures and shortcomings. The Constitutional objective of providing free and compulsory education upto to age of 14 is far from being achieved. Questions of access, quality and the establishment of an egalitarian system of education to prepare the ground for achieving the socio-economic objectives enshrined in the Constitution continue to dominate all discussions on educational development. The divide between the rich and the poor, the urban and the rural, continues to widen. The growing unemployment among the highly educated youths raises many questions about the economic relevance and functional utility of education. These issues, together with the questions concerning the apparently contradictory phenomenon of the feverish quest for degrees, mismatch between education and employment and the decline in the credibility of the examination system, have all been matters of serious concern.

In 1985, the Government announced a comprehensive review of the education policy of 1968. The contemporary state of education and the issues, problems and the policy options arising therefrom were put together and offered in a challengingly candid document for discussion and response throughout the country. On the basis of the consensus which emerged from this countrywide debate, a new policy was framed by the Government in 1986.

The 1986 policy had a positive approach and content. It declared that education is a unique investment in the present and the future. It resolved that all children who attained the age of about 11 years by 1990 will have at least 5 years or its equivalent of schooling and further that, by 1995, all children will be provided free and compulsory education upto the age of 14. It also declared that by 1990 and 1995, vocational courses would respectively cover about 10-15% of the higher secondary students. It reaffirmed that education will be treated as a crucial area of investment for national development and survival and that it will be ensured that from the Eighth Plan onwards the investment in education will exceed 6% of the national income.

The 1986 policy was widely acclaimed. The approbation of the policy came mainly because of its commitment to allocate larger resources, the concretisation of policy statements into a Programme of Action and the setting out of a time frame for the attainment of its basic objectives. There were also certain reservations against the new policy mainly because of the impression of its elitist aberrations. It was argued by some educationists and social activists that schemes like autonomous colleges, Navodaya Vidyalayas, etc., promoted elitism and thus compromised the egalitarian goals of our Constitution.

In May 1990, a Committee was appointed to review the 1986 policy. In its report entitled 'Towards an Enlightened and Humane Society', the Committee recommended several modifications in the 1986 policy. It proposed, *inter alia*, that the right to education be declared as a fundamental right; the scope of Article 45 of the Constitution be enlarged to cover early childhood care and education; greater emphasis be placed on vocationalisation of secondary education; and measures be taken for the transformation of the Navodaya Vidyalaya scheme.

SIn respect of resources, the Review Committee endorsed the 1986 policy statement that at least 6% of the GNP should be earmarked for education. It also recommended that all technical and professional education which confers greater employability (output) among the recipients should be made self-financing with the costs necessarily being paid for by the beneficiaries. It recommended a proper increase in the fees (linked to the cost of recurring expenditure and levels of income of parents of the beneficiaries) payable by students going in for higher education. It suggested a recovery of 75 per cent, 50 per cent and 25 per cent depending upon the income levels of the parents.

The Central Advisory Board of Education appointed a Committee in July, 1991 to review the implementation of the 1986 policy keeping in view the report of the Review Committee submitted in December, 1990. The CABE Committee in its report submitted in January, 1992, urged a larger allocation for higher education and suggested that it should be complemented by other measures like :

— prioritisation within the education sector in the matter of allocation of Governmental resources;
— progressively making higher, technical and management education, largely self-financing by revising the fee structure with proper support to the needy students by way of student loans; and
— institutional finances for development of educational infrastructure.

Meanwhile, in the latter half of 1991, in the context of an acute resource crunch, the Government began exploring measures for raising additional resources for development and effecting economy in government expenditure. A major economic reform package was announced which included deregulation, liberalisation and greater participation of the private sector in developmental efforts. The announcement of these measures has had its impact in the education sector too. Towards the end of 1991, the Government suggested a freeze on grants to the institutions funded by the Central Government. The Central Universities, the Institutes of Technology, the Institutes of Management, etc., were told that during the Eighth Plan period the grants provided by the Central Government will be frozen at the level of 1991-92. The implication of this freeze was that the incremental allocation normally provided annually would not be available hereafter and the institutions concerned may thereby be forced to generate some of the resources required for this purpose. A possible method considered for this resource generation was the levy of a higher rate of recovery from the students who at present pay 5% or less of the annual recurring expenditure. The Institutes of Management responded with a hike in fees from Rs. 600 to 6000 per annum. The IITs too are considering a similar increase. The Central Universities, however, have not taken any decision in this matter. They have demanded that the Central Government should review its decision to freeze grants.

The system of higher education in the country presently consists of about 200 universities, 7500 colleges, about 50 lakhs students and 2.85 lakhs teachers. The estimated annual expenditure on higher education was about Rs. 2200 crores in 1990-91. It is estimated that during the 8th plan (1992-97), an additional 10 lakhs student will be seeking admission to higher education. This would imply that the existing facilities will have to be expanded by incurring around 20% over and above the present levels in terms of capital and revenue expenditure. If the Government will not be able to provide for this increase, where are these resources to come from?

The resources required for the maintenance and unavoidable expansion of the existing system of higher education continue to be a matter of serious concern. Questions relating to the revision of fee structure involving higher levels of recovery, greater private participation in the establishment of educational institutions and creation of endowments are all being discussed extensively.

Against this background, Supreme Court's judgement (in Mohini Jain's writ petition against the State of Karnataka) of July 30, 1992 declaring the Right to Education as a Fundamental Right and its ruling that the State is under a constitutional mandate to provide education at all levels and for all citizens assumes great urgency and significance.

EXCERPTS FROM THE JUDGEMENT*

THE ISSUES

I. Constitutional/Legal Issues

The Supreme Court has held that the right to education flows directly from right to life; the right to life under article 21 and the dignity of

* Not included

an individual cannot be assured unless it is accompanied by the right to education. It has further ruled that :

(a) The State is under a constitutional mandate to provide educational institutions at all levels for the benefit of the citizens.

(b) The State may discharge its obligation through state-owned or state-recognised educational institutions.

(c) Charging capitation fees in consideration of admission to educational institutions, is a patent denial of citizens' right to education under the Constitution. It is arbitrary and violative of Article 14.

(d) The only method of admission to the medical colleges in consonance with fair play and equity is by way of merit and mereit alone.

What are the implications of the above pronouncements of the Supreme Court, more particularly :

— Can an individual or a group of individuals now demand that an institution be set up by the State for their professional education? How would the Court enforce this right to education?

— How do private professional institutions meet their costs if they are prohibited from charging higher fees? If they can levy fees only at the rates prescribed by Government, who will meet the balance of costs? Is the State in a position to meet them? If not, does it imply that recognised institutions cannot be set up at all?

— What is the criterion for judging merit? Does not the criterion of merit vary from institution to institution? Could all students securing above 60 or 70% marks in science subjects not be considered as meritorious?

— Article 41 speaks of right to work, right to education and right to public assistance in certain cases. But it is qualified by the important phrase "The State shall, *within the limits of its economic capacity and development*, make effective provision for securing…"

— To what extent has/is this practical constraint been/to be taken into account by the judiciary in developing the scope of 'right of life' (Article 21).

— Are the 'right to work', 'right to health', 'right to shelter' not as basic as 'right to education'; since 'dignity of man' is inviolable, how far can the State go?

— The judgement also speaks of the mandate of the Constitution to the State 'to eradicate poverty' and observes "The State action or inaction which defeats the constitutional mandate is *per se* arbitrary and cannot be sustained."

— What follows if poverty has not been eradicated by the State? Can the Government(s) and/or its functionaries be held acccountable for inaction and therefore, for contempt? Can the Court take some enforcement measures in this direction?

— Is not the citizen's right to education circumscribed by the State's economic capacity and development as acknowledged in Article 41?

— The right to education can only be enjoyed by the citizens subject to the State's economic capacity. Is the state not justified in raising that capacity by asking the beneficiaries to share the cost of education?

— The judgement makes exception only in case of foreign students and NRIs.

— Why could not the children of rich parents be made to pay higher fees within the country too? On what logic could this classification be defended?

— The judgement has been made prospectively applicable. So the students already admitted will have to pay high fees.

(i) What about the existing institutions—are they to be closed down or is the State to pay them the difference between what they can chage as fees and their actual costs?
If they want to survive, are they not likely to take recourse to clandestine dealings with students?

(ii) What about the students admitted after the date of judgement i.e., July 30, 1992? Are their admissions to be cancelled and money refunded?

II. Issues Concerning Education

— How is 'education' to be defined in the context of 'right of education'?

— Can there be an inherent right to all citizens to get any education at any level that they seek?

— Should not the right to education be confined to a minimum level that should be common to all citizens?

— What is the significance of the provision for free and compulsory education upto 14 years enshrined in Article 45?

- Where individual choices determine the areas and levels of education, is the State obliged or mandated to provide for the universal enjoyment of that right?
- If right to education is concomitant to fundamental rights, which every citizen can claim, how can issues like curricular differentials, professional education, vertical mobility etc., which involve selectivity, be addressed?
- What would be the legally permissible limits in the creation of facilities for highly specialised education? Who would determine these limits?
- Would not such limits be subject to challenge as they would become artificial and arbitrary hurdles in the way of enjoyment of a citizen's fundamental right?
- In this view, is it not likely that 'merit', which might justify selectivity, may become an arbitrary criterion which can be challenged?
- The right to education can become a major issue for litigation in the future.

III. Issues Concerning Levy of Fees

- What is 'tuition fee'? The Supreme Court has not defined tuition fees. It has accepted what the State has prescribed at the lowest level as tuition fees.
- What is capitation fee? The court has held that charging capitation fee as a consideration for admission is wholly illegal. In this view, capitation fee is the price paid for buying admission. The difference between fee paid for 'tuition' and 'admission' is implicit.
- What is the 'economic fee'? The State has to incur considerable expenditure to provide for education. Free education as a concept is limited to education upto 14 years of age. Beyond that age, the beneficiaries may share the cost of education. How much do they share? What proportion of the cost can be transferred to the citizens?
- There is nothing in the judgement, or in the Constitution, that sets any limit to such sharing. It follows therefore that :
- State will be free to recover the full cost or transfer to the citizens only a part of it, the balance being treated as a subsidy.
- Tuition fees, once prescribed and uniformly levied, would be legally permissible. What is legally not permissible is the exercise of economic power in buying admission by those who do not,

on their own merit, deserve such admission. In this view, even if tuition fees are prescribed on a 100% cost-sharing basis, there would be no violation of the 'right to education'.

— Would a scheme of fees based on a judicious blend of the following elements be valid, in the context of this judgement?
— the unit cost of education;
— the income of parents;
— merit (by virtue of having secured the prescribed minimum marks or more in the relevant examination/admission test);
— Govt./bank loans to students belonging to weaker sections from the same group of meritorious students to enable them to pay the same fees; loans being repayable in instalments after they start earning; or scholarships to meritorious poor students.

(It would, however, have to be assumed that the fees for medical education so determined may approximately be Rs. 1 lakh per annum).

IV. Issues Relevant to Policy

The Court has held that "every citizen has a right to education under the Constitution. The State is under an obligation to establish educational institutions to enable the citizens to enjoy that right. The State may discharge its obligation through state-owned or state-recognised educational institutions. When the State Government grants recognition to private educational institutions, it creates an agency to fulfil its obligation under the Constitution."

— What is the importance of this observation?
— Is State the exclusive provider of education, either on its own, or by creating agencies which it aids, or recognises?
— Is there a role for private enterprise in education? A role which is not necessarily charitable, or philanthropic?
— If there is a role for private enterprise and how can it be distinguished from a 'pious, religious or charitable' purpose and a profit-propelled, risk-taking, commercial enterprise?
— Can education not be conceived as an industry, in the service sector, governed by market forces of supply and demand?
— While State may provide elementary education free of cost, is it illegal for a large number of private schools to provide the same education at a cost, or price?

— The levey of a higher level of fees by private schools has come to be accepted by the State and the society and no question of individual right or State's obligation seems to have been raised in this context.

— If State resources for education have to be supplemented with private resources, there has to be some incentive for private individuals/organizations to promote education. Establishing insitutions, employing people, creating facilities, etc., require investments and the cost on such investments and their maintenance will have to be met by those who seek the benefit from these institutions. Will the 'right to education' make this private participation difficult and leave the field entirely to State?

— How is quality of education ensured? Quality is a function of several inputs. It cannot be ensured merely by insisting on uniformity. Someone has to pay for those additional inputs.

— Higher education essentially has to be selective. Selectivity involves competitiveness. Better institutions attract better students. Those who provide better education have to do so at a cost. They will have to levy an economic fees. Would that violate the 'right to education'?

— While State may subsidise higher education and technical education, private individuals and agencies will not. Does right to education necessarily involve a right to subsidized education? The answer should be 'no'. In that case, will not asking students to pay for the education they receive inhibit their right to education?

— In higher and technical education (which is selective, differentiated and specialised), there can be no universal right as in the case of food, clothing and shelter. Has this distinction not to be taken into account?

— Has man-power planning (turning out as many professionals/ technicians only as can be absorbed by the economy), been at the basis of our educational planning?

Can it be? Have we the competence to make reliable manpower forecasts ?

Should it be ? Considering the fact that manpower planning is restrictive and denies access to higher education to large numbers of the people. What about the self-employment sector? Who will determine the number of people who will be self-employed and how?

THE DEBATE

1.THE OPENING STATEMENTS

G. Ram Reddy

The judgement has far-reaching implications for the education system, especially the system of higher education. Since both the UGC and the AIU are concerned with higher education, they have jointly convened this colloquium to discuss the implications of the judgement.

The UGC is a statutory body charged with the responsibility for the promotion and coordination of university education and the determination and maintenance of its standards. In the performance of these functions, the UGC may enquire into the financial needs of the universities; allocate and disburse grants to them; establish and maintain common services and facilities; recommend measures necessary for improving standards; advise Central and State Governments regarding the establishment of new or the expansion of already existing universities; and specify, through regulations, the fees that can be charged for various programmes of study.

The Commission has taken a number of steps for the development of universities and for the coordination and determination of standards. However, till now, not much has been done about the regulation of fees.

At present the higher education system consists of institutions set up by the Government and also others set up under its auspices by private agencies. The latter group of institutions comprise aided and unaided institutions. The fees charged by government and aided institutions are nominal. They are charging hardly any fees. The fees levied by unaided institutions vary from institution to institution and State to State.

It is in this context that the specific issues raised by the judgement have to be considered. The broad issues to be considered are :

* the nature and force of the linkage between the Directive Principles and Fundamental Rights;
* the extent to which the enjoyment of the right to life can reasonably be regarded as dependent upon the exercise of the right to education;
* whether the State can assume the obligation to provide education at all levels or is it entitled to decide upon its spread and diversification on the basis of societal needs as well as the constraints of resources; and more specifically;

* the full qualitative and dimensional significance of the State having been made subject to a constitutional mandate to provide education as a fundamental and legally enforceable right of the citizen.

The framers of the Constitution desired removal of illiteracy in 10 years. Even now only 53% of the population is literate. Presently only 6% of the relevant gae group is enrolled in higher education. This might be a narrow access. But what percentage would constitute a desirable access? If no resources are available, how can the State provide education?

The education provided by the State is heavily subsidised. If private institutions cannot charge fees at a rate higher than government rates, why and how can they come forward to provide education at the same highly subsidised rates? How and where do we draw a distinction between public good and private gain?

The judgement quotes with approval the views of the President of the Medical Council of India that we are already producing surplus medical manpower and that there is no need for expansion of medical education. If a view is put forward that like other kinds of education, medical education too is a fundamental right, how do we reconcile it with the view of the President of the Medical Council? If we export human capital, we also receive substantial remittances in foreign exchange.

There is a view that all is well with the government institutions and that they maintain a high quality while the private institutions do not do so. Is this view valid?

Finally, about the Constitution itself: every Constitution has a context and a background. When our Constitution was framed, socialism was the ruling philosophy. It now appears that this context has changed, or is changing. The question, therefore, arises whether the Constitution itself does not require changes.

Ms A.S. Desai

The judgement has come at a time when the universities in the country are facing a major financial crisis. The Government says that higher education must pay for itself so that more of the public funds can be allocated to elementary, adult and non-formal education.

Education cannot be self-sufficient. To most people, education is a means of achieving a better social position in life. Lack of access to education leads to social polarisation. A State committed to the welfare of its people cannot ignore education, health and social welfare.

How much of the cost of education can the State bear? How much of it can the student meet? Most people spend on education in the hope of a better future. But except in a very few professional courses, education does not now guarantee access to jobs and assured income. It is only in near-full-employment economies that education can be linked with assured future income.

We need to identify not only the legal issues but also the social dimensions of the issue so that we can place education in the context of the societal system of which it is a part.

S.K. Agrawala

The Supreme Court has ruled that the right to education flows directly from the right to life. In recent times, the Court has been elaborating the principles that constitute right to life. Life in this context is not confined merely to animal existence; it is living a life of dignity.

Similarly, with reference to the quality clause, under Article 14, the Court has been interpreting this principle also in a wider perspective. It has been holding that any thing which is arbitrary, unjust and unfair militates against the principle of equality.

We have made an attempt to identify the issues arising from the judgement. These issues have been listed in the papers circulated to all participants. These are not exhaustive, nor are these the only issues requiring consideration. We have made an attempt only to provide a framework for discussion. For this, we have grouped the issues into four categories comprising the constitutional/legal issues; issues concerning Education; issues concerning levy of fees; and issues relevant to policy. We will discuss these issues in four sessions, each session devoting itself to one of these themes.

2. CONSTITUTIONAL/LEGAL ISSUES

Madhava Reddy

In the Mohini Jain case, the Supreme Court examined the question : "is there a 'right to education' guaranteed to the people of India under the Constitution?" To appreciate this point, various provisions of the Constitution, its Preamble, Articles 21, 38, 39(a) and (f), 41 and 45 have all to be read together and cumulatively. The Court acknowledges that 'right to education' as such has not been guaranteed as a fundamental right under Part III of the Constitution. However, it has held that a cumulative reading of the above provisions makes it clear "that the framers of the Constitution made it obligatory for the State to provide education for its citizens." The objectives so prominently pronounced in the Preamble and Article 38 cannot be achieved without providing education to the large majority of the citizens who are illiterate. The objectives promised in the Preamble are sought to be achieved by guaranteeing fundamental rights to each individual which he can enforce through courts of law.

The directive principles in Part IV, according to the judgement, have also the same objective. It is education which brings forth the dignity of man. The framers of the Constitution were aware that seventy per cent of the people were illiterate. They were hopeful that within 10 years, illiteracy would be wiped out. It is this hope that is reflected in Articles 41 and 45. Article 41 recognises an individual's right to education. Although the directive principles cannot be enforced from the context and the language, it is also apparent that these were not intended to be mere pious declarations.

The Court has held that "the directive principles which are fundamental in the governance of the country cannot be isolated from the fundamental rights guaranteed under Part III. These principles have to be read into the fundamental rights. Both are supplementary to each other. The State is under a constitutional mandate to create conditions in which the fundamental rights guaranteed to the individuals under Part III could be enjoyed by all. Without making 'right to education' under Article 41 of the Constitution a reality the fundamental rights under Chapter III shall remain beyond the reach of the large majority which is illiterate."

The Supreme Court verdict goes on to say that the "right to life under Article 21 and the dignity of an individual cannot be assured unless it is accompanied by the right to education. The fundamental rights guaranteed by the Constitution including the right to freedom of speech and expression and other rights under Article 19 cannot be appreciated and fully enjoyed unless a citizen is educated and is conscious of his individualisic dignity."

On the basis of this reasoning, the Supreme Court has ruled that "the State Government is under an obligation to make endeavour to provide educational facilities at all levels to its citizens." The Court has further held that "the right to education, therefore, is concomitant to the fundamental rights enshrined under Part III of the Constitution. The State is under a Constitutional mandate to provide educational institutions at all levels for the benefit of the citizens."

While making these pronouncements, the judgement omits the expression "within the limits of its economic capacity and development" appearing in Article 41. The expression "at all levels" is an innovation of the Court by judicial activism. While declaring that the citizen's right to education is a fundamental right, the Court does not seem to have gone into the question of the individual's fundamental right to pursue the kind of education that he chooses at his cost, or his right to establish and administer educational institutions. Generally, the Court has been holding the view that an individual cannot enforce his fundamental right if it involves the abridgement of the fundamental right of another. In the case of the minorities' right to establish and administer institutions of their choice, the Court has held that this right cannot be enforced at the cost of the fundamental rights of others.

In its judgement, the Court has also dealt with the legality of the system of capitation fees. It holds that "the State is under an obligation to establish educational institutions to enable the citizens to enjoy the said right. The State may discharge its obligation through state-owned or state-recognised educational institutions. When the State Government grants recognition to the private educational institutions, it creates an agency to fulfil its obligation under the Constitution. The students are given admission to the educational institutions—whether state-owned or state-recognised—in recognition of their 'right to education' under the Constitution. Charging capitation fee in consideration of admission to educational institutions, is a patent denial of citizen's right to education under the Constitution."

According to the judgement, the State action or inaction which defeats the constitutional mandate is per se arbitrary and cannot be sustained. Capitation fee makes the availability of education beyond the reach of the poor. The state action in permitting capitation fee to be charged by state-recognised educational institutions is wholly arbitrary and as such violative of Article 14 of the Constitution of India. The capitation fee engenders a clear class bias; it enables the rich to secure admission while the poor has to withdraw because of financial inability. A system that denies admission to a meritorious student because he has no money is patently unreasonable. The Court therefore rules, "charging of capitation fee in consideration of admissions to educational institutions is wholly arbitrary and as such infracts Article 14 of the Constitution."

The third major issue considered by the Court was the provisions for regulation of fees contained in the Karnataka legislation of 1984. Under this Act, the State Government had notified that students admitted against government seats in private medical colleges shall pay Rs.2000; Karnataka students (other than those admitted against government seats) shall pay Rs. 25000; and Indian students from outside Karnataka shall pay Rs. 60000. The legislation which was enacted ostensibly to curb the evil practice of collecting capitation fees permits the managements to admit students at their discretion in exchange for substantial sums of money. The Court holds that when the Government has prescribed Rs.2000 as the tuition fee for students admitted to government medical colleges and also for students admitted against government seats in private medical colleges, it has a responsibility to see that colleges established with government permission and run with its recognition, are prohibited from charging more than Rs. 2000. The Court, therefore, declares that Rs. 60000 permitted to be charged from students from outside Karnataka "is not tuition fee but in fact a capitation fee and as such cannot be sustained and is liable to be struck down."

There is nothing in the judgement that debars the entry of private enterprise in the field of education, especially higher and professional education. They are free to function under the scheme of state-recognition. The Chairman UGC has said that the UGC has been empowered to lay down the norms for regulation of fees for courses offered by universities and colleges. One consequence of the judgement is that while prescribing the norms of fees, the UGC or any other agency empowered to do so, has to ensure that the fees prescribed by them do not violate the citizen's right to education.

The findings do not apply to foreign students and NRIs. It could not have been the intention of the Court that private institutions are only for foreigners and NRIs. That there are irregularities and corruption in the private sector does not mean that it should be totally closed down; it calls only for regulation. If the State is the provider of education, it can also regulate, provided the regulations are within reasonable limits. These regulations would be necessary in education as the State will also have to concern itself with certain essential standards.

The judgement has raised several issues. According to reports, petitions have already been filed for a review of the decision. For instance, a person has claimed that the verdict has adversely affected his fundamental right to education for which he can pay any price. The ruling that merit along shall determine admission will also be a matter for litigation. What will happen to all those students who qualify in the entrance tests, but cannot be admitted to medical colleges for want of seats?

The whole matter is now before a Constitution Bench. The highest Court in the country has corrected itself more than once. For the present however, the judgement of 30th July, 1992 holds the field. It is, therefore, the law of the land today. Those of us who are concerned with education have to arrange our affairs, adjust our policies and conduct ourselves accordingly.

Anand Sarup

It is not necessary for us to imagine so many things that the judgement did not say. To my mind, the Court addressed the issue in a limited fashion. And the limited question was whether a medical college functioning under the scheme of recognition by the Government could charge more fees than what the Government itself has prescribed for its own institutions. The Court says that the Government may fulfil its obligation to provide for education through state-run or state-recognised institutions. A careful persual of the judgement will make it clear that practically all the contentious issues arise from the fact and the implications of 'recognition by the State'.

In view of the above, I would like to straightaway question why so much importance is or should be accorded to recognition? There is really no reason as to why all activities in the sphere of education should be carried on under the broad umbrella of government recognition. Anyway, what is so wonderful about the performance of the Government in the realm of education? Be that as it may, as long as an institution depends upon the Government for acquiring credibility, identity and the legal authority for its activities, it must accept its subordination to Government. It, therefore, seems logical that any one who is essentially the creature of the government recognition should not be entitled to charge a fee or levy higher than what is charged by the government in its own corresponding institutions. The need of the hour, in the context of the constitutional imperative, is not only to enforce the views of the Supreme Court in the matter of higher education but also, much more purposefully, in the case of primary and elementary education where money power is much more openly and extensively at play creating an unbridgeable chasm between the rich and the poor.

The moment this dependency relationship created by government recognition is dissolved, the issue of subrodination of non-government institutions to government regulations about course curricula, routine of the teaching-learning process and limitations about fees etc., would become inoperative and irrelevant. For example, if a private institution were to go out of the ambit of recognition and enter the academic areas on its own strength and if people are prepared to pay whatever it demands on the basis of its own reputation, without the props of government recognition, the whole scenario would undergo a fundamental change. Therefore, the question as to whether a state-recognised institution can charge more than a state-run institution is quite separate from the major and distinctly different question regarding a general enhancement in fees in government and government recognised institutions.

While it is true that the judgement of the Supreme Court has limited the fees that can be charged by government recognised institutions but it is also true that nowhere in the judgement has a limitation been placed upon the extent to which fees might be enhanced by the Government. Only the question of whether a government recognised institution could charge more than the fee of Rs. 2000 has been discussed. In fact, the Court has not gone into the question or the right or wrong of Rs. 2000. The judgement does not, therefore, suggest that there can be no general rise in fees or that fees cannot be raised to an economic level. So, the judgement does not pose any problem in so far as the raising of fees is concerned.

Thirdly, the Court has discussed the issue whether or not there should be a ban on the establishment of additional capacity in the private or public medical colleges. The observations made by the Court clearly indicate that any one dealing with medical education, in fact with anything in the gamut of higher education, within or outside Government, is free to discuss the justification for, and the merit of, opening new medical or any other kind of colleges. The Court recognises that the Government may eventually say that there is a demand but it is not in a position to provide the requisite facilities since its economic capacity does not permit further investment. The fact that this issue has been discussed makes it clear that the Government cannot be compelled to open more colleges irrespective of the needs, priorities and resource constraints.

As for Prof. Reddy's qeustion about the need for seriously considering what changes, if any, need to be incorporated in the Constitution, it does seem necessary to go into the matter in all seriousness not only with reference to the judgement on education, but even more so, with reference to the economic policies we are pursuing, moving away gradually from the egalitarian objectives written into the Constitution. We cannot ignore the fact that the Constitution seeks to establish a socialist state which incorporates concepts which have lost their appeal for us since these have been exploded elsewhere. We cannot ignore the fact that the present discussion about the right to education becomes all the more important when it is juxtaposed against the scenario in which heirs of inherited wealth, like their feudal forbears are able to jump the queue once again to acquire the expertise to control the economy and the politics of the country.

Amrik Singh

I do not feel very enthusiastic about this judgement. What it has said about the right to education is very eloquently argued. But what does it mean? Does it mean that a child who does not have access to elementary education today will now have the access because of this judgement? The answer is obvious.

While the courts can pronounce, they cannot go beyond this. The whole question of who will have access and how, is still for the State Governments to prescribe. Their policies are going to be what they are. It is, therefore, my apprehension that this judgement will not get implemented. Consequently it may not lead to any concrete action. Hence my lack of enthusiasm. Nevertheless, there is no denying that the judgement is still a step forward because what the judgement now says had not been said all this time.

In 1984, the UGC was empowered to prescribe the fees for all higher education programmes offered by colleges, universities and the IITs. There was already a proposal to make the All India Council for Technical Education a statutory body. Perhaps, the UGC did not want a rival. Hence the amendment. But the fact is that so far the UGC has not prescribed the fees for any course.

Questions have been raised about the role of private colleges. I want to know if there is any country in the world, barring perhaps the ex-communist countries, which does not permit private initiative in education. If the rest of the world is going this way, how can India remain an exception?

Since we are discussing legal issues, I would like to raise the question of fees charged by private schools. We all know that many private schools charge high fees, ranging from 200 to Rs. 1000 per month. Is the judgement going to apply to them also? I wish it does

In that case, we will finally see a shift in he balance of social and political power in the country.

The Supreme Court has examined the question of fees in a limited context. The Karnataka Government enacted the legislation in 1983. Since there were many capitation-fee colleges in the State, some of them as old as 20 years or more, the Act provided for a 5-year period of transition. It was during this period that the scales of fees were worked out; Rs. 2000 for government seats and Rs. 60000 seats for the management quota. It was this process of selling seats and the extortion of money that brought the issue to the Supreme Court. Let us face up to the fact that now the rich people have entered the field of education and have started minting money. To accommodate them, all norms have been violated by those in power. In Maharashtra, the universities were divested of the power to grant affiliation and that power was taken over by the State Govt. When questions of opening private medical colleges come up, whether in Andhra Pradesh, Karnataka or Maharashtra, the universities were bulldozed into granting affiliation and the State Medical Councils too were bulldozed to grant recognition. (The State Medical Councils can grant recognition to practise within the State).

I would like also to refer to the question of recognition by Government which Mr. Anand Sarup has raised. We have in the country a large number of professional bodies set up by the Centre—in Architechture, Engineering, Medicine, Pharmacy, Dentistry, Accountancy, Management and so on. These bodies were set up to lay down norms and they have done so. But our talent for diluting everything has ensured that these norms are not applied. In my view, the source of all trouble is that we have made all these professional bodies dysfunctional. But I still hold the view that the question of recognition should be left to the professional bodies.

Some of us would recall that an amendment to the Medical Council Act was moved in 1987. One of the objectives of the amendment was to ensure that prior approval of the Medical Council of India was obtained for opening a new medical college. The bill got referred to a Joint Select Committee. Five years and three governments later, we stand where we were. But the Supreme Court judgement made it necessary for the Central Government to promulgate an ordinance to require prior clearance of the Medical Council for establishing a medical college. This was the lacuna sought to be remedied five years ago but was sabotaged. It had now to be done. That indeed is a happy outcome of the Court's verdict.

The major source of all our problems is corruption. We all know that the Courts cannot root out corruption. Unless we tackle the issue of corruption, there will not be any lasting solution.

V. M. Dandekar

The Chairman has observed that today the judgement is the law of the land and we should abide by it. It sounded as if it was something given to us by God and we must suffer until the same God decrees otherwise.

There was another observation about the socialistic pattern of our Constitution. I think the framers of the Constitution did not talk about socialism. It came later. Even so, the constitution-makers made a distinction between elementary education and other kinds of education. The Supreme Court has not taken this distinction into account, which is very clearly spelt out in the Constitution. I will, therefore, make a very general and simple proposition : whatever is free and compulsory must be available to all; what is not free must be paid for. It is as simple as that.

We all know the conditions in which the large majority of our people live. Whether it is in the matter of health, drinking water, or whatever else, the conditions in the country are not such that would ensure the dignity of the individual. We see inequalities in every walk of life. No one makes the point that every citizen has a fundamental right to five-star meals without paying for it. Therefore, there is no justification for singling out education for a special treatment.

Amrik Singh seems to be saying and he has quoted the President of the Medical Council, that there are too many doctors in the country. If so, how is it that the doctors are making so much money? How is it that so many young men and women are prepared to pay vast sums of money for admission to medical colleges? Who undertakes our manpower planning? What is our competence to undertake manpower planning? People are lining up with so much money for admission to medical colleges, engineering colleges, as also to B.Sc., B.Com. and B.A. The fact is that they find it worthwhile. So long as a degree holder gets more than what an uneducated man gets, there will be demand for higher education.

If there is a demand for medical education, medical colleges will come up. If these colleges are not very good, they will produce some kind of a doctor, who will be better than having no doctor at all. If these do well, they will survive. Sometime ago, the Maharashtra Government decided that there will be no more schools in the State.

Soon enough, the government realised that it was better if the youth are in the colleges and not on the streets. The fact is that people are putting a market value on education. They demand higher, technical and professional education. They are prepared to pay for it.

Amrik Singh mentioned the role of professional bodies in granting recognition. They do not in my view inspire much confidence. They monopolise the profession. This is what the American Management Association does. This is what the Indian professionals do.

The socialist system collapsed. It took them 80 years to witness that collapse. We have had socialism for 40 years. Should we wait for another 40 years to see it collapse?

D. Swaminadhan

The judgement is said to be under review already. Therefore, I do not know how, what we are going to say is relevant. I would, however, point out that there seems to be a certain contradiction in the judgement itself. In the first part, the judgement declares that every citizen has a right to education and that this right flows from the right to life. It follows that the State should provide education to all those who demand it, be it higher, technical, medical or other professional education. If there is a demand, the State is under an obligation to provide the facilities to meet that demand.

Later in the judgement, the Court rules that admission to educational institutions should be on merit and merit along should determine admission. What does it mean? Merit means competition and selectivity. In that case, how is it that all those who seek admission can enforce their right? I think there is a contradiction here. I may be wrong, but I think I have a point.

G. Ram Reddy

Since questions of contempt of court have been raised, as organisers of the colloquium, we would like to seek some clarification. Since the issue is before the Constitution Bench, are we debarred from discussing the judgement? If there is indeed any contempt of court, we would like to close the discussions here.

Madhav Reddy

Prof. Baxi will bear with me, it won't be contempt. Especially a colloquium like this.

Upendra Baxi

This is a meeting of very prominent people. We may have very honest differences of opinion. We might even be angry. Even if there is no law of contempt, we make our points in ways that do not denigrate or demolish other national institutions. That would not be contempt.

The University of Delhi has intervened in the writ petition before the Court. The University is of the view that both the issues arising from the judgement, namely, that there is an enforceable fundamental right to education under the Constitution and that the whole system of charging capitation fee for admission to educational institutions is unconstitutional, deserve to be supported. Hence the observations that I will be making here are purely in my personal capacity and are not in my capacity as the Vice-Chancellor of the University of Delhi.

There is some confusion. There is a distinction between fundamental rights and directive principles. But in recent times, the judiciary has been creating more rights which are not specifically provided in the Constitution through judicial activism. For instance, the judges have created rights concerning due process of law, right to bail, right to privacy, right to environment and so on. About three months back, there was a verdict on right to health. This activist role has established a new tradition and created more rights. There may be many views about judicial activism. But we all welcome this new tradition.

The right to education is in fact the right to access to educational institutions; right to primary education; right to literacy. The State has a duty to fulfil this right at all levels. This right to access must be guaranteed by the State. Secondly, merit has to be observed in making admission. The Court has not gone into the question of how merit should be determined. But, the Court has held that those who do not have merit cannot buy admission. What the "teaching shops" across the country are providing is not education. Therefore, the responsibility to provide for education devolves on the State Governments.

Now, points have been made about the economic capacity of the State to provide for education. We all know that the Government is under tremendous pressure to cut down public expenditure. This is a conditionality imposed by the IMF. On the other hand, there is a conditionality of the Constitution. Judges have been saying for over 40 years that conditions should be created for the enjoyment of the fundamental rights guaranteed by the Constitution. Judges are the only people who care for the Constitution. Others criticise the Constitution and repudiate it for their benefits. Judges maintain the Constitution and derive no benefits. They face only criticism, hostile or friendly.

We have all a right to change. So has the judiciary. In our own time, we were once socialists, we were marxists; now, we are post-marxists, we have heard those who have sculpted the national policy on education of the Government of India asking what is wonderful about government. That is how we change.

The judgement says that the citizens have an enforceable fundamental right to education. What is this education? Is it merely admission to an institution? Is it the award of a degree? Or is it only access to the formal system of education offered by the universities and colleges? We all know that the Indira Gandhi National Open University and the other open universities in the country are developing good programmes of distance education. Is it not possible for the citizens to enforce their right to education through the means of distance education? What should be the content of the education to which all people have a fundamental right? It is to be educated about the scheme of our Constitution and the values of liberty, equality and fraternity that the Constitution enunciates. Equally important are the teaching materials and the teaching methods. The material and the method have to be non-communal, eco-friendly and gender-free.

I would like to refer to the timing of the judgement. During the last few months, the central universities and many of the state universities also, were facing a resource crisis. The so-called grant freeze has placed them in a critical situation. The judges could not have been unaware of this crisis. The fundamental right to education that the judgement has upheld prohibits the state, prohibits as a matter of duty, from reducing grants to the institutions which are already in existence.

Questions have been asked whether for the enforcement of the right to education, people can ask for the establishment of more colleges, because they have merit. This is an issue that the courts will have to decide case-by-case. What is significant is that the judgement is an important beginning; it also has given us a great opportunity.

M.V. Pylee

The judgement has upgraded the preamble of the Constitution and the directive principles of State policy into fundamental rights. We all know that the Constitution itself makes a clear distinction between fundamental rights which are enforceable and directive principles which are not. The Supreme Court itself has held in several cases that if there is a conflict between the fundamental rights and the directive principles of State policy, the fundamental rights will prevail.

The preamble of the Constitution is a general statement. It reflects the long-term objectives of the nation. It gives us a general idea about the directions in which we should be moving and the manner in which we should be arranging our affairs. It cannot, therefore, in my view be of the same nature as fundamental rights.

While framing the Constitution, Dr. Ambedkar was asked about the relevance of Part IV which contained only 'pious platitudes'. Dr. Ambedkar replied that the people of this country will be voting governments in and out of office every five years. Those who fail to conduct the affairs of the nation according to these principles will be voted out of office by the people of India.

There are several universities which permit students to appear privately in their examinations without formal attendance in class-rooms. This facility has given room for private enterprise to step in and provide coaching to prepare students to take the examinations. These private coaching institutions (they are called Parallel Colleges in Kerala) are subject to no regulation or recognition. They charge what they like. Their fees are several times more than what the formal system levies. No questions have so far been raised about their right to charge higher fees.

It is important to realise what constitutes a right and what constitutes a matter of policy. In formulating policies, the State has to take into account various factors that are crucial to the implementation of those policies. The courts cannot take over this function.

Kishore Gandhi

The judgement does not take into account the social and political realities prevailing in the country today. There has been a significant paradigm shift in our economic policy; from a controlled economy to a market-friendly, liberalised economy. There have to be corresponding changes in all sectors of development to reflect this shift in policy and in our political, social and bureaucratic structures.

In a situation of acute resource crunch, we are already spending large amounts on universities. The higher education system and the universities are pampered with the tax payers' money. We have been talking about raising resources from other sources. From the alumni, from the NRIs and so on. These have had no impact so far. The NGOs (non-governmental organisations) are possible the only source that can try and raise some resources. Perhaps, more self-financing institutions might be an answer.

Prof. Baxi mentioned distance education in the context of the enforcement of the right to education. Unfortunately, the distance education system is still to develop professional education programmes in engineering, technology or other areas. Therefore, those who seek education in these areas cannot turn to the distance education system.

Ms A.S. Desai

There are several factors that contribute to the dignity of life. Of all these, education is the very critical factor from which many others flow. While basic nutrition or shelter can be purchased, the awareness that enriches life and improves its dignity comes through education. Education has thus a specific context and a place. It cannot be clubbed with everything else.

I am surprised that we take the line of thought that there is so much polarisation in society that we have to live with it. The judgement has a legal context; it has also a social context. If we look at the judgement in the social context and not in its purely legalistic context, we would appreciate that the right to education has several implications. Everyone—be they doctors, lawyers or technologists—is making us pay heavily for their services because they have paid heavily for their education. It is again the poor who will suffer because they can pay neither for their education nor for various services. These realities cannot be ignored. Access to education will be denied to the poor even if they have merit; secondly, they cannot compete in the market because they are poor. The market will enrich only those who can afford; the poor will continue to remain deprived.

If there is increasing demand for professional and technical education, it is because it increases the earning capacity of the people. It adds even to the dowry potential. If the market forces were to operate freely, the poor people, the women and a number of others who deserve education may not be able to secure professional education. Even the system of loans and scholarships may not help them much because it is these categories of people who may not be able to compete successfully in the employment market.

V.D. Karad

The judgement is not against private institutions; the Court has disapproved only the differential fee structure. It says that there should be no discrimination in the matter of levying fees between students from different states.

C.R. Mitra

The Supreme Court has not defined capitation fee in the legal sense. It has only vaguely talked about extortion. Nor has the Court given a legal definition of the term education in the context of the right to education. Here again there is a reference to educational institutions at all levels. Secondly, the Court was considering a specific case relating to the admission of a student to a medical college. In dealing with this specific case, the Court gives a verdict of far-reaching consequence to all education and at all levels.

All over the western world, private enterprise plays a role in education. In India too, private enterprise has and will continue to have, a major role to play. There are many institutions in the private sector and in the industry, which make significant contributions to human resource development through education and training. Their role may be invisible, but it is effective and efficient too. The verdict of the Court does not go against them.

We have borrowed many things from the western world. Most of our institutions are built on their models. There is nothing in our legal system that is not inherited from the West. So too is our education system. In recent years, British higher education has changed significantly. The Oxford and Cambridge universities have changed. The British University Grants Committee has been abolished. Its place has been taken by a University Funding Council. British universities are now talking about marketing and pricing education. Why can't we also change according to the need of the times?

It seems to me that we are lost in semantics. There is a verbal onslaught, a verbal polarisation, in whatever we attempt to do. Globalisation, privatisation, liberalisation, commercialisation : we try to read too much into this and in the confusion that follows, we seem to lose our sense of direction.

Anand Sarup

Much of our reaction to the judgement is conditioned by, if I may say so, the lack of internal consistancy and the lack of reasoning in the judgement itself. We cannot discuss the implications of the judgement by ignoring the fact that some basic issues are connected with education.

Education has a character and as an activity, it has a role which goes beyond mere acquisition of knowledge or expertise. It differentiates people in a fundamental way, socially, politically and economically. Therefore my point again is: in a democracy can inherited wealth be allowed to be the basis for access to education and the benefits that it confers?

Whatever one might say, our Constitution has an egalitarian goal. If we read its provisions together and cumulatively, we cannot miss this message. I have no quarrel with those who ask for changes in the Constitution to bring it in line with the market-oriented policies already adopted by the Government. But I would like to ask the advocates of market economy and liberalisation to come out in the open and initiate a debate on what changes we need to make in the Constitution and what will be the short and long term consequences of these changes.

B.E. Avhad

In a democracy, judicial activism not only authorises, but requires the courts to legislate. In constitutional law, judicial law-making is inevitable. The Supreme Court had held in 1984 that the right to live with human dignity enshrined in Article 21 derives its life breath from the directive principles of state policy. It is against this background that the recent judgement holding that the right to education is guaranteed under the Constitution deserves to be appreciated. It is true that this judgement has come in the context of the position obtaining in Karnataka in the field of medical education but it does pose some questions of general and national importance.

While interpreting personal liberty with reference to individual dignity, the right to education has been given conflicting treatment. Right to education is not included in Chapter III of the Constitution as a fundamental right. Article 45 enunciates a directive principle of state policy rather sharply in stating that the State shall provide free and compulsory education to all children upto 14 years of age. The rule of interpretation requires the exclusion of what Article 45 specifically omits to include. It certainly excludes children above 14 and thus all of higher education.

The basic necessities of life—food, clothing and shelter—could not be guaranteed by the State of all even after so many years of independence. These necessities must rank above the rest. Higher education cannot be given a higher priority.

3. ISSUES FOR EDUCATION

Anand Sarup

The issues for our consideration have been lised and circulated. This provides an adequate framework for our discussions. We could attend to many more issues and problems as we go along. In the circumstances, we need not stand on formalities. With your permission, I request Prof. Khanna to initiate the discussion.

S.K. Khanna

I would like to raise a couple of issues associated with the growth of education in the country. But before that, it is necessary that we redefine the concept of education so that there is greater clarity. Is education only for the general enrichment of the citizens' consciousness? Or is it for acquiring knowledge and skills which can be offered in the market-place to earn a livelihood? We will, I believe, have to answer this question sooner than later.

When the constitution was adopted, the scenario was very different. The population was about 250 millions or so. The manpower requirements for the development sectors were reckoned on that basis. The situation has changed considerably since then and by the year 2000, our population will have crossed the 1000 million mark. The number of universities has already gone up from 25 at the time of independence to about 200; the number of colleges has risen from about 700 to over 7500; the number of students has increased from about 2 lakhs to 45 lakhs. We do not know what kind of manpower needs the country will face in the year 2000 and what kind of educational network will have to be created.

We all know that there is considerable mismatch, direct or indirect, visible or invisible, between education and employment. Almost 52% of the total enrolment in the higher education system, in the humanities, social sciences etc., are not tied up with any employment sector. The remaining 48% which include professional education (teacher education, engineering, medicine, law) are also not really related to the relevant professional employment sectors. They may or may not be absorbed by the concerned sectors. Still some 30000 students are known to be in the private sector, in the engineering and medical, colleges.

The annual rate of expansion of higher education today is 5%. The participation ratio in higher education is just about 6% of the relevant age group. The available infrastructure does not permit any increase in this rate of participation.

It is time that we took a second look at our constitutional goals and objectives. The framework designed for 250 million people cannot meet the aspirations of 1000 million. We have to redefine our goals.

Anand Sarup

The basic issue is one of expansion. We know that this expansion cannot be supported with government resources. Therefore, we have to explore as to what other avenues are available to raise the required resources? Certainly the state can and should control expansion and in this context, be enabled to give directions so that expansion meets the needs of the society better. Even otherwise, it can create conditions in which people obtain resources for education from the market place which they can pay back when they begin to earn. Alternately, it can recognise private institutions and by this act of patronage enable them to charge capitation fees which would, besides providing resources for expansion, allow any one with money in his pockets to walk upto the counter and buy an admission, irrespective of his or her aptitude and academic performance. What will a poor boy or girl whose parents weren't rich do is a moral question which will have to be faced sooner or later.

One problem arises because education has not been defined. A problem arises also because people now have a right to education and there is apprehension that a person might go up to the court and ask for facilities in a field in which skills and knowledge are not needed by the rest of society. It would be difficult to meet such demands since these might involve public expenditure of considerable magnitude.

There are questions of relative priorities between primary education, elementary education, higher education etc., which will have to be sorted out while responding to the right to education. There is also the question of how much more than the fees for government schools one pays for education in the so-called 'public schools'. Should we not consider the consequences of the judgement for these schools and demand that they downscale their fees to the extent possible, to the level of government schools? If we have to lay the foundation of an egalitarian society, we will have to begin with the schools. Those who come out of the highly expensive/elite schools have no idea about how ordinary people live.

D.Y. Patil

Primary education is still not mass education. Technical and medical education is available only to a small number.

I am glad I started capitation fee colleges. I know the agonies of the rural people. I have studied in rural schools, rural colleges. I suggest that all private institutions at all levels should allocate 30% of their seats to rural students. Their tuition, boarding, lodging etc., should be free.

Vast areas of land are available in our cities. Land price in Bombay is four time higher than the construction cost. If parts of this land are allotted to promoters of private educational institutions rather than to building contractors, they could approach financial institutions for loans to construct building, buy equipment and provide other infrastructure for educational programmes. Students who seek admission to these institutions could be asked to deposit Rs. 5000 each for raising the margin money required for the loans. This is one way to eradicate illiteracy and also to clear the slums in the cities.

As for medical colleges, hospitals can be asked to finance the education of students. Those poor boys and girls who have secured 70% or more marks can be paid the cost of their education which they could repay after graduation by working in those hospitals. Grant of exemption from payment of income tax is another way of attracting donations to educational institutions.

The Government colleges attract many rich people. Why should our poor masses support their education? Even in the technical/vocational institutions we spend about Rs. 2700 per student. If he repays at the rate of Rs. 10 per month, it could raise substantial resources. We cannot afford education of all the people at public cost.

The Agricultural Universities have vast areas of land attached to them. How many of them use this land for productive purposes? If they did, they would generate enough resources for the maintenance of Agricultural Universities.

V.M. Dandekar

The judgement is incidental to the charging of capitation fee. It has to be understood in the context of the existing system of higher education, its management, its styles and methods of opereation and so on. Moreover, an impression has been created that there is a resource crunch; otherwise all is fine. The fact, however, remains that the entire education system is being run in the interests of teachers who have created a monopoly for themselves. Unless you enter this government sponsored monopoly system and go through the prescribed processes, you cannot get a degree and if you do not have a degree, you have no access to employment.

I suggest that teachers should be accountable to the students directly and no one else: not to the Medical Council or any other professional body. Even in reputed colleges in the country, there is no teaching. The reason is that teachers have an assured income, power acquired through unions and automatic promotions.

The reciprocal situation is that students are irresponsible. To turn out a standard product, you need a regulated system and the stamp of a university. I was a great enthusiast of autonomous colleges. How many colleges came forward? Not even the most reputed colleges have opted for this status. Why? This is because no colleges have any pride in their products. No teacher wants to own his product. It is in the context of this system of organised education that the judgement should be interpreted.

Unless we change this system, no improvement is possible. We might begin with teacher accountability. A teacher might be attached to a university or a college which may provide him with infrastructural facilities. He should cease to be a salaried employee. He should like doctors, lawyers, engineers etc., function as a professional. If one is a good teacher, students will come to him. He should charge them directly and pay to the host institution a fee for using its facilities. If he does not perform, he will fade out as a teacher and end up as a clerk in a nationalised bank.

One may ask as to what will happen in respect of those subjects which are commercially unviable because through these no marketable knowledge is acquired. I believe that notwithstanding this, good teacher, whatever he teaches, will be in demand. We need not worry about manpower planning. The market will balance the demand and supply.

During these discussions I heard someone refer pejoratively to 'teaching shops'. We have no cause to denigrate them. I have seen long queues of students before the so-called teaching shops when the classrooms in colleges are empty. The reason is that our education is oriented to examinations and students are more confident of passing these through tutorial classes rather than through recognised educational institutions.

One word about subsidies. If we are subsidising education, we should know our priorities. We should know how much we are subsidising and whom. Subsidies should be only for the deserving.

Anand Sarup

The sheer quality of Prof. Dandekar's presentation leaves one breathless. It will take a great deal of effort to understand each statement that he has made and examine its validity. Nevertheless, I do hope that somebody from the organised system here will join issue with him.

G. Ram Reddy

It is very difficult to challenge Prof. Dandekar. Once you accept his premise you have to go along with him. But do you? Who will implement his proposal on teacher accountability? Is there a political will to change the system and dismantle all the existing structures? Who will buy the argument that teacher should sell his service directly to the students? It is all very well to propound theories without realisting the implications of their execution. May be, there is some merit in what he says, I will accept that. But is it the only way to make the teacher accountable? What he is suggesting may be very interesting and tempting but, I am afraid, it is simply un-workable.

Upendra Baxi

There is considerable scope for introducing factors like accountability and responsibility in the system. But changing a whole system is an entirely different ball game like making changes in the Constitution. These changes will come because IMF will not give us money without our meeting the efficiency criteria laid down for us. These are exogenous changes. System changes always are.

Some time back the University of Delhi set up a system to ensure regularity in teaching. Teachers were asked to articulate the standards of responsibility and professional behaviour and stand by them. The question thrown back to us was : how about the accountability of the members of the Governing Bodies, of the Principals or of the Vice-Chancellor? They would also have to be accountable in a similar fashion. Similarly with students too, a number of issues will have to be sorted out. In good universities, I am talking about massive assembly line universities—not about IITs, IIMs, etc.,—students struggle hard to get admission. The bulk of them are serious about pursuing their studies. They do not go on strikes. At any rate, there are no strikes to demand that the libraries remain open till 9 p.m. (they close at 6 p.m.) or to demand chnages in the curriculum. But the question is : can we change without touching the existing politics of the students union structure? The intersection between student unions and party politics involves a certain amount of political intrusion on the campuses.

A mention was made about the unpopularity of the concept of the autonomy of private colleges. We must understand that there is so much politics around the opening of these colleges. They offer an opportunity to mobilise funds for political campaigns. How do we change these situations? My appeal to all political parties is to agree to a self-imposed moratorium of five years on pursuit of any kind of political agenda on the campuses.

The kind of sweeping criticism one heard demoralises the honest minority of well-meaning teachers. My worry is that such criticism will only lead to the loss of a major national resource. I agree that considerable scope exists in increasing accountability and promoting excellence. Nonetheless I wish that we were less global in our denunciation and more imaginative in our recognition of the positive elements that exist in the system.

We should not ignore some positive consequences of the judgement. The right to education can be enforced by a student who has merit, who has paid the fees according to the prescribed rates, against bad management of education. He can take the institutions to court if the teachers do not take classes; if they are absent, if the examinations are delayed; and if the results are not announced in time. The institutions will be held accountable for the loss of time of students. There is enormous possibility for mobilising courts in ensuring better management of education.

Anand Sarup

For most people, going to court is a harrowing experience. It is alright for Professors of Law and retired Judges to talk about the facility of judicial remedies to secure claims and enforce rights. But, I do not know if the ordinary people would accept that being able to go courts represents a solution.

The judgement does not say what fees should be charged. It does not postulate that the State should provide free education, or no-cost education. Those who provide education can charge a fee. If they charge an economic fee, and if there is a window from which the students can take loans, then a different scenario emerges. The students, their parents and the Banks will all start asking : are the teachers doing their jobs properly; are the laboratories adequately equipped; is it not possible to curtail the duration of different programmes; and so on. A whole new culture will emerge and a certain environment for accountability will get established. The judgement, from this view-point, has very significant consequences for the processes of education.

N.C. Nigam

We have widened the scope of discussions to include important and significant issues. We are touching a very fragile system. Pricing education is not an innovation. The system of paying teachers according to what they teach is in vogue in many countries. For instance, in Germany, teachers are paid a basic salary; in addition they receive a payment on the basis of the number of students who go to their classes. There are many Universities who charge their students on a per hour or per credit basis. These practices create their own consequences. There are mutual obligations and responsibilities. If the teachers do not take classes, students go to the Dean and not to the Court. And they get what they had paid for.

I do not agree that students and teachers, across the board, have lost a sense of responsibility. We should not globalise the issue. My experience in the IITs suggests that students in these institutions seldom miss their classes. It is a matter of tradition. Some traditions are too strong to be easily overhauled. But I do agree that the pressure of the environment is against such traditions. We cannot easily dismantle these traditions and create a new structure.

Ramlal Parikh

There are three principal issues that the judgement raises. The first is the definition of the concept of education. I think it is important that we make a distinction between education and schooling. Conditioned as we are to the institutionalised system of education, we seem to think that it is the only way of education. There are several ways to educate people; the non-institutional forms provide equally efficient methods of education.

My first, point, therefore, is that right to education should not be understood merely in terms of right to schooling; it is he right to access to any means of learning—formal, non-formal, distance, open and so on. There should, therefore, be no problem about enforcing the right to education. In fact, I would go to the extent of suggesting that for the next ten years, we should not expand the institutionalised system of education. We should go for alternative modes. Education goes beyond institutions. Degrees should not become more important than education. In several countries, continuing education programmes are organised on large scales. That is the way in which the fundamental right to education is secured.

Secondly, what does the right to education mean to the individual? Education enhances one's capacity to learn, it increases the ability to educate oneself, acquire more knowledge and apply that knowledge in work and in life. This is the basic education that people need. This basic education can be provided through non-school programmes. Through programmes of literacy, adult education, functional literacy and so on. Expansion of more primary schools is, therefore, not the answer. That would only mean construction of more school buildings, which is not education.

Now, if a village does not have any facility for basic education, I hope someone can start a public interest litigation against the State for its indifference, insensitivity and lack of concern.

My third point is the urgency for reforms in education. We need to reorganise and reorient the existing curricular system. We need to introduce greater flexibility and more openness in the system. For instance, why do we insist on 8 papers of three hours each for a degree programme? We must deformalise the system. Let the learners determine what they want. A system so deformalised, open and unstructured can serve a much larger number of students.

C.R. Mitra

It seems to me we are assuming that the be-all and end-all of education is schooling and the passing of examinations. Prof. Dandekar suggests that teacher accountability can be ensured if teachers are paid by students directly. But let me say that there are teachers who made me love the subject; there are also teachers who are adroit in teaching how to pass the examinations.

The Supreme Court judgement has provided an external impulse to discuss the health of the system. The grant-freeze has come only now, but we have been discussing and diagnosing the ills of the system for long coming up always with off-the-cuff solutions. The fact of the matter is that our system is fractured and it is with this that we hope to fulfil all our expectations.

I made an attempt to estimate the contribution the orthodox system makes to our stock of professional manpower. I have tried to compare these with the contribution from what I call the invisible system, which is neither non-orthodox nor non-formal. I am referring to the training industry, in the public and the private sectors. They contribute over 5 lakhs per year to our stock of professional manpower—a much larger number than what the orthodox system turns out. The market recognises it but the cost of this education and training is not reflected in the education budget of the nation. Can we force this system to come out in the open and become visible? Let us not go on multiplying the models of the fractured system.

To expect that courts will transform societies is to be anti-historic. It is only a system which is dynamic and alive to the needs of a knowledge-intensive, fast-moving, high-technology seciety that can respond to and manage changes.

What is the basis for the assumption that IITs teach the best curriculum? The crucial issue for relevance is that of curricular differentials. These institutions, at least those of them in the professional and technical fields, which provide teaching in what the work-place needs, can be said to be offering relevant education. That makes all the difference. We do not hear any body talking about curricular differentials in the non-professional colleges.

We seem to get trapped by the norms that we set. For most professional programmes, we have very rigid norms; so much by way of buildings, so many teachers, so much equipment and so on. If we look around the world, it should be possible for us to see that it is the difference in the curricular structures that mark the best from the ordinary.

Let us not imagine that privatisation is a mere rescue operation to help the government at a time of financial crisis. Let us look at privatisation as a positive initiative coming from private institutions, not to emulate government, but with worthy alternate proposals for responsible investment on sound business principles with an obligation to subject their curriculum to any test of relevance and a new direction. Let us see it as a new movement in education.

Anand Sarup

We all agree that there is tremendous scope for improvements and changes in the system. We also agree that the system should have greater flexibility; students should be free to study what they want, and teachers should be free to teach what they like. There are also ways of raising resources, directly or indirectly and we should consider alternate modes of education to provide greater opportunities to people.

The Supreme Court has made several assumptions. It assumes that the employers want educated and trained people: it assumes that there are people who want education. Since the number of people who want education is far in excess of the places available, a kind of discrimination takes place on the basis of the capacity to pay. Since education helps develop a full-fledged human being, who must live a life with dignity, the State will not be doing its job even in respect of the right to life, unless it also provides for education. The Court has now said that if you do not get what you want, you can come to the court to enforce your right. Is it objectionable? Is it practical? We should address ourselves to these issues and decide as to what is or is not possible or desirable.

Ms A.S. Desai

We are talking about alternatives. We seem to be thinking that private institutions are bad. Let me say that private institutions are neither better nor worse than government institutions. I am the product of a private institution and am proud of it.

What is important are the cost differentials. The differentials that create problems of access. Can loans be the answer? Even here there may be a problem of economic inequality. A student from a relatively rich background takes a loan, completes his education and gets employed. From then on, he is on his own. He can repay the loan from his earnings. On the other hand, there would be poor persons who also take loans, but soon after taking up jobs have to assume the responsibility to support their families and parents. The two situations are not equal therefore. There is, moreover, the problem of unequal access to employment. The poor person usually takes longer to get employed. Even then, he might have to enter at lower rungs and gradually move up. All these severely restrict his repaying capacity.

My suggestions, therefore, are : admissions should be by merit; the government should subsidise the education of the poor on a sliding scale (not by loans); and when students leave the system and become earning members, they should pay a tax on their degrees. Similarly, we should evolve a scheme for those who go away from the country after getting their basic education and professional training.

Finally, government should consider the allocation of two to four per cent of the allocation for all sectors of development to education. The community, as a whole, is the user of educated and trained manpower. It is, therefore, appropriate that it shares the cost of education.

G. Ram Reddy

I have a worry. May be, I have a limited vision. But, I am afraid we are not focussing on the real issues. To me, the issues are :

Firstly, we have a 6% access to higher education today. Do we expand it and if so, how much?

The second issue is of dependence on the State. What shall be the extent of this dependence? Today, the State spends a little over 3% of GNP on education. The New Policy of Education envisages that 6% or more will be spent. We talked a great deal in the new education policy on how to make the system work. How does it work?

Thirdly, the question of Right to Education; upto what level elementary, secondary, or higher education levels, does this right operate?

Fourthly, the cost. Who meets the cost? The State? The students? Prof. Dandekar said what is free must be available to all and what is not, must be paid for. Do we go along with it?

And finally, merit. How will merit be defined? For instance, can the students coming from rural areas and those studying in Delhi be assessed on the same scale?

M.V. Pylee

I want to introduce a new element into the discussion. Can we not see education as an industry in the service sector? In the same manner as there are hospital services, transport services, entertainment services, etc. The Supreme Court has some time back, held that university is an industry. It was of course, in the context of adjudication of some labour law case. Nonetheless, the question is worth considering.

Education is important for the development of the human personality. But how will a child who has nothing to eat, develop its personality with education alone?

There seems to be an assumption that education is the monopoly of the State. Why? Even so, there are class distinctions in state monopolies. For instance, in the railways which are a state monopoly, some people travel by second class, some by first class, and some by air-conditioned class. The principle here is that those who want better services must pay for it. So in education. The State needs to provide free education only upto the elementary stage. Beyond that stage, the beneficiaries must pay.

It seems to me that people are thinking in terms of the State providing free medical education, free engineering education as a matter of duty. I do not agree. I do not think anything will happen if the existing colleges are dismantled. There is no teaching and learning there any way. We should not invest any more money in this system.

Ms A.S. Desai

If education has to be developed as a service, how are you going to do it without any investment?

M.V. Pylee

Let me clarify. What I said is that those who derive any benefit from a service should pay for it. When I said everything is free, I was referring only to the existing fee structure, the nominal fee that we pay. For instance, the annual tuition fee for a post-graduate course in a university was Rs. 90 some twenty years ago. When the university proposed an increase in that fee, it was resisted. Even today it is Rs.90. My suggestion is that people should pay for higher education and that what they pay should be related to the cost.

Krishan Thapar

The judgement highlights and flags an important duty of the State. It has raised what was in the directive principles of state policy to the level of fundamental rights. If the State has failed to fulfil its obligation, what is wrong if the Court says it failed.

Today we are asking as to what should be the definition of education. What were we doing all these 45 years? If we did not know what education is all about, what provisions were we making? The real problem is that there are vested interests in education. They are quibbling about the judgement. There is criminalisation of education. There is a nexus between politicians and a new class of profiteering educationists. That is the problem.

There were, in the past also, movements in education in the private sector such as DAV institutions, the Khalsa colleges, the missionary schools. Today, what happens? A medical college is opened. Students are admitted. Teachers are appointed. The Medical Council does not recognise the college. The students join the politicians. What can you do? We have no exit policy even for industrial labour. How can we have an exit policy in a new field in which we are inducting new entrepreneurs?

The State should provide more resources for education. It has the resources. It is spending enormous amounts on less important sectors. The State cannot say it has no money for human resource development. If the structured system cannot be dismantled, it can be reshaped and developed.

Mr. Patil has made a concrete and practical suggestion. He has pointed out a method for raising resources. What we need is the efficient utilisation of the resources for education. The judgement has, in several ways, served a historical need. The promulgation of the ordinance on establishment of medical colleges was one important fall-out of the judgement.

S.K. Agrawala

A single judgement of the Supreme Court cannot be considered the final word in the development of law. It is part of a continuous process. The basic points arising from the judgement in Mohini Jain's case will be developed further by the Court in course of time.

Questions of education cannot be considered except in the context of two basic principles, namely, the economic capacity of the State and the need to ensure equity and access. Do we say that the State should provide education to all citizens, at all levels, without taking into account the economic capacity of the State? The answer to this question will come only through further refinements made by the Court in course of time in subsequent cases.

Inequity enters the system because all institutions do not offer the same quality of education. There are private institutions which, while providing better education, charge heavily. If one were to insist on settling the question of equity, then the quality of the majority of state-run schools has got to be improved.

Beyond the level of free and compulsory education provided by the Constitution, all education must be paid for on its unit cost. Here again the question of equity and equality arises. How can the poor people afford the cost? Can schemes of loans and scholarships improve equity and access? Ms. Desai had expressed some apprehensions. In any case how far can we take the principle of equity? Aren't there inequalities associated with birth? Aren't there questions about first generation or second generation learners? We need to make a beginning some where.

I agree that education which enhances the earning capacity must be paid for. That education is not just for public good alone; there is a private gain also in it. But I do not agree that while charging fees according to unit cost for those who can pay and concessional fees for the economically weak, a discretionary quota at the disposal of the management, to be allotted to the highest bidder to meet the development cost etc., will solve the problem. That can only distort the system further.

Amrik Singh

There is no justification for raking up the question of public *vs* the private enterprise in education. All over the world, where there are private educational institutions, such a thing has not happened. It is true that in education, wherever there is private enterprise, the profits go to the academic entrepreneur and not to the teachers.

What we need to do is to order our priorities in the system of education. Education of children upto the age of 14 years is the responsibility of the State; beyond that stage, the State needs to provide only a facility or a service. I would say, therefore, that the State is under an obligation to provide education upto the age of 14 years. It should divest itself of the responsibility to provide education beyond that age.

Someone raised the question of subsidised education. What is happening now? With such low levels of recovery, higher education is already subsidised heavily. Who gets the benefit? Not those who really deserve: therefore, my plea that higher education, especially professional and technical education, must be paid for at an economic rate.

Prof. Reddy asked whether we need to widen access to higher education and increase enrolment. Looking at even the current levels of enrolment, which is about 6 per cent of the age group, one wonders whether all those who are there deserve to be there? I would say that not even two per cent are there in search of education; the rest are not serious about education.

Finally, the issue of merit. What is merit and how is it to be assessed? Again, I would urge strongly that these issues are left better to the professional bodies and a more rigorous system of accreditation.

S. Venkateswaran

Education is a continous process. It proceeds from one stage to another. If an institution is good and offers good education, it will attract good students. Good students who are also prepared to pay for their education. In BITS, Pilani, we charge Rs. 8000 as annual fees. The fee is the same for all courses, engineering, science or social science. Still, we get very good students. The cut-off point for admission to any programme was 94 per cent this year.

If teachers are capable and do take their classes and students pay full attention to their studies, they are also prepared to share some reasonable increase in cost. It should be possible even in government institutions.

V.D. Karad

There is no system of fixing responsibility for any failure in our country. Our examination system is a great failure.

Upendra Baxi

The Supreme Court has said only what the educationists have been saying all along. After listening to the views expressed here, I get a feeling that the Right to Education can be enforced only through market-friendly and World Bank sponsored ways.

V.M. Dandekar

The Planning Commission seems to think that we have much more money than what we really have. I do not know where this money comes from. It will be necessary for the government to freeze the salaries and allowances; it will also have to increase the fees. If the grants are reduced on a progressively increasing scale, most of the good institutions which are offering worthwhile education, will turn out to be self-supporting. The others will gradually fade out.

4. LEVY OF FEES

M.V. Pylee

The limitations of the State's economic capacity in providing proper educational facilities have been explicitly noted in Article 41. The determination of priorities among sectors that increase peoples' income on the one hand, and education which increases their earning capacity, on the other, has to be understood in this context. Ironically all these priorities notwithstanding, a larger allocation of our resources for education has gone to higher education, even as measures for removal of illiteracy have not had adequate resources.

If education in a fundamental right, every one has a right to get the type of education he wants. Professional education which enhances the individual's earning capacity is always at a premium. Education confers both direct and indirect benefits. Direct benefits like financial returns get completely localised in the individual; indirect benefits get diffused and the society as a whole benefits. As long as education confers the ability to earn an income during his life time, it should be treated as an income-generating asset built into the individual himself.

Our higher education is heavily subsidised. The fee covers only a tiny fraction of the public cost. Students flock to the universities because of low cost; education, in consequence, has become valueless in society. There is no reason why rich people should be subsidised. Pricing education to recover the full cost can be an effective instrument in regulating admission to higher education. In this scheme of things no one will be denied admission because he/she is poor, if he/she shall merit. It should be possible to convert the present grant-in-aid system into a loan system. If funds are routed through students as repayable loans, students can then pay the full costs. It will make the students sensitive to what is happening in their institutions; it will add to their dignity as they have a responsibility to pay back what they got.

The whole scheme of private colleges in medical education was initiated because government had no funds. Private colleges were allowed with the hope that higher education need not be subsidised and that full costs can be recovered through a self-financing scheme of education.

A tentative estimate shows that the education of a medical graduate might cost Rs. 2½ to 3 lakhs. The recovery in government colleges is no more than 2 to 3 per cent of the total cost. The Karnataka Government, while prohibiting the charging of capitation fees, has prescribed fees at a scale that would recover the full cost. The differential scales have an income-redistribution effect. Under the scheme, 40% of the seats in private medical colleges have become available for admission on the same basis an in government colleges. The private colleges thus subsidise medical education in the government sector. Where do they get the money from? It is not the system which is at fault. It is the framework set for its functioning and implementation which is at fault. Since there is no way of detecting illegal payments at the time of admission, the presumption is that heavy sums change hands, in addition to the higher levels of fees.

Funds for cross-subsidies (for students admitted against government quota) have to come from the income of the colleges. If the full cost for producing a medical graduate is Rs. 3 lakhs and if the college can charge only Rs. 10000 (at government rates), how can it provide the remaining Rs. 2.9 lakhs? The private colleges will refuse to provide such subsidies. Then what follows? 40 per cent seats which were available as government quota will no longer be there.

There is no alternative to a self-financing education system. For such a system to emerge, several measures are necessary. First, right from inception, all medical colleges, whether governnment or private, should provide all the required facilities. Second, every student desirous of taking admission to medical colleges should appear in the entrance examination. Only those who score above a prescribed minimum should be admitted. Subject, of course, to the requirements of the reservation policy. Third, the fees to be charged should be equal to the full cost both in government and private colleges. The poor should be given scholarships and freeships, or repayable loans. A 14% return on investments to the management is not too much to concede.

One last point and that is, there should be full transparency in working out the cost and it should be made known to the public.

Amrik Singh

The source of all trouble is that we do not charge the full cost from the students who are going for professional education. Professional education, in my view, is an area in which we can begin with the implementation of the policy of recovering full cost. I do not think that we need to worry unduly about any serious protests or resistance. Take the case of IIMS. They raised the fees from Rs. 600 to Rs. 6000. There were no protests. My point is that people are prepared to pay. And we must force the issue.

I do not think that we should be talking about any subsidy for professional education. Yes, recovery of full cost will go against the poor people. They should be brought within the loan system. I do not think we can consider education as an instrument in the process of equalisation. On the other hand, what we should be doing is to create conditions to ensure equality of opportunities to all.

We should guard against a possible misuse of the loan schemes. In our country, the capacity to pay is always underestimated. In most states now, the reservation percentages go upto 50. In one form or another, they are recipient of scholarships or subsidies. Therefore, meeting the cost of their education is only a notional adjustment; it does not involve transfer of money in real terms.

My plea, therefore, is : recover the full cost in professional education; provide grants to institutions on the basis of the per student cost as in UK; no person should be allowed to leave the country within three years of his graduation as in France; and bring the professional bodies centre stage in the matter of norm-setting and enforcement.

Madhava Reddy

We are discussing fees in the context of the Supreme Court judgement. The courts do not lay down statutes; nor do they lay down policies. The limited question before the Supreme Court in the Mohini Jain case was equality under Article 14. Why should a student admitted to the same college for the same course pay Rs. 60000 when another student has to pay only Rs. 2000. It was in this context that the 'right to education' concept was considered.

What is fee? It is a charge that a person has agreed to pay in return for a service. What is tuition fee? It is a charge paid to an institution to cover the cost of teaching, libraries, laboratories, etc. Capitation is generally understood as a tax and not as a fee. So what a private college can collect is only fees and not tax. They have no authority or right to levy taxes. They can realise a fee only for the services provided by them.

If a private entrepreneur takes a loan to establish a medical college, how is he going to service the loan? In the context of the judgement, he cannot charge a higher fees than what the government prescribes. There are problems here. Even at the primary level, charging fees higher than what government schools do might violate the equality principle. Whatever mechanism is set up, whatever arrangements are settled, equality under Article 14 has to be ensured.

That raises the question : who will finance higher education and how? Why should the ordinary tax payer meet the cost of higher education when other pressing areas like drinking water, health etc., are crying for funds. I would urge that provision of higher education at cost should be given a chance. At the same time, we should evolve a fee structure that does not discriminate against merit.

Ms. A.S. Desai

The determining criteria for admission to an institution should be the merit of the student and the quality of the institution. We should try out the loan scheme. In my view, education should be considered as a leveller and not something that polarises people and societies. In the loan scheme, we should also remember that students will have to pay a higher fees which they will have to recoup by charging a higher professional fees. The cost of services will then become dearer. A tax on degrees, as I said earlier, could generate resources that can be recycled into the systems.

I.P. Anand

In my view it is not the judgement as such, but the issues raised by it, which are the most significant. For a generation of our people, soon after independence, public schools were not so much in demand. But today it is these schools which are thriving, charging fees as they like. They are in great demand, throughout the country. That is a change.

Those of us who are associated with private institutions know that state policies discourage resource generation. Whatever funds are raised are adjusted against grants. So there is no incentive for resource generation.

I think we have too many regulatory mechanisms. These mechanisms tend to take a fragmented view of growth and development. In higher education, I do not see the need for both UGC and the AICTE. The two could be integrated.

In technical and professional education, for a number of years, there has been no worthwhile expansion. We went on proclaiming that we are producing enough manpower. The emergence of the capitation fee colleges is a logical sequence of this inertia on the part of the State Governments. The Central Government, the UGC and also the AICTE were also a party to this situation.

In our institution, the Thapar Institute in Patiala, we raised the fees about five years ago. We also introduced a loan scheme. It has been working very well. The only caution I would like to add is that fees charged in the year of entry should stay at the same level till the completion of the relevant programme of study; there should be no midway increases.

Finally, I am convinced that higher education requires the cooperation of the corporate sector. Corporate resources are the answer to the problems of development in higher education and professional education. You should allow private initiative, give it a free hand. Let us not discourage private institutions.

G. Ram Reddy

I would like to know what would be the response of the corporate sector to an initiative to come together like this and consider ways for their involvement in education.

I.P. Anand

The corporate sector has always responded positively to such initiatives. In population programmes, rural development, etc., for instance. They have also been involved in human resources development programmes. Most of them are running their own programmes. So they would in my view respond positively to any initiative that you might take.

Anand Sarup

The logic of the Supreme Court judgement is that an institution functioning under the umbrella of state recognition cannot charge a fee higher than what the state-run institutions charge. It applies as much to primary and secondary schools as to higher education institutions. I would like this issue also to be considered.

N.C. Nigam

I would confine my observations to professional education and technical education within that. There is no a *priori* choice that the government system is good and private system is bad. Each has to be scrutinised independently. Having worked in the IITs and in a private institution, I am convinced that it is the private institutions which are more innovative and are willing to experiment.

There is no denying the fact that the right to education is circumscribed by the economic capacity of the State. But who will decide the economic capacity? The State? The Courts? The public? Similarly who will decide the rights? I think the right to education can be determined only on the basis of merit—merit prescribed on the basis of transparent criteria and made known in advance. In the IITs we have tried the aptitude test, but its reliability is still to be established.

We have talked about private initiative. What is the motivation for private initiative? I think it can only be the commitment to the cause of education. It cannot be the profit motive.

How do we decide what kind of institutions can be recognised? I suggest two basic conditions. One, only those institutions which have provided the basic infrastructure, building, equipment, staff. I am referring only to the botomline. This should apply to both private and government institutions. The second and it is mainly for private institutions, the Governing Bodies should consist of men of high public distinction. It should be insisted upon.

Having said this and since we are on the issue of fees, I would like to share some data with you. When the IITs were set up, I am referring to the data given in the IIT Kharagpur report in 1950, the per student per year cost was estimated as Rs. 1800. The corresponding cost in UK then was Rs. 1700 and in the USA Rs. 4000. What is the situation today? In the IITs, the annual per student cost is Rs. 55000. The corresponding costs in the UK and USA are Rs. 240,000 and 400,000 respectively. In the ordinary engineering colleges, the estimated cost today is between Rs. 14000 and 15000. (All these figures are for undergraduate education).

When the IITs were set up, the idea was that 10% of the operation costs should be recovered as fees. So, the fees were prescribed as Rs.200. On this basis, today we should have been charging a fee of Rs.5500. But the fees remained what they were. We are not tying to increase it.

The resources for education can come only in two ways : through fees or endowments. We do not have the concept of endowments for government institutions but for private institutions, endowments are absolutely necessary. It could be a one-time grant, or an endowment built up over a period of time. We tried this experiment at the Thapar Institute. We suggested the induction of corporate members into the Governing Bodies who would make an initial contribution on nomination and then keep paying an annual fee. The Institute offered its services in return, in the form of R & D, consultancy and so on. To introduce these innovations, we ran into enormous difficulties with the AICTE and the Ministry of HRD.

One last point. We should not encourage fee differentials on the basis of States from which the students come. We should institute a 20% reservation of seats in every institution for students from other States with everybody being charged the same fees.

V.M. Dandekar

I would go along with the proposition that we should charge full-cost fee. But I would only say : let us do it gradually, over a period of, say, five to seven years.

The specific issue that I want to address here is about the private non-aided colleges. We have talked about how they would find resources. Till about a couple of years ago, there was a provision in the Income Tax Act that donations to charitable purposes would be exempt from tax. This provision was withdrawn. Why can's we revive it? If we do, I am sure there would be many industrialists who would be prepared to make substantial donations to educational institutions. They might say that a hall, a block, a laboratory should be named after them. What is wrong with it?

Secondly, the government have announced several schemes to attract unaccounted money for specific purposes. No questions were asked about where the money came from. Why can't we do it for education?

Thirdly, I am again talking about private non-aided colleges, what is wrong if they were to make a profit? Yes, a profit, or a surplus, if you like. A profit that would be ploughed back into the institution, for its development. I am not taking about a profit that could be distributed amongst the sponsors or promotors.

Fourthly, the non-government, non-aided institutions should be left free to charge whatever fee they want to charge. I think the Supreme

Court judgement is against charging different fees within the same institution. So, if all the students are charged the same fees and if there is no discrimination in this matter, what fees they should charge should be left to their judgement.

Madhava Reddy

The Court said no discrimination in fees between government colleges, government seats and also seats earmarked for the management in private colleges.

V.M. Dandekar

I do not buy that argument. If you are not giving any aid, you have no right to prescribe all these things. All that recognition means in such cases is that the students can appear in the university examinations. Nothing beyond this is contributed by the recognising authority.

M. Anandakrishnan

I do not know how much heat you feel about the Supreme Court judgement in Delhi. In Madras, in Tamil Nadu and Andhra Pradesh generally, it has generated considerable heat, if one goes by the public response to the judgement.

A number of basic issues arises from the judgement. First, there is a need to increase the intake in higher education, particularly in professional and technical education. There is so much demand for seats in institutions which offer professional education. Second, the State has lost the capacity to fund higher education. It is not just a question of priorities alone. Even if all higher education institutions were closed, we would not be able to provide drinking water to all our villages. So what are the alternatives available? We have been talking about various methods of resource mobilisation through cess, levies, donation, endowments etc. I for one have been canvassing the idea of an Education Development Bank. Like the ones that we have in Agriculture or Housing. As Prof. Dandekar said, we permit even black money to be deposited in these funds. Then why not for education?

We are suggesting recovery of costs from students of professional education. It is very important. But for that we should know what the costs are. We should also know what would be an economic rate of recovery. Prof. Nigam mentioned some figures. Rs. 55000 in IITs and Rs. 15000 in engineering colleges. One can suggest any thing between Rs. 10000 and Rs. 100000 as the annual cost for engineering education.

Now, we need to make this costing more precise and scientific. What is an economic recovery? Here again, there may not be an agreement. So much debate on this question is going on. The World Bank is sponsoring so many seminars and workshops on this question. One can suggest anything between 10 per cent and 90 per cent as economic recovery. We are not going to settle these matters here.

Having said this, let me point out two major points of failure in our system. The first is that our national institutions, including the professional bodies, did not anticipate these developments. They were not able to adjust their policies and programmes according to emerging situations. Secondly, to put it mildly, our experience with the AICTE has been dismal.

Questions are asked as to why we cannot raise resources from industry. If we go to industry seeking support in a genral way, we would not get any response. Why should industry support higher education? It is not their responsibility. If on the other hand, we seek specific programme-based support, I am sure the response will be positive. For instance, the Anna University sought support from industry for a Bio-technology programme. We convened a conference like this. 20 industrialists participated. Each one pledged a support of Rs. 5 lakhs. Within 24 hours, we created a corpus of Rs. 1 crore. So was it in respect of Printing, Mining and Petrochemicals. I am confident that this kind of support will always be available from the corporate sector.

The real issue goes beyond all these matters. The real issue is the nexus between corrupt politicians and the greedy promoters of education. Political parties feel that they have unearthed a major source for funding political campaigns through educational entrepreneurship. The capitation fee colleges have become symbolic of this discovery. Five years back admission to a medical college in Tamil Nadu cost Rs.50,000. Now the cost of admission has risen to Rs. 5 lakhs. It was Rs. 20,000 in an engineering college. It is Rs. 1,50,000 now. When another party comes to power, they will demand more funds. The capitation fee will go up. The real answer lies in our ability to insultate education from political interference.

J.B.G. Tilak

The Supreme Court judgement is about capitation fees. We seem to be shy of talking about capitation fee colleges. What are they? Why are they opened? What is the motive behind their establishment? How do they secure recognition, or affiliation? How do they appoint teachers or admit students? We seem to be avoiding a discussion on any of these issues.

There is a need to rationalise fee structure. Some have argued for recovery of full cost. Some have even suggested making profits, or generating surpluses through these. The argument advanced is that there are afterall people who can pay and why should it matter whether the surpluses are or are no reinvested in education!

The votaries of privatisation are arguing for monetary gains even at the cost of justice and equity in education. It is not a choice between equity and efficiency, it is a choice between equity and monetary gain or profits.

Nowhere in the world, whether in the developed or developing countries, contribution of fees to the cost of higher education in the public sector exceeds 25%. In India, it is about 15-20 per cent. Even in the private institutions in the USA, the share of fees is about 35% of the cost. The fees charged by private universities is about 4 times the fees in public institutions.

According to official statistics, the recurring cost per student in medical colleges in India was Rs. 9000 (in 1983-1984) and Rs. 5000 in engineering colleges. There is no rationale for charging a fee of Rs.50000 or a capitation fee of Rs. 10 lakhs. In our country, the so-called private aided colleges rely on Government for 90% of their recurring expenditure. Are these private colleges in the real sense of the term?

If we have to deal with the problems confronting us certain policy initiatives will be inescapable. First, capitation fees will have to be prohibited, not just by law alone, but by uprooting the evil from the system. Secondly, private enterprises in education, unless they make the capital investment out of genuine philanthropic motives, should not be allowed to open colleges. They could invest elsewhere for making their profits. Thirdly, admission should be strictly on merit, on the basis of a common entrance test and those who quality should be offered admission. There could be a differential system of fees depending upon the paying capacity with provision for free tuition in deserving cases. Finally, as in some other countries, a distinction can be made between home students and foreign students, the latter being charged the full cost.

There is an euphoria of market equilibrium in India because of which everybody is getting to believe that demand and supply will balance in the long run. It is too optimistic to expect the market mechanism to ensure efficiency within the existing structures. What will happen if we produce too many engineering and medical graduates? The experience of the late 1960s with engineering graduates should not be forgotten.

S. Venkateswaran

I fully endorse the points made by Dr. Mitra and Mr. Anand. But I would like to add a little data, even at the risk of repetition. We have heard widely different statements about costs and recoveries and it has been asserted that nowhere in the world is the recovery more than 35% or so. We at BITS, Pilani charge Rs. 8000 as the annual fee. Our income from fees, or recovery of costs, is 65-70 per cent of the recurring expenditure. The lowest percentage of marks obtained by students admitted this year was 95% in the case of engineering programmes and for economics and biology 94%. We had seven rank holders from various State Boards. Our fee is the same for all programmes, undergraduate, postgraduate and Ph.D., and also for all subjects, economics, engineering or biology. The point I wish to emphasise is that a higher fee is not a deterrent. I do not think there would be any problem if we can offer good quality education at affordable fees and if you do not compromise on merit.

D.Y. Patil

I fully support the views expressed by Dr. Venkateswaran.

M.M. Ansari

We have discussed at length the sociological perspective of education in the context of equality, justice etc. We need also to look at the economic perspective, especially when we are discussing costs and recoveries. I wish to make a point or two about costs.

What we should recover from the students, or the beneficiaries, should be the economic costs. These costs vary across institutions, across programmes. If we look at the components, there is one major element—the salaries. Though the pay scales, thanks to the UGC, are uniform, the staff structure is not. There are universities in which the number of Professors is more than the number of Readers and Lecturers put together! Then, if we look at the pay structure of the non-teaching employees, there are variations across States, since their pay is linked to the pay scales in the State Governments. The question, therefore, arises as to which scale of costs are we going to apply : those in the central universities or in the state universities? or costs per subject?

On the other hand, if we go by the normative costs, the difference between the norms and the actuals is so wide that the picture derived from the unit costs will become totally distorted.

There are other problems associated with determination of incomes. Examination fees are a major source of income for most universities. Do we take these as tuition fees? Many universities generate considerable resources through distance education programmes unrelated directly or indirectly to their regular programmes.

The graduate profile is also important in discussing the economic issues of education. For instance, what is the graduation ratio? How are the graduates accepted in the market?

Therefore, when we are considering economic fees, my suggestion is that we need to also develop methodologies for determining costs, analysing them and establishing reliable norms.

Kishore Gandhi

From the discussions so far, one gets a feeling that there is a conflict of interest between government institutions and private institutions. This conflict extends to the conceptual levels in the perception of education as a fundamental right or as a profit yielding activity.

Private educational institutions need not be looked upon as aberrations. In the context of the process of economic reforms liberalisation and deregulation, I see no reason why we cannot ask the industrialists to step in and make investments in education. We have heard how successfully cost-effective changes were made at the BITS and the Thapar Institute. These may still be the exceptions, but these models appear to be replicable.

Resource generation requires people with the necessary dynamism. Most of our Vice-Chancellors are men of letters, scholars and intellectuals. They are not successful fund-raisers. So, we should develop some method by which people who can raise funds come to be associated with the universities.

B.E. Avhad

The Supreme Court, in the earlier part of its judgement, has defined capitation fee as the premium paid for admission. Later on, it has also held that any fees charged in excess of what the government has prescribed as tuition fees in its colleges, will also be deemed to be capitation fees. As far as tuition fees are concerned, there does not appear to be much of a problem. There is a cost involved in teaching. What you realise to meet that cost, in full or partially, can be called tuition fee. There would be no difficulty about it.

Another interesting point emerging from the judgement is that today capitation fee colleges in Maharashtra charge Rs. 12000. If tomorrow, the State Government decides to recover the full cost and raises the fees to Rs. 12000, it will cease to be capitation fees. So, if the differential in fee is governed by any philosophical considerations, it is acceptable. My plea, therefore, is that judicial activism should not be allowed to encroach upon the regions of philosophy or legislation.

If it is left to the courts to define education, all education at all levels, whether for private gain or for public good, will come within the ambit of fundamental rights. That should not happen. The priorities within education must have relevance in determining what constitutes the right to education.

When this matter came up before the Court a couple of days ago, new issues were raised. For instance, it was argued that the judgement has denied a person his fundamental right to gain admission by paying a capitation fee. Another institution argued that the judgement is a denial for the right to freedom of association guaranteed by Article 19.

While structuring the fees, we have to ensure that the priorities within education are kept in view. For example, primary, secondary, undergraduate, postgraduate, specialisation, super specialisation and so on cannot be treated at par. The fees should be on a graded scale, based on what constitutes public good and what would help in the accrual of private gains.

V.D. Karad

Dr. Tilak read out some figures to show per capita expenditure on education. He said the annual expenditure on medical education was Rs. 9000. I have the figures released by the Government of Maharashtra. These figures are very authentic. They state the annual per capita recurring cost of medical education in the state. For one medical college, it was Rs. 46000 in 1990-91; Rs. 66000 in 1991-92 and estimated as Rs. 88000 in 1992-93. There are figures for other colleges with minor variations. But the reality is that we incur a huge expenditure and not just Rs. 9000 as Dr. Tilak has stated. The capital cost involved in setting up a medical college is Rs. 12 to 15 crores. This is the kind of resources that the unaided colleges have to raise.

I agree that fees should be cost-based. Students would be prepared to pay a high fees if they are assured that they will receive good education. We attract good students at the Maharashtra Institute of

Technology, even though it is unaided. Our students have been performing well.

My suggestion for the private unaided medical colleges is that 10-15% seats should be reserved for the economically backward classes, 20% for the management and upto 70% for the government. It will be from this 20% quota that the management will raise all the resources required to run the college.

Ms. A.S. Desai

I would like to emphasise only one point. When the fees are raised and the loan system is introduced, womens' education will suffer. In most middle-class families, the benefit of the loan will go to the boys only. As far as the girls are concerned, the attitude will be that she will get married and go away, so, how are we going to repay the loan? We have to keep this aspect in mind.

5. MATTERS OF POLICY

D. Swaminadhan

Right to education has to be understood in terms of access to education. It has not been interpreted in terms of provision of free education. If we read all the pronouncements made in the judgement together, we will notice that there is no time frame indicated for providing education to all citizens, or at all levels. It would follow that the State can provide the facilities at its own pace and according to its capacity. The constitutional mandate for providing free education upto 14 years of age is obvious. When it comes to higher levels of education, at what cost are we going to provide it?

The judgement is not against any general enhancement of fees. It prohibits only capitation fee. One major implication of the judgement for the policy on higher education is that we need to provide facilities for those who seek higher education. They can, of course, be asked to bear a major part of the burden through increased fees. Perhaps, even at unit cost

But there is another major implication. The judgement says admission should be on merit. Assuming that merit is determined by an entrance test, it would follow that all those who have qualified in the entrance test should be deemed to have acquired a right to admission. In reality, the seats available are always far below the number of eligible candidates. In the light of the judgement of the Supreme Court, will the State be obliged now to set up more colleges to accommodate all the candidates who have requisite merit?

I had occasion to say earlier that merit involves some kind of selection and, therefore, I have a feeling that 'education as a universal right' and 'admission on merit' are concepts that are not mutually compatible. We need to think about it seriously.

The Eighth Plan which has just been finalised sets out the policy perspectives. Universalisation of elementary education and removal of illiteracy are the highest priority. In higher education, the emphasis is on access and cost-effectiveness. Open universities and distance education programmes are to be expanded to meet this objective. The plan also envisages levy of a user charge for higher education from the concerned sectors as is done in the case of electricity, transport, irrigation, etc.

The policy also envisages mobilisation of resources through private initiative and greater involvement of voluntary organisations with appropriate 'checks and quality'. It suggests that fees should be raised, but they should not be exhorbitant. It calls for schemes of scholarships and subsidies for the benefit of Scheduled Castes and Tribes and other deserving categories.

In Technical and Management education, the plan notes that there is an urgent need to raise fees. The IIMS has raised the fees and so will the IITs. It says that increase in fees should be accompanied by adequate provisions for the weaker sections.

Overall, the policy framework favours a higher recovery of costs from the beneficiaries; greater efforts to mobilise resources from non-traditional sources; involvement of private initiative in expanding higher and technical education, which, however, should not degenerate into commercialisation; and substantial provision for subsidising the education of weaker sections.

Amrik Singh

We should address this issue of increasing demand for professional education. My own views may be heretical. But, during the last quarter of a century or so, we are witness to a significant rise and consolidation of the middle class in the country. Their aspirations and attitudes are very important. Otherwise how is it that in both engineering and medicine, when the country has a surplus of manpower, the demand for education continues to rise. And people are prepared to pay any price for it. This demand has nothing to do with the manpower requirements in the employment sectors.

Some 15 per cent of our medical manpower is migrating to the developed world. Now, should we be training this manpower for the benefit of other countries?

We claim that we are making efforts to regulate the supply of trained manpower according to the employment needs. But what is the reality? During the plan discussions, expansion of health-care services is considered. It is discovered that there is considerable shortage of nurses. A decision, is therefore, taken to set up 12 more nursing colleges. In the end, however, 12 more medical colleges come up instead. How do we expand the health-care services without para-medical personnel? The analogy applies to engineering as well. Everyone wants to be an engineer. No one wants to be a technician. This attitude has brought about a distortion not only in our education system but also in our functional efficiency. This is the background against which the increasing demand for professional education has to be appreciated. It is not the genuine market forces that are at play. It is the rising expectations of the middle class, which are unreal and of course, corruption which seeks to exploit these expectations.

Coming to another issue. It is alright that the UGC and the AIU have come together to organise this colloquium. But may I ask why the AIU and the UGC cannot intervene in the writ petition which is now before the Supreme Court? As the University of Delhi did, for example. There have been occasions in the past when the AIU had taken such initiatives. For instance, AIU did intervene when matters went to court on the *enbloc* promotion of students even though they had not appeared in the examinations either due to political agitations or due to the war with Pakistan, or something else. On such occasions, AIU had taken the position in the court that it was for the University to consider and decide as to who should be promoted to the higher classes and how. The State Government has no *locus standi* in this matter. I think now there is a need to take a similar initiative. The UGC and the AIU should both consider this matter and intervene in the writ petition.

What has emerged from these discussions in the last two days? That private enterprise has a role; you cannot shut it out, legally, constitutionally or otherwise. That the State cannot provide all the facilities for higher education to all the people is another view. A third is that some part of the costs of education should be recovered and that some kind of regulation is necessary for the private initiative to play its part. I would only like to add that let this regulatory mechanism be not of the traditional bureaucratic type. That would give room for the politicians to intervene and there can be no means to cleanse the system of corruption. That is why I continue to hold the view that the professional bodies should be allowed to play their part. These bodies should be of professionals and academics, not politicians. Some views were expressed about the experience of AICTE. Now, let me point out that the Act provides that the Minister incharge would be its first President. But the first President only. We have had five ministers since the Act was passed. All of them were Presidents of AICTE. Why did this occur? Was it legal?

V.M. Dandekar

I think Amrik Singh was putting it too mildly when he said that the reason for excess demand for professional education was the rising expectations of the middle class. The reality is something else. I shall be blunt. We, the educated class, are paying ourselves too much. Payments that the society cannot afford. We sit on Pay Commissions, expert committees and so on. That is one reason why this excess demand for education; it increases your earning capacity.

My second point is about migration. For the last twenty years, I have been talking about it. We should not worry too much about it. I would put only one condition. People who migrate must make remittances; not loans and deposits, but regular remittances.

We all lament corruption. What is the remedy? If we must learn any lesson from the experience of the former Communist countries, it is that regulation breeds corruption. If there is corruption in education, it is only because we have made too many regulations.

One last point. I am repeating it. No improvement is possible unless we make teachers accountable directly to the students.

V.C. Kulandaiswamy

The judgement, in my view, has created more problems than it has solved; it has created more confusion than clarity in the area of education. We all agree that the Government has a responsibility to provide for education. But creation of facilities for education is not the sole right of the Government, to the exclustion of every one else.

Till today, nobody ever questioned the high level of fees charged by schools. But when Government stipulates that fees should be regulated according to the rate prescribed, the issue of higher fees will be taken to the Court. We all know that many people, including those from low-income categories, borrow money and enter into a debt to educate their children in these schools in the hope of getting them admission to engineering or medical colleges. This raises a major policy issue.

When it comes to higher education, I would like to point out the total bankruptcy of the Government in the matter of manpower planning.

In the late 1970s, the AICTE said that the country is already producing enough engineering manpower and that no more engineering colleges or polytechnics need be established. Even the State Government (of Tamil Nadu) was denied permission to set up one or two engineering colleges or polytechnics in the backward areas.

During 1985 to 1987, the Tamil Nadu Government sanctioned 30 more engineering colleges and over 100 polytechnics under what is known as self-financing system. I had then thought that these institutions would be closed down in two years because no students would go to them. After seven years, the capitation fee has gone up instead.

The engineering colleges in the country are finding it very difficult to get teachers. There is a scarcity of appropriate manpower for this. But the Government wouldn't admit that.

In Tamil Nadu, these self-financing institutions have invested about Rs. 500 crores. This has come entirely from the private sector. If it had not materialised there would have been no expansion of engineering education in the State. Not only engineering colleges, there are Arts and Science colleges, Dental and Medical Colleges and Law colleges under the self-financing system. Almost a parallel system. They are attracting large numbers of students.

As far back as in 1960, the Mudaliar Committee recommended that we should have three nurses per doctor. Even 32 years later, our annual output is 8000 nurses for 18000 doctors. Who is going to establish the nursing colleges to make up this deficiency?

Now, a word about merit. There are meritorious students who are not able to join government colleges and avail of subsidised education. If only the students with 90% or more marks can go to government colleges, where do those with 85-90% go? They too have merit. Why prevent them from getting medical education for which they are prepared to pay? Why should we insist that they should go only for subsidised education?

The judgement and the issues raised by it call for a close look at the higher education policy. We need to evolve a new policy which would encourage private initiative. What we should discourage is only commercialisation of education and diversion of resources raised for education to other purposes.

Anand Sarup

The judgement does not say anywhere that ther should be no expansion. I would, therefore, agree that let expansion go on until the laws of demand and supply force the issue. We have all made the point that there should be some regulation, of this kind or that. If there has to be regulation, who will perform the task? Can we think of a mechanism that will substitute the role of Government? If someone other than Government assumes the responsibility, wherefrom would it derive the authority to regulate? So sooner or later, we come back to the issue of political intervention and corruption.

There is one more issue which concerns the all important sectors of school education. About elementary education, some one mentioned that all over the country, not merely in cities, but in rural areas also, there is an unprecedented demand for public school type education or English medium schools. People are prepared to pay for it. They do not want to study the local languages, the local culture. I am myself associated with a school the students of which are not likely to go beyond Matriculation, or the Higher Secondary stage perhaps. But the parents demand that they should be taught in English. Why? So that they can claim that they are products of English medium schools! At times it leads one to wonder whether there are two Indias. What has happened to the issue of equity? Can we claim that our school system promotes an equitable society and thus helps to achieve the egalitarian goals of our Constitution.

One word about the demand for manpower. A recent study has shown that among engineers and doctors, there is gross under-employment. Engineers are doing the work of technicians. This is a very important matter since it represents a very large volume of inessential expenditure?

V.M. Dandekar

Let us not be so romantic about egalitarianism. If there are private schools which claim they are offering better education and if in the perception of the students and their parents there is indeed a difference, I think they are paying for that difference in the type of education provided. On that issue, I am not with you. I do not think it is bad.

Secondly, about English medium schools. Why are they so popular? In all our selections; interviews, wherever they are, there is a premium for English. It is only natural, therefore, that people, as a matter of deliberate choice, seek English medium schools.

N.C. Nigam

I do not agree with the view that whoever has merit has also a right to education. The view taken was that if 6000 students have qaulified in an entrance test and if there are only 1000 seats, the remaining 5000 should also get admission, since they have acquired the right to admission on merit. It is not so. The right to education is circumscribed by the limits of economic capacity; limits set by the Government and the legislature in the case of public institutions and the society and some 'benefactors' in the case of private institutions.

Dr. Amrik Singh raised the question of surplus manpower and the migration of engineers and doctors. The fact is that these countries need manpower. And where there is a need, people will move in. Let us not be critical about it. There is a certain degree of globalisation taking place in economic activities. This migration is also a consequence of that globalisation.

I think we seem to be too optimistic about the market mechanism. We are saying all the time that all will be well when once the market forces take over. I am sorry that I am not able to share that optimism. In our country, the market mechanism is still not strong. It is not the market but patronage that regulates our activities. Some kind of a market regulation has started emerging only in the last one year or so. Let us not depend too much on that now. I would go to the extent of saying that there is a lot of public deception in the way colleges are opened and students are admitted.

M.V. Pylee

One comment on market forces. In Kerala, there are over 600 schools which have no students. There are only teachers. The State Governnment has decided to close them down. This is how market forces come into operation.

N.C. Nigam

The UP government enacted a law declaring malpractices in examination as cognisable offences. The pass percentage fell to 19. That is how the system of regulation works.

M. Anandakrishnan

There is no disagreement on the role of private sector. What we are debating is whether or not the current model of private participation is satisfactory. If it is not, what alternate model of participation can we develop? We have to address this issue.

On the question of merit, let me give some examples. In Tamil Nadu, 35000 students appeared in the entrance test for admission to engineering colleges. 20% qualified with 90% or more marks. There are only 1000 seats. Similarly, some 13500 students qualified in the medical entrance test. There are only 950 seats. If all these students have to be admitted, are we going to open so many more colleges?

If we want to rely too much on market forces, let me warn you by giving one example. In May this year a person was offered admission in an engineering college for Rs. 80000. He did not take it. Two months later, he approached the college. He was asked to pay Rs. 1,50,000. See how the market forces had come into play!

In the capitation fee colleges, only 5% of the students are women. What does it suggest? No one is prepared to borrow money for the eudcation of girls. They will get married. Who will repay?

It is all very well to say that fees collected for education should not be diverted for any other purpose, but are there any accounts of what was collected? The managaements who collect capitation fee do not give any receipts. Who will know what money was collected? The whole system should be transparent but it is difficult to imagine how this can be achieved.

If you pay Rs. 10 lakhs to buy admission, what kind of professional ethics can you expect from the person when he begins to earn?

C.R. Mitra

My position is that we are in a critical situation. There is no way except to look for alternatives. A paradigm shift is necessary. A lot was talked about middle class aspirations. The fact is that the middle class is successful. That is our dilemma.

In our country we have witnessed the development of curricular differentials, starting with IITs. Several years ago, undergraduate programmes were launched in Computer Science. Much later, more or less the same programme was repackaged into Master's degree programmes. The contents did not change much. But the packaging did. At the same time, we have also seen some institutions, both within the established system and outside (they are not getting grants) develop programmes in collaboration with the industry and successfully launching them. This is what I call the new entrepreneurship in education. Not selling seats and collecting money. But developing a curricular structure that carries the aspirations of the students with the needs of the work place. That should be the movement for the future. Let us look at our policy initiatives from this perspective.

We have a weakness for regulations. We love them when we regulate. We have them when we are regulated. My point is that there is tremendous scope for private initiative but it will blossom only if the initiative is allowed to blossom in the best interests of society within, if you like, a set of well-designed and transparent system of management. To my mind that would require that we develop a comprehensive system ot accreditation whereby all programmes, whether of government or the private sector, are subjected to a rigorous evaluation by professional groups. There can be no half-way house here.

Let me respond to a point made about market froces and patronage. Why patronage? Because our desire is to regulate and not to open up. We do not trust anybody; instead we insist on how the rest of the world should behave. Therefore, we regulate. When we regulate, we tend to patronise. We overlook weaknesses and shortcomings. We do not use sound objective professional criteria in making our judgements. So, the system of patronage arises. And that definitely gives room for all kinds of malpractices and corruption.

S.K. Agrawala

I wish to react to the suggestion that AIU should intervene in the writ petition. Judging by the reactions to the verdict from those assembled here, there does not appear to be any consensus on most of the issues. Unless a consensus emerges and a consistent approach develops, the AIU, its President or the Standing Committee cannot take a definite position and intervene in the petition. I hope after this colloquium, we would be able to discuss the matter within the AIU and develop a consistent approach to the problem. That would take some time.

It was pointed out that the judgement does not provide a time frame. I do not agree with that view. The judgement is effective prospetively, from the day it was delivered.

Another point with which I find myself unable to agree is the question of merit. When somebody is adjudged meritorious by whatever criteria you may evolve, his right to education would become enforceble. If there are no institutions, he can demand that institutions be set up. I do not think that economic capacity of the State can come in the way of enforcing his right. That the judgement has not taken this into account is another matter. That is a criticism of the judgement.

S.K. Khanna

What we have been saying in the last two days clearly establishes that the existing system of higher education in its present form cannot grow any further. The future growth of the system will necessarily be in the private sector and not in the area that is now supported by the Central and the State Governments.

From this premise, may I venture to make a policy hypothesis? The enrolment in the Central and State government institutions should be frozen at the present levels. All resources now available with these institutions should be used for improving the quality of the education provided by them. We know that the enrolment is growing at an annual rate of 5%; there is no way to contain this. It is time, therefore, that we took bold and imaginative steps to encourage private participation in higher education to absorb the additional enrolment in the years to come.

The private sector has to be approached with sensitivity; not through bureaucratic regulatory models. Let us consider whether we can through legislative processes develop clear guidelines for private agencies to establish universities with adequate resources and endowments. If we make it possible for private universities to be established, there could be a healthy competition for the good of the system. The existing pattern of growth of private institutions in a few States will then give way to a new national pattern, which might provide high quality of education and possibly low capitation. In my view, it would enable good institutions to survive.

I suggest that the statutory bodies should provide the framework for a new approach like this.

Upendra Baxi

When learned and responsible people become self-opinionated, it is adviseable that they remain learned and responsible. There has been a lot of loose thinking and loose talking here. When we say regulations are bad, no body comes forward with the suggestion that all regulatory bodies including the UGC, should be wound up. No body mentions the amendment to the UGC Act brought forward in December last to confer more regulatory powers on the UGC. Only a handful of us opposed it. What happened to the philosophy of globalisation then? It seems to me that we reflect a pathology of ambivalence and indecision on every single issue. We must stop revelling and luxuriating in this kind of moral opportunism when I make this kind of comment, I include myself among the guilty.

Economists and lawyers have developed comprehensive theories on costs of regulation. There is a body of knowledge on cost-benefit analysis. There is also a highly developed body of knowledge on models of privatisation. I have not seen any body bringing up such models for discussion around this table. True, we heard tentative, incidental, ambivalent views on privatisation from distinguished individuals here. To me these appeared to be their personal views. I have not heard any one explaining what globalisation means and from where the concept has originated.

We are talking about changes. We do not seem to be articulating what these are, logically and consistently. These are all matters of great relevance and significance. If a distinguished experienced and articulate group like this cannot articulate a vision of these changes, how are we going to initiate a national dialogue? So let us take a non-wobbly, consistent and logical position. Let us say : abolish UGC, ACTE and all other regulatory bodies; reject the report of the Gnanam Committee; and also that globalisation means privatisation which means placing education in the hands of private enterprise for making profits. Let the contradictory views also be cogently and succinctly expressed. Let us then place both the views before the public. Then only we can have a meaningful dialogue and eventually a mandate for action. My plea on the issues under discussion to everyone who is anybody in education is : let us stand up and be counted.

C.R. Mitra

We have done our homework and presented our views as logically and precisely, as we can. I do not know whether we can let some one question our honesty and integrity.

V.C. Kulandaiswamy

I would like to make four brief points. First, the Supreme Court judgement has made it possible and necessary for us to consider in what manner and in what form, the private sector can play a role in primary, secondary and higher education. They have been playing some role in a particular manner. What new direction it should take, what policy initiatives and changes are necessary for the purpose, is a major issue.

Secondly, Dr. Nigam referred to the sluggishness of the market forces. I agree, the market reaction is known only when the product has come out. As far as education is concerned it is already too late. At the same time, there are no reliable yardsticks to assess manpower needs.

Having accepted that private sector has a role, we may say two things : one, there should be a strong conditionality of acceptable quality and two, there should be a reasonable quantity and some economic discipline. While we agree that there should be no excessive regulation, we do not agree that there is no need for any regulation whatsoever. What is needed is that the composition of the regulatory bodies should be reviewed and made broad-based enough to inspire confidence and credibility. Normally they are autonomous; but essentially they are governmental in their behavioural characteristics.

Thirdly, about the brain drain. Many people go abroad, as students or as employees of various organisations or as international civil servants, etc. There are no data available about the remittances they make. Unless such data are available for study and has been analysed, we cannot conclude that their migration serves any national interest.

Finally, some surplus in production is a pre-requisite for quality. When demand and supply are equal, the market mechanism will tend to compromise with the quality of the product.

Amrik Singh

As a quick response to what Prof. Kulandaiswamy has said let me state that initially, education including universities, were in the list of State subjects. As Dr. Karad said, it is the State Governments which decide and implement policies on education. The Centre, however, has the responsibility for coordination and determination of standards in higher and technical education. It is in pursuance of this role assigned to the Centre that a large number of professional bodies were set up. The UGC is the oldest among these. There are other bodies too, in architecture, engineering, medicine, law and so on.

The sad thing is that the very body politic which created those bodies has made them redundant. The regulatory functions assigned to those bodies have been taken over for manipulation by the political bosses. Somewhere along the line, they have lost their credibility. Our only salvation is the recovery of the public confidence in these professional bodies. If private enterprise has to perform its functions properly and in the public interest, professionalization in the realm of regulation will also become necessary. Besides even as the educational institutions function within the discipline of regulations, there should be a totally independent system of accreditation as well for regular and periodic evaluation of these institutions.

THE AGENDA FOR ACTION

I. Right to Education—Towards A Better Understanding

In the context of education as an enforceable fundamental right, it is necessary to understand and appreciate its consequences at the conceptual and practical levels. The issues and problem on which greater clarity is required are :

(i) *The levels of education* : Education can be divided broadly into : (a) the kind of training which provides basic knowledge, the skills to apply that knowledge and the capacity to learn on one's own and (b) the kind which differentiates people in a fundamental way and enhances their earning capacity. In other words, at one level education enriches the quality of life generally among all people and at another level, it enriches the individual from the professional vocational point of view. What is the level of education up to which individuals should have a right to equal treatment, because it enables them to lead a life with dignity?

(ii) *State's responsibility* : Is it reasonable to expect the State to bear the entire responsibility for providing education at all levels when it has not been able to provide even the minimum amenities of life to large sections of our population or would it be more reasonable to carve out an area in education which would constitute the unreducible minimum of the State's responsibility and leave the rest to be provided for jointly by the State and various sections of the community? Does the provision of free and compulsory education in Article 45 upto the age of 14 years help in the articulation of this division of responsibility? Even if no distinction is made between different levels of education, would not the 'limits of its economic capacity referred to in Article 41 of the Constitution circumscribe the enforcement of the fundamental right to education.

(iii) *Merit* vs *right* : How is merit going to be determined for the purpose of admission to educational institutions? Will not the concept of merit come in conflict with the right to equal treatment? There has, therefore, to be some areas in education in which the right to equal treatment is assured and others in which merit alone determines the operation of the right to education?

(iv) *State's obligation towards meritorious students* : There can be situations in which a number of students, who have merit, determined on whatever criteria have been prescribed, are not able to get placements in the courses of their choice. Do they have a right to demand enhancement of the facilities for accommodating them? How will the citizens' right be enforced if the economic capacity of the State does not permit the provision of more facilities?

(v) *Right and Access* : What does the right to education imply? Should it be confined only to access to educational institutions imparting formal classroom instruction? Could the State not discharge its obligations by securing access to any one of the organised systems of learnings? In this context, Open Education, Distance Teaching, Non Formal Education, etc., can provide the required access

II. New Perspectives for Policy

A major consequence of the judgement would be to delineate an area in education (free and compulsory education till the age of 14 years for example) in which, within a range the right to equal treatment in the matter of quality and fees is guaranteed. Conversely, there will be another area in which the right to access would, on the one hand, be qualified by consideration of merit of the individual beneficiary and on the other, by the economic capacity of the State to provide the requisite facilities. Several policy options suggest themselves in- this context. These will have to be examined in depth and new initiatives will have to be worked out and articulated. Some of the alternatives are :

(i) *Recovery of full-cost* : Higher education, especially technical and professional education must pay for itself. There is an increasing demand for education at this level as it enhances the earning capacity of the beneficiaries. Private gain from this kind of education is more pronounced than public good. The beneficiaries should, therefore, bear the full cost worked out on critical evaluation of the relevant qualitatively acceptable and cost-effective institutions.

(ii) *State subsidy* : Higher, technical and professional education need not be subsidised by the State for every body. Graded subsidy should be available only to specially deserving students and others from the weaker sections and the economically backward groups. In developing new policy initiatives, questions of equality of opportunity should receive due consideration.

(iii) *Reforms in the system* : Significant changes have to be made in the existing system. Some of the changes urgently required are :

(a) curricular revision and reorientation to link education with the present and foreseable needs of the work place;
(b) structural changes in the programmes of study permitting greater autonomy to the learners in selecting and combining courses and determining the duration, etc;
(c) greater flexibility and openness in the management of institutions and programmes;
(d) modification of the examination system;
(e) development of systems of accreditation of programmes and institutions by peer groups and professional bodies interalia, to encourage better utilization of infrastructure through networking; and
(f) definition of the professional responsibilities and standards of conduct of teachers and their enforcement preferably through self-regulating mechanisms.

(iv) *Manpower planning* : So far our attempts at manpower planning have been neither successful nor effective. What alternative methods if any, should be developed to determine the extent of facilities to be created to meet emerging needs in the newly emerging areas of specialization. It cannot be left entirely to the market equilibrium of demand and supply.

(v) *Establishment of new universities* : If public funds to finance higher education continue to shrink it will become necessary to take a second look at the policy that universities must be established only by the State? Can we not open up the area of university education to non-governmental agencies? Can non-governmental agencies not be encouraged and allowed to create endowments and Trusts to establish and manage Autonomous Universities with a lot of elbow rooms for innovation in respect of curricula, teaching-learning methodologies and functional linkages with different types of industries and infrastructural activities. Perhaps the articulation of this idea of possibly establishing new self-supporting universities functioning without the props of government recognition could lead to a more dynamic alternative to the present system.

(vi) *Education and industry* : Can certain areas of education and training be opened up to private enterprise to be run as specific purpose ancillaries. If these enterprises can design and develop curricula which, because of their relevance, may respond more specifically to the needs of the employment market. It could be left to them either to function within the overall discipline of a system of professional accreditation or establish their credibility on the market place on the strength of their own performance.

III. Resources for Education : Alternatives to State funding

At present the State is the main provider of education. The contributions from all non-governmental sources, including the fees charged from students, do not account for more than 15-20 per cent of the total expenditure on education.

Although the participation ratio in higher education is still only about 6% of the relevant age group and the current rate of growth of enrolment is only about 5% per year, the Eighth Five Year Plan does not envisage any major increase in enrolment in the institutions imparting formal education. On the other hand, this plan calls for a significant expansion of the Distance Education System because of the assumptions about its cost-effectiveness. It also talks about higher rates of recovery from students and greater participation of non-governmental organisations in the provision of education.

It is necessary to develop consistent, logical and practical approaches to resource mobilisation for higher, technical and professional education. Some options are :

(i) *Increase in Fees* : The rate of recovery from students at present does not account even for about 5 per cent of the operational expenditure of most institutions. It is necessary that the rate of recovery is stepped up progressively to a more economic level. The rate of economic recovery has to be worked out carefully. The idea and the many corollaries of Technical and Professional Institutions becoming self-supporting in course of time will also have to be considered.

(ii) *Cost Analysis* : Attempts have to be made to develop and introduce systems of costing in education to improve cost-consciousness. This is necessary also from the point of view of informing the public about the costs involved in various types of education and asking them to share such costs fully or partially.

(iii) *Institution-Industry Relationship* : Mutually beneficial linkages between educational institutions and the user agencies of manpower have been talked about for a long time. No concrete steps have, however, been talked so far to develop such a relationship either for resource mobilisation or for advance planning for trained manpower. In order to quicken the process of inter-action, universities and individual institutions should be given some of the resources only if they raise matching resources from the private sector. As a matter of policy, the resources so generated should not be adjusted against grants; on the other hand, institutions should be asked to create endowments from such resources, wherever possible.

(iv) *Educational Development Bank* : A detailed working paper should be prepared either by the UGC or by the AIU for detailed discussions on the possibililty of establishing an Educational Development Bank on the lines of the National Housing Bank. The Project should be so formed that it may attract unaccounted money also.

(v) *Corporate Finances* : The involvement of the corporate sector, through donations or endowments, or by creation of constituencies for membership on governing bodies, etc., might be explored.

THE PRIVATE SECTOR—A NEW ROLE

It is necessary to define the role that the private sector can play in the development and funding of education. The entry of the private sector need not take the shape only of commercial propositions for profiteering through the patronage of Government. Private resources can and should be mobilised as investment propositions, even for establishment of new universities, by creating endowments and setting up Trusts to manage them. The whole concept will have to worked out in some detail (also suggested elsewhere). The possible models are :

(i) *As in the School Sector* : There is a significant private sector in school education. It has been functioning for several years. Most of them have, however, been charging increasingly higher fees (much higher than university fees) for secondary education while education at this level is free in most government-run schools. Inspite of this, the demand for admission to such schools is continuously rising. Does the fee structure in these schools conform to the principles laid down in this regard in the Supreme Court judgement under review. Can a similar pattern at the higher education level be conceived?

(ii) *A new model* : Can private (non-governmental) organisations come forward to support education on a completely self-sustaining basis? They may provide good education and transfer the entire cost to the students. If all students admitted to such institutions exclusively on merit are charged the same fees, determined and announced in advance and if there is no discrimination in this matter, they would assume a new role by replacing the present practice of a minority of undeserving students buying admission merely on the basis of their economic power. It will also substantially eliminate the corrupt practices associated with the selling of seats.

DEREGULATING EDUCATION

Dependence of the education system almost entirely on state funding has very naturally encouraged the State to subject the education system to increasingly greater controls and regulations. The whole situation which is no longer sustainable requires review and radical reorganization. The issues to be addressed in this context are :

(i) To what extent is regulation unavoidable? What really would happen if the system is dregulated substantially? Would deregulation not encourage the representatives of various professions to come together and set out the norms for their profession and for the survial of the system ensure that they are observed in letter and spirit?

(ii) Can the existing external mechanisms for regulation not be replaced by internal mechanisms within each professional area, with greater transparency in their functioning?

(iii) Would not the emergence of professional bodies and organisations on these lines pave the way for objective accreditation of institutions and programmes without any external interference?

In short, can the whole culture of control be replaced by a system combining self-imposed discipline and automatic forfeiture of entitlement to financial and other forms of support?

APPENDICES

Text of Supreme Court Judgement in Mohini Jain vs State of Karnataka and others*

---

* Please see Appendix-3.

LIST OF PARTICIPANTS

1. Dr. D.Y. Patil
   President
   D. Y. Patil Education Society
   Flat No. 104, 10th floor, Madhuli
   Opp. Nehru Planetarium
   Dr. Annie Besant Road, Worli
   Bombay 400018
2. Prof. V.M. Dandekar
   Director
   Indian School of Political Economy
   Senapati Bapat Marg, Pune
3. Prof. M.V. Pylee
   Director General
   Asian Institute of Development & Entrepreneurship
   Cochin University Junction
   Cochin 682022
4. Prof. Upendra Baxi
   Vice-Chancellor
   University of Delhi
   Delhi 110007
5. Dr. M. Anandakrishnan
   Vice-Chancellor
   Anna University
   Madras 600025
6. Dr. C.R. Mitra
   I-1751 Chitranjan Park
   New Delhi 110013
7. Prof. V.C. Kulandaiswamy
   Vice-Chancellor
   IGNOU
   New Delhi 110068
8. Dr. D. Swaminadhan
   Member
   Planning Commission
   Yojana Bhawan
   New Delhi 110001
9. Dr. N.C. Nigam
   Director
   HT, Hauz Khas
   New Delhi 110016
10. Shri I.P. Anand
    Shivathene Centre
    16, Nizammuddin East
    New Delhi 110013
11. Mr. Justice Madhava Reddy
    B-202, Sector 14
    NOIDA, Ghaziabad, U.P.
12. Prof. Ashoka Chandra
    Director
    Institute of Applied Manpower Research
    I.P. Estate
    New Delhi
13. Prof. V.D. Karad
    Director
    Maharashtra Institute of Technology
    Plot No. 19, Rajpath Society
    Opp. Vanaz factory, Faud Road
    Pune 411038
14. Dr. Amrik Singh
    2/26 Sarvapriya Vihar
    New Delhi 110016
15. Prof. G. Ram Reddy
    Chairman
    University Grants Commission
    New Delhi 110002
16. Dr. (Miss) A.S. Desai
    (President, AIU)
    Director
    Tata Institute of Social Sciences
    Sion Trombay Road, Deonar
    Bombay 400088

17. Prof. S.K. Khanna
Vice-Chairman
University Grants Commission
New Delhi 110002
18. Shri Anand Sarup
D-15, DDA Flats,
Saket
New Delhi
19. Prof. S.K. Agrawala
Secretary
Association of Indian Universities
New Delhi 110002
20. Dr. S. Venkateswaran
Director
Birla Institute of Technology and Science
Pilani 333031
21. Prof. Ramlal Parikh
Vice-Chancellor
Gujarat Vidyapith
Ahmedabad 380014
22. Shri C.R. Pillai
Director
IGNOU
New Delhi 110068
23. Dr. J.B.G. Tilak
Sr. Fellow
N.I.E.P.A.
17-b, Sri Aurobindo Marg
New Delhi 110016
24. Shri M.M. Ansari
Joint Director (Research)
Association of Indian Universities
New Delhi 110002
25. Dr. Kishore Gandhi
Faculty Exchange Building
Banaras Hindu University,
Varanasi
26. Shri Krishan Thapar
Former Member, Planning Commission
Apartment 324, Tower No. 1
Greater Kailash, New Delhi
27. Dr. (Mrs.) D.M. De Rebello
Joint Secretary,
Department of Education,
Ministry of HRD, Govt. of India
New Delhi
28. Shri B.E. Avhad
Advocate,
Dnyandeep, 19/1B/1,
Kothrud
Pune 411029

Index

CICIL LIST

CONCEPTS IN COMMUNICATION, INFORMATICS & LIBRARIANSHIP

(CICIL)

General Editor: **S.P. AGRAWAL**

CICIL-1 Development of Library Services in India: Social Science Information/**S.P. Agrawal** Rs. 150

CICIL-2 Development of Documentation in India: Social Science Information/**S.P. Agrawal** Rs. 250

CICIL-3 UNESCO and Social Sciences: Retrospect and Prospect/**S.P. Agrawal** and **J.C. Aggarwal** Rs. 250

CICIL-4 INDIANA : A Bibliography of Bibliographical Sources/**M.K. Jain** Rs. 200

CICIL-5 Dimensions of Library and Information Science: Kaula Festschrift/**V. Venkatappaiah** (Eds.) Rs. 600

CICIL-6 Book Numbers: Some Indian Methods/**M.P. Satija** and **S.P. Agrawal** Rs. 100

CICIL-7 National Policy for University Libraries in India: Problems and Perspectives /**N.B. Inamdar** and **L.S. Ramaiah** (Ed.) Rs. 250

CICIL-8 Media Utilisation for the Development of Women and Children/ **B.S. Thakur** and **Binod C. Agrawal** Rs. 150

CICIL-9 Terrorism: An Annotated Bibliography/**Susheela Bhan** (Ed.) Rs. 275

CICIL-10 Transnational Library Relations: The Indo-American Experience/ **M.B. Konnur** Rs. 175

CICIL-11 Geography of Marketing and Commercial Activities in India (Documentation on Research Information)/**R.S. Dixit** Rs. 130

CICIL-12 Information India 1988: Global View/**S.P. Agrawal** and **J.C. Aggarwal** Rs. 200

CICIL-13 Women's Education in India: Historical Review, Present Status and Perspective Plan/**S.P. Agrawal** and **J.C. Aggarwal** Rs. 360

CICIL-14 Cultural Communication in India: Role and Impact of Phonograms/**J.M. Ojha** Rs. 220

CICIL-15 Second Historical Survey of Educational Development in India: Select Documents 1985-1989/**S.P. Agrawal** and **J.C. Aggarwal** Rs. 490

CICIL-16 Documentation Encyclopaedia of UNESCO and Education/ **J.C. Aggarwal** and **S.P. Agrawal** Rs. 800 (set of 2 parts)

CICIL-17 Attitude Towards Information: A Study of Post-Graduate Teachers and Researchers in Social Sciences/**N.G. Satish** (in press)

CICIL-18 Librarianship and Bureaucratic Organisation: A Study in the Sociology of Library Profession in India/**P.K. Jayaswal** Rs. 175

CICIL-19 Literature Search/**K.A. Isaac** Rs. 150

CICIL-20 Child Education in India: Index to Scholarly Writings in Indian Educational Journals and Newspapers since independence/ **S.P. Agrawal** and **Naresh Kanta** Rs. 100

CICIL-21 Lok Sabha and Vidhan Sabha Elections in India 1989 & 1990: Process and Results with Comparative Study of Manifestos/ **S.P. Agrawal** and **J.C. Aggarwal** Rs. 250

CICIL-22 Islamic Studies in India: A Survey of Human, Institutional and Documentary Sources/**Mohamed Taher** Rs. 180

CICIL-23 Panchayati Raj: An Annotated Bibliography/**N.B. Inamdar, N.G. Satish** and **Anil Takalkar** 290

CICIL-24 Information India 1989-90: Global View/**S.P. Agrawal** and **J.C. Aggarwal** Rs. 500

CICIL-25 First Handbook of Psychological and Social Instruments/**Udai Pareek** and **T. Venkateswara Rao** Rs. 500

CICIL-26 Educational and Social Uplift of Backward Classes: At What Cost and How? Mandal Commission and After/**S.P. Agrawal** and **J.C. Aggarwal** Rs. 275

CICIL-27 Mass Media and New Horizons: Impact of TV & Video an Urban Milieu/**H.R. Trivedi** Rs. 180

CICIL-28 Indian Writings on Education: An Indicator to Indian Educational Journals Grouped by Subject Deseriptors 1979 to 1986 (in two parts)
S.P. Agarwal Rs. 900 (per set)

CICIL-29 Nation in Crisis/**S.P. Agrawal** and **J.C. Aggarwal** Rs. 200

CICIL-30 Information India 1990-91: Global View/**S.P. Agrawal** and **J.C. Aggarwal** Rs. 500

CICIL-31 Development of University Libraries in India after Independence/ **O.P. Gupta** Rs. 270

CICIL-32 Handbook on Child : With Historical Background/**Pramila Pandit Barooah** Rs. 320

CICIL-33 Weaker Section in Indian Society : Undiscovered Past, Uncertain Present and Unpredictable Future : Index to Writings in Indian Scholarly Journals and 10 National Newspapers Classified under 1500 Descriptors 1886-1990/**S.P. Agrawal** and **Rajeev Kumar Sharma** Rs. 600

CICIL-34 Communication Informatics and Librarianship in India : An Introductory Guide to Publications Based on a Survey of Libraries in Capital City of India/**S.P. Agrawal** and **Pushpa Rani Sharma** Rs. 720

CICIL-35 Problems of Collection Development in Special Libraries/**M.S. Sridhar** Rs. 225

CICIL-36 National Information Resources for Social Sciences in India : Mobilisation, Dispersal and International Enhancement/**S.P. Agrawal** Rs. 225

CICIL-37 Modern History of Punjab : A Look Back into Ancient Peaceful Punjab Focusing Confrontation and Failures Leading to Present Punjab Problem, and a Peep Ahead : Relevant Select Documents/ **J.C. Aggarwal** and **S.P. Agrawal** Rs. 400

CICIL-38 India Information Sources : Economics and Business/**Kyllikki Ruokonen** and **Manohar Lal** Rs.

CICIL-39 Educational Planning in India : With a Slant to Educational Financing and Administration, Vol. 1, Reports of Committees and Commissions, Five Year Plans, Statistical Tables/**J.C. Aggarwal** and **S.P. Agrawal** Rs. 650

CICIL-40 Integrated Library System : Two Case Studies : Latin America and India
Maria Luiza Rigo Pasquarelli, Rosaly Favero Krzyanowski, Ines Maria M. Imperatriz and **S.P. Agrawal** Rs. 160

CICIL-41 Social Science Information in India: Effort towards Bibliographical Control/**S.D. Vyas** Rs. 300

CICIL-42 Higher Education in India Since Independence: U.G.C. and Its Approach
O.P. Gupta Rs. 360

CICIL-43 Government and Politics in India: A Bibliographical Study of Contemporary Scenario Chronicling Rajiv Gandhi Era/**S.P. Agrawal** and **Rajeev Kumar Sharma** Rs. 500

CICIL-44 Second Handbook of Psychological and Social Instruments/ **D.M. Pestonjee** Rs. 300

CICIL-45 Development/Digression Diary of India; 3D Companion Volume to Information India: 1990-91/**S.P. Agrawal** Rs. 200

CICIL-46 Development/Digression Diary of India; 3D Companion Volume to Information India: 1991-92/**S.P. Agrawal** Rs. 300

CICIL-47 Information India 1991-92: Global View/**S.P. Agrawal** and **J.C. Aggarwal** Rs. 500

CICIL-48 Committees and Commissions in India 1974, A Concept's Project, Compiled by a team of professionals guided/ **Virender Kumar** (Vol. 12) Rs. 450

CICIL-49 Committees and Commissions in India 1975, A Concept's Project, Compiled by a team of professionals guided/**Virender Kumar** (Vol. 13) Rs. 450

CICIL-50 Committees and Commissions in India 1976, A Concept's Project, Compiled by a team of professionals guided/**Virender Kumar** (Vol. 14) Rs. 450

CICIL-51 Committees and Commissions in India 1977, A Concept's Project, Compiled by a team of professionals guided/**Virender Kumar** (Vol. 15) (in four parts) Rs. 450 each

CICIL-52 Committees and Commissions in India 1978, A Concept's Project, Compiled by a team of professionals guided/**Virender Kumar** (Vol. 16) (in two parts) Rs. 450 each

CICIL-53 Subject Guide to Communication, Informatics and Librarianship in India (Based on a Survey of Library Holdings in Capital City of India)/**S.P. Agrawal** and **Pushpa Rani Sharma** Rs. 400

CICIL-54 Restructurring of Library and Information Science Curriculum/ **A. Tejomurty** Rs. 250

CICIL-55 Committees and Commissions in India 1979, A Concept's Project, Compiled by a team of professionals guided/**Virender Kumar** (Vol. 17) (in two parts) Rs. 450 each

CICIL-56 Committees and Commissions in India 1980, A Concept's Project, Compiled by a team of professionals guided /**Virender Kumar** (Vol. 18) (in two parts) Rs. 450 each

CICIL-57 Third Historical Survey of Educational Development in India/ **S.P. Agrawal** and **J.C. Aggarwal** Rs. 700

CICIL-58 Model Library Legislation/**Velaga Venkatappaiah** Rs. 400

CICIL-59 Indian Library and Information Science Literature (1990-91)/ **Sewa Singh** Rs. 525

CICIL-60 Librarianship and Library Science in India/**Mohamed Taher** and **Donald Gordon Davis, Jr**. Rs. 350

CICIL-61 Comprehensive Glossary for Library & Information Science/ **O.P. Gupta** Rs.300

CICIL-62 Information India 1992-93:/**S.P. Agrawal** and **J. C. Aggarwal** Rs. 500

CICIL-63 Automation of Libraries and Information Science/**R.K. Shukla** Rs. 250

CICIL-64 Modern History of Jammu and Kashmir **J.C. Aggarwal** and **S.P. Agrawal** Rs. 1500 (per set of 2 vols.)

CICIL-65 Library and Information Science: Emerging Trends:/**Sister M. Esperanza,** A. C. Rs. 250

CICIL-66 Mental Retardation in India (A Bibliography)/**S. Venkatesan** and **V.G.D. Vepuri** Rs. 275

CICIL-67 Information India 1993-94: Global View/**S.P. Agrawal and J.C. Aggarwal** Rs. 500

CICIL-68 Information Behaviour of Scientists and Engineers:/**M.S. Sridhar** Rs. 500

CICIL-69 Uttarakhand: Past, Present and Future/**J.C. Aggarwal** and **S.P. Agrawal** Rs. 750

CICIL-70 National Information System in Education: A Comparative Study/**S. L. Verma** Rs. 650

CICIL-71 Not Published by us.

CICIL-72 Not Published by us.

CICIL-73 Second Historical Survey of Women's Education in India/**S.P. Agrawal** and **J.C. Aggarwal** Rs. 600

CICIL-74 Library and Information Science: Parameters and Perspectives/ **R.G. Prasher** (Ed.) 2 Vols. Set Rs. 1500
Vol. 1: Library and Information Science: Basic
Vol. 2: Information Science, Information Technology and Its Application

CICIL-75 Third Handbook of Psychological and Social Instruments/**D.M. Pestonjee** (in two volumes) Rs. 1100 per set

CICIL-76 Information India: Global Views 1994-95 & 1995-96/**S.P. Agrawal** and **J.C. Aggarwal** Rs. 500

CICIL-77 Development of Education in India: Selected Documents 1993-94/**S.P. Agrawal** and **J.C. Aggarwal**

